TEACHING
SECONDARY

English

READINGS AND APPLICATIONS

Second Edition

TEACHING SECONDARY

SECONDARY

English

READINGS AND APPLICATIONS

Second Edition

Daniel Sheridan

University of North Dakota

LEA LAWRENCE ERLBAUM ASSOCIATES, PUBLISHERS

2001   MAHWAH, NEW JERSEY   LONDON

Lawrence Erlbaum Associates, Inc., Publishers
10 Industrial Avenue
Mahwah, New Jersey 07430

Cover design by Kathryn Houghtaling Lacey

Library of Congress Cataloging-in-Publication Data

Teaching secondary English : readings and applications / [edited by] Daniel Sheridan.—
2nd ed.
    p. cm.
Includes bibliographical references and index.
ISBN 0-8058-2871-0 (pbk. : alk. paper)
    1. English language—Study and teacing (Secondary)—United States. 2. Language arts
(Secondary)—United States. 3. English language—Composition and exercises—Study and
teaching (Secondary)—United States. 4. English literature—Study and teaching
(Secondary)—United States. I. Sheridan, Daniel.

LB1631.T33 2000
428′.0071′273—dc21   00-023072
                                                                              CIP

Books published by Lawrence Erlbaum Associates are printed on acid-free paper,
and their bindings are chosen for strength and durability.

Printed in the United States of America
10 9 8 7 6 5 4 3 2 1

*This book is dedicated to Judy Sheridan,
the best English teacher I know.*

Contents

3

Choosing Texts   82

4

Teaching Writing   134

5

Teaching About Language   215

6

Joining the Profession   **295**

Appendixes   **313**

Preface

This new edition of *Teaching Secondary English* has been a long time in the making. I began planning it in the fall of 1996 and had begun the writing by early 1997. Then came the flood that devastated the Red River Valley of the North in April of 1997. For those of us in Grand Forks (ND), East Grand Forks (MN), and surrounding communities, the flood waters did more than take away our homes; they also altered our work-a-day lives forever, leaving behind a new set of priorities and (for me at least) a new kind of flexibility. Rather late in life, I learned a lesson about the inevitability of change. So in an odd and traumatic way, the flood helped shape the revision of this book. A year was lost, but when I returned to the project I found that I was more willing than before to see the book anew and make some significant changes.

Much, of course, is like the 1993 edition. As the chapter titles indicate, the range of the book is the same. I still think that the best kind of methods text does not try to cover everything. Teaching literature, writing, and language is basic to our profession, and instructors are invited to supplement this book, as I do, with other texts and materials that suit the special interests and needs of their students. The format of chapters is similar: each has a brief introduction in my words, followed by readings and some attempt to apply concepts to teaching situations. About half of the text, as before, consists of an anthology, allowing students to hear the voices of a variety of people with a range of attitudes. And the purpose has not changed. I have always wanted this to be a readable book that balances content knowledge with methodology, theory with practice, problem-posing with suggested solutions.

Still, those of you familiar with the first edition will notice some major changes. For one thing, this book is shorter than the original, unusual in this age of "new and expanded" editions. I hope, too, that the book seems tighter and more usable to you. I made a real effort to drop sections, even material that I like and still use in my own classes, if they did not seem to relate to the surrounding articles and applications. Moving each application to a position following an article was another effort to provide a kind of cohesion that was missing in the earlier, looser edition. For the same reason, I have provided introductions and study questions to accompany readings, and writing assignments at the end of each chapter. So, although the skeleton of the book is like the 1993 version and some of the material is the same, there has been a great deal of rearrangement, and much of the actual text is new.

With these changes, I hope that the philosophy of the book is clearer. For example, when it comes to the teaching of literature, I remain a proponent of the reader-response school of thought, but now I have tried to address the implications of that position more directly. And the same is true with all the other issues that inevitably arise as one seeks to explore what it means to "teach English." Thus, as in the first edition, there is a lot of problem-posing and discussion of tensions for the teacher, but now I hope students are given more help in figuring out their own attitudes toward those problems and tensions. I have worked even harder at establishing the right tone, writing in a voice that addresses the student/reader directly and avoiding the evasive abstractness of educationese. To summarize . . .

Distinctive Features of the Book

- It focuses on a few central concepts in the teaching of secondary English.
- It provides an anthology of readable articles on topics central to the teaching of English.
- The applications ask students to explore problems and issues related to the articles.
- Student readers are addressed directly without talking down to them.

Features New to This Edition

- It is shorter, tighter, and easier to use.
- The opening and concluding chapters more directly address the concerns of new teachers.
- As an anthology, it is updated (of the 22 articles, 14 are new to this edition).
- Each essay is preceded by a brief introduction and followed by questions for further thought.
- The applications are fewer but more extensive and more fully integrated with the rest of the text.
- A writing assignment has been provided at the end of each chapter.
- Interviews with college students are included in chapters 1 and 6.
- There are updated bibliographies at the end of each chapter.

This edition, then, is a thorough revision of the 1993 version. Indeed, as I worked on the book after the flood waters had receded and my life resumed a somewhat normal course, the work seemed to take on a life of its own. I hadn't expected that "doing a second edition" would be all that interesting and enjoyable, but I was wrong. The book kept changing and changing, and (in my post-flood mood) this seemed to be appropriate. But isn't that always the way it is with revision when you let it happen? I confess to you that I'm rather proud of this version of *Teaching Secondary English*. It is, I think, a better book. I hope you'll agree.

Acknowledgments

I would like to acknowledge the help and cooperation of students and colleagues at the University of North Dakota. In particular, I owe a debt of gratitude to Gabrielle Albertsen, Debbie Luth, and Nicole Poolman, whose ideas you will encounter in chapters 1 and 6. I would also like to thank my faculty writing group for their hard-headed but always supportive comments: Harmon Abrahamson, Victoria Beard, Colin Hughes, Cindy Juntunen, Melinda Leach, Libby Rankin, David Rowley, Lothar Stahl, Tom Steen, and Denise Twohey.

I am grateful as well to the dedicated work of secondary teachers in the area's schools. Teresa Tande and Betty Van Vugt are mentioned explicitly in the text, but I would also like to thank Kerry Jaeger, Sharon Knowlton, Vicki Peake, and (as always) Judy Sheridan.

Finally, I have appreciated the suggestions of the reviewers: Philip D. Bowles, Point Loma Nazarone College; A. David Capella, Wabash College; Sara D. Jonsberg, Montclair State University; Kyoko Sato, California State University, Northridge; Myles Striar, Boston University; and Rebecca Sullivan, Luther College.

1

English Teachers

Introduction

Who Teaches English?

Who teaches English? In one sense it is an impossible question to answer, for when I look at the teachers I know and the teachers-in-training with whom I work, I see a bewildering array of types. They are young and old, aggressive and laid-back, political and apolitical. They come from teachers' colleges and universities. Some love Henry James and others find his work unreadable. Some are into pop culture, whereas others are deeply traditional. Some write poetry; others are afraid of poems. They all love (or hate) grammar. They are mostly women but seem to resist prevailing gender stereotypes. And even the trait that I once believed to be the mark of all English teachers—that they talk a lot—has proved unreliable, as I encounter more quiet students who want to teach English. No, there is no single type who teaches English. I might agree or disagree with so-and-so's beliefs about teaching grammar; I might argue with someone's love of James, dislike of Dickens, or passion for Poe; I might believe that we need more men in the field. Still, I know that there is no formula for success—and so there is hope for you and me.

Though there is no one type who teaches English, there is, however, a stereotype, a cartoon image of the English teacher that persists in the popular imagination. She looks something like Miss Grundy from the old *Archie* comics—her hair, normally in a prim bun, coming loose as she loses herself in a passage from "Thanatopsis." She has an inexplicable love of ancient literature (pre-World War II when I was an adolescent, but nowadays pre-Vietnam) and an irritating habit of correcting people's language. She seems to be cast from a different mold entirely—vaguely "literary" or weird. Although I know of no one who fits this stereotype, I feel its power each time someone reminisces about a teacher who enthused about *Romeo and Juliet* or whenever people tell me they must watch their language in my presence.

A public image like this is a mixed bag, suggesting a combination of fear, respect, and affection for English teachers. Like all stereotypes, it has within it a kernel of truth, one that may help us understand more fully who teaches English—and why. If we restated things, we would discover that most English teachers have a deep engagement with literature and a firm understanding of the power of language. In a culture that has, to some degree, marginalized literature and that insists on overly simple views of language, English teachers are bound to seem a bit strange. They remain believers in language, especially the power of the written word.

In the readings of this chapter, you will encounter a few English teachers. For example, Keith Reins, in "A Target on the Blackboard" (pp. 7–13), reflects on his varied experiences in the classroom. His teaching practices have changed quite a bit over the years, and yet there is something constant throughout: He has tried to stay true to the love of language and literature that brought him to English in the first place. And there are the three young women who, at the beginning of their journey into the profession, speak so earnestly and wittily about their hopes and fears. "Where's That Fairy Dust When You Need It?" (pp. 15–20) is all about anxiety, the greatest of which is the fear that we will not be "prepared." But even these three beginners reveal, in both what they say and how they say it, the basic love of language that one expects of an English teacher.

The Field of English

But what do they *do*? What is the discipline of an English teacher? From what I have said so far, you might conclude that teaching the English language is the main topic. That is true enough, from one vantage point, but it can be confusing. An English teacher is not necessarily a linguist, although he or she does need to know something about linguistics. It would be more accurate to say that English is the study of language in action, chiefly in reading and writing, but also in speaking and listening—that is, in the various ways in which we use language to negotiate the problems of life. But, you might say, this is a broad claim, which scarcely seems to limit the field at all.

That is the point: The field of English resists limitations. Unless we are willing to reduce the field to a limited set of skills, the English teacher has to deal with more than just the manner in which things are read and written. What language refers to, the content, is part of English too. To cite just a small example, I know a high school English teacher who regularly assigns a short story in which the word *roe* appears. For her it is not just a word: It is an experience, one that her students have not had. So she buys some caviar (an inexpensive brand) and lets her students taste it. A jar of caviar is one of her teaching materials; it is part of English.

So we can be content to say that English is the study of language only if we recognize that language is a way of exploring life itself. That is a daunting prospect, as Gabby, Debbie, and Nicole tell us in "Where's That Fairy Dust?" There is so much to know, some of it "teacher knowledge" (how to form response groups, what to say on a weak rough draft), some of it "literary knowledge" (how metaphors work, what Shakespeare's stage was like), and much of it "life knowledge" (the feelings of a parent, the taste of caviar). No wonder English teachers sometimes yearn for the limitations and certainties of math! But remember that you already know a great deal, as do your students, and that is the starting point of all real learning. (If you doubt this, shoot ahead to the second interview, "I'm Going to Get Paid Today!" in chapter 6.) And remember, too, that the most important kind of knowledge—knowledge of your students—is within your grasp. Yes, it will be years before you are a wise old hand like Reins, but if you are willing to pay close attention to your students, you will soon become knowledgeable in this crucial area.

Obviously, the scope of English and its fuzzy boundaries can be a challenge, one that makes the curriculum hard to pin down and sometimes causes us to lose sight of our goals. But there are also advantages to working within a loose and sprawling field. There is maneuverability within such a discipline, so that the teacher is left with a great deal of freedom. It isn't that English can be whatever we want to it be, but that we must, of necessity, choose part of the field to begin with, and that choice is usually up to the teacher. Even a beginning teacher will make a lot of choices about what to teach and how to teach it.

Moreover, the inexhaustible range of materials means that we never have to grow stale. As we have seen, that can be scary if you focus on the responsibility to know everything. But consider it, for the moment, as an opportunity. The field includes more than just the great books; it also allows us to work with the Ann Landers column in this morning's newspaper, the poem you read in *English Journal* last night, the outrageous junk mail that offered you a "free" condo in Florida, and the short stories written by last year's ninth graders. With this range of material, there is no excuse for staleness. And the same applies to writing. It is not necessary to assign the same kinds of papers over and over again, especially if we have grown tired of reading them. There are lots of things for students to write, not just papers or themes, but letters and ads and journals and stories and poems and whatever will help them learn strategies for communication. Adopting this expanded view of the curriculum takes some time and energy and a little imagination, but it pays off in the long run. Good English teachers have folders full of materials, assignments, and teaching ideas filed away "just in case."

Approaches to English

But if English is endlessly various, how can we make sense of it? What is it, after all, that we are trying to accomplish as English teachers? To begin to answer that huge question, it might help to consider the different elements of the learning situation: the student (the *who*), the subject (the *what*), and the skills to be learned (the *how*). Of course, these are interrelated, and we must not forget the teacher's role in it all. But I am thinking for the moment of the various emphases that English teachers adopt, and these three elements—student, material, and language skills—seem to play the most important roles.

For example, we can focus on the students. What should English do for them? In what used to be called the Human Growth and Development school of thought, the language arts are seen as routes to self-development, or, in Maslow's famous formulation, "self actualization." People become more complete, more thoughtful (perhaps better?), as they improve in reading, writing, speaking, and listening. According to this way of thinking, the most important thing about language is its connection to our sense of identity. Language use can help us reach external ends (it is a means of learning about the world), but more importantly it helps us grow as people. So English teachers sometimes say that they don't teach books but instead teach kids.

Of course, many teachers do not think this way. For them, language is primarily a means to an end, and that end is knowledge of a factual sort. They focus on the content of English, which usually means the books to be read. This leads us to the Carrying on the Tradition school of thought, a view espoused most publicly by E. D. Hirsch, Jr., and former Secretary of Education William Bennett. Both favor a fixed core curriculum for all students: a more standardized set of readings that would connect students to one another, in a shared culture, and to the past, in a shared tradition. The emphasis here is on the conserving role of the English teacher, who is seen as the transmitter of what is worth reading and studying. Thus, English teachers sometimes say that no student should graduate without having read certain texts.

Finally, there is the Skills for Living school. Clearly, the traditional language arts—reading, writing, speaking, and listening—can be thought of as language skills. These can be kept broad or can be broken down into subskills, like phonics or word attack in reading, fashioning sentences or organizing in writing, articulation in speaking, or focusing one's attention while listening. These are skills for living and might even be equated, at some level, with thinking skills. And so English teachers sometimes speak of the skills that students need to "survive" in the world.

Each of these schools of thought has its own special legitimacy. True, each can be reduced to its least common denominator: self-esteem for its own sake (Human Growth and Development), memorization of facts from a list (Carrying on the Tradition), or focusing on grammar and usage in the place of writing (Skills for Living). But these are extreme positions. Moreover, these schools of thought are not mutually exclusive. For example, it is hard to imagine a serious English teacher who would not subscribe, at least in part, to all three. For most of us, however, one approach is predominant, serving as a foundation for the others and providing us with a personal philosophy of teaching. You too will need such a philosophy, some ordering principle for your work, some sense of your goal, and it is not too early to begin asking now if you lean toward one or all (or none) of these approaches.

It is worth considering the goals of English for another reason as well. Nowadays education has become highly political. Everyone—and not just politicians—has something to say about what schools should be teaching "our kids." The climate of opinion thus influences schooling, as it has always done, causing certain approaches to be in style and others out of style. For example, the Skills for Living philosophy is currently very popular. It was prompted by the 1983 report of the National Commission on Excellence in Education, "A Nation at Risk," and has since been gathering force. At the moment, we see it in the push toward teaching for specific assessable "competencies," which is being promoted in a number of states. A trend like this reminds us that schools are not isolated from the larger culture and that education is itself subject to change.

English, in particular, goes through phases. For instance, the past twenty-five years have seen the rise of a movement in composition that emphasizes the process of writing itself and deemphasizes the teaching of grammar as a separate subject. Although lately there has been a renewed interest in the teaching of grammar, this "process" approach is still very current, and one result is that more genuine writing seems to be taking place in secondary schools now than there was twenty-five years ago. The teaching of literature, on the other hand, has yet to undergo this type of change. It is true that psycholinguistic studies of the reading process and reader-response schools of criticism have begun to influence some classroom practice, but, on the whole, the process of reading does seem to be neglected in favor of the read-first/analyze-later approach to literature. This, I hope, might change, but regardless of what happens in this instance or that, you can expect your professional life to be affected by changes and trends, both positive and negative. So it is wise to pay attention to trends.

Individual Teachers

This brings us back to individual English teachers. The big picture is important, to be sure, but teaching is first and foremost a personal activity, something individuals choose to do. The two readings in this chapter are basically reflective pieces: In the first, an experienced teacher looks back over his career, whereas in the second three neophytes talk about their own strengths and weaknesses, trying to peer into their own futures. In the applications that follow each reading, you are asked to reflect on your own. What were your English teachers like? In what ways would you expect to be like them? Do you share the attitudes and fears of Gabby, Debbie, and

Nicole? In the final assignment, should your instructor choose to use or adapt it, you will be asked to explore your own motives for becoming an English teacher. Thus the focus, here at the start, is on the individual teacher and his or her own motives.

As you read about these teachers, and as you remember your own, bear in mind that teaching is always a local activity. These people are acting as individuals, yes, but they are embedded in complex situations that constrain their behavior. This sense of embeddedness heightens their individuality, reminding us that although we can learn from them, we cannot achieve much by simple imitation. And even if we could become like them, would that really help us? They are simply examples of English teachers at work, worth thinking about because their work raises all kinds of interesting questions about preparation, about interaction with students, about goals, about a host of other things. They are a place to begin, the first of many subjects in what I trust will be a lifelong conversation about the teaching of English.

A Target on the Blackboard

Keith M. Reins

As Keith M. Reins tells it, his becoming an English teacher had something to do with a teacher he never met. His older brother's English teacher, Mr. Anton, was able to bring Reins to the experience of reading literature. From there Reins takes us on a brief journey through his reading tastes, which eventually led him to teach speech and English. The journey, of course, has only begun, for Reins is the kind of teacher who keeps changing and growing. As you read this article, think about what attracted him to English in the first place and what keeps him teaching English.

"A Target on the Blackboard" appeared in English Journal, *Vol. 85. No. 5 (September 1996); copyright 1996 by the National Council of Teachers of English. It is reprinted with permission.*

In his sociological study of the teaching profession, *Schoolteacher*, Dan Lortie identifies "The Continuation Theme" as one of the primary motivators for becoming a teacher (1975, 29–30). Simply put, people who liked school as students often decide to work in schools as adults. It's possible that one of the motivators for staying in the profession—going the distance—may be the extent that continuation is realized. Sadly, the crush of daily responsibilities can make reflection upon practice, motivation, and even job satisfaction impossible: we forget the reasons we became teachers in the first place and wonder if we remain in the classroom only out of habit. Horace, the fictional Everyman-as-teacher in Theodore Sizer's *Horace's School*, commiserates for us all as he dwells upon the realities of his profession which amounts to a class load of 132 students:

> Spending just five out-of-class minutes per week looking at the work of each student and, at least once a month, talking privately with the youngster, would take a total of ten hours—ten hours of enervating work, two hours every evening, Monday through Friday, week after week. (Sizer 1992, 4)

But this is nothing new: every English teacher with a calculator has done the math, and there is still the Homecoming Dance to plan.

Reflection is important—necessary—not only to evaluate how we are doing in the classroom day-to-day, but also *why* we are there at all. We need to make time to examine ourselves as learners and teachers, to knot the threads of literacy that connect our own school experiences to the fabric of our classroom practices.

For me, ironically, the opportunity to reflect came during a period of unemployment following a move. Coming off of a 15-year run of bell-to-bell nonstop teaching, I filled the time at a university completing an advanced degree, mainly taking workshop writing classes, freelancing for an educational publishing house, and thinking and thinking. I thought about my own literacy and my classroom practice; I thought about a teacher I never knew who taught me to read and why I became a teacher.

BEGINNINGS

In 1969 my older brother was a senior at Fairview High School. There was a new English teacher in town, and my brother came home from his first day in Mr. Anton's Senior English class with orders to purchase four books. A quarter of a century later, my parents *still* talk about scouring that small, midwestern town for those strange titles, *The Jungle, The Prince, Rabbit Run*, and *The Catcher in the Rye*.

Meanwhile, I was suffering the dismal pangs of 9th-grade adolescent angst at Bess McGovern Junior High School. My reading up to that point had been lackluster. In 7th grade, Miss McClacky made us read *Evangeline*. She handed out ugly little olive drab paper-bound editions of the poem that carried the same fetid odor as my mother's nursing books that I secretly spirited into my bedroom, savoring the gruesome depictions of surgeon's operating tools. Eighth grade is a blank, and in 9th grade Mrs. Vlasic taught us *The Merchant of Venice*. I didn't understand most of it, but I did like the part about removing a pound of flesh and Portia's clever arguments that prevented the mutilation. It sort of reminded me of my mother's nursing books.

My own reading had been equally uninspired. I don't know if I had ever read a novel. I read nonfiction about whatever subjects were fleetingly appealing to a puerile boy, mostly books with big pictures about wars and guns. But it was 1969; wars and guns were quickly losing their appeal. I needed something different. So one day, for no reason other than boredom, I picked up one of Mr. Anton's books. Probably because the cover was an attractive bright red, I selected *The Catcher in the Rye*. That vermilion paper cover held the first book that was important to me and began with the first sentence I ever loved:

> If you really want to hear about it, the first thing you'll probably want to know is where I was born, and what my lousy childhood was like, and how my parents were occupied and all before they had me, and all that David Copperfield kind of crap, but I don't feel like going into it, if you want to know the truth. (Salinger 1945, 1)

The sentence was a springboard, and I plunged in, dove deep, stayed down a long time, and came up gasping for more. I was fully unprepared for what I had just read—the humor, the irreverence, the language, the prostitute, the pimp, the perverts. It was so extreme! I had found what I needed, and I would have more! I couldn't believe they were reading this stuff in high school, and I sure couldn't believe that any *parents* knew about it. So I kept it a state secret, just between Mr. Anton and me. The best teacher I never had, I imagined him in front of the class: dark and intense; long, coarse hair falling wildly over his eyes; pacing the floor like a caged tiger; slashing hands through the air in savage gestures; reading vivid passages from graphic books like *The Catcher in the Rye*. I also imagined a parade of Salinger's books, and I would read them all, one after another in my private little Illicit Lit. class.

So I went to the library and sought out *Franny and Zooey*. Checking out, I eyed the librarian nervously, for I had recently been expelled from the local theater for the crime of attempting to view *Easy Rider* at the age of 14. Surely my favorite author's books were just as poisonous to young minds as any motorcycle film. I didn't read the book right away but saved it for a long drive to Chicago I was taking with my father the next weekend. I loved trips to Chicago—the noise, the clutter, the crush of strange people, the smells, the Vienna Hot Dogs—but I hated the ride. Six hours in a Chevrolet station wagon with a father who does not listen to the radio is just shy of a lifetime in adolescent years. This ride would be different, though, for I had *Franny and Zooey* to keep me company.

With the trip underway, I began my subversive reading and experienced my first deep disappointment as a reader. I hated *Franny and Zooey* as much as I loved *Catcher*. But in my disappointment I became a better reader, for I learned to discriminate and trust my responses. I didn't hate the book arbitrarily; I hated it because it had no action, no irreverence, and no humor. It was a very long ride to Chicago.

Going back to class, I tried *The Prince*, but it had nothing to do with me, and it certainly wasn't funny. I picked up *Rabbit Run*, but it seemed slow and ponderous—over my head. I read a few pages, then flipped through it, randomly looking for anything of adolescent interest. I didn't finish it then and still haven't.

As a last resort I started *The Jungle* and was rewarded with my second important book. It wasn't funny, but it was vivid, intense, and extreme. The striking word pictures of the Chicago stockyards fed my voracious senses and taught me the difference between showing and telling with the written word. It was like driving by a bad car accident and not being able to keep from looking. The intensity of the conflicts heaped upon poor Jurgis and the physical response of tension and release I felt as I read taught me how a good writer can manipulate a reader. And I discovered irony: the image of the stockyard workers losing balance and falling into vats of lard never left me. The second sentence that I ever loved concluded the gory scene:

there was never enough of them [workers who had fallen into the lard vat] left to be worth exhibiting—sometimes they would be overlooked for days, till all but the bones of them had gone out to the world as Durham's Pure Leaf Lard! (Sinclair 1905, 102)

HIGH SCHOOL READING

When I entered high school, Mr. Anton left. Even so, my English classes were interesting. I believe now that creativity was valued over academic style, and I had a lot of fun. We read *The Spoon River Anthology* and went to a cemetery to do gravestone rubbings. We did a lot of speech and drama, went to the Guthrie to see *Of Mice and Men*, produced radio and television commercials and ad campaigns, and did some creative writing. It was very hands-on and experiential—an intuitive embodiment, I think, of John Dewey's "New Education"—and I got a lot out of it, but I don't remember much about what we read. I do remember being bored with *In Cold Blood, Huckleberry Finn,* and *Macbeth*.

Having exhausted the curriculum of my private reading class while still in junior high, I returned to nonfiction. Music had taken the place of war and guns in my life, so I read about musicians. By accident, I stumbled across the third book I loved, *Really the Blues*, the autobiography of jazz musician Mezz Mezzrow.

Mezzrow was the first white man to play in black jazz bands. He eventually moved to Harlem, giving himself over completely to African American culture and being accepted by that society as well. He also became a heroin addict, as did so many jazz musicians, and went to prison. In his autobiography he wrote vividly and realistically of music and performing and both the thrill and horror of narcotics abuse. Mezzrow led an extreme life, and he portrayed it vividly in prose. Though I didn't realize it at the time, a pattern to my reading had developed. I liked extreme literature. I had neither the interest nor the skill to appreciate subtlety. Capote's intricate and compelling prose was wasted on me. Twain's wry humor evaded me. Shakespeare's pretty poetry was out of the question. I needed freak shows of the mind.

READING IN COLLEGE

In college I eventually evolved into a speech major, and my advisor told me I'd better get a minor in English, so I said okay and trotted off to Analysis of Literary Forms class. If Mr. Anton was the teacher who taught me to read, then Dr. Lesh was the professor who taught me *how* to read. His approach was quite structured, but structure was what I needed at the time. I remember him telling us about "close reading." He drew three concentric circles that looked like a target on the board. In the center was a circle that represented the author. Nobody could get in that circle because the writer obviously knew more about his own life and work than anybody else ever could. The next circle contained the learned scholars who through diligence and intellect can squeeze just about every last drop of meaning from a piece of literature after a lifetime of monastic dedication to their craft. The third and final circle was for the rest of us common schmucks. Our job was to try to get from the outside of that circle to at least the inside of it by learning close reading. This sounds just awful, but I really needed a model for thinking, and my professor gave it to me.

But his selection of literature made the job easy. First we read *The Bell Jar*. If Holden Caufield was my Yang, then surely Esther Greenwood was my Yin, as extreme in her own way as Holden was in his. From Sylvia Plath I learned that prose can be poetic, and I learned that well crafted word pictures can make my skin stand on edge, as in her description of Esther regaining consciousness after her suicide attempt, "A chisel cracked down on my eye, and a slit of light opened, like a mouth or a wound, till the darkness clamped shut on it again" (Plath 1971, 139).

Next we read *Black Boy*, Richard Wright's autobiography. I loved his sentences that scratched at my senses with the violence of the kitten he hanged when he was 6 years old, "It gasped, slobbered, spun, clawed the air frantically; finally its mouth gaped and its pink-white tongue shot out stiffly" (Wright 1945, 12). I read Wright's short stories on my own and concluded that the African American experience has been so extreme that I should read more about it. I went on to read and savor more work by Wright as well as Ralph Ellison, Ernest Gaines, Claude Brown, Julius Lester, and Alice Walker.

A particular favorite is Walker's book of short stories about African American women, *In Love and Trouble*. Her darkly humorous description of Rannie Toomer in "Strong Horse Tea" vexes my emotions, mixing anger and pity with guilty amusement and distaste:

> Rannie Toomer's little baby Snooks was dying from double pneumonia and whooping cough. She sat away from him, gazing into the low fire, her long crusty bottom lip hanging. She was not married. Was not pretty. Was not anybody much. And he was all she had.
>
> "Lawd, why don't that doctor come on here?" she moaned, tears sliding from her sticky eyes. She had not washed since Snooks took sick five days ago and a long row of whitish snail tracks laced her ashen face. (Walker 1967, 88)

We read other extreme literature. I was surprised by the sexual frankness of Sylvia Plath's poem "Daddy" and Allen Ginsberg's "Howl." Randall Jarrell's fleeting poem, "The Death of the Ball Turret Gunner," taught me that there is power in what is not said. I appreciated the almost evil irony of Ambrose Bierce in "An Occurrence at Owl Creek Bridge" and selections from *The Devil's Dictionary*. I discovered that literary forms themselves can be extreme when I read John Barth's "Lost in the Funhouse." Then something strange happened. I read *Huckleberry Finn*, which I had despised in high school, and actually enjoyed it! I appreciated the craftmanship of Emily Dickinson who could say more with fewer words than anyone else. I recognized a great contrast between Dickinson and Walt Whitman who painted his catalogues of word pictures with broad strokes of the pen. I was moved by the hopelessness of the conflict in Kate Chopin's *The Awakening*. I enjoyed the folksy innocence of Richard Wilbur's "Digging for China." Without trying, I had learned to appreciate literature that was not extreme. I could read and understand subtlety.

BECOMING A TEACHER

A few years later, I became a junior high speech teacher. Remembering the fun I had with creative, hands-on activities in high school, I tried to do the same. We did a lot of readers' theater. Since a local African American radio station welcomed my students to perform on their air, and because I had become a reader of black literature, we adapted scripts from the works of Richard Wright, Langston Hughes, Julius Lester, and Alice Childress. If extreme literature had worked for me as an adolescent, I figured it would probably work for my students. I became an habitual abuser of mimeograph machines. Fairy tales were certainly extreme, so I xeroxed them and let my

students adapt them into children's theater. We added music and sound effects and hit the road, touring local grade schools with our tales. We also read children's books, memorizing the gist of the stories and constructing book costumes out of big cardboard boxes. We then performed in grade school classrooms and library story times as talking books.

Then the school closed down, and I became an English teacher at a wonderful team-taught middle school on the other side of town. About this time I started taking graduate classes in English to fill in the considerable gaps in my training as an English minor. I discovered the writing process in a class called "The Teaching of Writing," and it changed my life. Writing didn't have to be a sudden thing. I learned to use journals and small groups for developing ideas and to dedicate the lion's share of class time on the front end of writing assignments in prewriting. It made perfect sense: you can't build a house if you don't have the raw materials of lumber and nails; you can't build a composition if you don't have the raw materials of ideas and time. I didn't realize it then, but later I would use the same concepts to teach literature.

Though English at the middle school was not a reading class as such (there was a separate reading class), I never liked to segment the language arts, so I found ways to use reading in my classes. I started out each class period reading to my students. My favorite novel for 7th graders was Robert Newton Peck's *A Day No Pigs Would Die*. In its own way it was extreme with humor and graphic description. I could always count on an audible response during the scene of Pinky's butcher. The young narrator summed up the complexity of emotion adolescents sometimes feel about parents they usually love but sometimes hate, saying, "I hated Papa at that moment. I hated him for killing her and hated him for every pig he had killed in his lifetime . . . for hundreds and hundreds of butchered hogs" (Peck 1972, 137). We spent time reading King Arthur tales, and then we wrote our own. Most of all, we read and responded to each other's writing.

TEACHING HIGH SCHOOL

Then I moved away and became a high school English teacher. I would actually teach literature. I had 11th graders, so American literature, of course, was on the agenda. And, of course, we would start with the Puritans. I pored over the big, yellow anthology for hours, reviewing my Puritan lore and lingo. I applied Puritan dogma to Anne Bradstreet's poetry. I looked for symbolism in Jonathan Edwards' sermons. I learned how to correctly pronounce *huswifery*. It was tough going, and for some reason it never occurred to me that if it was hard for me, it would be impossible for most 11th graders. (I've since decided that the real power of the Puritans is that they make everybody else seem so interesting.) I met my first real literature class, a wonderful and tolerant group that I will never forget, and I actually drew those three concentric circles on the board the very first day.

I drew a target on my board but missed it by a mile. You don't have to be an expert marksman to know that if you're teaching someone to shoot, they will have a much easier time hitting a big target than a small one, and I had given my class a tiny target. The reason that I had learned to read literature at all is because my two favorite teachers had given me great big targets that were hard to miss like *The Catcher in the Rye* and *The Bell Jar*. Only after I had had success with the extreme was I able to appreciate the subtle. So I started over.

I started reading to my 11th graders at the beginning of class. I read *Black Boy*, perhaps the perfect book for reading aloud because it is so episodic and each scene can be read in five minutes or so. Some days students volunteered to do the reading for me, and we adapted several episodes for readers' theater presentations. We used journals to respond to ideas in *Black Boy*. I asked the students to write about their earliest memories, or times they were in trouble, or times they were in pain, or times they took a stand. These were the same kinds of experiences Wright wrote about in his autobiography. We read from the journals and talked about our experiences as well as Wright's. It was just like teaching writing; if you spend time developing ideas before a discussion, then you have things to talk about during the discussion. We wrote our own personal narratives, and they were good.

The school had copies of *The Catcher in the Rye*, and I asked my students to buy *The Bell Jar*. They were so thrilled about putting aside the big yellow anthology, I think they would have bought me a new car if I'd asked. As we read the books, the students wrote in their journals about what they found in them. I wrote several suggestions on the board each day. *Write about something you find in the book that is funny. Write about something you can relate to. Write about a similar experience you have had. Write about something in the book that annoys you.* We always had things to talk about, and the discussions were driven by the students' thoughts, memories, and insights. We discussed the two main characters and wrote dialogues that Esther and Holden might have if they went on a date. One boy wrote nothing, explaining that neither one of them would actually get around to going on the date. He had a point. During a discussion, a girl said, "Holden doesn't want to do anything, and Esther wants to do everything, and neither one of them can do anything." Bullseye.

I think I finally became a pretty good literature teacher, but it's very, very hard work, harder even than teaching writing. I'm glad I stuck with it and went the distance. And I'm glad I found a good role model in Mr. Anton, the inspiration for my personal "Continuation Theme." It's a strange thing to have a favorite teacher that you've never met. I can't really say that I have continued in his tradition since I never saw him teach, but sometimes I imagine myself in front of the class: dark and intense; long, coarse hair falling wildly over my eyes; pacing the floor like a caged tiger; slashing hands through the air in savage gestures; reading vivid passages from graphic books like *The Catcher in the Rye.*

WORKS CITED

Lortie, Dan C. 1975. *Schoolteacher: A Sociological Study.* Chicago: The University of Chicago Press.

Peck, Robert Newton. 1972. *A Day No Pigs Would Die.* New York: Alfred A. Knopf.

Plath, Sylvia. 1971. *The Bell Jar.* Toronto: Bantam Books.

Salinger, J. D. 1945. *The Catcher in the Rye.* Toronto: Bantam Books.

Sinclair, Upton. 1905. *The Jungle.* New York: The New American Library, Inc.

Sizer, Theodore R. 1992. *Horace's School.* Boston: Houghton Mifflin.

Walker, Alice. 1967. "Strong Horse Tea." *In Love and Trouble.* New York: Harcourt Brace Jovanovich.

Wright, Richard. 1945. *Black Boy.* New York: Harper Collins Publications, Inc.

For Further Thought

1. Reins mentions Dan Lortie's discussion of "The Continuation Theme," the idea that "people who liked school as students often decide to work in schools as adults." Was this Reins's experience? How would you characterize your own experience in secondary schools? In what way has it influenced your decision to become a teacher?

2. What attracted Reins to literature—that is, what did he like about the literary experience? How does this compare or contrast with your own experience as a reader? What, in the end, attracted you to the study of English?

3. Think about the teacher who drew a target on the blackboard. How would you evaluate this as a metaphor for what should happen in the English classroom? Note that Reins himself seems uncomfortable with it—and changes it later in the article.

4. Reins says that teaching literature is "very, very hard work, harder even than teaching writing." Do you agree or disagree? Explain your answer.

Application 1.1:
Remembering Your English Teachers

My teachers in seventh and eighth grade were my personal stereotype of high school English teachers. They were prissy, "old maid" types, one of whom even carried a wooden ruler with her for discipline. They both emphasized grammar, grammar, grammar, and we had a lot of work-sheets. My last two English teachers were far different. Miss H. was young and beautiful. The boys in class were in love. Mr. D. was overweight, sloppy, and sarcastic. They were both cool and reserved, and demanded excellence of us. They exposed us to the twentieth century rather than the nineteenth.

> *I really don't know what the "real" image or stereotype of English*
> *teachers is supposed to be. I like to think that I have something of all*
> *my teachers in me somewhere. I just hope I got the admirable quali-*
> *ties instead of their bad points. (Sandy Holmgren)*

The teachers of our past are like ghosts that haunt our professional lives. And ghosts, as we know, can be benevolent or malevolent. So Sandy is right to worry about the effect her teachers have had on her: She hopes these ghosts will shape her work for the better, though it might not turn out that way. In either case, however, she recognizes that they will play a part in her life as a teacher.

Is Sandy doomed to act out the roles given to her in the classroom? No, I think we must reject the deterministic view that we are bound to teach the way we were taught. Sandy need not teach "grammar, grammar, grammar" or use "a lot of work-sheets." Nor need she be "cool and reserved." Instead, she can focus on the admirable qualities, like demanding excellence and exposing students to the twentieth century. But if we are to make choices like these, we must first come to terms with the teachers whose behavior gave rise to the choice in the first place.

The biggest danger is *not* remembering, *not* reflecting on our experiences with teachers as students. For example, I know that Mr. B., my tenth-grade English teacher, was not among the best teachers I have had. He was smart and funny and kept us on our toes, but he was also a wise guy who too often used humor to attract attention to himself. I know this, and yet there are times when I hear Mr. B. in my own voice when I am teaching. I literally have to tell myself not to imitate him. To do that, to be conscious of his influence, I first have to remember.

Of course, remembering teachers is not always a matter of conjuring up ghosts so we can avoid their example. Far from it. Most of us have fond memories of English teachers, which is one reason we want to join their profession. Here, for example, is Scott Winter's memory of Mrs. J., his senior English teacher:

> Mrs. J. taught Honors English as a college course and expected college
> work in return. The following fall I basically retook her class in col-
> lege. Most of the books were even the same.
>
> The book I remember reading is *Siddhartha* by Hermann Hesse.
> Mrs. J. talked about the book until everyone understood it and had an
> opinion on it. Then I remember her telling us that people carried this
> book around with them in the 60's because they could relate to it, and
> that made sense to me. That's where I had the "fabulous reality" that I
> could relate old literature to my own life (which sounds hokey, but I
> mean it).
>
> I also remember Mrs. J. meeting with my parents during Open
> House Day. My parents sat down at her desk. She smiled. She leaned
> forward. She said this: "Your son is one of the laziest boys I've ever
> taught." She leaned back. She smiled again.
>
> My parents loved her. The result: I made the first essay deadline of
> my life. I wrote a 20 page paper on "The Dark Side of Mark Twain."
> She gave me A's across the board. And she was smug about it. Then

she gave me a B on my report card. I think she was smug about that too.

That's the best teacher I had in high school. I loved her without knowing it.

"I loved her without knowing it." But, of course, another student might not have loved Mrs. J. Another student might have considered her intrusive and found her grading to be unfair. And yet she was good for Scott and probably for the vast majority of her students.

It's time to remember our teachers, time to realize more consciously whom we loved and admired and whom we found to be wanting. It's time to think about the impression that these ghosts from our past made on us.

Some Things to Consider About Your Teachers

1. List your English teachers from grades seven through twelve. Write a brief paragraph on each, in which you describe the teacher's behavior.
2. Choose one of your teachers and examine his or her influence on you. You might think of the teacher as a positive or negative role model—someone you would like to emulate in your teaching or someone whose example you would like to avoid.
3. Think about the three approaches to English described in the introduction to this chapter: Human Growth and Development, Carrying on the Tradition, and Skills for Living. Which of your teachers, if any, seem to fit into a particular school of thought? Which approach do you lean toward at this stage in your career?
4. Make an overall judgment about your English teachers. Taken as a group, were they good or bad? This might be difficult, but try to make the judgment. Be prepared to explain why you reached this conclusion and what it has to do with your decision to become an English teacher.

"Where's That Fairy Dust When You Need It?" (A Conversation About Student Teaching)

Gabrielle Albertsen, Debbie Luth, Nicole Poolman, and Dan Sheridan

Note: This is the first of two interviews. The second, "I'm Going to Get Paid Today!", appears in chapter 6. In it, these students discuss their growth as teachers.

Gabrielle (Gabby) Albertsen, 26, was raised in Georgia and California. At the time of the interview, she was pre-paring to student teach in a seventh-grade classroom. Nicole Poolman, 24, was born and raised in the Minneapolis/St. Paul area. Having graduated from college, Nicole returned to finish her education courses. Nicole was preparing to student teach with tenth and eleventh graders. Debbie Luth, 21, was born and raised in northern

Illinois. Because she wished to be certified in ESL as well as English, Debbie would not be student teaching for another year.

One evening these three English majors talked with me about student teaching—especially about their hopes and fears. What follows are excerpts from that conversation. As you read the interview, you will notice three kinds of concerns surfacing: worries about their academic background, questions about teaching practice, and concerns about being able to exert authority in the classroom. You might also notice that these three young women have different personalities and different kinds of concerns. See if you can tell them apart, by "voice," as you read. I began by asking what they feared the most about student teaching. Interestingly, Debbie (who is farthest away from student teaching) began by expressing her deepest fear.

Debbie: I feel insecure about English. And though I know I've learned a lot, I'm not sure I'll ever know enough. Maybe that's one of the problems with English. I'm tutoring two students in math, and with math you learn this and you learn that, and it's all right there. With English, there are so many billions of books out there, and so many different ways to write, that it's hard to feel that you can ever get a grasp on it all.

Gabby: And yet at the same time, that's to our advantage. Yes, it makes me uncomfortable, but there's just such a wide variety of stuff to pick from.

Nicole: My number one fear is just being completely incompetent once I'm in there. I know that as a teacher, you're never supposed to be afraid to say, "I don't know the answer to that," but I'm afraid that I'm going to be saying "I don't know" all the time.

Gabby (laughs): You can begin every morning with, "I know nothing, nothing at all."

Debbie: Or write it on the chalkboard, "I'm new at this. I don't know what I'm doing."

Dan: *So when would you expect to be expert enough to feel like a "real" teacher?*

Gabby: After twenty years! But you see, for me, it's not just not having read every single solitary thing I could ever possibly teach, which is just impossible; it's also having stuff to go along with that. Knowledge about the authors, sure, but also photos and activities—anything at all.

Nicole: Other works by this author, their lives, history, everything that makes English interesting when you're listening to a teacher lecture about it. It's all the stuff that I don't really know. I know that we can start from scratch and do the research, but it's not the same.

Debbie: Not the same as being able to pull it out of your head. Actually, I'm more concerned about walking into the teacher's lounge and there's people who have been teaching and reading for 20 years, and they will know so much more than me. I want to feel confident about myself enough so that I can walk into that classroom and teach, but if I just walk out of the teacher's lounge where there are people who know so much more than me, it's hard to feel confident.

Gabby: Well, I know that I have super high expectations for myself and so I expect to be able to do just a billion times more than is actually possible. And so when I get in there for the first time, and I have no idea what's going on, that's just going to crush me. But that's kind of the way it's supposed to be, I guess. Not that you're supposed to go in and just fail right off the bat, but I think we admire those people because they've been doing it for such a long time—to expect to have that kind of knowledge is just unrealistic.

*　*　*

Dan: *So what do you want?*

Gabby: I want a big book of lesson plans. I can read the material the night before. I want to know *how to teach.*

Debbie: It's hard to know what students will find interesting. True, all those facts might be interesting to us, but facts can be boring. And so it feels sometimes like it's all magic. You don't get a handout that says here's how to make the difference between boring facts and fun facts. If that were written somewhere, it would be all so much easier.

Gabby: They ought to teach magic in college.

Dan: *Do you think it's the teacher who has the magic?*

Debbie: Teachers, and their knowledge of the students. You'd have to know students well enough to know how to do it.

Nicole: Half of my fear is not knowing where the magic is. You think, if you just know all the answers, you're going to come out a teacher. And you realize in the end that you aren't going to find the answer. Darn it.

Debbie: Darn it.

Nicole: And that's another thing I'm scared I won't be able to do. How to read a class, read a group you're speaking to. Are they listening? Do they care? Are they paying attention? That's a skill that can't be taught.

Gabby (referring to her summer work with young kids): You know, I'm finding that it's not as hard as I thought it would be. With the kids I'm working with, you know exactly what's going on with them—because it's on their faces. Even with older [secondary school] kids, you really still kind of know. I think it's not as hard as we want to make it.

Debbie: I can do that. And I can make the lesson plan. And I can read the stuff the night before. But when you put it all together, at the same time, where you're trying to think about the stuff

you're going to cover today, and the stuff to say about it that's interesting, and the kids you want to watch, and the ones you want to slow down for . . . there's just so much that it's overwhelming. There's so much *stuff* to think of.

Dan: *Yes, it's complicated, isn't it? You're afraid that you won't be able to attend to all that stuff—at the same time?*

Debbie: I'm afraid that there will be so many balls to juggle at once, that they'll all come crashing down.

Gabby: I think that at some point within the first few times you're up in front of the classroom, you realize that you're losing this one and this one's dozing off, and I think there's got to be some sort of "click." You think, "Okay, I have to speed up for this one, I have to say things a couple of times for this one, I have to move this way." There's just got to be some point where it just kind of clicks.

Dan: *You seem to be saying that, if you do look at the students, you trust that you'll be able to make the adjustments. To teach.*

Gabby: I think so. It's kind of sink or swim. For the first few days or however long it takes, when you're trying to get your bearings and the kids are trying to figure you out, there has to be some point where it just has to change—you have to be able to do everything for those kids, plus remember what's going on, or your classroom will be chaos.

Debbie: That's the fear.

Dan: *But Gabby is saying, it can't be that hard because people do it all the time. She trusts that she can do it. And I have implicit trust in the three of you. I understand the fears (I have them myself), but I know that you'll do well—especially, once you stop worrying about how much you know and start thinking more about* these *kids and what they need to be doing to learn. That's an important turn in* anybody's teaching, and that's something that will happen to you in student teaching. When I supervise your student teaching, I'll see it happen.

Gabby: Will you let us know when it happens?

Dan: *Of course I'll let you know. If I knew in advance, I'd bring flowers on that day. I just know when I see it. It doesn't happen just in one day, but something does happen. The student teacher realizes, "Yes, I can do this."*

Gabby: I wish there was something they could give us before we began, so we'd know we could do it. I know I'm not going to sleep the night before.

* * *

Gabby: I hope I can be "Mrs. Albertsen" this time. I don't want to be in front of that classroom and be "Gabby."

Dan: *Your cooperating teacher will introduce you as Mrs. Albertsen, and then you are Mrs. Albertsen.*

Gabby: Good. I think that sets up a barrier, whereas when I'm just Gabby, I can still be one of them.

Debbie: That's another thing. We're so close in age, at least I am. This summer I saw the Girls State kids from high school, and . . . well, I'm not a tall person, and I'm not all that big, and these kids are much larger than me, and they look more developed and more mature, and it is threatening. Age gives you something.

Gabby: Yes, there's a thirteen-year-old girl in the summer program where I work, and she's easily three inches taller than I am. She's going to be in 7th grade!

Nicole: I'm afraid that I'm going to get treated the way I treated student teachers when I was in high school. We were atrocious to them. We didn't give them any respect; we didn't listen to them; we didn't acknowledge their authority in any way, shape, or form; we treated them worse than we would treat a substitute teacher.

Dan: *What was the cooperating teacher doing all this time?*

Nicole: Not much.

Gabby: Wouldn't they jump in? (laughs) If the cooperating teacher doesn't jump in, I'm taking a whip to school.

Dan: *Is discipline a serious worry for you—controlling kids?*

Debbie: Very serious for me.

Gabby: It's not something that's ever worried me.

Debbie: But you're a pretty tough cookie, Gabby.

Gabby: It's thinking of stuff to *do*. I'm going to have to have a billion things to do in one week.

Dan: *Do you think there's a connection between this need to be the expert (to know all that stuff that Debbie mentioned) and this need to be the adult (to be Mrs. Albertsen), and this need to be in control (not to tolerate misbehavior)? They all seem to fit together—all this need to be taken seriously, to believe in yourself as a teacher.*

Gabby: Well, sure, we want to be in charge.

Debbie: But when you were listing those, they have different fear levels for me. About knowing the stuff: I can get no sleep the night before and I can figure it out. Now when it comes to the power/control issue, you can't stumble. You stumble and they're all watching you.

Dan: *Well, if you had the magic, they would just listen to you.*

Gabby: Where's that fairy dust when you need it?

Debbie: I think I need more practice. Not just teaching, but the more I'm around students, the less anxious I'll be. I mean, why should they be so threatening? That was me four years ago. The more I'm around them the more human they seem, the less threatening.

* * *

Debbie: Do you know what I got afraid of today? There I am, faithfully writing down something the teacher said in poetry class, and I think, "I have all these notebooks, and these will be my bible when I start teaching, and here I am taking professors' words as truth, and maybe it's all going to be *wrong*." I don't feel that any of the knowledge that I have (which is so little) is guaranteed in any way.

Dan: *That's the scary part. It has no authority since it came from people like your poetry prof and me.*

Debbie: So I'm screwed.

Dan: *Think of all the mistakes you've heard teachers make. Did they really matter so much? You're probably the only one who's writing these things down.*

Debbie: Maybe. And I admit that I discovered one good thing about teaching English. When I'm working with my math students, it's very hard to teach something to students who don't know the stuff that goes before it. The nice thing about English is that it's a lot more flexible; you can basically start almost at square one. It's not the same regimented thing. I like that. It's not like you can't start writing a persuasive paper until you've "achieved" grammar, whatever that means. You just work with it where you're at. . . .

Dan: *I think a lot of this anxiety is in your heads. It's almost like, "If you really believe that you're a teacher, then the kids will believe it; and if you don't believe you're a teacher. . . ."*

Gabby: That's exactly it.

Nicole: It sounds like a Disney movie.

Debbie: I believe I can! I believe I can!

Nicole: Click your heels three times and you become a teacher.

Debbie: It obviously feels like that. Take a theater arts person. They've learned a lot about reading things and writing plays. And they've caught some common sense about teaching people. It feels like a theater arts person would be just as prepared to teach English as I would. I don't have any *answers*. I can sum up my knowledge in two sentences: "It depends" and "Look at the students."

Gabby: But the theater arts people care about it in a different way. They want to act it out. We love the words and the way they're written, and they love saying the words. They want to be up on the stage *doing* Shakespeare, and we want to be *explaining* Shakespeare and *loving* Shakespeare and encouraging kids.

Nicole: I think that the person who has been going through an English education program has a focus. It's my focus . . . and yours too, Debbie, because you always have that notebook and you're always writing things down, and looking at it from the perspective of "Someday I'm going to teach this." Whereas that other person has just been a learner the whole time. So I think that in itself would make the difference.

Gabby: That is a good answer. But, you know, I still want my big bag of lesson plans. I want to have them to use right off the bat. I want all the answers before I have to ask the questions.

Nicole: This past month I was taking all the stuff from both methods classes and putting them into files. And one thing I noticed was that I came out of one class with a huge file of stuff, but I didn't really think about that stuff, though I was glad I had it. And when I left the other methods class, I didn't have much stuff but I felt that I had thought about teaching so much more. So I thought it was a good balance.

Debbie: And when I went through my stuff, I found that I had this big file on ESL; and I had this huge file on how students develop; and I had a huge file on learning styles, and all this background stuff. But when it comes to actual lesson plans, all I have are those NCTE books and even those are so sketchy.

Dan: *So you need more stuff in these methods classes?*

APPLICATION 1.2

Debbie: Stuff is great.

Gabby: No, no more stuff.

Dan: But you said you wanted a huge bag of stuff.

Gabby: No, that's not what I said. I have a big bag of stuff. What I want is a big bag of stuff I can *use!*

Dan: You're going to do fine, Gabby.

Gabby: All that stuff that teachers brought to our class. It was great. I'm going to read all that later. But right now I want what they *do*. I want *how they do it.*

Dan: The problem, Gabby, is that what makes it work is not written down in a neat little sheet of paper that you can Xerox. And if it is and you try to do it that way, then it comes out different. But you need both, don't you? Stuff and your own ideas. As Nicole said, stuff without thinking is not all that useful. You have it, but you don't know what to do with it.

* * *

Dan: So what do you need? What should the university have done differently for you?

Debbie: Oh great! It's a little late now!

Gabby: I always love that question. "What should we have done for you?" It's sink or swim. "What should we have done for you?" A life vest maybe?

For Further Thought

1. Gabby, Debbie, and Nicole are all good students, people who stand a very good chance of success in teaching. Yet all three express some pretty serious anxieties. Is this natural? How would you react to them if they were *not* afraid?

2. All three agree that they don't know enough: about literature, writing, teaching, students. And, oddly, all three know that they are being unreasonable: as beginners, they aren't supposed to know as much as veterans. But knowing this doesn't seem to help much. Imagine that you are a friend listening in. What could you say to Gabby, Debbie, and Nicole to make them feel more confident?

3. Gabby's final comment on sinking or swimming makes explicit an idea that is latent in many of their remarks. They fear that there really isn't anything they can do to prepare for teaching, that they have to learn to teach by teaching. What do you think? Is it really sink or swim?

4. Make a prediction about these three students. How do you think they will feel about these issues after having student taught? Write out your thoughts and then look ahead to "I'm Going to Get Paid Today!" (pp. 304–310).

Application 1.2:
What Makes an Effective English Teacher?

> . . . *teachers with more successful patterns of classroom behavior tended to have strong interests in many areas, to prefer student-centered learning situations, to be independent, to have superior verbal intelligence, and to be willing to allow nondirective classroom procedures. Teachers with less successful behavior patterns tended to prefer teacher-directed learning situations, to value exactness, orderliness, and "practical" things, and to be less tolerant toward the expressed opinions of pupils. They were also more restrictive and criti-*

cal in appraising the behavior and motives of other persons. (William H. Peters, "Research on Teaching: Presage Variables," in Effective English Teaching, *p. 29)*

In recent years, educational research has begun to focus on teaching effectiveness. Researchers look at learning outcomes (measurable or observable indications that learning has occurred) and ask what produced that learning. Obviously, there are some difficulties with this enterprise. One needs a clear sense of the desired outcomes, and in a field like English there is some disagreement on that point. And there are so many variables that need to be accounted for when you ask why students learn or fail to learn: variables in the students, the social environment, and the curriculum. So we ought to approach such research with some healthy skepticism.

Still, some interesting results have emerged from this research. The data support the general notion of a student-centered classroom, one in which students are encouraged to seek answers to problems in an active way. Peters (1987) cites other research that named "tolerance of ambiguity and preference for complexity" as further hallmarks of good English teaching (p. 38). We may infer that the traits of a successful English teacher are an understanding of the complexity and ambiguities of language, along with a willingness to let students explore language in fairly fluid situations. These traits seem quite different from that fussy sense of correctness that some associate with our discipline.

However, ambiguity is precisely what concerns the three students in "Where's That Fairy Dust?" "I want all the answers before I have to ask the questions," says Gabby, expressing an attitude that is fairly typical of beginning teachers. Uncertain of their own authority and put in a situation where they have to "act like a teacher," they attend primarily to the subject matter and fall back on questioning techniques that only confirm the teacher's preconceived ideas. Moreover, they fear the loss of control that seems to accompany fluidity in the classroom: They want things to be predictable. As Debbie says, "We want to be in charge."

So it seems that the very qualities which make for effective English teaching are the hardest for a young teacher to acquire. There is some truth in that, and yet there is hope, too—for the beginning teacher has energy, enthusiasm, and a greater possibility for direct rapport with teenagers. Moreover, student teachers like Gabby, Debbie, and Nicole are willing to try new things; they are too young to have gotten into a rut. The key, as I say in the interview, is to keep one's eye on the students—advice that Debbie throws back at me as the sum total of what she has learned about teaching in college. That, and "it depends"—the ultimate statement about ambiguity and the need for flexibility. Debbie is being ironic, of course, but she is no slouch when it comes to figuring things out. Although she laments that need for flexibility, she also rejoices in it. (Look at the way she contrasts English and math.) And although she knows that "looking at the students" is not sufficient to make her a good teacher, she also knows that she can't get by without it. (See her remarks on this subject in the follow-up interview in chapter 6.)

Debbie, along with Nicole and Gabby, is wrestling with a problem that beginning English teachers face. They know that English stops being interesting and worthwhile as it is reduced to formulas, but they want the formulas anyway. Hence their joking about magic and fairy dust. They know that exploring ambiguity is central to their mission as English teachers, but at this stage in their careers they want clarity. Hence their desire for answers and their humorous irritation with me as I refuse to provide them. They know that they will need to be flexible, but that seems to leave the door open to chaos. Hence their wistful longing for a whip. And yet this very sense of humor, with its heavy doses of irony, suggests a strength that is common among beginners: Their very willingness to laugh at themselves and their dilemma is perhaps the best indication of their promise as teachers.

Some Things to Consider About Effective English Teaching

1. Examine Peters's language, looking for contrasts or oppositions that explain his values. For example, "strong interests in many areas" seems to be contrasted implicitly with "narrowness." "Student-centered" is used to suggest an opposing term, "teacher-directed." Describe some of these oppositions and discuss your reaction to them, thinking about whether one side of the opposition is necessarily "good" or "bad."

2. In *Making the Journey*, Leila Christenbury (1994) lists the following "characteristics of good teachers." They (1) like people (young people in particular), (2) can be flexible, (3) can draw appropriate conclusions from classroom observations, (4) listen actively and attentively to students, (5) have a sense of humor, and (6) have a sense of intellectual curiosity—both their own and their students' (pp. 35–36). Apply these criteria to one of your English teachers, describing how he or she fit (or failed to fit) Christenbury's idea of a good teacher. How are these characteristics like or unlike Peters's traits of effective English teachers?

3. Using either Peters's or Christenbury's criteria for good teaching, evaluate your own promise as a teacher. Where do you think you excel? Where might you experience some problems?

Writing Assignment: Telling Your Story

I've loved English since I first began reading and writing, but I can't say why. My family had books in the house when I was younger, but my brothers and friends preferred fighting to reading. I remember lying on the living room floor in the sun, reading book after book, while my brothers would be shooting baskets or playing catch. I read everything I could get my hands on. (Steve Slavik)

On the first day of a methods class I usually ask students to write about why they are here. At first it seems like an odd question to ask. "Why am I here? Because I want to teach English, of course!" But why do you want to to teach English, and what route have you traveled to arrive in this class?

We could, I suppose, take some things for granted: that you *like* English, for example. I think that is a prerequisite, although most of us will admit that we are enthusiastic about some parts of the discipline and only mildly tolerant of others. Steve Slavik is an enthusiastic reader and and avid writer, but he confessed in class to have little taste for grammar. That seems OK to me. Another student might be more reluctant about writing but enthusiastic about drama and language study, including grammar. That too is OK. It is important to allow ourselves these enthusiasms and to learn effective ways to teach the things that we merely accept. And can we assume that you are good at English? Here perhaps we might pause and ask what is meant by *good*. We might agree that English teachers should read and write well, but there is no fixed standard in this regard. And, as we have seen, most of us—like Steve—do not feel equally competent in every aspect of the discipline.

But how much you like English or how good you are at it is not the issue here. You do not have to justify anything. Tell us instead how you came to prefer English. What actually happened in your life? For Steve, the desire can be traced back to early childhood and to parents who supported his tastes and abilities, even as his brothers indulged other tastes. For Katie, another methods student, English "came alive" in sixth grade when a teacher asked her to write something that seemed interesting and then praised Katie's work. For Jennifer the process was different: It stemmed from her own struggles with family and academic problems in high school and the power of writing to help her deal with those issues. She hated high school (the opposite of the "continuation theme"), but, almost for that very reason, Jennifer wants to be a high school teacher.

* * *

Tell the story of why you are here—taking a course in the teaching of English. Begin wherever you wish, as early as you like, but end your narrative with your enrolling in this course.

For Further Reading

Christenbury, Leila. *Making the Journey: Being and Becoming a Teacher of English Language Arts.* Portsmouth, NH: Boynton/Cook, Heinemann, 1994. A very readable book aimed at the beginning English teacher. Christenbury uses narrative and a wealth of classroom examples to illustrate issues and strategies for the teaching of English.

Elbow, Peter. *What Is English?* New York/Urbana, IL: Modern Language Association/National Council of Teachers of English, 1990. Elbow was a participant in the English Coalition Conference in 1987, a meeting of teachers on all levels that explored core issues in the teaching of the language arts. Elbow's book describes those conversations, both in his own voice (the regular chapters) and in the voices of other participants (in interludes). A very readable book that addresses important issues.

English Journal. Periodically, *English Journal* devotes an issue to a particular aspect of teaching English. Note especially "The Newest Members of the Family" (February 1995), on the experiences of teachers new to the profession.

Flood, James, Julie M. Jensen, Diane Lapp, and James R. Squire, eds. *Handbook of Research on Teaching the English Language Arts.* Sponsored by the International Reading Association and the National Council of Teachers of English. New

York: Macmillan, 1991. You probably will not need to consult this, but if you are ever asked "what research says" on a subject, this is the place to look. A surprisingly readable reference book.

Hillocks, George. *The English Curriculum under Fire*. Urbana, IL: NCTE, 1982. Short essays on challenges to the English curriculum, especially from the back-to-basics movement. Still relevant today.

Meyer, Richard J. *Stories from the Heart: Teachers and Students Researching Their Literacy Lives*. Mahwah, NJ: Lawrence Erlbaum Associates, 1996. A book full of stories about how we come to be literate, aimed at helping teachers reflect on their own stories of literacy.

Peters, William H., ed. *Effective English Teaching: Concept, Research, and Practice*. Urbana, IL: NCTE, 1987. An article by Peters is cited in Application 1.2. The other essays in this collection discuss effective teaching research from other points of view.

Small, Robert C., Jr., and Joseph E. Strzepek. *A Casebook for English Teachers: Dilemmas and Decisions*. Belmont, CA: Wadsworth, 1988. The authors pose a series of "cases" or situations, followed by questions, suggestions, and further readings.

Tchudi, Stephen, and Diana Mitchell. *Exploring and Teaching the English Language Arts*, 4th edition. New York: Longman, 1999. A comprehensive book on the teaching of English, with chapters on literature, writing, drama, and mass media.

2

Reading Literature

Introduction

Teachers of Reading

Teachers of reading? Isn't that the job of the elementary teacher or reading specialist? What does it have to do with teaching literature? Everything, I'd say, for I want to suggest here that teaching reading and teaching literature should not be distinct enterprises. Traditionally, of course, they have been considered to be different. Working on the theory that students already know how to read and that the business of the classroom is to talk about texts, teachers have made assignments that students read on their own. Then, having done the reading, students come to class and the talk begins. This might consist of lecture or discussion, but the pattern is the same: read and then talk.

Both of the assumptions behind traditional practice—that secondary students "already know how to read" and that the business of the classroom is to talk about texts that have already been read—need to be examined more closely. We might ask, for example, if it is helpful (or even accurate) to talk about reading as a static skill, a set of mental activities that, once learned, enable us to read all kinds of texts. How would our ideas about teaching change if we thought of reading as a form of thinking that changes continually as we grow as thinkers and as texts challenge us to think in different ways? And what about those texts? Is that what we are teaching? If so, are they the same for all readers and for each of us as we develop as readers?

As teachers are fond of saying, "There are no easy answers," but the three readings in this chapter begin to address some basic issues. Louise Rosenblatt, Robert Probst, and Nancie Atwell present their ideas in different ways, but they all treat reading as an activity, something that readers *do* with texts. In their insistence that reading involves the active creation of meaning by the reader from the text, they stand in opposition to the notion, so prevalent among students, that reading is really just "picking information up off the page." Thus, these authors talk about reading in ways that are alien to many students who seem honestly to believe that their job is to look at the book, whereas the teacher's job is to tell them what it means. On the contrary, reading, as it is described in these essays, is work that the student/reader must do.

Of these three essays, Louise Rosenblatt's "A Performing Art" (pp. 29–35) is the oldest and most general. Yet Rosenblatt's point of view is still very relevant today. In essence, she argues that the experience of reading is an active performance on the part of the reader—an evocation of meanings that are only implicit in the literary text. Hence the mission of the English teacher is to help students understand "the lived experience" of a literary work. This can be difficult, and it certainly involves a change of heart from traditional notions of teaching literature. We need the courage, she says, "to admit to our students that the actual business of recreating a work is difficult and tricky and sometimes frustrating, but always exciting and challenging" (p. 33).

If Rosenblatt is theoretical, Robert Probst is more specific and practical. In "Reader-Response Theory and the English Curriculum" (pp. 41–51), he fleshes out Rosenblatt's idea of reading and applies it to a classroom situation. In the next essay, Nancie Atwell asks a crucial question about the teaching of reading in secondary schools: If our job is to help students become proficient readers, and not just to analyze texts, why aren't we spending more time on reading itself? "Making Time" (p. 55–66) offers a rationale for organizing one's classroom as a reading workshop.

Reader Response

The position taken in the Rosenblatt and Probst pieces is known as *reader response*, a term that has become something of a catchword. It is used to describe a wide variety of approaches to teaching, some of which are antithetical to each other. It sometimes indicates an anything-goes attitude toward interpretation: A text is essentially empty of meaning, and readers are free to make it mean whatever they like. This view, almost a parody of reader-response criticism, is not what I mean here. Rather, I am using the term in Rosenblatt's transactional sense: Meaning is created by the reader through an active engagement with the language of the text.

Response is a complex process—not just a matter of feelings, although the reader's feelings surely matter. Response is intellectual as well as emotional, and more. It is linguistic (a use of language), social (at least in schools, where books are read with other people), and even physical (the state of our bodies can influence how we read, and what we read can affect our physical state). Therefore, the response that we have as readers is not usually an orderly, linear march from the beginning to the end of the text. It involves guessing and making mistakes, backtracking and sometimes wandering, and it can mean reacting in several, even contradictory ways to the same aspects of the text. And though it sometimes results in a unified interpretation, it need not reach that stage.

So although it is usually necessary for teachers to create a reading schedule for longer texts, we cannot assume that all (or even most) students have read at the same rate and in the same way. These differences among readers go beyond variations in fluency and comprehension; on a more basic level, the reading experience is different for each of us, because what we bring to the text is different. How different, of course, depends on who we are: There will be less variety in the responses of students with similar language backgrounds, who have been educated in the same way and who hold similar values. But there will still be considerable variety, especially when the text is ambiguous or open to a number of coherent interpretations. Our task as teachers, then, is to find a way to recognize the multiplicity of student responses without suggesting that the text can mean whatever we want it to mean.

Tensions for the Teacher of Literature

It is reasonable to think of reader and text as engaging in a creative tension—between, say, the attitudes that students bring to *Huckleberry Finn* and the commentary on racism that Twain is providing. In this case, the encounter with the text invites responses, some of them racist, which might then be modified. Of course, some students might not be open to that invitation, which results in another kind of tension. But the main point still holds: When students read actively, literature can do things to readers—intrigue, please, puzzle, anger, move them in some way. Because texts are invitations to respond and think, in the best classrooms the tension between reader and text is acted out in lively discussion.

But where is the teacher in all this? As the Probst and Atwell articles make clear, the role of the teacher need not be that of expert interpreter, at least not exclusively. It is true, of course, that as teachers we bring more literary and life experience to the act of reading, so we have much to offer our students in our expert role. But if our main goal is not to tell students what we know but to help them learn on their own, then we need to consider other roles, like that of coach or guide. Thus, when Probst positions himself as a questioner in the classroom, or Atwell takes on the role of correspondent between and among members of a reading group, they are adjusting to the multiple demands that teaching literature places on people. And there is tension here as well, for it is not always easy to know when to take charge and when to let go, especially when we know that students need us to do both.

As we have seen, the tension between reader and text is not a negative thing; it is actually an opportunity for learning and creativity.

And the same can be said of the tensions that develop in the literature classroom—these too are opportunities. It might help, for example, to think of the classroom experience in dramatic terms, with
these players: active student readers, a judicious teacher, and a text
that challenges everybody. This is what one sees in "Provocations"
(pp. 72–78) the John Rouse essay that concludes the readings for
this chapter. We get to see Mrs. Martinez, a veteran teacher in an inner-city school, conduct a discussion on a Native American trickster
story. The atmosphere, one could say, is "full of tension," of a creative sort. Teachers like Mrs. Martinez are not interested in making
those tensions go away; they want to work with them to provoke
thought. Tensions are, after all, signs of life, energy, and thought.
They are among the many reasons we gravitated to the teaching of
literature in the first place.

A PERFORMING ART

Louise M. Rosenblatt

Louise Rosenblatt is one of the fore-most proponents of what has been called the "reader response" approach to literature. Actually, Rosenblatt does not use that term. The Reader, the Text, the Poem (1978), a book that describes her theoretical grounding, is subtitled "The Transactional Theory of Literature," and that is more like it. Throughout her long career, Rosen-blatt has been concerned with the way readers and texts engage in a transaction, each influencing the other in the creation of meaning. As you read this essay, first published in 1966, ask yourself how reading, as you know it, can be described in terms of "performance." Is it true, for instance, that, like musicians with sheet music, we perform the text as we read?

"A Performing Art" was first pub-lished in English Journal, *Vol. 55, No. 8 (November 1966); copyright 1966 by the National Council of Teachers of English. It is reprinted with permission.*

Those who seek to praise the riches of literature have often been well-served by Keats' image of the reader as a trav-eler "in the realms of gold" coming upon a great work like "some watcher of the skies/When a new planet swims into his ken." But this suggestion of a remote object gazed upon with awe may reinforce the current, almost hyp-notically repeated, emphasis on "the work itself" as distinct from author and reader. Fortunately, in another sonnet, "On Sitting Down to Read *King Lear* Once Again," Keats provides a counterbalancing image, which does justice to the reader's involvement in the literary work:

. . . once again the fierce dispute
Betwixt damnation and impassion'd clay,
Must I burn through.

Imaginative literature is indeed something "burned through," lived through, by the reader. We do not learn *about* Lear, we share, we participate in, Lear's stormy induction into wis-dom. In *Huckleberry Finn,* we do not learn *about* conditions in the pre–Civil War South; we live in them, we see them through the eyes and personality of Huck. Even while we chuckle at his adventures and his idiom, we grow into awareness of the moral dimensions ap-propriate for viewing that world. Whether it be a light-hearted lyric of Herrick's or a swiftly-paced intellectual comedy of Shaw's or a brooding narra-tive of Hardy's, a reading is of necessity a participation, a personal experience.

The literary work is not primarily a document in the history of language or society. It is not simply a mirror of, or a report on, life. It is not a homily setting forth moral or philosophic or religious precepts. As a work of art, it offers a special kind of experience. It is a mode of living. The poem, the play, the story, is thus an extension, an amplification, of life itself. The reader's primary pur-pose is to add *this* kind of experience to the other kinds of desirable experi-ences that life may offer.

No one else can read a literary work for us. The benefits of literature can emerge only from creative activity on the part of the reader himself. He responds to the little black marks on the page, or to the sounds of the words in his ear, and he "makes something of them." The verbal symbols enable him to draw on his past experiences with what the words point to in life and literature. The text presents these words in a new and unique pattern. Out of these he is enabled actually to mould a new experience, the literary work.

It is this experiential aspect which differentiates the literary work of art from other forms of verbal communication. *Imaginative* literature happens when we focus our attention on what we are sensing, thinking, feeling, structuring, in the act of response to the particular words in their particular order. Even the most modest work—a nursery rhyme, say—demands attention to what the words are calling forth within us. In its highest form, as in Keats' reading of Shakespeare, such absorption in what we are evoking from the text produces feelings of being completely carried out of oneself.

As the reader submits himself to the guidance of the text, he must engage in a most demanding kind of activity. Out of his past experience, he must select appropriate responses to the individual words, he must sense their interplay upon one another, he must respond to clues of tone and attitude and movement. He must focus his attention on what he is structuring through these means. He must try to see it as an organized whole, its parts interrelated as fully as the text and his own capacities permit. From sound and rhythm and image and ideas he forges an experience, a synthesis, that he calls the poem or play or novel. Whether for a nursery rhyme or for *King Lear*, such an activity goes on, and its complex nature can only be suggested here. The

amazing thing is that critics and theorists have paid so little attention to this synthesizing process itself, contenting themselves usually with the simpler task of classifying the verbal symbols and their various patterns in the text.

In the *teaching* of literature, then, we are basically helping our students to learn to perform in response to a text. In this respect we are perhaps closer to the voice teacher, even the swimming coach, than we are to the teacher of history or botany. The reader performs the poem or the novel, as the violinist performs the sonata. But the instrument on which the reader plays, and from which he evokes the work, is— himself. The final lines of a poem by Yeats are sometimes used out of context to suggest the fusion of so-called form and substance in the work of art itself.

> O body swayed to music, O brightening glance,
> How can we know the dancer from the dance?

In this image of the dancer, who under the spell of the music makes of his own body the formed substance which is the dance, we can also prefigure the reader: under the guidance of the text, out of his own thoughts and feelings and sensibilities, the reader makes a new ordering, the formed substance which is for him the literary work of art. The teacher of literature, especially, needs to keep alive this view of the literary work as personal evocation, the product of creative activity carried on by the reader under guidance of the text.

Critical theory during the past few decades has made this emphasis suspect, however. Building on one facet of I. A. Richards' work, the "New Critics" and their sympathizers did much to rescue the poem as a work of art from earlier confusions with the poem either as a biographical document or as a document in intellectual and social history. A mark of much twentieth-century criticism became its avoidance largely of the social and biographical approach to literature. This moreover, was paralleled by a reaction against impressionist criticism. Walter Pater, for example, became the exemplar of the reader too preoccupied with his own emotions to remain faithful to "the poem itself." The reaction from impressionism fostered the notion of an impersonal or objective criticism, which, avoiding also the historical and social, busied itself with exploitation of the techniques of "close reading." This tended to treat "the poem"—or any literary work—as if it existed as an object, like a machine, whose parts can be analyzed without reference either to the maker or to the observer (or reader). Those who have been indoctrinated with this critical emphasis are especially shocked at insistence on the literary work as experience. They misinterpret this as an invitation to an irresponsible emotionalism and impressionism.

There is, in fact, nothing in the recognition of the personal nature of literature that requires an acceptance of the notion that every evocation from a text is as good as every other. We need only think of our successive readings of the same text, at 15 or 30 or 50, to know that we can differentiate. Undisciplined, irrelevant or distorted emotional responses, and the lack of relevant experience or knowledge will, of course, lead to inadequate interpretations of the text. The aim is to help the student toward a more and more controlled, more and more valid or defensible, response to the text.

This does not imply, however, that there is, as with the mathematical problem, one single "correct" reading of a literary text. This raises very complex and thorny problems concerning the criteria of soundness to be applied to any interpretation. However, this question is much more difficult to set-tle in theory than to face in practical interpretation of particular texts. We may not be able to arrive at a unanimous agreement concerning the best interpretation, say, of *Hamlet* or of "The Second Coming," but we can arrive at some consensus about interpretations that are to be rejected as ignoring large elements in the work, or as introducing irrelevant or exaggerated responses. Recognition that there is not a single interpretation which the teacher can impose still leaves room for a very stringent discipline. This can be carried on at the simplest or the highest level.

First, we can always move from our personal responses and interpretation back to the text. What in the text justifies our response? This is what the scientist would call our "control," the means of avoiding arbitrary and irrelevant interpretations.

Second, we can make clear the criteria, the framework of ideas or knowledge, or the standards of evaluation, that we are bringing to bear on our experience. We may sometimes find that differences are due not to a misreading of the work but to a very different set of expectations or bases of judgment.

More is involved than just the need for a reaction from current pseudo-scientific "objectivity" or "impersonality." More is implied than merely reinstatement of the social, historical, philosophic, or ethical approaches to literature. We must place in the center of our attention the actual process of literary re-creation. As teachers of literature, our concern should be with the relation between readers and texts. This would change the emphasis in much that we do.

We would not forget, of course, that the text was an event in the life of an author, that he produced it at a particular moment in his life and in the history of his world. But we would not forget, either, that the text becomes an event in the life of each reader as he recreates it.

What, then, are some of the implications of this emphasis on the personal nature of literary experience? Above all, our business is to contribute to a continuing process of growth in ability to handle responses—linguistic, emotional, intellectual—to literary texts. This means that our aim is to improve the quality of our students' actual literary experiences. We must seek to bring to our students at each stage of their development sound literary works in which they can indeed become personally involved.

This may seem simply to repeat a cliché of education, that students should be given works suited to their interests and level of maturity. Often, however, the search for appropriate works is perfunctory, and habit or convenience or economy intervenes. Sometimes, the notion of "interest" is oversimplified or superficial, as when works dealing only with teen-age problems are offered to adolescents, or when youngsters are allowed to go on indefinitely following one type of reading—science fiction, say. Nowadays, for the Advanced Placement youngsters, especially, the error is to look only at the works, and to be pleased at the number of "great works" or works of high technical complexity being read, rather than at the *quality of the actual reading experiences*. (I hear, alas, of *The Waste Land* in the ninth grade and *The Magic Mountain* in the eleventh. Extreme instances, perhaps, but symptomatic.)

It may be that the youngster reading *National Velvet* or *Johnny Tremain* will have a fuller, more sensitive, more responsible literary experience than the student who is so unready to handle the demands of the *Divine Comedy* or even Henry James that he falls back on criticism of criticism of criticism, and never develops a literary technique of reading and assimilating for himself.

Those struggling to face the challenge of education for the culturally disadvantaged have been least able to ignore the fact that the reader can read only out of past experience and present interests. Here, however, the danger is to focus too exclusively on the external life of the reader. What he brings to the text is not only an external environment and special dialect, but also fundamental human emotions and relationships. Probably many of the works which do treat essential human relationships but are considered remote from the interests of the disadvantaged reader are not so at all; they are made inaccessible by being expressed in a "standard" dialect which the youngster must learn almost as a second language. Materials treating the immediate environment and problems of the slum child have their important uses, but mainly as bridges, leading the young reader to learn how to enter through the printed page into the whole culture surrounding him.

When the young reader is confronted with the text—whether it be *The Pearl* or *The Scarlet Letter* or *Hamlet*—first of all we should seek to foster his having a personal experience with it. His efforts and his attention should be focused on re-creating it sensitively and responsibly. He should be encouraged to bring to the text whatever in his past experience is relevant, his sensuous awarenesses, his feeling for people and practical circumstances, his ideas and information, as well as his feeling for the sound and pace and texture of language. We know that in a reliving of the work, he does not read coldly, arriving first at something called "the meaning" or the paraphrasable sense, and *then* starting to feel or think about it. In an actually creative reading, all these things may go on either at the same time or in many different phases: emotional response, the formulation of ideas, and tentative general views about the emotional attitudes, the characters or the situations that the work treats. The young reader needs to learn how to suspend judgment, to be self-critical, to develop and revise his interpretation as he reads.

To do justice to the text, then, the young reader must be helped to handle his responses to it. Yet the techniques of the usual English classroom tend to hurry past this process of active creation and re-creation of the text. The pupil is, instead, rushed into peripheral concerns. How many times youngsters read poems or stories or plays trying to memorize as many random details as possible, because such "facts" will be the teacher's means for testing—in multiple answer questions—whether they have read the work! Or students will read only with half a mind and spirit, knowing that this is sufficient to fill in the requirements of a routine book report: summarize the plot, identify the principal characters, describe the setting, etc. Even the search for meaning is reduced too often to paraphrase that simply dulls and dilutes the impact of the work. The concern with theme often relies too much on high-level abstractions, while the analysis of techniques becomes a preoccupation with recognizing devices—the scanning of verse, the labelling of "types," the listing of symbols, the recognition of recurrent myths.

Our assignments, our ways of testing, our questions about the work, our techniques of analysis, should direct attention to, not away from, the work as an aesthetic experience. In applying the accepted treatments to the work, we must remember that all the reader has to deal with is whatever he himself lives through in his interchange with the text.

Hence, I should like to see our classrooms more often places in which we have the courage to admit to our students that the actual business of recreating a work is difficult and tricky and sometimes frustrating, but always exciting and challenging. Instead of hurrying the youngster into impersonal and so-called objective formulations as quickly as possible, the successful teacher of literature makes the classroom a place for critical sharing of personal responses. Awareness that others have had different experiences with it will lead the reader back to the text for a closer look. The young reader points to what in the text explains his response. He may discover, however, that he has overreacted to some elements and ignored others. Or he may learn that some word or image has triggered a fantasy or awakened some personal preoccupation quite alien to the text. (I. A. Richards, long ago, reported in *Practical Criticism* on the many pitfalls awaiting the reader.) Such exchange of ideas, such scrutiny of the reasons for response, will create awareness of the relevance of critical terminology and will develop ability to handle more and more demanding texts. Discussion of personal responses, of the text-as-lived-through, can thus give rise to a truly "inductive" study of literature.

The more we teachers understand the linguistic demands of a particular work, the better able we shall be to help the young reader. But we cannot do this by formulas for reading, or by simply requiring the mouthing of the right answers to the right questions. Passive acceptance of the teacher's interpretation can bring only pseudo-understanding, verbalizing about, rather than experience of, the work. Even the skills and knowledge to be imparted can so easily become substitute ends in themselves. The identification of the "persona" of the poem, or the definition of the nature of irony, or the statement of the theme, or the recognition of a mythic pattern—the journey, the oedipus situation—it is hard to keep in mind that these are not the ends or the justification of our teaching. These are means by which the reader can handle or describe his response to the clues offered by the text. But their value as means lies always in their helping the reader to enter more fully into the total experience by which he organizes, re-creates, the work for himself.

We may not always be able to look over his shoulder while the student is having a real literary experience, but we can do at least two things. First, we can be very careful to scrutinize all our procedures to be sure that we are not in actuality substituting other aims—things to do *about* literature—for the experience *of* literature. We can ask of every assignment or method or text, no matter what its short-term effective-ness: Does it get in the way of the live sense of literature? Does it make litera-ture something to be regurgitated, ana-lyzed, categorized, or is it a means toward making literature a more per-sonally meaningful and self-disciplined activity? And, second, we can create in our classrooms an atmosphere of give-and-take and mutual challenge; through this, we shall surely find indi-rect evidences of the real literary expe-riences, the sources of growth.

A consequence of such an approach is that as the student clarifies his sense of the work, he becomes aware of his own attitudes, his own notions of what is important or desirable; he broadens his awareness of alternatives of behavior and aspiration. Willy-nilly, the English classroom, if it is a place where litera-ture really resides, becomes the arena for a linkage with the world of the stu-dent. What he brings to literature, what he undergoes through the medium of the literary text, how he is helped to handle this in the classroom, will affect what he carries away from it in enhanced sensitivities to language and to life.

When I made some remarks of this nature not long ago at a meeting of col-lege teachers of literature, one of them exclaimed, "Good heavens! You don't propose to have kids read stories in or-der to learn that they mustn't steal cars! Or concentrate on stories about teen-age dating?"

He was echoing what has been gener-ally a wholesome reaction against cer-tain kinds of too-literal use of literature: for example, the emphasis on extracting a message or moral or lesson, or the use of stories as a springboard for get-ting youngsters to talk out their prob-lems and release tensions. This use of literature has probably not been as widespread as some think, and actually no one denies the therapeutic potentiali-ties of such use of literature by people trained in such matters. Nor is the read-ing of poetry as an art threatened be-cause John Stuart Mill found in Words-worth's poetry the experience through which he overcame a severe mental de-pression. But I agree that such didactic or therapeutic aims should not replace directly literary concerns. The teacher of literature seeks primarily to help stu-dents to read so well that they may de-rive any and all possible benefits from literature. On the other hand, the anti-septic reaction of the extreme disciples of the so-called purely literary ap-proach, who fear any moral or psycho-logical concern, tends to negate the full nature of the literary work of art.

Here, then, is another important im-plication of the emphasis on the essen-tially personal character of literary ex-perience: it forces us to recognize that in the classroom, if we are to keep liter-ature alive, we cannot completely sepa-rate the technical, the aesthetic, from the human meanings of the work.

Perhaps a very simple and modest il-lustration will suffice, drawn from a dis-cussion by a group of verbally not very gifted high school seniors, most of whom were destined for vocational or technical colleges or institutes. One of the girls responded with intense indig-nation to the story of a man who had left his wife and child and run off to sea. The other pupils objected to her un-qualified condemnation. They pointed out the many clues to the father's unhappiness, his boredom with monotonous routine work, the dreary apartment, his nagging wife, and his yearning for the romance of far-off exotic places. Some of these clues were in descriptive details, in items like a picture on the wall which took on symbolic meaning in relation to all the other details. The story was certainly not very complex, but it sufficed to provide the occasion for what amounted to a group process in "close reading." By the time the discussion ended the girl realized that, no matter what her opinions about a husband's responsibilities, she had missed the insights the story offered into personality and the conflicting needs of husband and wife in the situation.

From one point of view, the girl's learning was merely a matter of becoming aware of literary devices and narrative development. From another angle, she had to some slight degree simply acquired a broader moral stance, in which passing of moral judgment was tempered by understanding of motives and human needs. I see these as two indivisible facets of the same process of growth in ability to read and respond in a balanced way to the literary work. (Probably none of the youngsters in that group was ready to be amused at the trick ending of the story or to decide on whether it was a sound ending—which again, even for so frail a literary work, would involve the human implications of the story as well as its technical dexterity.) When we are helping students to better techniques of reading through sensitivity to diction, to tone, structure, image, symbol, narrative movement, we are also helping them to make the more refined responses that are ultimately the source of human understanding and sensitivity to human values.

When there is active participation in literature—the reader living through, reflecting on and criticizing his own responses to the text—there will be many kinds of benefits. We can call this "growth in ability to share discriminatingly in the possibilities of language as it is used in literature." But this means also the development of the imagination, the ability to escape from the limitations of time and place and environment, the capacity to envisage alternatives in ways of life and in moral and social choices, the sensitivity to thought and feeling and needs of other personalities. The youth will need to grow into the emotional and intellectual and aesthetic maturity necessary for appreciating the great works of literature in our own and other languages. As he does this, he grows also into partnership in the wisdom of the past and the aspirations for the future, of our culture and our society. The great abstractions, love, honor, integrity, compassion, individuality, democracy, will take on for him human meaning.

Keats, you recall, ends his sonnet on sitting down to read *King Lear* once again, with the lines:

> But when I am consumed in the Fire,
> Give me new Phoenix-wings to fly at
> my desire.

Keats saw himself about to be completely "consumed," absorbed in, the reliving of the play. But he anticipated that he would emerge reborn to even greater freedom and creativity. This is indeed the paradox of the intensely personal nature of the reading of the literary work: it is a kind of experience valuable in and for itself, and yet—or perhaps, therefore—it can also have a liberating and fortifying effect in the ongoing life of the reader.

For Further Thought

1. Rosenblatt says that the aesthetic experience of literary reading is different from that of other kinds of reading. Cite some examples of other kinds of reading, explaining how you think the experience is different from that of reading literature.

2. Rosenblatt writes of the New Critics and techniques of close reading. Find out more about the New Critics—perhaps by interviewing an English professor. How much of your experience in the English classroom, in secondary school or college, was influenced by this school of thought?

3. Consider the distinction that Rosenblatt makes between learning things *about* literature and the experience of literature itself. How much analysis of literature do you think is appropriate in secondary classrooms? As a teacher, how much time would you devote to the consideration of figurative language—metaphor, for example, or personification?

4. Many of Rosenblatt's references are to literary works assigned in the upper secondary grades or in college. (Atwell, a middle-level teacher, will adopt a very different emphasis.) Do Rosenblatt's ideas hold true for all kinds of literature, regardless of level? Can you make the same case for the value of the literary experience if you are talking about Hinton's *The Outsiders* or another young adult novel?

5. In the next-to-last paragraph of the essay, Rosenblatt describes the benefits of the literary experience. Do you accept this list of benefits, or would you want to make some distinctions? How do these benefits match up with the three schools of thought described in the introduction to chapter 1? If you disagree with Rosenblatt, where would your emphasis be?

Application 2.1:
A Look at Three Lesson Plans

Louise Rosenblatt discusses the teaching of literature in fairly general terms, which is appropriate in a discussion of one's philosophy of literature. That is the value of her work: She asks us to consider what we believe to be true about literature, about reading, and about teaching. For everyone's teaching practice is ultimately based on a set of beliefs.

Let's begin to examine the relationship of beliefs and practices by looking at three lesson plans that have been adapted from the work of three real teachers. They are, to varying degrees, traditional in their approach to literature. But here I need to clarify the intent of the exercises that follow. For although the selection of readings reveals that I lean toward a reader-response philosophy of teaching of literature, I am not at all certain that this philosophy necessitates one particular classroom approach. Nor is it clear to me that any given set of practices ensures that one is being "true" to one's stated philosophy. So much depends on the spirit with which one does something. For example, I have seen students work in response groups where the agenda was clearly set by the teacher; it looked very free and open, but students knew exactly what they were "supposed to do." And I have seen front-of-the-room teachers who were amazingly in touch with students and their genuine responses to literature. Still, one does have to make choices, so it is good to consider which practices are most in keeping with your philosophy. That is what we are after: a clarification of our own beliefs about reading and teaching literature.

The three lesson plans were written for different students on different grade levels, and though they are based on slightly different understandings about teaching literature, they have two things in common. First, each teacher has found it useful to write a daily plan—that is, they are planning within the frame of a fifty-minute period. True, they are working within a larger frame (a unit or semester plan), but the individual lesson is still the primary unit of instruction. Second, and more important, is that each teacher has determined, in advance, a goal for the lesson, some place he or she wishes to go with the literature. Those goals, as you will see, are different in each plan, and some more than others seem to value the students' response to the text. Nonetheless, these plans seem fairly traditional, in the sense that the teacher's agenda is fairly fixed.

Plan 1: A Teacher-Led Discussion

In the first plan, a twelfth-grade teacher is conducting a poetry unit that includes work about the four seasons. They come now to e. e. cummings's "in

Literature Plan 1 (Twelfth Grade)

TOPIC: e. e. cummings's "chanson innocent" ("in Just-spring")

OBJECTIVES: To provide students with several experiences of the poem; to help them clarify certain images (the balloonman especially); to demonstrate how a poem changes with successive readings and with more information.

TIME: One fifty-minute period

Objectives	Activities	Time
Students will settle into English class. Students will have a chance to anticipate the main idea of the poem—to help them connect with the poem more readily.	Settling-down time (take roll, etc.)	5
	Introduce the idea of spring: Show pictures of spring scene, ask students for childhood memories of spring (list on board, as images).	5
	Read the poem aloud. Students jot down questions. Then read it again.	
Students will share ideas about the scene and action of the poem—to establish a baseline understanding.	Discussion: Focus on setting. ("When and where is this taking place?") Note three possible meanings of "In Just-spring." "Who are the characters and what are they doing?" End with questions about spring—is it like our jottings on the board?	10
	Read the poem again, telling students to pay close attention to the balloonman.	
Students will struggle with the troubling element in the poem—to appreciate the dissonance created by the balloonman and to begin to work through that dissonance.	Free writing: Write your feelings about the balloonman. What is he like? How do you feel about him?	15
	Discussion: How does this figure change (liken the technique to a camera focusing). Who is goat-footed (the devil? Pan?)? Explain about Pan and the woods and "panic." Ask students about freedom in the spring—what are you free from? How is spring a wild time?	
	Read the poem once more. Any final reactions?	
	Show pictures again and sum up ideas about spring from the cummings poem. Ask students to make a list of images and memories of spring, the images on one side of a piece of paper, and the actual events on the other side.	10
Students will see what others have written—to enrich their ideas.	Share your ideas with a neighbor and ask any questions that seem appropriate.	to the end of the class
	Tomorrow: We will read a few more poems about spring and begin to write one of our own. I will write one too.	

Just-spring." This teacher loves the poem and has taught it many times. She knows from experience how a poem can "grow" as it is read and reread, so she constructs a lesson that, she hopes, will reveal that to students. In addition, she feels that certain points of information will help students interpret and appreciate the poem—in particular, the use of the Pan image. Her plan takes the traditional form in which objectives are listed for each activity and particular amounts of time are allotted to each. The time line is flexible, she says, but experience has shown that she can get this work done in fifty minutes.

Some Things to Consider About Plan 1

1. Respond to the content of the plan. Did you read this poem, or poems like it, in high school? How were such classes conducted? If there were allusions or tricky figures of speech in the poetry, how did the teacher handle them? What was your reaction?
2. The lesson is fairly directive, that is, the teacher knows where she is going and expects students to follow that lead. What are the advantages and disadvantages of this approach?
3. The teacher wants to get to the Pan image in the poem. How important is that? What would you think if students discussed the poem and Pan was never mentioned? Suppose you were in this situation, having mentioned Pan, and a student said that you were "reading into" the poem. What would you say?
4. Find the cummings poem (if your instructor has not already provided it), read it, and then discuss how you would spend a fifty-minute class period on this poem with a class of seniors. Explain the ways in which your approach differs from the teacher's lesson plan.

Plan 2: Introducing a Novel

The second plan is the work of a tenth-grade teacher who is about to launch into Golding's *Lord of the Flies*. The class has just finished a writing unit that had no particular connection to the novel. He always teaches this novel, claiming that it "works well" for sophomores, and this is when the books are available. But because students are coming to the novel cold, he knows that he needs to do some prereading. The desert island scenario is intended to focus students' attention on the situation of the novel and to bring out whatever "baggage" they attach to that situation. Beyond that, this teacher mainly wants to get students into the story. He knows that the beginning is the toughest part of any book, and that he has better success in getting students to do the assigned reading if he spends some class time getting them started.

Literature Plan 2 (Tenth Grade)

TITLE: Prereading for *Lord of the Flies*

GOALS: To evoke in students' minds the idea of being stranded on a desert island; to deal with preconceptions; to get students "into" the story.

REMINDERS: _____

Content	Strategies
Key concepts: being stranded, the island as Eden, the island as a survival problem, children versus adults	1. Show pictures of islands. ("How do you feel?") Get reactions in brief free writing. Show ads with Edenic pictures (get further reactions and talk).
Materials: pictures of islands: ads that show Edenic islands	2. Inventory: "Imagine that you are stranded on a desert island. Make a list of the things you will need to survive. Think of physical needs—but also social and emotional needs. Write out your list."
Chapter 1 of *Lord of the Flies*	3. Discuss lists, putting examples on the board.
	4. Raise question of adults versus children in discussion: What advantages or disadvantages would a group of children have compared with a group of adults?
	5. Begin reading chapter 1, up to the arrival of the boys when Ralph blows the conch.

Evaluation	Notes (Next Day)
Check to see that free writing and inventories are done (circulate and check off in grade book).	1. Get student responses to chapter 1 in a brief response statement.
In discussion, attend to students' expectations: that the island will be a paradise, for example, or that children will have physical problems but not social problems because they are more "innocent" (listen carefully).	2. Discussion: Ask questions about survival skills, social organization, and general ability to cope. "Are these kids coping well?"
Tomorrow: Students will finish chapter 1. Check on their expectations: Will these children survive? Will they get along? How are they coping?	3. Predictions about the future: the struggle for leadership? Piggy's role? Will they find food?
	4. Begin chapter 2 and then pick up the pace, assigning the rest of chapter 2 and all of chapter 3.

Some Things to Consider About Plan 2

1. Respond to the content of the plan. Did you read *Lord of the Flies* in high school? What motivated you to read it (assuming that you did)?

2. Consider the idea of prereading. Did you have teachers who got you started this way? Was it helpful? What, if any, dangers might there be in this approach?

3. Look at the strategies section and the way verbs are used. Who is the implied subject of those verbs? (For example, who puts items on the board? Who will read the text? Will it be read aloud?) What are some other ways to conduct this part of the lesson?

4. Discuss how you might introduce a class of sophomores to *Lord of the Flies*. If you have not read the Golding novel, choose another book, like *To Kill a Mockingbird*, that might be assigned in tenth grade. Explain the ways in which your approach differs from the teacher's lesson plan.

Plan 3: The Use of Questions

In the third plan, an eighth-grade teacher has assigned Shirley Jackson's "The Lottery." Expecting students to have some difficulty with the story, she has devoted some time at the end of the previous period to introducing it and reading the opening section aloud. In this respect she is like the tenth-grade teacher who prepares his students for *Lord of the Flies.* But she is also like the twelfth-grade teacher in that she has a fairly definite goal for students: They are to "appreciate the power of community values and rituals." With this explicit goal, she plans a set of activities that lead students through factual, interpretive, and evaluative considerations. The core of the lesson, however, is a discussion based on a series of prepared questions.

Literature Plan 3 (Eighth Grade)

Topic: "The Lottery"

Goal: Appreciate the power of community values and rituals

Context: Students have read stories and poems, including some by Native American writers, in which the traditions of elders are valued. "The Lottery" will be followed by Jessie Stewart's "Split Cherry Tree," in which values and traditions come into conflict.

Prereading (previous class period): A discussion of lotteries (definition, how they work, why people participate, example of our state lottery); brief introduction to the story, including the date of publication; start reading the story (at least five paragraphs, but no further than the beginning of the lottery itself); students finish reading the story for today.

Opening activity: Recall exercise. Students are asked to recall something from the story, and I put these items on the board. These will be mostly plot developments, but other things (physical items like the black box, things people said) will surface too. I try to group items as I put them on the board. Everyone must contribute, even if what they say repeats what someone else said. This activity should help students remember the story in some detail.

Consolidate the plot: Go around the room and have students retell the story quickly. Be sure they understand when and where the action takes place. Expect some students to say that it happened long ago and far away. Point out details of contemporary America if need be.

Discussion questions (interpretive and evaluative):

What kind of town is this? What kind of people live here? What is their attitude toward the lottery?

What public functions does the lottery serve (initiation rite, census, public holiday)? What might have been the original purposes of the lottery (sacrifice for good harvest, scapegoating)? How aware are the people of these purposes? If we agree that people are not aware of the original purposes of the lottery, why then do they do it?

Do you think people can really act this way? Can you think of examples of things we do simply because they have always been done (wedding customs, holiday customs, dress)? What do you think about the power of tradition to cause people to behave in these ways? Is Jackson's example of a blood sacrifice too extreme, or do you think it could happen? (Cite examples of human "pack behavior.")

Activity (if time permits): Conduct a black-balling exercise. Students draw papers from a black box, and the "winner" suffers some mildly unpleasant consequence (for example, extra points for everyone except the winner). Students will write in their journals about their participation in this activity (what school traditions conditioned their behavior) and the fairness of it all.

Homework: Finish the journal entry (if not done in class) and then write at least a paragraph on the following situation: Your parents have started a business that requires your labor. They plan to take you out of school to be "home schooled," but in private they say that there really won't be much schooling. "You're old enough to be a working person now," they say. Write about how you would feel in this situation. We will begin to read "Split Cherry Tree" in class tomorrow.

Some Things to Consider About Plan 3

1. Respond to the content of the plan. Do you remember reading "The Lottery" in school? At what grade level? How did you react to the story? This story is frequently challenged by persons who feel it is destructive of traditional values. Do you think this teacher is taking a risk by assigning it in eighth grade? (Look at Edward Jenkinson's essay on censorship in chapter 3.)

2. Describe the teacher's role in this class. How much freedom does she afford students to arrive at their own interpretations? How do the teacher's planned questions function in this lesson? Are they constraining? Freeing? Could they be both?

3. Teachers, English teachers in particular, ask a lot of questions, and often those questions are ways of "getting said" things that the teacher feels need to be said. Try rewriting this plan, with similar goals, without asking any questions. For more on the issue of questions, confer Susan Hynds, "Challenging Questions in the Teaching of Literature," in *Literature Instruction: Focus on Student Response*, Judith A. Langer, ed. (NCTE, 1992), pp. 78–100.

4. Find "The Lottery" and read it. Then write a paragraph or two in which you discuss how you would deal with the story under the same circumstances. Explain the ways in which your approach differs from the teacher's lesson plan.

READER-RESPONSE THEORY AND THE ENGLISH CURRICULUM

Robert E. Probst

Like other reader-response critics, Robert Probst relies on Louise Rosenblatt's description of the literary experience as a transaction between the reader and text. In this essay Probst discusses the nature of that transaction and then draws out some implications for teachers—goals for a literature program, principles of instruction, and questions for reading and writing. All are geared toward exploring connections between the work of literature and the lives of students.

"Reader-Response Theory and the English Curriculum" appeared in English Journal, Vol. 83, No. 3 (March 1994); copyright 1994 by the National Council of Teachers of English. It is reprinted with permission. "Sign for My Father, Who Stressed the Bunt" from Armored Hearts, copyright 1995 by David Bottoms, is reprinted by permission of Copper Canyon Press, P.O. Box 271, Port Townsend, WA 98368.

> *Double, double, toil and trouble;*
> *Fire burn, and cauldron bubble.*

RESPECTING THE TEXT AND RESPECTING THE READER

There's something rotten in the state of Denmark, to mix plays, if not metaphors. Perhaps not rotten, but tumultuous, at least, with reader-response advocates, deconstructionists, cultural critics, feminist critics, new historicists, narratologists, and a few die-hard New Critics, all clustered around the cauldron, tossing their newts' eyes, rats' tails, and bats' wings into the tumbling, bubbling theoretical stew. If we aren't careful, when the hurlyburly's done, we may have forgotten that the purpose of literature programs in the elementary and secondary schools is to develop readers, not literary scholars and critics.

A few of our students will write us appreciative letters several years from now telling us of the joys and agonies of their doctoral research in seventeenth-century poetic forms or their pursuit of Melville's white whale, three of them will publish in *PMLA* or *New Literary History*, two will come home to debate feminist readings of Hemingway at the local college, and one lonely but diligent scholar will travel to England, become buried in the library at Oxford, and produce a brilliant and unreadable Freudian analysis of the significance of the three witches. Most of our students, however, are going to be elsewhere. They'll be in some line of work far removed from the literary world. They should, nonetheless, be readers. They should be people who enjoy literature, who read it willingly, even enthusiastically, and who respond to it and think about it in ways that enrich their emotional and intellectual lives.

To teach them, and to design English curricula for them, we need to keep in mind who they are and where they are headed. If they aren't scholars, if they don't have the instinctive love of books that probably led us into teaching English in the first place, how then do we approach them? How do we justify the time and energy we ask them to expend upon imaginative inventions, the hours we expect them to spend reading and writing, hours they might prefer to spend watching television or roaming the streets? Or—since the explanations and justifications we offer them are unlikely to be persuasive anyway—perhaps the more important question is, How do we teach so that the

experience with literature is its own justification, so that the time spent talking and writing is compelling enough that it doesn't require formal defense?

We must try, first of all, to *respect the natural influence of literary texts upon readers.* Louise Rosenblatt argues that the teacher's influence should be "an elaboration of the vital influence inherent in literature itself." Our first task, if we accept that position, is to make sure that the literature has the chance to work its effects upon the readers, to make sure that we don't get in the way, substituting other matters for that vital influence. The literary experience, then, although it may involve learning about history, biography, genre, technique, and the other elements into which literature is too easily subdivided, is first of all the immediate encounter between a reader and a book. Texts and lessons should begin here, assisting the students to articulate and investigate that influence rather than replacing it with peripheral matters. The literary text must not be reduced to exercise or drill, but must be allowed to live as a work of art, influencing the reader to see and think and feel. Into the context of that natural response, whatever it may be, other tasks, other questions, may be introduced, but the influence inherent in the work itself must be respected and must be of primary concern in the classroom. We must respect the text.

Implicit within this vision of literary experience is a *respect for the uniqueness of the individual reader and the integrity of the individual reading.* We have tended in the past—influenced strongly by the professional tendency to insist upon the rightness of certain readings, upon conformity to established interpretations—to seek consensus in the classroom. Teachers who guided us to a select group of pre-eminent critics reinforced the notion that there was a perfect reading hiding out there somewhere. We didn't have it—obviously—but the best, the most widely-published critics, might lead us to it. One thing we learned quickly was that our own, private, personal experiences would do little to help us find it. They were idiosyncratic, unique, almost deviant, and the poet clearly could not have had them in mind as he wrote, so they were better disregarded and ignored if we hoped to find the right reading, the correct interpretation.

If literature is to matter, however, if it is to become significant in the reader's life, then those personal connections become hard to deny. Meaning lies in that shared ground where the reader and text meet—it isn't resident within the text, to be extracted like a nut from its shell. Rather, the meaning is created by readers as they bring the text to bear upon their own experience, and their own histories to bear upon the text. Robert Scholes goes so far as to argue that reading text and reflecting upon our lives are essentially the same intellectual process:

> Learning to read books—or pictures, or films—is not just a matter of acquiring information from texts, it is a matter of learning to read and write the texts of our lives. Reading, seen this way, is not merely an academic experience but a way of accepting the fact that our lives are of limited duration and that whatever satisfaction we may achieve in life must come through the strength of our engagement with what is around us. We do well to read our lives with the same intensity we develop from learning to read our texts. (19)

So we must respect readers and their readings, too.

This is not, of course, to say that texts mean anything we want them to mean—it's obviously possible to misread, to misunderstand a word, or miss a point. When we argue that a writer holds a certain belief, that a character has certain values or goals, we obligate ourselves to offering evidence and logic that sustain our position. Our reasoning, when we do so, may be weak or it may be strong. In a debate about such matters of inference one argument may well prove to be more persuasive than another. The point remains, however, that a work may mean to a reader what it did not mean to its author. It may trigger responses, evoke memories, awaken emotions and thoughts that could not have been predicted by the writer. And those associations may be of much more interest and importance to the reader than anything the writer could have predicted.

Consider, for the sake of a concrete example, responses to this poem by David Bottoms:

Sign for My Father, Who Stressed the Bunt

On the rough diamond,
the hand-cut field below the dog lot
    and barn,
we rehearsed the strict technique
of bunting. I watched from the infield,
the mound, the backstop
as your left hand climbed the bat,
    your legs
and shoulders squared toward the
    pitcher.
You could drop it like a seed
down either base line. I admired your
    style,
but not enough to take my eyes off the
    bank
that served as our center-field fence.

Years passed, three leagues of
    organized ball,
no few lives. I could homer
into the garden beyond the bank,
into the left-field lot of Carmichael
    Motors,
and still you stressed the same
    technique,
the crouch and spring, the lead arm
    absorbing

just enough impact. That whole
   tiresome pitch
about basics never changing,
and I never learned what you were
   laying down.

Like a hand brushed across the bill of
   a cap,
let this be the sign
I'm getting a grip on the sacrifice.

It's difficult for many students to read such a text as this without finding their minds wandering beyond the words on the page to extraneous matters. Of course, we'll argue that they aren't extraneous to the reading but simply external to the text. Students have spoken of their own experiences playing baseball (or if not baseball, some other sport that required the same concentration and practice), of fathers or mothers or other teachers who tried to get them to accept something difficult for youth to accept, and of their own slow realization that sacrifice was occasionally necessary. Other students will speak of still other matters we can't foresee. One young reader said that it simply evoked a "sense of loss," a sad awareness that the times he and his father had played football together were now past and seldom thought of. Adult readers, some with children of their own, have their own perspectives on the poem, perspectives shaped by their unique histories. For some teachers, the text has called to mind resistant students, students to whom they have struggled to teach concepts unpalatable at the time. If such other matters—thoughts of our parents and our children, our own memories and dreams—are awakened by the poem, are they not part of the literary experience, part of our own encounter with the text, and shouldn't they be welcomed into the discourse?

The poem may invite some readers to reflect on their own mothers or fa-thers, to speculate that much of a parent's rejected teaching was well-meant and ultimately significant. If so, if the reading enables a reader to see some aspect of his or her own life more clearly, to articulate a chapter of a personal story so that it makes sense, then it would be hard to assert that this reading was insignificant. Nor does attention to those personal elements preclude addressing other issues we might want to attend to in the English class. The concept of metaphor, for instance, is clearly worth discussing in the context of this poem. Paying attention to the readers' responses, however, doesn't necessarily obviate consideration of metaphor. In fact, the discussion of responses is likely to lead directly to an opportunity to define and discuss metaphor. Once students have pointed out that the "sacrifice" in the last line of the poem is more than just a ball tapped down the third-base line, that it suggests other sacrifices, larger sacrifices, once the class begins to see that the moment on the ball field represents the relationship between the man and the boy, that it is a metaphor for the teaching and learning, then we may observe that they have discovered the concept of metaphor, and help them define it with their own perceptions about the poem. The concept is more likely to register upon students if they come to the definition through concrete experience than if they are first given the definition and then asked to go out into texts and search for examples.

Those fundamental assumptions—that our students are not professional literary scholars, that the literary experience is at first personal and unique, that there is validity to unique and divergent readings, that we must respect and trust both the text and the reader—lead us to six goals for literature instruction, goals that might direct the design of programs or textbooks.

GOALS FOR THE LITERATURE/ WRITING PROGRAM

1. *Students will learn about themselves.* That is the English program's greatest and most sadly neglected potential. The essential content of our writing is, after all, our own experience. Literature is, above all else, a reservoir of conceptions of human possibilities; it is about life. Rosenblatt says that "of all the arts, literature is most immediately implicated with life itself," and Kenneth Burke refers to literature as "equipment for living." It isn't purely academic, simply a scholarly exercise, but rather it speaks of the human condition and invites us to reflect on our own. If a reading of the Bottoms poem offers us a chance to see ourselves more clearly, to tell something of our own story, to grasp our own experience more firmly, then that opportunity should be pursued. It is likely to result in more readers who see value and significance in literature and who will therefore be more likely to read on their own after schooling ends for them.

2. *Students will learn about others.* The English program ought to humanize us, ought to make us more sympathetic and understanding of one another. When the human questions that literary works raise are emphasized in the classroom, and when the differing responses of the students are respected, it has the power to do so. If the Bottoms poem is simply an opportunity to teach the distinction between metaphor and simile—one of the more useless distinctions in the literary lexicon—there is little to do but learn definitions and memorize examples. But if the influence is inherent in the work itself, which may be to evoke thoughts of parents and children, of teaching, of lessons learned and taught, forgotten and remembered, of lost opportunities, of sacrifices made and not made, then

the encounter with the poem is a chance to learn about both oneself and one's classmates. And it may not be possible for students to understand themselves well without the background of their peers. They may need in part to define themselves in terms of similarities and differences with others around them. The literature and their own writing give them that chance.

3. *Students will learn about cultures and societies, their varying concepts of the good life, of love and hate, justice and revenge, and the other significant issues of human experience.* If we are to come to understand ourselves, we will have to do so, at least in part, by coming to understand the larger groups to which we belong. Those cultures and societies are the background against which we define ourselves as we accept or reject what they value, struggle against the limitations they impose, or celebrate the visions they offer.

4. *Students should learn how texts operate, how they shape our thought and manipulate our emotion.* Respect for the students' unique readings doesn't imply that readers should look only into their own memories and associations, that literary texts are simply catalysts to introspective meditations. Texts are more manipulative than that, and they *do* work upon us, encouraging us to see things in certain ways, to notice and value one aspect of a situation rather than another; if the reading is to contribute to our intellectual growth, we need to be able to see those effects and understand them. The power of the text imposes responsibilities on the reader.

It's appropriate to ask, for instance, how "Sign for My Father" suggests that more is at issue here than baseball strategy. Students might be encouraged to notice that the word "sacrifice" carries several meanings; that the narrator's stance is that of one for whom many years have passed ("three leagues of organized ball, no few lives") so that the bunt is likely to be of less significance to him now; that Bottoms plays upon the contrast of the glorious home run and the lowly but important sacrifice; that games are often offered as metaphors for life. Such observations should, as often as possible, emerge from the natural discussion of responses. Some students, almost inevitably, will offer the suggestion that this poem is about more than baseball, leading directly into the analysis of text suggested here with questions that their own comments imply: "Why is it about more than baseball?" "What makes you suspect that?" "What do you see emphasized in the poem that suggests a broader significance in the mind of the author?" "What do you hear in the responses of classmates that indicates some larger issue has come up?" Such questions, growing out of the responses of the students, will lead into the appropriate analysis of text without substituting it for the human reactions that come first.

5. *Students should learn how context shapes meaning.* Meaning resides neither in the text, nor in the reader. In fact, it resides nowhere. Rather, it happens, it occurs, it is created and recreated in the act of reading and the subsequent acts of talking and writing about the experience. As the game exists only in the playing, the dance only in the dancing, so meaning exists only in the active encounter of reader and text. That encounter, however, occurs within a context. The reader may meet the text alone, or surrounded by thirty other restless readers; may come to it happy or sad, troubled or at peace, hungry or satiated; may love baseball or hate it; may have made the team or been cut. Events in life outside the classroom, outside the text, frame readings and either light them or cast them into shadow in various ways.

A student who brings to "Sign for My Father" a history of bitter conflict with a father, for instance, may see the poem very differently from one who carries pleasant memories of playing catch in the back yard. A student who has recently lost a parent may have a hard time reading the poem at all. A young woman with no interest in sports may see it as a male poem by a male poet about male experience and reject it utterly, though, when that did happen on one occasion, another woman asserted that *she* knew more about baseball than any man in the room, and that furthermore the poem was as much about parent-and-child or teacher-and-student as about father-and-son, a perspective that welcomed the female reader as well as the male. Each of us comes to a literary experience from other experience, against the backdrop of which we read. Those circumstances inevitably shape our reading.

6. *Students should learn about the processes by which they make meaning out of literary texts.* We have tended to deceive students about those processes by hiding from them our own struggles with texts. Typically, teachers come to class with meaning already made. That is to say, they understand the poem or play. They've read it, read about it, decided what's significant in it, figured out what's worth discussing, what problems there are to solve, what questions there are to answer, what, in sum, the text means. And students consequently don't get to see readers in the act of making meaning out of texts. Instead they are deluded into thinking that meaning is outside of themselves, that it lurks somewhere out there in the world, perhaps hidden in the text, perhaps buried somewhere in the recesses of the teacher's mind, but definitely outside themselves. Meaning comes to be something they have to find, or worse, that someone will provide for them, rather than something they must make and take responsibility for. They learn that the process of thinking about a literary work consists of answering questions posed by an authority, hoping that the interrogation will lead to some clearer vision of the text.

Students need instead to learn that literary meaning is largely an individual engagement, that it results from the creative effort of a reader working with a text, and that the reader may work in various ways. Answering someone else's questions is only one way to work for meaning. Inferential reasoning is only one of many valuable strategies to apply to texts. The explicatory paper is only one of the suitable genres in which to write about literary experience. There are other productive ways of dealing with texts and readings, and students need to know and appreciate them. One of the most valuable is in some ways a departure from the text. It is to tell your own story as it was evoked by the literary work. The Bottoms poem, for example, often awakens memories and associations that are compelling and interesting, though they leave the text far behind. When those stories rise to the surface, students seem almost driven to tell them, or if the stories are more dangerous and frightening, to write about them. Too often those stories are lost, listened to politely, perhaps, and then swept aside to let the class get down to the serious business of interpreting and analyzing. When that happens, students are taught that their lives are less significant than the imaginary lives of the characters in the text, that their thoughts are less important than those of the writer, that making sense of their own lives is less important than analyzing how writers make sense of theirs.

But if literature is a valid way of dealing with experience, if narrative and poetry and drama are forms that help us comprehend and cope with human events, then it seems reasonable to invite students to use those forms in their own lives, to reflect upon their own experiences as Bottoms must have reflected on his to write that short, elegant poem. Students might be encouraged to choose the form appropriate for their response—a letter perhaps, or a personal narrative, or a poem, the writing of which might be aided by drawing upon "Sign . . ." as a model. Or, if it serves the student's purpose, a problem-solving essay, a traditional, expository paper.

These six goals might guide the development of a literature and writing curriculum devoted to cultivating in students a love of reading and an ability to draw upon literary experience to enrich their own lives. Such a curriculum proposes to develop readers and writers rather than literary scholars. Encompassing all of these goals, implicit in them, is the over-arching goal that *experiences with literature will yield pleasure—aesthetic, intellectual, emotional, and social—for students.* That is not to say that the work will always be fun or that class will seem a game, but that there will be rewards, intellectual and emotional, for students. They will have the satisfaction of seeing more clearly who they are, who their classmates are, what they value and reject. They will have the intellectual pleasure of solving problems and analyzing challenging texts amid the emotional pleasure of participating in literature's celebrations of life.

PRINCIPLES OF INSTRUCTION

In pursuit of these goals several principles for instruction might guide the design of instruction.

1. *Invite response to texts.* Everything we do in the classroom should make clear to students that their responses, emotional and intellectual, are valid starting points for discussion and writing. Students must not feel, as they so often do, that they are irrelevant in the process, that they are interchangeable, that they could be replaced by anyone else who would sit there taking the same notes while the class proceeded along exactly the same path. Instead, they have to realize that they are an integral part of the process, that literary meaning requires their presence and participation.

2. *Give students time to shape and take confidence in their responses.* They need an opportunity to reflect and to articulate their reactions and their questions before they hear those of others. Unfortunately, students are too often encouraged to do the opposite. Professors who announce at the beginning of a course that "the critics important for you to study are these . . ." tell us that it's more efficient to read those critics early, find out what it is we are to think, and then read the literary works and think those thoughts. The questions that often follow selections, those questions that call for information or that pose a particular textual problem, tell crafty students that nothing else needs to be attended to in the reading. Instead, we need to encourage students to verbalize their own responses, to articulate their own questions, preferably before hearing those of others, to ensure that their concerns will be addressed and will inform the work of the class.

3. *Find the links among students' responses.* Those points of contact, the similar stories, the shared reactions, and the dramatically contradictory readings will enable us to encourage communication among students and will demonstrate the possibilities for different points of view and for profiting from the exploration of those differ-

ences. The similarities observed will underline their shared humanity, and the differences will remind them of their uniqueness.

4. *Invite discussion and writing about self, text, others, and the culture of society.* Literary experience and writing should be opportunities to learn about all these elements. The temptation to focus exclusively on the text is strong— it gives us surer footing, a solid ground on which to build. The divergent readings and responses can be so varied, so digressive, that they become confusing and chaotic. If, however, we begin to think of the literature classroom as a workshop in which students may be doing many different things, then we may grow easier with the notion that in response to one text some students are writing letters, others poems, others are arguing about the author's intentions, others about the values they themselves hold, and others still are improvising alternate possibilities for a scene drawn from the text.

5. *Let the talk build and grow as naturally as possible, encouraging an organic flow for the discussion.* In the interest of devising and conducting well-crafted lessons, we've often tried to foresee exactly where the talk would go. We've built carefully designed edifices of questions that enable us to conclude, just before the bell rings, "Thus we have seen that Bottoms, in 'Sign for My Father,' means . . ." Although some lessons may need to be taught that way, because we think that some point very much needs to be made, too often those lessons steal from the students the opportunity to explore their own readings. Students should feel free to change their minds, to explore, to follow the talk wherever it leads.

6. *Look back to other texts, other discussions, other experiences, and for-*

ward to what students might read next, what they might write tomorrow. As the classes proceed, we need to search for opportunities to connect today's discussion with yesterday's essay, today's novel with tomorrow's play. Meaning grows not only out of the encounter of reader and text, but out of the rich interplay of other readers and other texts as well, and out of the tight bonds between the act of reading and the act of writing in the students' lives.

QUESTIONS FOR READING AND WRITING

These principles suggest a sequence of issues or questions to consider in teaching both reading and writing in the secondary English program. Our problem is to figure out ways to help students do something that they must do largely on their own. They need freedom if they are to discover the significance of the text for themselves and learn to find their own way through literary works. On the other hand, they need assistance and guidance so that they may learn a repertoire of questions, strategies, attitudes, and skills, that will enable them to enjoy literature.

The questions we raise to help students read and write are critically important because they should support without restricting. Here, for instance, is a hypothetical set of questions, offered as an example of the kind of inquiry that might guide without too tightly confining, that might support the students' readings without dictating precisely what they will do with texts. All these questions are generic—none are tied directly to a specific text. All of them would have to be reworded for lower grade levels, and perhaps supplemented with questions directed specifically at the text of the moment, but they might suggest the approach and the emphasis for the classroom. Implicit in

this sequence of questions is the opportunity, or perhaps requirement, that students write and talk about their perceptions. These questions can't be treated like the short-answer questions often provided at the end of a selection simply to see if students did their homework.

The first question asks students to focus on what took place in their minds as they read:

1. Read the text and record what happens as you read—what do you remember, feel, question, see . . . ? Afterwards, think back over the experience. What is your own sense of the text— does it have any significance for you; does it recall memories; does it affirm or contradict any of your own attitudes or perceptions?

Such a question invites readers to observe themselves reading, to respect their thoughts and feelings and examine them for their significance. It asserts that they and their primary reactions are important and will constitute much of the substance of the class.

The second question then asks them to concentrate on what was going on in the text. Even such a simple task as paraphrasing has the potential of revealing differences in readings, differences in judgments of characters, differences in the attitudes and beliefs of the students:

2. What did you see happening in the text? You might paraphrase it—retell the event briefly.

or

What image was called to mind by the text? Describe it briefly.

or

Upon what did you focus most intently as you read—what word, phrase, image, idea? What is the most important word in the text?

The third asks them to compare their readings with those of other students.

Its purpose, at least in part, is to begin to build the society necessary for the discussion of literary works. It attests to the importance placed upon *readings*, as opposed to texts, and affirms the importance of dialogue about unique readings as a way of coming to understand texts and ourselves as readers:

3. Please discuss your readings with your partner (or in a small group). Did the text call to mind different memories, thoughts, feelings? Did you make sense of it in different ways? What similarities and differences do you notice in your experiences with the text? What might account for those differences?

The fourth question asks them to reflect on the context of the reading: that is to say, the classroom setting and any related works that come to mind. It serves as a reminder that meaning is complex, that it demands attention to matters outside the text, even outside one's self:

4. Does this text call to mind any other literary work (poem, play, film, story— any genre)? If it does, what is the connection you see between the two? How did the circumstances—this room, this group, other events in your life— influence or shape the reading?

And the fifth asks them to consider how meaning has evolved, changing and taking shape, during the course of reading and talking and writing about the text. It reaffirms the extremely important notion that meanings are fluid, that they develop, evolve, grow; that meaning is not a static entity, a unitary and unchanging thing to be found, dusted off, admired for the moment and shelved:

5. How did your understanding of the text or your feelings about it change as

you talked? How did you respond to it— emotionally or intellectually? How did you think about the text—did you analyze it, examine your own associations and memories, react to the observations of your partner, or something else?

If we designed instruction around such questions as these, we would be asking students to learn something about themselves, about texts, about other readers and thus about their society, about contexts (the classroom setting, other literary works, and so on), and about the processes by which meaning is made from literary texts and human experience. For them to read intelligently and to write well they have to be aware of all of those elements—they all contribute to meaning. The writing that students would undertake in such a curriculum would, of course, be diverse in both mode and content. Traditional essays about literary works, those answering questions about the author's intentions or values, about the characters' beliefs and motivations, or about similar issues, are reasonable and valuable assignments, so the curriculum should attend to the interpretive, analytical essay. Students will write it more effectively, however, if the essay is part of a real dialogue in pursuit of meaning and significance. Interpretive essays will be most appropriate when there is real disagreement about a text, and then the talk might lead into the writing of more extended and carefully planned argument than oral discourse allows. Those papers themselves could become the substance for further work—students could even be asked to write analyses of the arguments of their classmates. But *all* of the work should be devoted to making sense of literary and human experience in a way that respects the uniqueness and the integrity of the individual reader. In a curriculum that respects the student's role as a maker of meaning, the expository, analytical essay would be only one of the genres in which students would be asked to perform.

Much of the writing we ask students to do might be personal narrative, perhaps the telling of one's own stories as they are called to mind by reading. If poetry and fiction are legitimate ways of making meaning, then we should have students try their hands at them. Students of music aren't asked just to listen and appreciate; they are invited to hum a tune or pound on a drum. Literature students should similarly be asked to hum a poem once or twice during their schooling if they are to come to understand the genre as fully as they might. There are, after all, various possible ways of making meaning out of experience, literary or otherwise, and students should learn to exercise some responsibility in choosing among them. They need to know that telling their own stories is a perfectly legitimate, respectable act, as significant as explicating a text.

Our primary goal in the English curriculum is not to make literary scholars of all of our students. It is to make them readers and writers, independent and self-reliant thinkers who employ language and literature to enrich their lives. If we keep clearly in mind what we are about, it should be possible for all our toil and trouble to yield an English curriculum that accomplishes that for many of our students.

WORKS CITED

Bottoms, David. 1983. "Sign for My Father, Who Stressed the Bunt," in *In a U-Haul North of Damascus.* New York: Morrow. 22.

Burke, Kenneth. 1957. "Literature as Equipment for Living." *The Philosophy of Literary Form: Studies in Symbolic Action.* New York: Vantage. 253–62.

Rosenblatt, Louise M. 1985. Language, Literature, and Values." *Language, Schooling, and Society.* Ed. Stephen N. Tchudi. Upper Montclair. New Jersey: Boynton. 64–80.

———. 1968. *Literature as Exploration.* 3rd ed. New York: Noble.

Scholes, Robert. 1989. *Protocols of Reading.* New Haven: Yale UP.

For Further Thought

1. Probst discusses the literary experience as a transaction between text and reader. In your own words, describe the nature of that transaction. Then respond to it: Is this the way you are accustomed to thinking about how meaning is created from texts?

2. Think about Probst's six goals for a literature/writing program, and then apply them to your own experience. How did your experience in secondary English classes accord with these goals? What about your college English courses? What other goals might there be for studying literature?

3. Think about Probst's six principles of instruction, and then apply them to a particular teacher. How does this teacher's work reflect (or fail to reflect) these principles? Are there other, equally valid principles of teaching literature, or do you agree with Probst that these are paramount?

4. Choose a short work of literature (perhaps a poem, short story, or essay), read it, and then apply Probst's five teaching questions to it. Write your response to each question, and then add a paragraph in which you comment on the use of questions as a guide for teaching.

5. Reconsider the reader-response position on literature, and then write a few paragraphs in which you discuss the value of this approach for the teacher of English. Consider problems as well as advantages.

Application 2.2:
Working With Student Response

Each lesson plan in the first application pays some attention to student responses—that is, each in its own way seriously attempts to involve students in their own learning. Still, one would not immediately identify any of the lessons as embodying a reader-response approach. The teaching practices described in those plans are not specifically aimed at drawing out student response to the reading experience. So the question arises: Are there classroom methods or approaches that are more in keeping with the principles of reader-response theory?

Response Questions

To help answer that question, we might work from a set of principles for reader-response instruction, like those offered by Robert Probst in the preceding essay. Probst describes the following principles of instruction: (1) invite response to texts; (2) give students time to shape and take confidence in these responses; (3) find the links among students' responses; (4) invite discussion and writing about self, text, others, and the culture of society; (5) let the talk build and grow as naturally as possible, encouraging an organic flow for the discussion; and (6) look back to other texts, other discussions, other experiences, and forward to what students might read next, what they might write tomorrow (pp. 47–49). We need not insist, of course, that any teaching practice adhere strictly to these principles, and we can admit that some of them might apply to practices based on another theory (to the lessons described in Application 2.1, for example). But they do seem like a reasonable starting point to examine classroom practice that seeks to value the response of student readers.

One kind of practice is suggested by Probst himself. At the end of the essay, he presents a sequence of five questions that might guide instruction in the study of literature. The questions ask about (1) the student's immediate experience of reading the text, (2) her attention to certain features of the text, (3) her response to the text in comparison with that of a classmate, (4) connections she might make between this text and other experiences, including other texts, and (5) changes in the student's understanding or feeling as a result of having read the text. It is clear that Probst sees these questions as prompts for short in-class writings (response statements) as well as directions for small-group and whole-class discussion.

Some Things to Consider About Response Questions

1. Probst's questions are intentionally generic—that is, they are general enough that they might be used with any work and adapted to any level. This poses a dilemma: Using them repeatedly might grow stale after a while, but changing them to suit the work in question might direct student responses to particular things the teacher has decided to be important. How would you use these questions?

2. Choose a text you have read recently and write two short response statements, about a paragraph each, on the first two of Probst's questions. Then

comment on the use of short in-class response statements. Did your teachers ask you to write about your reading in this way? How valuable did it seem to be?

3. Probst's approach honors student responses, but teachers have responses as well. As a teacher, how and when would you offer your own response to the text? Explain your decision.

4. Recall the teacher who assigned "in Just-spring" (pp. 37–38) and wanted students to see the Pan motif. What might she say about a series of questions that do not direct students to anything in particular in the poem?

5. Choose a literary text and a grade level. Then write a plan in which you use Probst's questions, or variations on them, to create a response-centered lesson. Consider all the practical issues: When will students write, how will they talk to partners or in small groups, how will you conduct class discussion? Then critique your own lesson.

Leading a Discussion

Probst presents a very organized model for tapping into student response to literature, but we know that, in actual practice, things can be less predictable. This is implied in one of his own principles: "Let the talk build and grow," he says, "as naturally as possible, encouraging an organic flow for the discussion" (p. 48). The direction of talk is left, it seems, in the hands of students; they can take it where they will, which introduces a large element of uncertainty in planning. Yet, even here, there is a tension at work, for it is not clear that students are completely "in control." For one thing, they *have* to respond; they do not have the option to turn it over to the teacher, which is what some might prefer. Moreover, in "encouraging an organic flow," the teacher is making decisions about which responses to elicit from students, which to linger over, which to redirect. Indeed, it is the teacher who decides what is "natural" or "organic" in the first place. In other words, even in a response-centered classroom, the teacher is actively making decisions. To get a sense of how these decisions might work themselves out in the classroom, we can refer to Mrs. Martinez, the teacher described in an essay that appears later in this chapter. To work with this application, you will have to read "Provocations" (pp. 72–78).

As John Rouse describes her, Mrs. Martinez is the *agent provocateur* in the classroom: "Her manner was not at all challenging but rather inquisitive, innocently offhand and unassuming. She would make a remark that touched a sensitive spot and so startle a person into self-revelation or self-exposure while she listened in a most interested and sympathetic way" (p. 73). This connects to Rouse's notion of what makes a good teacher: "A teacher is one who gives not instruction but provocation, so that the learner, startled into making an assertion, begins an individual movement towards some as yet uncertain goal" (p. 72). It is essential to Mrs. Martinez's classroom approach that she provoke responses in students, without saying very much herself. In her lesson on the Trickster story, then, she reads the text, asks a very simple question, and then allows the discussion to develop, encouraging or provoking on occasion. How and why she provokes students are what concern us here.

Some Things to Consider About Mrs. Martinez's Lesson

1. Reread "Provocations," with attention to what Mrs. Martinez does after reading the Trickster story. How does she initiate discussion? How and when does she speak thereafter? After the discussion, how does she interpret student response to the story?

2. Consider the larger context of Mrs. Martinez's teaching—that is, things she might have done before the lesson to make it possible. These would include her attitude toward students (the conversation in the teacher's lounge), her provocative approach, her behavior at the beginning of class, and the routines that she has set up. How important are these factors? Could the lesson have "worked" without them?

3. How directive is Mrs. Martinez? Does she know, in advance, where this lesson will go? Think too about her reaction to the accusation that she manipulates kids. What does she seem to mean by manipulation?

4. From the point of view of some teachers, this lesson would seem to end on an inconclusive note. Do you think that is true? How important is closure in the teaching of literature? What might Mrs. Martinez say on that subject?

5. Imagine that you are John Rouse, student teaching with Mrs. Martinez. Imagine, too, that at the end of the lesson, she suggests that you take over another class of juniors after lunch. This is a scary proposition, but since Mrs. M. has provoked, you end up agreeing. You want to use the same Trickster story, but feel that you cannot do it so "effortlessly" as Mrs. Martinez. Devise a plan of your own for getting students to respond to the story.

Small Groups and Response

Mrs. Martinez is adept at leading a discussion of the whole class, but even so (as her student teacher observes), only a few students participated. She argues that all were listening, and that the conversation is the main thing, whether one speaks or listens. This might be so, and yet many teachers feel that the large group or the whole class is not the best setting for a discussion of student responses to literature. Patrick Dias (1992) puts it this way: "the large-group format with the teacher up front is inhospitable to . . . deeply personal engagements" (Dias, p. 137). He prefers the small-group format, "which, as opposed to whole-class discussion, multiplies the opportunities for individuals to try out and formulate their ideas" (p. 140). Dias has therefore developed a small-group procedure, used mostly in teaching poetry, intended to help students explore their responses to literature with a minimum of teacher intervention.

Dias's procedure works like this: (1) Groups are formed (perhaps six students per group); (2) each group chooses a reporter; (3) the teacher distributes copies of a poem and reads it aloud, inviting questions about unfamiliar words; (4) the poem is read aloud again, this time by a student; (5) within the group, one member reads the poem aloud; (6) each member in turn reports an initial impression of the poem; (7) students discuss the poem one section at a time; (8) students reread the poem if necessary; (9) about twenty minutes into the discussion, the teacher gives a five-minute warning that reports are due; (10) groups report in turn, without notes, with the order of reporting shifting from day to day; (11) if there is time, the class discusses different interpretations and the poem might be read again. Dias describes these steps in much more detail, but that is the gist of it: multiple readings, a lot of small-group discussion, and some sharing of ideas.

Some Things to Consider About Dias's Small-Group Procedure

1. In Dias's procedure, the teacher facilitates the whole process and sometimes provides information but does not do any interpreting for students. In this sense, they are left on their own. What assumptions about poetry, young readers, and the goals of education seem to lie behind this approach?
2. Obviously, this approach calls for a heavy reliance on small-group work. What were your experiences with small groups when you were in high school? What are some of the pros and cons of small groups?
3. Think about this procedure. Why does Dias use it primarily for teaching poetry, as opposed to short stories or parts of a novel or play? How would the procedure have to be adapted to work with "The Lottery" or a section of *Lord of the Flies*?
4. Find Patrick Dias's article, "Literary Reading and Classroom Constraints: Aligning Practice with Theory," in *Literature Instruction: A Focus on Student Response*, ed. Judith A. Langer (NCTE, 1992), pp. 131–162. The steps I have outlined are adapted from that article. Dias goes on to describe the procedure in practice as students discuss Ted Hughes's poem, "The Thought Fox." Respond to the lesson as Dias describes it: How realistic does this small-group procedure seem to be?

MAKING TIME

Nancie Atwell

Nancie Atwell is the best known proponent of the workshop approach to teaching reading and writing. In "Making Time," she describes her work with eighth-grade students in Boothbay Harbor, Maine. The essay deals with both reading and writing, which Atwell sees as parallel activities, but her attention (like ours in this chapter) is on reading. As you read, think about the assumptions that underpin Atwell's approach to reading, especially the idea that reading in school should mirror the reading we do outside of school.

"Making Time" appeared in To Compose: Teaching Writing in High School and College, *ed. Thomas Newkirk (Portsmouth, NH: Heinemann Educational Books, 1990). A revised version of the essay appears as chapter 2 of* In the Middle: New Understandings about Writing, Reading and Learning, *2nd edition, Heinemann, 1987. It is reprinted with permission from Nancie Atwell.*

> My education was the liberty I had to read indiscriminately and all the time, with my eyes hanging out.
> *Dylan Thomas*

My sister called with good news: their offer was accepted. She, her husband,

and my nephew Eric were about to move to a new house, one with actual closets, a two-car garage, a big yard with shade trees—and an above-ground pool. Bonnie called to break the good news, and to warn me. "Please," she asked, "whatever you do when you visit us, promise you won't let on to Eric that Atwells don't swim."

My sister wants us Atwells to pretend that learning to swim is not a big deal. Specifically, she wants to be able to dress Eric in life preservers and introduce him to their pool without any adult relatives betraying our longstanding panic about deep water. Bonnie remembers the swimming lessons of our youth—how our parents conveyed their own unease in the water, how their eyes worried, and how we kids kept our feet firmly planted, touching bottom, and refused to put our faces in the water. We were no fools. We believed our parents when they showed us that learning to swim was going to be difficult and dangerous.

My sister knows that her smart little boy, like all humans, learns at least as much from the implicit as the explicit. In defining conditions necessary for learning to take place, Frank Smith (1982) refers to incidents of teaching, implicit and explicit, as "demonstrations." We humans are surrounded by demonstrations; everything anyone does "demonstrates not only what can be done and how it can be done, but what the person doing it feels about the act" (171–72). We learn by engaging with particular demonstrations, as I learned more by engaging with my parents' inadvertent demonstrations concerning deep water than from all of their good, explicit advice about stroking, kicking, and breathing.

In our classrooms each day, we explicitly teach and students learn; this is a fact, Janet Emig writes, that "no one will deny. But," she continues, "to believe that children learn *because* teach-

ers teach and only what teachers explicitly teach is to engage in magical thinking . . ." (1983, 135). It is magical thinking for me to believe I convey to the students in my classroom only my good, explicit advice about writing and reading. The information that comes out of my mouth when I talk is at least equaled by implicit data. Every minute that they observe me I'm providing demonstrations with which eighth graders may or may not engage. I can never account for what each learns through the ways I teach.

As the ways my parents approached deep water taught me tacit lessons about swimming, so the ways we approach writing and reading in the secondary English classroom convey inadvertent messages to our students about writing and reading. Recent studies of language arts instruction in U.S. schools, particularly Applebee (1982) and Goodlad (1984), give us a pretty clear picture of exactly how we are approaching writing and reading. We know:

- Our students spend little of their time in U.S. classrooms actually reading: on average, 6 percent at elementary, 3 percent at junior high, and, at high school, just 2 percent of a typical student's school day is devoted to reading.
- Our students spend little of their time in U.S. classrooms actually writing. Only 3 percent of the writing our students do in school is composing of at least paragraph length.
- Our students spend most of their time in English classes listening to their teachers talk about writing and reading. Between 70 and 90 percent of English class time is devoted to teacher talk, either lectures or directions.
- When our students are asked to what extent they participate in

choosing what they'll do in class, 55 percent of elementary school kids report having no say. *Two-thirds* of students in grades seven through twelve, students who might reasonably be expected to take on greater individual responsibility, report they do not participate in any way in deciding what they'll do in class.

Teachers mostly decide what students will do in language arts classes. We choose and assign texts, generally one chapter or chunk at a time to be read by the whole class as homework then discussed or formally tested in the following day's session, at the end of which another part of the text is assigned. We present lectures on literary topics and require our students to study and memorize various bits of literary information—characteristics of the New Criticism, the chronology of Shakespeare's plays, lists of Latin roots, literary definitions—followed by exams where students report back what we said and assigned them to memorize. They also complete worksheets and textbook exercises concerned with punctuation, capitalization, sentence structure, paragraph organization, word analysis, and parts of speech. Finally, on occasion their homework consists of a writing exercise where the subject of the writing is an idea of the teacher's.

We talk about the importance of writing clearly and gracefully and reading well and widely, but we seldom make class time for students to write and read, seldom accommodate students' knowledge or choices, and seldom do our students see us writing or reading, see their teachers entering or captivated by the world of written language. Our students are learning from us. The question is, what exactly are they learning? What inadvertent messages do we transmit via this standard approach to the teaching of English? I've begun to try to make explicit the tacit lessons I learned as a student, as well as those I conveyed to my own students for too many years:

- Reading and writing are difficult, serious business.
- Reading and writing are performances for an audience of one: the teacher.
- There is one interpretation of a text or topic: the teacher's.
- "Errors" in comprehension or interpretation will not be tolerated.
- Student readers and writers are not smart or trustworthy enough to choose their own texts and topics.
- Intensive, repetitive drill and preparation are necessary before you can read and write independently.
- Reading and writing require memorization and mastery of information, conventions, rules, definitions, and theories.
- Reading and writing somehow involve drawing lines, filling in blanks, circling, and coloring in.
- Readers break whole texts into separate pieces to be read and dissected one fragment at a time. Writers compose whole texts one fragment at a time (punctuation marks, spelling, grammatical constructions, topic sentences, paragraphs, and so on).
- Reading is always followed by a test, and writing mostly serves to test reading (book reports, critical papers, essays, and multiple choice/fill-in-the-blank/short answer exams).
- Reading and writing are solitary activities that you perform as a member of a group. Readers and writers in a group may not collaborate, as this is cheating.
- You learn about literature and composition by listening to teachers talk about them.

- Teachers talk a lot about literature and composition, but teachers don't read or write.
- Reading and writing are a waste of the school's time.
- You can fail English yet still succeed at reading and writing.

I know these demonstrations from the inside, as an avid reader and writer who read and wrote only dreaded, assigned texts during my high school years. And I know these demonstrations as a junior high English teacher who spent years teaching the junior high English curriculum, alternately spoon-feeding and force-feeding one text or assignment after another to my students, dosing them with my English teacher notions of basic skills, appropriate topics for writing, and Great Works of Literature.

Some of this was the same Great Literature I'd been dosed with too, but had eventually come around to loving in college. I was incredulous when I read *Pride and Prejudice* at age twenty, convinced it could not be the same novel I'd suffered through my sophomore year in high school. It took me longer than that to give Willa Cather a second chance. I finally gathered my courage last summer and reread *My Antonia*, eighteen years after barely passing a multiple-choice test on the novel. My list of reconsidered readings goes on and on: *Anna Karenina, The Scarlet Letter, Crime and Punishment, The Mill on the Floss, Hamlet, Moby Dick,* and *The Canterbury Tales* (which, I discovered, when I finally got hold of a copy minus the standard high school ellipses, were bawdy).

I was a good reader as a teenager but a different reader—and person—than today. When I was ready for complicated and complex themes and language, those books were there, waiting for me to enter and enjoy. It took me a very long time to consider the implica-

tions of my experience as a developing reader for the students who struggled through my courses. My only models for teaching literature were university English education courses that perpetuated lit-crit methodologies, and those high school English teachers whose classes I'd endured in my teens. Glenda Bissex (1980) observes, "The logic by which we teach is not always the logic by which children learn." My assumptions about my role as an English teacher blinded me to the illogic of my teaching.

I teach reading and English, as two separate, daily courses, to all of Boothbay Harbor's eighth graders. A few years ago, on the heels of research showing that sustained silent reading boosted students' reading comprehension, I began letting reading class students choose their own books one period each week, and they began driving me crazy. Daily at least one eighth grader would ask, "Are we having reading today?" We had reading every day—or at least that was my impression. Once again I bypassed an implication for teaching, clinging to each week's four days of curriculum and one day of reading.

My breakthrough in reading finally came by way of writing. Drawing on the work of Donald Murray (1985), Donald Graves (1983), Lucy Calkins (1983), and Mary Ellen Giacobbe (1983), as well as our own classroom research, teachers at my school transformed our daily English classes into writing workshops. I'm going to define a writing workshop as a place where writers have what writers need. Writers need Mary Ellen Giacobbe's three basics of time, ownership, and response (1983).

Writers need regular time set aside in *school* for them to write—time to think, write, confer, write, read, write, change their minds, and write some more. Writers need time they can count on, so even when they aren't writing they're anticipating the time they will be. Writers need time to write well, to see what they think, shape what they know, and get help where and when they need it. Good writers and writing don't take less time; they take more.

Writers need choices. They need to take responsibility for their writing: their own materials, subjects, audiences, genres, pacing, purposes, number of drafts, and kinds of changes to be made, if any. When we invite student writers to choose, they write for all the reasons literate people anywhere engage as writers—to recreate happy times, work through sad times, discover what they know about a subject and learn more, convey and request information, apply for jobs, parody, petition, play, argue, apologize, advise, make money.

Finally, writers need help discovering what they'll choose to do with the time at their disposal. They need response, not at the end when it's too late for our advice to do them any good, but while the words are churning out, in the midst of the messy, tentative act of drafting meaning. In school, this help comes in the form of conferences with the teacher and other students. In writing conferences, students read or describe their writing. Responders begin with information. They listen hard to the content of the draft, then tell what they hear, ask questions about things they don't understand or want to know more about, and invite writers to reflect on what they have done and might do next (Graves 1983).

When I allow time, ownership, and response, I'm expecting that students will participate in written language as writers do, that they'll use the writers' workshop to tell their stories. And they do, writing every day for forty-five minutes, an average of twenty finished pieces each year. My whole-group instruction is limited to a mini-lesson of five or ten minutes at the beginning of class on an issue they or I have identified in their writing (Calkins 1986). Mini-lesson topics include skills issues, such as methods for punctuating dialogue and checking for consistent voice or tense, and process issues: how to brainstorm to find a title, showing rather than telling, deleting and adding information, narrowing the focus of one's content, lead writing.

After the mini-lesson I find out what each writer will do that day, recording my students' plans, and for the remainder of the period writers write. They discover topics, confer with other writers and with me as I move among them, draft, revise, and, when they've made their best meanings, edit and publish. All the while I offer questions and options. Mary Ellen Giacobbe calls this "nudging"—that gentle guidance designed to move students beyond where they are to where they might be. In all of this, the key is time—regular, sustained time to craft texts, seek help, and plan. Habitual writing makes students writers.

Habitual reading makes students readers. The same qualities that characterize writing workshop have come to characterize my reading course, now a daily reading workshop. I had help here, too, this time from my eighth graders. As they assumed responsibility for their writing, they showed me how their participation in written language could be enriched and extended through reading. The powerful connections that they made between their writing and reading dismantled brick by brick the walls I had erected separating writing and literature. In reading workshop, students have what writers *and readers* need: time, ownership, and response.

Readers need regular time set aside *in school* for them to read—time to think, read, confer, read, reflect, reread, and read some more. Readers need time they can count on, so that even when they aren't reading they're anticipating the time they will be. Readers need time to lose track of as they become absolutely caught up in the world of written language. Readers need time to grow.

Readers grow when they assume responsibility for deciding what and how and why they will read: their own materials, subjects, audiences, genres, pacing, purposes, number of readings and rereadings. When we invite student readers to choose, they read for all the reasons that literate people anywhere engage as readers—to live other lives, learn about their own, see how other writers have written, acquire others' knowledge, escape, ponder, travel, laugh, cry.

Finally, readers too need help discovering what they'll choose to do with the time at their disposal. They need response. People who read naturally talk with others as an extension of our lives as readers, sharing opinions, surprises, insights, questions, speculations, and appreciations. Readers don't need lesson plans, study guides, or teachers' manuals. Readers need a text and a listening friend.

Writers and readers need some kind of personal meaning. They need written language to make sense, to give shape to and challenge their worlds. Both writers and readers need to engage naturally and purposefully in the *processes* of written language.

Writers and readers *rehearse*, planning and predicting:

- What will I write?
- What will it be like?
- How will it be shaped by my prior experiences as a writer?
- What will I read?
- What will it be like?
- How will it be shaped by my prior experiences as a reader?

Writers and readers *draft*, discovering meaning:

- Where will these words I am writing take me?
- What surprises, disappointments, problems, questions, and insights will I encounter along the way?
- Where will these words I am reading take me?

Writers and readers *revise*, reseeing and reseeking meaning:

- Is this what I expected, what I hoped for?
- What do I think of those words on the page?
- What new thoughts do I think because of those words on the page?
- What makes sense? What needs to be changed so sense can be made?

Making time for students to read in school invites this engagement. I make time every day for a forty-five-minute reading workshop; last year's eighth graders, including eight special education students, read an average of thirty-five full-length works. Reading workshop, too, begins with a mini-lesson. We spend five or ten minutes talking about an author—Richard Wright, Robert Frost, Lois Duncan, S. E. Hinton—or genre. We read and discuss a poem or a short story by cummings, Updike, Wilbur, London, or one of the kids in the class, peeling away layers of the text and coming to meaning together. We focus on reading and writing processes, how we read and reread the text and how authors might have come to write as they did.

The rest of the period is devoted to independent reading. Students choose their own books, settle back, and dive in. I move among them for the first ten minutes or so, finding out if anyone needs my immediate assistance, and then I sit down and read too, my books and their books. I expect that they will read and discover books they love. But I also help, in conferences about their reading.

Most of my talk with eighth graders about literature is written down. We write because writing allows deeper, richer responses than speech, but we write in a special way. For the past two years, eighth graders and I have conferred about literature in letters, thousands of letters back and forth about books, authors, reading, and writing. In our correspondence we nudge each others' thinking. We confirm, challenge, extend, and suggest. And we engage in some serious, and not so serious, literary gossip.

For example, this is an exchange with Jennipher. We're calling each other "Robert" here because one week we happened to read or talk about four works by various authors named Robert; Jenn decided that we would substantially increase our chances of becoming published authors if we were white males named Robert, so she changed our names.

5/2

Ms. A. Robert,

Just to see what Anne Frank was going through was miserable. Her "growing up" with the same people everyday. I think she got to know them a lot better than she would have if they weren't in hiding, her mother especially. That sudden change, going into hiding, must have been hard.

It amazed me how much more they went downstairs in the book. [Jennipher had also read the Broadway stage play script of *The Diary of Anne Frank.*] And it seems so much bigger in the book. It also told a lot more of her feelings, right up until the end. It must have come suddenly—to see police come in and arrest them.

I'm going to read some Robert Frost poetry now.

J. J. Robert

P. S. I think she would have been a writer.

5/3

Dear J. J. R.,

I don't have any doubt—if she'd survived, she would have been a writer all her life. Her prose style is so lively, and her insights are so deep. And she loved to write.

We've talked about how movies alter (often for the worse) the books on which they're based. Plays can't help but do the same. All that inner stuff—reflections, dreams, thoughts and feelings—doesn't easily translate into stage action, although Hackett and Goodman tried with Anne's between-act voice-overs.

If you're hungry for more information on Anne, please borrow my copy of Ernst Schnabel's *Anne Frank: Portrait in Courage* when Tom Apollonio returns it to me.

Ms. A. Robert

5/10

Ms. A. Robert,

We missed you! You get used to peoples' voice. The switch is hard for me.

Robert Frost's poems are really good. "The Witch of Coos" seemed to me somewhere between Stephen King and Ray Bradbury. Kind of wierd, huh? I heard someone quote (kind of!) one of his poems. It was on "People's Court," (Dumb Show) and there was a fight about a fence. In the end the guy came out of the courtroom and was talking to the reporter. He said something like, "This goes to show—good fences don't make good neighbors." I almost freaked out.

Back to the books.

J. J. Robert

5/10

Dear J. J. R.,

They quoted Frost on "People's Court"? (You *watched* People's Court?) I need an aspirin.

N. A. R.

For half of last year, in addition to conferring with me in letters, readers conferred in letters to each other. One day in January, Jane and Arelitsa were passing notes in the back of my classroom. I asked, "What are you two doing?" and Jane said, "Oh, you'll be interested in this." She was right. Their notes were about Frost's "Nothing Gold Can Stay" and what it meant to them, two exuberant thirteen-year-olds gossiping about poetry, forging meaning together. So Jane and Arlee put their letters on overheads, shared them with my classes, and opened the door to students' exchanges about literature.

Suzy was one of my students that year. She started the year as a lip reader. She used only class time to read and said, "I guess reading is a pretty good thing to do, but sometimes I read and I don't know what I read." By May, Suzy had read nineteen novels. She said, "I really enjoy reading for pleasure. But I hate having books assigned. I can't get into them as much."

Through her own choice of books, time to read, and a place to reflect on her reading, Suzy got into books. She wrote the letter below, to her classmate Hilary, at home. It concerns *Mr. and Mrs. Bo Jo Jones*, a novel that Hilary loaned Suzy about a teenage shotgun marriage. In getting into her book, Suzy critiqued the lead and conclusion, connected the novel to her own life, predicted while she was reading what would happen, and made plans to reread.

Hilary,

It's about 12:00 (midnight). I just finished *Mr. and Mrs. Bo Jo Jones*. It was the best book I've ever read in my life.

The book was a slow start and got to be a little boring at times. But the end was fast and different. I loved it! I cried so much. Did you? (I hope so, 'cause I'll feel quite embarrassed about what I'm going to say!)

I didn't cry until right when the doctor and Bo Jo came in to say the baby was dead. It was strange?! I felt so sorry for her (even though it's fiction) for having that happen. Then at the Coffee Pot, when they said it was quits, I was so mad! I knew they were just getting to be very much in love, but thought it probably would be best. I knew for some reason that something good was going to happen when they met at the apartment.

When they sat down and talked and realized they wanted each other but couldn't face it until their decision, it was great. I cryed there too 'cause I was so happy for them! It was great how they went ahead three years and said how it was going. The book was great! I'd recommend it to anyone.

I almost forgot. Did you stop to think if that was you or someone you knew? I did and it seemed so terrible. I thought what if that happened, if I'd do the same. That's not how I wanted to say it, but good enough.

I might want to reread that in the fourth quarter, if you don't mind?

Well, that's all! Finally. I had to right this right now because it was so fresh and I just can't get over how good this book was.

                                                        Suzy

P. S. I hope you don't think I'm some sort of freak writing this!!!

Suzy,

Don't worry; you're not a freak! I'm so glad you liked the book. I know I sure did. I loved all the same parts that you did. I cried too; boy did I.

The book *What About Me?* must be funny. You've been laughing a lot while reading it. What's it about? Gotta go.

                                                        Hilary

Last year, Suzy and her classmates averaged at the seventy-second percentile on standardized reading tests, up from an average at the fifty-fourth percentile when fully twenty-one percent scored in the bottom quartile; last year, that figure was just two percent. In June of last year, ninety-two percent of my students indicated that they regularly read at home for pleasure, and when I asked how many books they owned, the average figure they gave was ninety-eight, up from September's fifty-four. This is the kind of evidence that convinces administrators. I am more convinced by some nonstatistical results.

My students discover that they love to read. Even the least able, most reluctant readers eventually find the one great book that absolutely impels them, and they are changed readers. For Tim, who never read at home and had never found a book he wanted to reread, the one great book was Jay Bennett's *The Dangling Witness*. Every day for two weeks he came into class, waved his copy of the mystery, and announced in an awed voice, "This is a good book. I mean, this is a *really good* book." Until Jay Bennett, Tim hadn't trusted that there was such a thing as a good book.

Eighth graders discover authors who write well for them. They learn names of writers whose books they can look for in bookstores and libraries: Frank Bonham, Lois Lowry, Madeleine L'Engle, Cynthia Voigt, Anne Tyler, Jack London, Susan Beth Pfeffer, Todd Strasser, Robert Lipsyte, Robert Cormier, Nat Hentoff, Farley Mowat, even, for those ready and willing, Shakespeare. Patrice was ready and willing.

5/17

Dear Ms. Atwell

I finished *Macbeth* today. The reason I decided to read *Macbeth* was because a girl at Skyway Middle School, who I am friends with, read it and really loved it.

I found that the three witches were my favorite characters. Many movies have used take-offs of these characters. *The Beast Master*, a movie I saw on cable, did. They used them differently, but they were used to tell the future.

Macbeth himself was, overall, a very confused guy. His wife made him kill the king, and he was hearing voices that told him to "sleep no more." Putting one of Shakespeare's plays into movie form could almost be as bad as Steven [sic] King, because of all the killing and walking around with people's heads.

I truly enjoyed *The Comedy of Errors*. I enjoyed the way the two characters called Dromio spoke. Every time they opened their mouths they spoke in riddles. The overall idea was very good and funny. The reunions were like this: 2 father-son, 3 husband-wife, 2 brother, and 2 owner-slave. There is one wedding. Some of the reunions are *very* technical.

Patrice

Eighth graders discover their own theories about literature. Patrice's remark about technical reunions has its roots in a discussion that had taken place about a month before. We were talking about Hardy's poem "The Man He Killed" and Mike said, "Ms. Atwell, I really don't like this poem. I mean, why couldn't he just say it in regular language?"

Mike had been reading Frost and Wilbur. He loved e. e. cummings. He wasn't asking for colloquial prose when he said "regular language."

I said, "Show me what you mean, Mike," and he read the line "We should have set us down to wet right many a nipperkin"—a word I'd had to look up the night before and could find only in our O.E.D.

I'd made a dumb assumption. I thought my kids knew language changed over time, that English wasn't just American and contemporary. So we talked. Over the next weeks kids began collecting and bringing to class examples of prose and poetry from other times. When they hit Shakespeare, I made copies of speeches from five of the plays and we looked at how the language differed within the plays, how Romeo and Juliet spoke one way, Macbeth another, and why. We began to puzzle out what makes a tragedy a tragedy and a comedy a comedy. They decided that just about everyone dies in a tragedy and a new order begins; in a comedy, almost everyone gets married, reinstated, or reunited. John said, "Yeah, just like on Love Boat." And from there we talked about basic plot conventions through all of literature, and how and where Shakespeare had borrowed his plots. Then they found and read to each other stories from Greek and Roman mythology.

They and I were collaborating as theorists, discovering, testing, and acting on literary principles. As readers, eighth graders discovered that literature is accessible; that literature is reading, and reading is sensible, interesting, and fun,

As writers, eighth graders discovered they could draw on their experiences as readers, trying out the themes, styles, and modes they read and finding their own voices in collaboration with the voices they love to read. Dede and Billy loved Robert Frost. They collaborated with him by borrowing the theme from "Nothing Gold Can Stay," Frost's poem about the inevitability of change:

Dawn

The lake sparkled
in the light of the moon.
Dawn was near—
it would be soon.

The clouds gave off a goldish light
and broke the silence of the night.

Now the dawn has come to be noon,
just like grown-up life—all too soon.

BILLY SNOW

Beyond the Light

The sunset is so lovely.
with its warm colors and bright glow.
I could sit and stare for hours
at the elegant sight.
Then I shiver
as a cold breeze blows—
to warn me of the darkness
and to warn me of the night.

DEDE REED

Luanne collaborated with John Updike. Her poem arrived at my house in the mail during April vacation, when Luanne was in the middle of basketball tournaments. She borrowed her subject, learning from Updike that basketball was a suitable poetic topic, and she borrowed a simile from his description of the "Ex-Basketball Player" whose hands were "like wild birds":

The Turnover

I was going for a lay-up
as I remember it;

the brown leathered ball
under my hands,
through half-court
and down toward the middle.

When suddenly the rhythm
stopped.

A hand came down
in place of mine—
like a bird doing
a wild dive:
Just empty space
between my hands
and the floor.

I stood there
wondering where I'd gone wrong,

when I looked up to see
two more points
added to the other side's score.

LUANNE BRADLEY

I've made some discoveries too. I've learned that by giving students more time to learn reading, I've given myself more time to teach reading. I have much less homework than in the old days of lesson plans, lectures, ditto masters, and essay tests. Reading workshop is a workshop for me, too, as I quietly confer with readers, answer letters, and read.

I've learned about adolescent literature, a genre virtually nonexistent twenty years ago when I was an eighth grader. My students introduced me to authors of juvenile fiction who write as well for adolescents as my favorite contemporary novelists—Atwood, Tyler, Heller, Updike—write for me.

I've learned to fill my classroom with books—novels, and also short stories, biographies, histories, and poetry, as many paperbacks as I can buy or budget.

I've learned that good, rich discussion of literature happens naturally when real readers are talking together, as opposed to the sterile, grudging responses given by too few students to my old, lesson plan questions. I've learned that the context of students' self-selected texts is ripe for high-level literary talk about such traditional teacher's manual issues as theme, genre, and technique, and that it's entirely possible to go beyond these to consider reading process, professional authors' processes, relationships between reading and writing, between one text or author and others, between literature and real life.

My students taught me that they loved to read. They showed me that in-school reading, like in-school writing, could actually do something for them, that the ability to read for pleasure and

personal meaning, like writing ability, is not a gift or a talent. It comes with the freedom to choose and with time to exercise that freedom. I learned that freedom to choose and time to read in school are not luxuries. They are not complements to a good literature curriculum. They are the wellspring of student literacy and literary appreciation.

If my class schedule were more typical—that is, forty-five minutes a day for English, including literature—I'd continue to give over class time to reading and writing. But I'd teach writing on three regular, consecutive days, so students would experience that sense of routine and continuity writers need, and follow it with two days of reading workshop, encouraging kids to take home over the weekend those books they read in class on Thursday and Friday. And I would continue to nudge, pointing students toward new topics, modes, styles, authors, techniques, books, and genres.

The most recent National Assessment of Educational Progress reports that American thirteen- and seventeen-year-olds do less reading, especially of fiction, than our nine-year-olds. In a feature in the *New York Times* about Americans' reading habits (Fiske 1983), Jan Marsten of the University of Chicago suggested that "there seem to be periods in the lifespan during which reading tends to drop off, including adolescence. It would hardly be surprising if people did less reading during periods of such upheaval in their lives" (1).

Secondary teachers know about upheaval in adolescents' lives. First jobs, first cars, first boyfriends and girlfriends are hallmarks of adolescence. So are a preoccupation with peers and participation in junior and senior highs' extracurricular activities. Reading necessarily takes a back seat as teenagers' worlds become impossibly full. A former student of mine anticipated April vacation of her freshman year by saying, "Ms. Atwell, I'm going to read six books this week. All of them are books I've been dying to read since Christmas. I just look at them and feel depressed. There's always something else I've got to do." When reading doesn't happen at school, it's unlikely to happen away from school, which means it's unlikely to happen at all.

English teachers can help. We help by giving reading—and writing—our highest priority; we do so when we make time for them to happen in our classrooms. What single, more powerful demonstration can we provide our students of the value we place on these activities? Encircling this are other compelling demonstrations—of the uses of literacy, of writing and reading as whole, sense-making activities, of the ways an adult finds meaning and pleasure in her own and others' written expression, of *all* students' rights as literate human beings.

Genuine, independent reading and writing are not the icing on the cake, the reward we proffer gifted twelfth graders who have survived the curriculum. Reading and writing are the cake. Given what we know about adolescents' lives and priorities, can we afford to continue to sacrifice literate school environments for skills environments? For multiple-choice and essay-question environments? For spoon-fed and force-fed environments? I say we can't. Making time makes readers and writers, and readers and writers can remake their worlds, using language to see and shape their lives as Jennipher did in her final letter to me.

6/8

Dear Ms. A. Robert,

I finished *Autumn Street*. It was excellent how she told it from her childhood view of things, her feelings and then how she was back in the present in the end.

Sunday morning was special. The cats were under my bed at 4:15 doing something, I don't know how they got upstairs. I took them down and looked out the window. Low and behold, sunrise! But no, it did not rise. All I could see was a golden strip across the sky. I pulled up a chair and put my feet up. I said "Nothing Gold Can Stay" in my mind without stumbling and found how Ponyboy could have felt in *The Outsiders*. After fifteen minutes when the sun didn't appear I went back to bed feeling new.

We're really going to miss you.
See you sometime.

J. J. Robert

REFERENCES

Applebee, Arthur. 1982. *Writing in the Secondary School: English and the Content Areas.* Urbana, Ill.: National Council of Teachers of English.

Bissex, Glenda. 1980. *GNYS AT WORK: A Child Learns to Write and Read.* Cambridge: Harvard University Press.

Calkins, Lucy. 1983. *Lessons from a Child.* Portsmouth, N.H.: Heinemann.

———. 1986. *The Art of Teaching Writing.* Portsmouth, N.H.: Heinemann.

Emig, Janet. 1983. "Non-Magical Thinking: Presenting Writing Developmentally in Schools." In *The Web of Meaning: Essays on Writing, Teaching, Learning and Thinking*, ed. Dixie Goswami and Maureen Butler. Portsmouth, N.H.: Boynton/Cook.

Fiske, Edward B. 1983. "Americans in Electronic Era Are Reading as Much as Ever." *The New York Times.* September 8.

Giacobbe, Mary Ellen. 1983. Classroom presentation to the Northeastern University Summer Writing Institute, Martha's Vineyard, Massachusetts (July).

Goodlad, John. 1984. *A Place Called School.* New York: McGraw Hill.

Graves, Donald H. 1983. *Writing: Teachers and Children at Work.* Portsmouth, N.H.: Heinemann.

Murray, Donald. 1985. *A Writer Teaches Writing: A Practical Method of Teaching Composition.* 2nd ed. Boston: Houghton Mifflin.

Smith, Frank. 1982. *Writing and the Writer.* New York: Holt, Rinehart and Winston.

For Further Thought

1. Atwell begins her essay with a picture of English teaching that borders on caricature. Did your English teachers act like this? Describe what you think is the "traditional" approach to teaching reading and writing.

2. Atwell writes of the three basics for learning through language: time, ownership, and response. How do you react to this trio of needs? Are they sufficient? Can you relate these basic ingredients of the workshop approach to the description of effective teaching presented in chapter 1 (pp. 20–22)?

3. Atwell is critical of the idea that teachers decide what students will do in language arts classes. What do you think about that? In what areas, if any, should the teacher decide? In which should the students be free to choose? Think about choices of what to read, when to do it, and how to show that it has been done.

4. Reconsider the workshop approach. What attitude does the teacher need to adopt to make it work? And, thinking very practically, what does a teacher need to do to make it work—routines, rules, bookkeeping, and other kinds of support? You could consult the second edition of Atwell's *In the Middle*.

6. According to James Moffett, "Nothing can be 'unstructured'; when we say that, we mean that we don't recognize the structure of what we're looking at" (*Coming on Center*, 2nd ed., Heinemann, 1988, p. 24). Think about the relationship of structure to freedom. How necessary is it for students to exercise freedom of choice?

7. Read the first section of *In the Middle: New Understandings about Writing, Reading, and Learning*, 2nd edition, especially chapter 2. What differences do you notice between this chapter and the essay you have read in our book? In what direction do you think Atwell is moving?

Application 2.3:
Adapting the Reading Workshop

The techniques we examined in the previous applications are based on the assumption that the teacher chooses the text. That is the bedrock on which the main tradition of literature teaching rests. But as we have seen, Nancie Atwell challenges the assumption that "student readers and writers are not smart or trustworthy enough to choose their own texts and topics" (p. 57). This is actually a bit of an overstatement, for Atwell admits that students do need "nudges" from the teacher, and in the second edition of *In the Middle* she backs off from many of the categorical statements she has made about reading workshop. Still, in the working out of her workshop approach, she tries to remain true to the premise that students learn the most about reading and literature when they have a large measure of control over what they read.

Relinquishing control of the reading curriculum is not easy, as Atwell herself acknowledges: Both editions of *In the Middle* describe her slow and sometimes painful conversion to the workshop approach. It is not as simple as merely letting students choose what they want to read. For one thing, there is the context to be considered. A teacher works within a school, which usually specifies something about the curriculum, and even if the administration is flexible, there are one's colleagues to be considered. Beyond that, there are the demands of district and state offices. In addition to contextual obstacles, there are instructional considerations: What are the teacher's goals? Do they require a certain level of reading difficulty, certain kinds of literary experiences, even certain texts? And finally, there are internal or psychological issues, for when we give over responsibility to students, we need to adjust our teaching roles accordingly. In this sense, teaching and learning are reciprocal activities: If we ask students to think of themselves differently as learners, we end up thinking of ourselves differently as teachers.

Two Contextual Issues: Textbooks and Mandated Testing

A number of contextual issues are raised by a ninth-grade teacher, Judith Whitley, in an *English Journal* article. Almost simultaneous with Whitley's decision to embrace the workshop approach, two external factors came into play. First, her Michigan school district ordered expensive new textbooks, which created pressure to use the new books and underscored the lack of resources for an Atwellian classroom library. Like so many teachers, Whitley had to face the fact that textbooks were determining the curriculum, and the curriculum was constraining her instructional options. Fortunately, Whitley liked the new textbook. She decided, therefore, to make it the centerpiece of a workshop-like classroom: Students chose selections from the book, and then wrote letters to each other, about their reading, in response logs. Then the other shoe dropped: "Michigan mandated that all public schools create an outcomes-based curriculum to increase student achievement scores on required proficiency tests. . . . These mandates demanded that we produce course syllabi and strict course requirements including comprehensive semester examinations" (Whitley, p. 15). Having a more cohesive reading list helped Whitley in devising mini-lessons to help the whole class prepare for the state-mandated tests. She concludes that use of a textbook is not antithetical to a student-centered methodology or to the principles of reading workshop (p. 16).

Some Things to Consider About Whitley's Adaptation

1. Judith Whitley says that she had to get over a prejudice against textbooks: "Until recently, I have felt the need to whisper the T-word" (Whitley, p. 15). This attitude is shared by teachers like Nancie Atwell and even Mrs. Martinez in "Provocations" (p. 77). So what *is* it about textbooks? How did you feel about them when you were a high school student? Why might using a textbook seem distasteful to so many students and teachers?

2. Find out more about standardized tests and other state mandates as they relate to the teaching of English. For example, the State of Minnesota has instituted "high school graduation standards," according to which students are tested in reading and math (beginning in eighth grade) and writing (beginning in tenth grade). Students must pass the test before graduating. Programs like these have serious implications for English teachers. Find out what your state is doing about "outcomes-based education" and standardized testing. What, in your opinion, are the pros and cons of your state's approach?

3. Whitley teaches ninth grade. Atwell taught eighth grade. Barbara Hoetker Ash (whose teaching is described subsequently) is also a middle school teacher. But how would a reading workshop work in tenth, eleventh, or twelfth grade,

where there is often a greater emphasis on covering a certain body of literature? Assuming that you are attracted to the workshop principle, how would you adapt it to, say, eleventh-grade English (which is typically a course in American Literature)?

4. Find Judith Whitley's article in the January 1998 issue of *English Journal*. Read it and analyze the beliefs about literature and reading that support her practice and suggestions.

An Instructional Issue: Reading Assignments for the Whole Class

Whitley's adaptation of the workshop approach is based on practical considerations having to do with materials and standardized testing. But other teachers who favor the workshop might hold some substantive reservations about certain of Atwell's techniques. For example, Barbara Hoetker Ash, a middle school teacher in Georgia, is enthusiastic about reading workshop but also sees the value of students reading assigned texts together. In an article in *English Journal*, Ash reminds us of the benefits that derive from shared reading experiences: the opportunity for students to share insights more readily, the creation of more efficient mini-lessons, and the chance to "learn what strategies other readers use" (Ash, p. 78). Her solution is to move in and out of reading workshop, alternating it with assigned readings that can be discussed in the large group, thus making reading more of "a social affair."

It is important to note, as well, that Atwell herself has become much more flexible, which means (ironically) that she is willing to allow for more direction from the teacher. This involves several changes in the reading workshop, not the least of which is a greater reliance on assigned readings. In so doing, she has become "a teacher with a capital T"—that is, one who is more willing to intervene, assist, and model adult reading behavior. It is interesting, too, that Atwell now describes herself more readily as a teacher of literature, not a teacher of reading.

Some Things to Consider About Ash's Adaptation

1. Ash's version of writing workshop might be considered a compromise position: She is willing to sacrifice some student "ownership" to gain the kind of shared learning that she believes comes with assigned reading and large-group discussion. In this she is like many teachers who adopt the workshop approach for only part of the school year. What do you think of that compromise? In what ways would you be inclined to adapt the basic idea of reading workshop?

2. In some respects, involving the entire group in a shared text or task is the most difficult of all tasks for the English teacher. Hence one of the appeals of the workshop approach: It helps solve the problem of involving the entire class. Yet this is precisely what Ash missed in the workshop. Think back on the instructional techniques described earlier in this chapter. How did those teachers address the problem of involvement?

3. In her *English Journal* article, Ash describes what she considers to be the "typical" treatment of literature in secondary classrooms "where a 'right' reading or interpretation is implied, if not openly espoused, and where students are usually quizzed and tested on aspects of the literary work (the

themes, the characters, the setting, the images, symbols, and the like)" (Ash, p. 77). Is this the way literature was presented in your experience? Whether it is true or not, what might be some of the strengths of this tradition?

4. Find Ash's article in the January 1990 issue of *English Journal*. Read it, and analyze the beliefs about the teacher's role that undergird her practice. In particular, you might think about her return to large-group instruction. How is what she is currently doing different from what she describes as the typical literature classroom? If there is a difference, do you think it is a matter of technique, attitude, or both?

Two Teachers' Stories

Teresa Tande and Betty Van Vugt both teach in northeastern North Dakota: Teresa works with eighth graders in the small city of Devils Lake, Betty with sixth, seventh, and eighth graders (depending on the need) in the small town of Manvel. In some ways their personalities and situations are different. Teresa is lively; Betty is more low-key. Teresa teaches in a middle school that is in the process of developing an integrated curriculum; Betty's school in Manvel is tiny and cramped like "an old-fashioned country school." Though both teach on the middle level, Teresa's background and orientation are toward the upper grades, Betty's toward the lower grades. Yet they are alike. Both graduated from state colleges in the upper Midwest; both are experienced, smart, and hard-working; both teach in relatively homogeneous communities; and both have spent a fair amount of time experimenting with reading and writing workshop.

Teresa had been teaching for sixteen years when she was introduced to the workshop approach at a National Writing Project summer institute in Minot, North Dakota. At first, she resisted the idea that her eighth graders could handle this kind of freedom. "I read *In the Middle* and argued with Nancie all the way," she says. It would surely lead to "chaos" because eighth graders didn't have sufficient "internal control." Still, she was attracted by the idea of affording students a greater measure of freedom. "I liked that, because with the freedom of choice came more accountability." So after all the arguing with Atwell, Teresa decided to do it. Because the writing side most attracted her to the workshop approach, she devoted three days a week to writing and two to reading. "I jumped in with both feet— reading and writing workshops, buddy dialogues, wide open choices."

The results, as Teresa tells it, were mixed—better than what she had expected, but not as good as she had hoped. Students wrote a lot in writing workshop (good), but they weren't working up to their potential (not so good). After a while, when the novelty wore off, they had trouble finding topics ("which is one reason I moved writing workshop to later in the school year"). The reading side was better, but also mixed. Students didn't always make the best choices ("Some of the boys chose comic books or magazines with lots of pictures"), and what they wrote to each other tended to be perfunctory. Still, she was encouraged. In subsequent years, she adapted both workshops until they seemed to fit the needs of her students and her own teaching style. Or rather, she continues to adapt it, for Teresa's teaching is always something of a work-in-progress.

Her current practice looks something like this: Students do reading workshop once a week, usually on Fridays, for the entire school year. This allows time on other days for assigned readings that can be discussed as a large group, creating a rough balance between teacher-directed literature activities and student-centered reading workshop. Choice of books is still pretty open, though comics and most magazines are not acceptable. Teresa is also less shy about nudging kids into more challenging materials. Her approach to writing workshop is described more fully in chapter 4. For now, all we need to know is that Teresa uses writing assignments and group tasks during the first semester to prepare kids for a six- to nine-week writing workshop in the second half of the year. Reading and writing workshops, she says, are extensions of each other.

Betty came to the workshop idea through a different route. Halfway through her first year teaching seventh graders at Manvel, she became discouraged with the "babyish" selections in the basal reader series and the endless grammar drills in the regular curriculum. So she called the local university, asked to talk to someone in the English Department, and found a professor who recommended *In the Middle*. "I read it over the Christmas holiday," says Betty, "and decided that I'd go for it." So, like Teresa but with less experience with middle-level kids and in the middle of the year, she instituted both reading and writing workshop, full-time. Because she had no classroom library, she used the public library in a nearby city to search for books "from Atwell's lists." It was somewhat makeshift, but Betty was pleased with the results. "All things considered, the kids did a really good job."

The following fall she was really prepared, with the system in place and a student teacher to help out. "But it was a disaster," she says. The new seventh graders wrote very little and complained about not having topics. They chose the shortest, simplest books or refused to read at all. "This group was less mature and they just couldn't handle it. By midyear, I had a huge number of deficiencies to report." So she had to retreat to the regular curriculum. That year was a learning experience, but Betty didn't give up entirely. For the past three years, she has been experimenting with both kinds of workshops. Like Teresa, she has decided not to begin the school year this way, but rather to wait until some sense of community has developed in her classes and students have some opportunity to internalize rules and discipline. She also tends to alternate workshop units with more teacher-directed units, for both reading and writing. Having pulled back considerably in that disastrous second year, she is now moving steadily in the direction of more freedom for students. But like Teresa, she knows that wherever she winds up will be a compromise position.

What strikes me most about these two stories is not the differences (which are real enough) but the similarities. Both teachers were attracted to the workshop approach because they felt the regular curriculum wasn't challenging enough for students. Both began their thinking with writing workshop because, as Betty says, "you can fool yourself into thinking you're teaching reading [it's hidden from view], but with writing you can't fool yourself at all." She's right: If students aren't writing, or if they are not improving, the fact is there in front of you—if you care to look. Both teachers began by "going whole hog" and then learned to pull back and find their own compromise positions. And in both cases those compromise positions resulted from a need to find their own proper roles as teachers. With the workshop approach, as Betty notes, "I would almost feel like I wasn't teaching. I wasn't sure I was doing my job." It took time for her to learn how to let go in some areas while intervening energetically in others. With both Betty and Teresa, that balance of letting go and exerting their authority continues to shift. They are always learning and growing, and their students learn and grow with them.

Some Things to Consider About the Teacher Stories

1. Comment on the two stories. Do you think Teresa and Betty are typical or atypical? In either case, what do the stories suggest about the way teachers go about changing their practice?

2. Try thinking of the workshop approach, not as a monolithic thing, but as an orientation toward students that could be put on a continuum. Draw a line and put those names on a line that shows "student choice" on one end and "teacher control" on the other. Where on that line would you put the following practitioners: Teresa Tande, Betty Van Vugt, Nancie Atwell, Judith Whitley, Barbara Ash, your eighth-grade English teacher? Then put yourself on that line.

3. Betty Van Vugt articulates one of the great fears of teachers who use the workshop approach: that somehow they are not doing their job. This goes beyond the fear that someone might be watching and misunderstanding; it is an internal problem. In your own words, describe the job of an English teacher. How does this relate to the issue of control?

4. In a paragraph or two, describe your attitude toward the reading workshop approach. Would you use it? When and in what manner? What kind of compromise would you strike?

PROVOCATIONS

John Rouse

What makes a good English teacher? Or rather, what is it that good English teachers do? While he was student teaching, John Rouse watched his co-operating teacher, Mrs. Martinez, and asked those questions. The key, he suggests, has something to do with provoking students. But what kind of provocation is the most effective?

"Provocations" appeared in English Education, *Vol. 20 (May 1988); copyright 1988 by the National Council of Teachers of English. It is reprinted with permission. For more stories about Mrs. Martinez, see* Provocations: The Story of Mrs. M. *Urbana, IL: NCTE, 1993.*

A teacher is one who gives not instruction but provocation, so that a learner, startled into making an assertion, begins an individual movement towards some as yet uncertain goal. Where an instructor would be concerned with the material to be covered by the class together, a teacher is concerned with the experience of individual learners. And will in fact separate learners, by whatever artful means, by cunning even, from the safe anonymity of the group in which they sit, for anonymity is an expression of the impersonal and the irresponsible. Provoked, the learner comes out of hiding long enough to express a feeling or thought which until then may have been hardly admitted or even recognized, reporting the world as beheld from one's own perspective so that a mode of being is revealed and opened to thought.

Mrs. Martinez was perhaps the most provocative person I have known, in school or out. But whether she had a natural talent for upsetting people or she had developed this skill over time with practice I hardly knew at first. Her manner was not at all challenging but rather inquisitive, innocently offhand and unassuming. She would make a remark that touched a sensitive spot and so startle a person into some self-revelation or self-exposure while she listened in a most interested and sympathetic way. She could make people feel uncomfortable while giving the impression that she was the one person truly interested in their distress. They listened to her, warily, expectantly.

Not that she talked very much. She was never eager to report her opinions or concerns or the events of her day, preferring rather to listen. But she wanted to make sure that something would be said worth listening to. So she would provoke people with a remark or a question, drawing out some individual response or personal story. And during the telling she was a most sympathetic and responsive listener, she charmed the soul by listening. In this way she collected many stories, she was interested in people. And sometimes she would tell a story herself, although when she was finished people often seemed uncertain of how to respond because they might have sensed a concealed message in the story, an oblique reference to one's own situation or character.

In a corner of the faculty room the bridge game had already begun, in another the math teacher sat at the desk marking student papers. "Well, what are we going to do in class today?" Mrs. Martinez said as we came into the room.

"Giving a test, of course," the math teacher said. "There's no point in trying to teach anything on the day before spring break."

"I've got book reports due," a bridge player said. "Why? What are you doing?"

"I haven't decided yet," Mrs. Martinez said. We settled down on the small couch. "Sometimes I like to find out what *they* have in mind."

"You mean you're going to make it up as you go along?"

"Well isn't that what we always do?"

"Some of us plan our lessons," a bridge player said.

"Yes," Mrs. Martinez said, "we should have plans." She turned to me. "You saw Mark waving as we came into the building? He said something very interesting yesterday. You see, he's scatterbrained, and I said to him awhile ago, 'Mark, sometimes I think that inside you there's a willful child,' and he laughed and said, 'willful child,' as though he'd never heard the expression before. Then he said, 'How old do you think the child is?' and I said, 'How old do you think? He said, 'Thirteen, maybe—fourteen?' and I said, 'Could be.' So now he's been coming to me all year, like yesterday, and he'll say, 'I think he's about sixteen now, what do you think?' " Outside we could hear youngsters shouting to each other as they crowded through the doors. "I took him on as my project," she said, "to see what I could do with him."

The math teacher said, "I know that Mark and he's trouble. Sounds to me like you're trying to play psychiatrist."

"Yes, I'm trying to change him."

"But we aren't trained for that!"

"It's manipulation!" one of the card players said. "That's what you're doing, you're manipulating the kid."

"Now you've got it!" Mrs. Martinez said. "That's right—I'm trying to get that boy to grow up any way I can."

"Well, I'm not a manipulator."

"Oh go ahead and try," Mrs. Martinez said. "You'll learn to enjoy it."

As we went out to her first class I said, "You've got them stirred up." I wanted to ask her if she'd done that deliberately.

"Oh," she said, "they'd rather argue with me than play cards. I do a public service."

We reached her classroom and I went to sit in the back, opening my notepad as the youngsters came in. They seemed big to me, these seventeen- and eighteen-year olds, and noisy. Soon I would be facing them myself, but as student teacher my first task was to sit and observe. Mrs. Martinez was standing at the door greeting each of the youngsters as they arrived. She did this every class period, every day. When I asked her why, she said, "Because that's the only time I'll be able to speak to many of them personally, these classes are so large." Soon all thirty were in their seats and Mrs. Martinez closed the door.

"Well," she said, "here's our last class before the vacation, and I think you have a rough day ahead of you. What should we do this period?"

"Let's have a study hall," someone said. "I got a math test coming up."

"Oh no!" someone else said. "Let's do something for us." He turned to Mrs. Martinez. "Tell us a story," he said. "You haven't told us a story in a long time." Everyone looked at her, waiting. "How about it?"

"I don't know about that," she said. "How much work have we done this week? Jack, what does the chart say?"

Jack, currently the class secretary, flipped open a notebook. "We heard all the committee reports except from Mark."

"He's not ready—are you Mark?" someone said. "Let's have the story."

"We got all our notes," Mark said, "but we haven't written it up yet."

"What is your report about?" Mrs. Martinez said.

"You know what it's about. You said we spend so much time in detention we might as well write about it. So we interviewed the teacher and the principal and all the kids. George got a lot of information—right George? He's been on detention all week. If you think we're bad news wait till you hear about some of those guys."

"I'm looking forward to it," Mrs. Martinez said. "If I fill in for you today with a story, will your group be ready with your report the day we come back?"

"You got it!" Mark said.

"All right—Jack, turn off the lights please. And Mark, pull down the shades." She reached for the chair behind her desk and pushed it into the room. "Let's gather round," she said.

She sat there in the semidarkness, among those youngsters settled into a waiting silence. "The last time we gathered here I told you about Trickster. Do you remember the story?"

"He was like a kid," one of the boys said. "He always wanted everything his way."

"It was *stupid*," Lois said.

"Yes, Trickster can be very foolish. What did he do that you thought was so stupid?"

"He had a fight. I mean, his left arm had a fight with his right arm. That's pretty stupid, if you ask me."

"And what did we decide that meant?"

"It's like your left hand doesn't know what your right hand is doing," one of the boys said.

"Yeah, he just couldn't get his act together," Mark said.

"All right. Now in this story you'll see that Trickster is still blundering along, learning everything the hard way. He still wants what he wants when he wants it and never mind anybody else. But he meets a woman who knows how to manage this kind of man, so he learns something new. It happened like this:

Trickster was coming along in the coolness of the morning, and as he came he saw a beautiful young woman. She was so beautiful that he stopped to enjoy her beauty, and he began to feel warm. "What a lovely woman you are," he said. "What is your name and where do you come from?"

"My name is Whirlwind," she said, "and I come from the southwest with the heat of midsummer."

"Oh that's a pretty name, Whirlwind," said Trickster. "As pretty as the rest of you. I think we ought to go along together. I will show you this fine country, and we can rest in the shade of those cottonwoods farther on."

"No," said Whirlwind, "I like to keep moving."

"Well, I'm the man who is always coming along," said Trickster, "so I'm willing to go along with you. I think maybe, we ought to get married, and then we will always be together."

"Oh," said Whirlwind, "I don't want to marry you. You have funny arms and funny legs and a funny voice, and that funny look on your face."

"I'm very goodhearted," said Trickster. "The way I look doesn't have a thing to do with that."

"Well," said Whirlwind. "I really don't want to marry anybody. I'm too young to get married."

"Oh no you're not!" said Trickster. "You're just right to get married. Why, anybody as beautiful as you are ought to get married right away while she's still young—before she gets old and fat and ugly, and nobody wants her."

"Well, I don't know," said Whirlwind. "My people say I'm very hard to get along with. Maybe I'd better not marry anybody."

"I'm not so easy to get along with myself," said Trickster. "Some people say I'm just mean, I'm so hard to get along with. That ought to make us a good pair."

"Of course," said Whirlwind, "when I really like somebody I'm willing to do a lot to get along with him."

"That's just the way I am," said Trickster. "Why, I'd do anything to make the person I really loved happy."

"Well," said Whirlwind, "you make us sound a lot alike."

"Oh we are!" said Trickster. "I think we'd be making a big mistake not to get married. It seems to me we're just made for each other."

"All right," said Whirlwind. "Then I guess we should get married."

Trickster was so excited that he came running to her with his arms wide open. He wanted to catch hold of her before she could change her mind and run away. But just as he caught hold of her, up she went in a cloud of leaves and grass and sticks and dust, carrying Trickster along with her.

She carried him away, far away, and then she threw him down on the ground near Saddle Mountain. "There!" she said. "Maybe that will teach you a lesson. Maybe now you'll believe what a person tells you the first time!"

And off she went, leaving him choking and sputtering in her dust, for she really was the whirlwind.

In the Trickster stories of the Plains Indians that Mrs. Martinez liked to tell, we hear of a time long before the present world, and of a being who is the creature of his appetites, not yet fully human. Trickster has no purpose in life at first beyond the gratification of his constant needs for food and sex, and so is obsessively self-centered, the enemy of anyone who tries to limit him. Each one of us has a Trickster unconscious, these stories suggest, and it must be brought into awareness and managed, lest it bring harm to the individual and everyone around. For Trickster blunders about instinctively, hurting and being hurt, falling into danger and escaping, and so gradually develops cunning and finally a conscience. Knowing neither good nor evil, he yet becomes responsible for bringing into the world an awareness of both. In short, the Trickster cycle tells of the coming into the world of human purpose—of the slowly developing human consciousness. And in the story of Trickster with Whirlwind we see him undergoing yet another lesson on the way to becoming fully human, for he has not yet learned to consider the desires of another, not yet learned to love.

There was a moment's silence. Her voice coming to us there in the semi-darkness had carried us away, and we needed a moment to return from Saddle Mountain to our chalkboarded room with yellow walls. Mrs. Martinez said, "Well, what can you say about that? Lois?"

"He was stupid!" she said. "He thought he could talk her into it."

"He wasn't so dumb," Jack said. "At least he had a line. I liked the way he did that—he wouldn't give up."

"Oh sure," Lois said. "Is that how you came on to Marci?" She turned to Marci: "How about it?"

"I have nothing to say."

"I don't need a line," Jack said, "I'm sincere—" and the others burst into derisive shouts, delighted.

"They don't call him Grab-ass for nothing," someone said.

"Come on guys—give me a break."

"He has a point, doesn't he?" Mrs. Martinez said. "I mean, you do have some sincere feeling when you're interested in someone, don't you? You're not just cold-blooded about it, like Trickster."

"All he wanted was a little fun," Mark said. "What's wrong with that?"

"Don't be stupid," Lois said. "He was trying to get her into the bushes any way he could, so she dropped him. That's all he wanted."

"They'll promise you anything to get what they want," Latasha said. "He was too pushy, he got what he deserved."

"But don't you believe in love at first sight?" Jack said. "He's got to get to know her, doesn't he? How can he do that if she's going to run away? She doesn't give him a chance." He turned to Mrs. Martinez. "What do you say?"

"Well, to win in love means that you have to think about someone else for a change, not just yourself. If a girl gives in to a boy too soon he doesn't learn anything, he can go on being selfish."

"Yeah, make it hard for them," Latasha said quietly—and those sitting nearby burst out laughing.

"Some girls can be pretty aggressive too, you know," Jack said. "How about that?"

"Don't give in to them too easily, Jack," Mrs. Martinez said, and the others laughed.

"Why do you always favor the girls?" Jack said.

"I don't, really."

But she gave the boys no favor, she kept them hungry and working for her. She was young enough once to do that through their sexual interest, and now she did it through her maternal attractiveness, she practiced an erotics of teaching. She was interesting to them as a teacher and as a person, and they enjoyed these exchanges with her, they wanted her attention.

No one spoke for a moment, and then Leo said, "I'll tell you one. There's a guy I know, Joe—from the neighborhood. He's a real nice guy, and he met this girl Anna, who was a real slut, but he really liked her a lot and they started going out together. And then we noticed changes in Joey, like he didn't talk to us anymore. So we didn't like her, and we all kept telling him to watch himself with her, but he wouldn't listen. So one day Joey and Anna were up in her room, and her parents came home and caught them fooling around. They freaked out, and so she said Joey raped her, and her idiot parents believed her. Joey went to jail for two and a half years!—and he only just got out last May. When he came out he saw Anna and he spit in her face and then he left." Leo looked around at the others. "So what do you say about that?"

"That's tough!" Mark said. "He got a bum rap."

"How do you know?" Marci said. "I'll bet there's a lot more to that story."

"I wonder how Anna might tell it," Mrs. Martinez said.

"You sound cynical, you know that?" Mark said. "I'll bet you've had some experiences. I'll bet you could tell a story. How about it?"

"I've already told a story today, " she said. "But there'll be another day."

When the bell sounded the youngsters lingered there in the dimness, talking, until Mark touched the light switch and the fluorescents flickered on. As they gathered their books and moved away I went up and sat next to Mrs. Martinez. "Well, what do you think?" she said.

"It was very interesting. But you know, some people would wonder what it had to do with reading and writing."

"But not you, of course." She smiled. "You see, I think there has to be conversation. Everything will come out of that. Reading and writing are only other ways to converse."

"But only a few of them were talking."

"That's true, but they all listened. And where are they going to hear real conversation these days? No wonder the art of conversation is dead, there's hardly anyone who can listen to it. People actually resent someone who has interesting things to say. Have you noticed that?"

"I haven't really thought about it." But I almost challenged this, she had such an air of self-confident certainty.

"Besides, " she said, "there's no way you can have a general discussion in a class this size. But some of these people have something to say that the others can learn from—there's always the chance that something really good will be said. I'm willing to take that chance. And you know—I was thinking about this yesterday—there's no public discussion about these things. I mean, boys talk with boys and girls with girls, which means they only gossip with each other. What did you think of the story Leo told?"

"He had me interested. You read these stories in the newspaper but you don't think about them happening among the young people you work with."

"I told a story about a woman who was justified in what she did to a man, and Leo counters with a story about a woman who was not justified. And did you notice that part about how Joey changed? He didn't talk with the other fellows anymore, he was always with Anna—and they didn't like her. It reminds me of that scene in *Marty* where his friends resent the girl for taking their buddy away. So who knows what really happened between those two? In the battle of the sexes the truth gets lost. Do they tell you these things at the university?"

"They talk about communication skills and sentence combining and lesson plans. But I was wondering—did you plan to tell that story today?"

"I was ready in case they gave me that assignment. But I think next time I should have copies of the story ready, and then we could have one of the boys read Trickster's part and a girl be Whirlwind. We could act out the story—that might be more interesting."

"I'm not sure I could work the way you do. I mean, come into a class and wait to see what's going to happen. The students would think I didn't know what I was doing. Aren't you supposed to give the principal your lesson plans for the week?"

"Oh I just put down page numbers in the textbook, like everyone else, and that satisfies him. Of course I never open the textbook." She looked at me intently. "Does that bother you? I'm wondering what you will say about me when you go back to the university."

"I'll say that you're a very interesting person."

But she was a puzzle to me at the time. How did she manage to maintain decorum in that classroom while being so provocative? Young people bring into a classroom a thousand secrets of pain and humiliation, so that one inept comment from her, or one personal remark blurted out by one youngster about another, could turn the entire class silly or sullen. What would have happened if the principal had come in and heard that talk about attempted rape while the textbooks went unused? What if some protective parent became concerned and complained? Yet she took these chances every day, carried along by her self-confidence. Much of her strength, it seemed to me, lay in her amused detachment, her ironic attitude toward the entire daily mechanism of the school. She had a casual manner.

Then it occurred to me that perhaps Mrs. Martinez saw herself as Trickster. For like Trickster she enjoyed disturbing the tranquility of routine, raising with some casual remark or question doubts about habitual ways of doing things. If disorder belongs to the totality of life, as Kerényi remarks, then the Trickster's function "is to add disorder to order and so make a whole, to render possible, within the bounds of what is permitted, an experience of what is not permitted." Mrs. Martinez said, "I'll tell you something I usually keep to myself. These young people are going to lead very routine lives, but here in my class life will not always be routine."

She had a kind of spiritual intensity, the intensity of an individual, exploring mind moved by a deep interest in other people. Language instruction was for her a way to provoke young people into expression so that they would become more individual and join her in a protest against things as they are.

For Further Thought

1. Think about Mrs. Martinez's qualities as a teacher: her relationship with students, her goals as an educator, the way she conducts her classes. List those qualities and then write a paragraph or two in which you describe her work.

2. What precisely does Mrs. Martinez *do* during the discussion of the Trickster story to provoke student response? What do you think of her way of handling students?

3. Mrs. Martinez writes no lesson plans and seems to decide what to do at the last moment. Would you say that she is unprepared or flexible? What does it mean to be prepared to teach? Could a beginning teacher work like Mrs. Martinez? (For some thoughts on planning, you might look ahead to "Paradoxes of Planning" in chapter 6.)

4. In the essay, John Rouse is a student teacher; Mrs. Martinez is his cooperating teacher. Think about their relationship. What is her attitude toward him, and how does she seek to influence him? What are some of the mutual benefits (and problems) for apprentice and mentor in this situation?

Writing Assignment: A Literature Lesson

By now you might be tired of analyzing and altering other people's lessons. You are ready to do one of your own. In fact, you might already have written lesson plans, either for the course you are taking or another course or a field experience. In any case, you are not an absolute neophyte. You know that a plan involves some kind of learning goal for students. It requires that you think of activities for students to perform. It might also need some thinking about evaluation—how you will assess student learning. You will need a timetable of sorts and some materials. And, surrounding it, there should be some sense of the context—what went before this lesson and what will follow it.

That's a lot to think about, and just to complicate matters, let me suggest two more things. First, there is a difference between preparing to teach and making a lesson plan. This distinction is explored in some detail in "Paradoxes of Planning," an essay in chapter 6, but for now you need only realize that an effective plan comes as the result of a certain kind of thinking. Before you decide what to do, you need to consider your students and their needs, think about the material and why it matters to students, and see yourself as an agent to help learning. If you have done that thoroughly, your plan can be quite simple, but for this assignment at least you need to show that you have done the preparatory thinking.

The second thing to consider is how you will test your plan. Of course, there is no single way to do this; when you are a veteran teacher, you will follow your instincts and experience and all will go well. But most of us, at least in the beginning, need to check our plans to see if they are actually leading students where we want them to go. So let me make three suggestions. (1) Look at the things students *do*. Are they active or passive? Will they understand why they are doing things? Can you explain why doing these activities will result in some learning? (2) Try altering the plan to see if it would work another way. Specifically, you might eliminate all questions from the teacher. This is useful, because we know that English teachers tend to play "guess what I'm thinking" and, in general, ask too many questions. Or you might find another way to alter your plan to test its effectiveness. (3) Show it to someone else and get some feedback. This is obvious, right? And yet you would be surprised how seldom students in education classes do this. They know that the writing process calls for drafting and sharing and revising, but they tend not to see lesson planning as a form of writing. It is. So you would be well advised to treat the act of planning as you would any other writing task, as a process that needs some careful attention.

In the following assignment, you will be asked to do some unusual things, and the resulting paper will look a bit odd because it will be produced in a series of parts. Your instructor, no doubt, will alter those parts in some way, which is entirely appropriate. The main thing is to think about what you are doing as you plan and to keep some kind of record of that process so you can look back on it and learn from it.

*   *   *

Choose a work of literature and write a plan for teaching it on a grade level of your choice. Plan one or two days to cover the material, which might necessitate doing only part of the work. Assume that you have multiple sections of classes of about twenty-five students, grouped heterogeneously (a range of ability levels, a mix of genders and backgrounds).

Your paper will consist of the following parts: (1) a lesson plan; (2) an explanation of the choices you made, including some discussion about students, goals, and context; (3) an earlier version of the plan, accompanied by a discussion of what you did to test it and how you changed it; and (4) an evaluation of the plan's strengths and weaknesses, including a discussion of your role in its execution. Attach to the paper appendixes that might help a reader understand it (a copy of the literature, activity sheets, etc.).

Note: An assignment like this would seem to favor a traditional approach to teaching—that is, to lead you away from the workshop approach. But this is not necessarily the case. You might wish to situate yourself in a workshop setting and plan a mini-lesson or two. Or you might have decided on some adaptation of the workshop that would be reflected in your planning. In any case, your paper should make clear your approach to literature instruction.

For Further Reading

Adams, Peter. "Writing from Reading: 'Dependent Authorship' as a Response." *In Readers, Texts, Teachers*, edited by Bill Corcoran and Emrys Evans (pp. 119–152). Upper Montclair, NJ: Boynton/Cook, 1987. Adams describes variations on "dependent authorship," that is, assignments in which students work within the confines of a text, extending or altering it.

Albritton, Tom. "Honest Questions and the Teaching of English." *English Education*, Vol. 24, No. 2 (May 1992, pp. 91–100). A sensible discussion of the way English teachers ask questions, urging us to make them honest.

Ash, Barbara Hoetker. "Reading Assigned Literature in a Reading Workshop." *English Journal*, Vol. 79, No. 1 (January 1990), 77–79. This essay is referred to in Application 2.3.

Atwell, Nancie. *In the Middle: New Understandings about Writing, Reading, and Learning.* 2nd edition. Portsmouth, NH: Heinemann, Boynton/Cook, 1998. This new edition is less dogmatic and in some ways more complex than the first edition of *In the Middle*. A "must read" for English teachers.

Beach, Richard, and James Marshall. *Teaching Literature in the Secondary School.* New York: Harcourt Brace Jovanovich, 1991. A comprehensive textbook on teaching literature.

Corcoran, Bill, and Emrys Evans, eds. *Readers, Texts, Teachers.* Upper Montclair, NJ: Boynton/Cook, 1987. A good collection of essays from a reader-response orientation, including the Peter Adams piece in this bibliography.

Dias, Patrick. "Literary Reading and Classroom Constraints: Aligning Practice with Theory." In *Literature Instruction: A Focus on Student Response*, edited by Judith A. Langer. Urbana, IL: NCTE, 1992, pp. 131–162. This essay is referred to in Application 2.2.

Hynds, Susan. "Challenging Questions in the Teaching of Literature." In *Literature Instruction: A Focus on Student Response*, edited by Judith A. Langer. Urbana, IL: NCTE, 1992, pp. 78–100. This essay is referred to in Application 2.1.

Karolides, Nicholas, ed. *Reader Response in the Classroom: Evoking and Interpreting Meaning in Literature.* White Plains, NY: Longman, 1992. An excellent collection of essays by Robert Small, Nicholas Karolides, Deborah Appleman, James Davis, Robert Probst, and others. Many of the essays contain examples of using particular works in secondary classrooms.

Langer, Judith, ed. *Literature Instruction: A Focus on Student Response.* Urbana, IL: NCTE, 1992. This collection includes essays by Arthur Applebee, Alan Purves, Robert Probst, and others. The Hynds and Dias pieces in this bibliography are contained in this volume.

Probst, Robert E. *Response and Analysis: Teaching Literature in Junior and Senior High School.* Portsmouth, NH: Boynton/Cook, Heinemann, 1988. A thorough discussion of teaching literature from a reader-response perspective.

Purves, Alan C., Theresa Rogers, and Anna O. Soter. *How Porcupines Make Love II: Teaching a Response-Centered Literature Curriculum.* White Plains, NY: Longman, 1990. A reprise of the original *Porcupines* book (1972) with a lively discussion of theory and issues related to response-centered teaching.

Rosenblatt, Louise M. *Literature as Exploration*, 4th edition. New York: Modern Language Association, 1983. The classic modern discussion of the teaching of Literature, originally published in 1938. "A Performing Art" (pp. 29–35) is included in this edition as a coda. A 5th edition (1995) is available through NCTE.

Smith, Frank. *Reading without Nonsense.* New York: Teachers College Press, 1979. A readable introduction to the psycholinguistic theory of reading.

Whitley, Judith. "The Textbook Isn't Dying in the 1990's." *English Journal*, Vol. 87, No. 1 (January 1998), 15–16. This essay is referred to in Application 2.3.

3

Choosing Texts

Introduction

Thus far we have considered the teaching of literature in terms of goals and methods, but what is the content of the literature curriculum? What should we be asking students to read?

The choice of any text is important—so important that its implications go beyond schools themselves. When teachers assign books in school, they place a value on them, promoting and promulgating them, thus helping create or reinforce what has come to be known as the literary *canon*, that is, the body of literature deemed worthy of being taught in schools. And because what we teach influences what people know and how they look at the world, the canon has come to represent—at least in the public imagination—something about the culture we live in. For many people today, changes in the canon reflect changes in the culture at large, changes that may be viewed as either progressive or dangerous, depending on one's politics. In the end, what we teach in the English classroom is a political issue.

Even within the reading workshop approach, the question of what to teach remains relevant. It is true that if students are afforded a choice of texts, then they share with teachers the responsibility of shaping the canon for that class. But questions regarding that canon are still relevant, and teachers continue to exert considerable influence. Moreover, as we have seen, reading workshop does not necessarily mean free choice for students all the time. Teachers who adapt Nancie Atwell's approach, and Atwell herself in her recent work, seem more and more insistent on the value of having students read together. It is important to remember, too, that the workshop approach is more common on the middle school level than in the upper grades, where coverage of a certain body of literature is usually a higher priority. Thus, eleventh-grade "American Literature" might vary from school to school and from teacher to teacher, but seldom would it involve the free choice of texts by students. Directly or indirectly, the choice of texts is something that teachers cannot avoid.

The Canon

Even as I write, the canon wars are going on, mostly on college campuses, but also on high school book selection committees and on the editorial pages of newspapers and magazines. Should English departments be teaching Milton and Pope, for example, or Margaret Atwood and Chinua Achebe? Should it be Emerson and Melville or the slave narratives of Frederick Douglass and Harriet Jacobs? Will it be the "great books" of "White males" or the rediscovered texts of women and other "marginalized writers"? In a recent case in San Francisco, the school board was asked to consider replacing some traditional texts (Shakespearean plays were among those named) with works by authors from ethnic groups underrepresented in the curriculum.

You might say that it does not have to be one or the other: We can and should teach both kinds of literature, side by side if possible. That is fair enough, and it is, in fact, the position of nearly everyone (including many of the San Francisco teachers in the case just mentioned). As you recall from chapter 1, English is a vast subject that embraces nearly anything in print or on the screen, so in theory everyone can afford to be moderate. Yet in practice, the English curriculum, on any level, is constrained by time (how much can be covered), money (how much we can afford to put in a book room), and our own expertise (what we actually know). Because we simply cannot assign everything that we wish to teach, we end up choosing, although not often in these extreme ways—Herman Melville *or* Harriet Jacobs. And in choosing what to teach, we act out of our literary and social values.

Choice is, therefore, inevitable and inevitably political. What is to guide our choices? The readings in this chapter offer a variety of perspectives, but it is useful to consider the issue first from the standpoint of history. English, as an academic subject, was formed in the midst of a developing concern over the canon. At the end of the last century, as now, curricular choices were influenced by reading lists. The most contentious issue involved control of the curriculum: Were those lists to be created by college professors, as a way of ensuring standard preparation within a particular (and quite traditional) canon, or were they to be developed by secondary teachers, as a way of fostering literacy in all students? That debate, which took place in the last decades of the nineteenth century and the first decades of the twentieth, led to the professionalization of high school English teaching.

It is instructive to be reminded of this, lest we think that the canon, indeed any canon, is somehow "above" historical context. Despite what some might say about timeless classics, a work of

literature and the value we ascribe to it are both shaped by historical
processes. Thus the canon of American literature is the result of
American history and represents a kind of political statement, a version of American culture—from someone's point of view. For example, E. D. Hirsch, Jr., author of *Cultural Literacy: What Every
American Should Know*, represents the conservative position on the
canon; as the title of his book suggests, Hirsch is concerned about
the cohesiveness or connectedness of American culture. Proponents
of "diversity," on the other hand, can be expected to espouse another
set of values (honoring pluralism and difference) and thus support
other kinds of curricular choices. The issue is explored later in this
chapter by Sandra Stotsky in "Academic Guidelines for Selecting
Multiethnic and Multicultural Literature" (pp. 96–105).

In this context Ken Donelson (pp. 87–93) offers us a glimpse at the
process of choosing course content as it might take place in the work-
aday world of teaching. In Donelson's view, we have a great many
choices to make, so we need to get down to the business of doing
it—accepting that our values will direct the show, whether we admit it
or not. As teachers we are on the front lines of the canon wars, selecting readings from textbooks, indeed choosing the textbooks themselves. As Donelson reminds us, it has always been this way; the only
difference now is that we are asked to be more thoughtful about it.

Reading for Young People

Part of our thinking must have to do with the interests and concerns
of the young people we are teaching. In "It's the THAT, Teacher" (pp.
109–113), Ted Hipple takes the position that the English teacher's
main job is to turn nonreaders into readers, hence the value of works
that appeal to the taste of adolescents. This is a familiar argument,
and a persuasive one, especially when it is reinforced by Hipple's assertion that there is now a canon of top-notch young adult (YA) novels
that can compete with the classics. But what do teenage readers like?

A difficult question, but it is possible to generalize a bit. Many adolescent readers like books with teenage protagonists, preferably
just a little older than themselves. At the middle school level, readers
especially like stories with linear plots and lots of action. They like
works that address their own concerns: not just drugs, sex, and
rock and roll, but love, self-esteem, and independence. All this is
true enough, if we leave lots of room for variations in taste, but there
is more, some of it problematical. Students like relevant works, yes,
but that may mean confirming their stereotypes of the world, especially in regard to gender. They like action, true, but they also identify with risk-taking and violence. They are concerned about the issues of adolescence, but they do not always agree with us (the adult
world) on many of those issues.

High-interest reading, then, is not always politically correct or
even moral by adult society's standards. Nor is it always well written.
It is easy to grant the value of the titles on Hipple's list of canonical
YA books, but some teenagers prefer violent crime stories, bod-

ice-ripper romances, and super-morbid gothics. Although we do not have to pander to that taste in the classroom, we should recognize that it exists. When we seek high-interest texts for students, we should examine them carefully, asking ourselves not just what they like but also what values are being promoted in the books we choose.

In addition, aesthetics should play a role somewhere in this process of choosing books. Depending on our teaching goals, we may not be concerned with transmitting the classics from generation to generation or with promoting Hirsch's version of cultural literacy, but we should, after all, be asking students to read good books. So it matters that Robert Cormier's *The Chocolate War* is, in my opinion, a better novel than S. E. Hinton's *The Outsiders*, and that Chris Crutcher's *Running Loose* is superior to Judy Blume's *Forever*. Those are literary judgments, and I offer them deliberately because all four titles appear on a list of "the best YA books of the year, 1964–1995" compiled by Ken Donelson (see *English Journal*, March 1997). My aim is not to second-guess Donelson but to underscore a point: Donelson's list is *his* list, just as Hipple's list is his own. It is not yours or mine. Lists can be useful, especially when they are put together by experts in the field like Hipple and Donelson, and, besides, one has to start someplace in coming to terms with the broad scope of young adult literature. But the ultimate judgment of which books are most worthwhile, both in themselves and for the particular students in our classes, is up to each teacher.

Questions of literary merit are complex and important. It is not just that we owe it to students to offer them the best works available; it is also true that we may have to justify our choices. As Edward Jenkinson points out in "Protecting Holden Caulfield and His Friends" (pp. 116–126), censorship is on the rise in this country. Even classics are not safe, as efforts to remove *Huckleberry Finn* from the curriculum make clear, so one cannot always appeal to a shared sense of "cultural literacy" to defend a text. Playing it safe is not the answer. The safest course of action, as it turns out, is to assign the best available works for your students, and to know why you made the choice.

Protecting Students

In the end, the question of what to teach has to take into account the student's right to read, or not read, a given work. Thus, we need to do more than protect books from would-be censors; we also need to be sensitive to students' needs and adopt a reasonable attitude toward their rights. Literature, as we know, can be disturbing. Indeed, it ought to be at least a little disturbing if it is to be worthwhile. The worst thing about censorship is that it seeks to deprive students of experiences, disturbing or not, through which they might learn. This is not to say, however, that there are no limits. If we bear in mind that reading assignments are seldom voluntary and that teachers have enormous power over the experiences of students, we will use that power wisely. Before viewing Roman Polanski's version of

Macbeth, for example, students should be warned about graphic violence—yes, even though it might seem tame to many of them. And they should know in advance that *Inherit the Wind* raises issues that, for some of them, will be controversial. Whether students should have the right to opt out, to read another work, is a question to which there is no general answer. You must decide case by case. But to pretend that students do not really get upset because this is "just literature" is to deny the very power of the arts to move and disturb us.

Just how difficult the matter can be is illustrated in the experience of an eighth-grade English teacher and one of her students. The class had been reading Bette Green's *Summer of My German Soldier*, and this boy was unusually quiet throughout the unit. Later, the teacher learned that the student was a victim of physical abuse and the family was receiving rather intense counseling. In his journal the boy wrote of how painful it was to read the book.

Was the experience "good" for the student? Perhaps, but what he felt at the time was the pain, not the learning. Should the teacher have warned students and presented options? Perhaps, but that might have been overprotective. I have no easy answers to this question. In my view—and this is ironic—the experience was good for the student (he did manage to write about it) but bad for the teacher (she is now very cautious about assigning this book). No, there are not easy answers, nor should there be. The moral to the story, if there is one, is this: Literature can do things to people. That is why we teach it. That is also why we need to be thoughtful and caring when we ask students to undergo the literary experience.

Canons to Right of Them, Canons to Left of Them, Canons in Front of Them, Volley'd and Thunder'd

Ken Donelson

Ken Donelson begins with an argument against list-making, but eventually he does what we all have to do: He makes a list of his own. The resulting canon for four years of high school English gives us something to think about, a starting point for discussion of what literature we might want to assign. More important perhaps is Donelson's discussion of why he chose these works. As you read, think about your own personal canon and your own reasons for including this work or that.

This essay appeared in English Education, *Vol. 17, No. 4 (December 1985); copyright 1985 by the National Council of Teachers of English. It is reprinted with permission.*

We are often told that it is the duty of the teacher of English to bring her pupils to "love" the classics. That she fails to do this, much or most of her time, is often the subject of complaint. . . . The teacher of literature should not feel that it is obligatory upon her to impart love for the classics, especially of all the classics, to her pupils. Rather is hers the less ambitious duty to make her pupils know and understand the works which they study. This is not a utopian idea. It is one which she can carry out. The "love" which is imparted is the personal affair of the pupils and must be left to take care of itself. It cannot be forced.

—*Louise Pound, "What Should Be Expected of the Teacher of Eng-*

lish?" English Journal 10 *(April 1921): 182–183.*

I noticed in the National Council of Teachers of English [NCTE] May 1985 *Council-Grams* that the Commission on Literature "found fewer reasons for satisfaction than for anxiety." I sympathize with the Commission, which noted that "the status of literature in education has been diminished by hostility, bigotry, ignorance, indifference, and neglect on the part of pressure groups" and went on to add, "If the current increase in censorship continues, eventually the only literature permitted in the classroom will be so bland and benign that it could not reflect the actual world in which students live."

Something even more troubling about the teaching of literature is happening, as NCTE's Commission on Curriculum noted in the same publication. To be more accurate, something that some people would like to see is happening as part of the educational reform movement—a return to the core curriculum in literature, standardization of literary texts across the country so that Jason in Maine and Sheri in Oregon would read the same materials. Theoretically, so the notion goes, American students would thus have a common background in literature or, as others put it, a common literary heritage. The issue was raised last year by the report of the Coalition of English Associations. Concerned that current reform movements were giving little attention to literature and less guidance to those seeking to reform English teaching, the Coalition listed what it called "Some Plain Truths about Teaching English." Among the five points:

1. English studies include both the study of literature and writing. . . .
2. So much excellent literature exists that different schools may reasonably make different selections of literature for their students. Many reports raise the question of what students should read. *A number suggest the importance of establishing a common body of literature* [my emphasis]. Students should read works that help them define and understand their own values and experiences and those of others. All students should read widely in the literatures from their own cultures and regions, from the pluralistic American experience, and from the world at large.

—from "Coalition of English Groups Faults Reform Reports," *English Journal* 73 (October 1984): 97.

More to the point, the notion that English teachers ought to teach a common body of literature came to public attention when William J. Bennett, then Chair of the National Endowment for the Humanities and now occupying a presumably even more august post, released a list of works that "every high school student ought to be required to read," or so most news stories announced. The list was determined "unscientifically," as the August 13, 1984, *New York Times* charitably termed it. A total of 325 people responded to invitations by Bennett, columnist George Will, and instructors of 1984 summer humanities institutes. The resultant canon would hardly surprise many literate adults—the top group included *Macbeth* and *Hamlet*, several American historical documents, *Huckleberry Finn*, the *Bible*, the *Iliad* and the *Odys-*

sey, *A Tale of Two Cities* and *Great Expectations*, *The Republic*, *The Grapes of Wrath*, and *The Scarlet Letter*. The closest any contemporary work came to making the list was *The Catcher in the Rye*.

An excellent list, one almost every English teacher would subscribe to, though for possibly quite different reasons. Most would admire its breadth in including many—though hardly all—of the greatest books ever written. Most would agree that the list might be used as a fair, if inexact, index of the background reading we'd assume of any good secondary English teacher. Some would agree that the list would make yet another fine addition to that endless collection of lists that students should consult in preparing for college. Some would admit shamefacedly, to themselves, that it was time to read books so widely endorsed and so much admired. A few might even go along with Bennett and agree that the list would constitute a good beginning for the English curriculum.

Why would so many English teachers admire the list and refuse to use it as the starting point of the reformed English literature curriculum?

> It is argued that since pupils will read popular literature anyway, we ought to teach the classics in school because otherwise they will never know anything about them. I do not say that the argument lacks merit; but it has an ugly aspect, when stripped of its sophistry. It amounts to admitting that because the classics are disagreeable anyway, we had better teach them in school along with the other disagreeable subjects. Moreover, it invalidates the very assumptions on which the teaching of the classics is based; the assumptions, namely, that their teaching will carry over into life.
>
> —Howard Mumford Jones, "The Fetish of the Classics," *English Journal* 18 (March 1929): 235.

For most English teachers, the reluctance won't stem from a lack of faith in the classics. English teachers became English teachers because they like to read; virtually all of them read and were taught the classics in college, and they'd love to communicate their enthusiasm about great books to younger students. Classics are important because they raise significant moral dilemmas, make some hard moral judgments, and tell the truth about humans involved in eternal human problems through imaginative prose and poetry. Classics challenge traditional and glib ideas and values, which make them exciting to read and teach, just as they are feared by censors (or should be feared *were* the censors to have read and understood the books).

Almost all English teachers would agree that there's not merely a place for the classics in English classes; these works are necessities, basics if you will. The problems arise when the listmakers begin to believe themselves and assume an infallibility about their lists. First, they assume that a canon of literature is easily established and easily applied to all schools. Second, they rarely list anything save the "tried and true," books that have successfully passed the test of time. Third, and a corollary of the second, they assume that contemporary literature, say of the last fifty years, would rarely enter the kingdom of literature teaching. Fourth, they assume that their lack of experience working with secondary school students somehow gives them objective judgment superior to those with that experience.

All these assumptions are very much open to question by real high school English teachers who are not impressed with an enthusiasm predicated upon ignorance. Granted, experience in teaching secondary school may not produce wisdom, but it does suggest to teachers what can work in ninth grade,

for example, and what is highly unlikely to work there. *Moby Dick* is one of the great works of literature, but attempts to teach it, complete or in altered or shortened form, in the ninth or tenth grades lead to almost certain failure. That comment should bewilder or puzzle no English teacher, but it constantly surprises listmakers.

Contemporary literature has a place in the English classroom, partly because it is simply more accessible to young people, partly because most of them who learn to like literature are likely to read more contemporary literature than any other sort throughout their lives. To ignore the present because it is the present is ignorance carried past absurdity. To ignore Salinger or Faulkner or Fitzgerald, to name three who were further down on Bennett's list, or Malamud or Bellow or cummings or Ellison or any number of other current writers is to pretend that nothing worthwhile is being written today.

To pretend that the classics, and only the classics, are worth using or teaching or recommending in literature classes is to play the arrogant snob and ultimately to be no friend of literature at all. The classics are worth reading, not because they're classics but because *The Divine Comedy* and *Don Quixote* and *Tom Jones* and *Bleak House* and *Persuasion* and *First Love*—to mention only a few personal favorites—tell how people felt and were like then and what people feel and are like today. And the classics are lively and exciting *if* the teacher cares about whatever classic is being taught and makes it come alive, no easy task when teaching many students who can barely read.

The upshot is that a canon of literature—whether it is for secondary school or the latest collection on a new book shelf—is not so easily established. Who will choose the canon?

What will the canon contain? What grade shall each work in the canon be assigned to? How many works in common should be listed? Should we list two from the canon to be taught every year? Three? Four?

I mused about that for several hours before I decided to play God and devise my canon of common works for each year of high school. I've ignored significant American historical and political documents since I assumed they should be taught where they will have the greatest effect, a course in American history. I'll make that same assumption about other significant historical and political documents like *The Communist Manifesto*, Aristotle's *Politics*, and Machiavelli's *The Prince* which surely would benefit from the context of classes in world history or economics.

After fooling around with several hundred titles (it's amazing how many excellent works deserve time in English class), I concluded that the list that follows is eminently sensible, teachable, and workable, defensible on literary quality and educationally worthwhile, but then my conclusion (based as it is upon my thoughts) will hardly amaze readers. It's a list that I could live with because the works cited are important to adults (at least this one) and interesting to young people.

My ground rules for establishing this canon were simple. On the assumption that all literate and sensitive English teachers will have their own favorites to add to my list of required, standard works, I kept the list short—two novels, two plays, and one Shakespeare play—for each of the four high school years. I added eight short stories to be taught each year, thus going one up on earlier listmakers. Though I added no titles of poetry, I assume that students will be awash in poetry all four years, for without poetry there can be no literature curriculum worthy of the name. I

assume that English teachers know enough good poetry to develop their own lists, again going one up on earlier listmakers who assume that English teachers are incapable of determining what is worth teaching. The list of poets from which to choose would be vast, but standard poets such as Dickinson, Shakespeare, Donne, cummings, Sassoon, Keats, Tennyson, Yeats, Poe, Pope, Hardy, Masters, Jeffers, T. S. Eliot, Roethke, Jarrell, and Thomas would certainly be included, just as contemporary poets like Jim Harrison, Diane Wakoski, W. S. Merwin, Adrienne Rich, Denise Levertov, X. J. Kennedy, Norman Dubie, Robert Francis, Anne Sexton, Donald Hall, Robert Bly, Donald Justice, Galway Kinnell, W. D. Snodgrass, and David Wagoner would be prominent every year.

Obviously, I believe in working with drama, both as a literary artifact and as a starter for improvisational drama and readers' theatre and more. I also assumed, what many others would do, that Shakespeare deserves to be read and acted every year.

Two major problems soon intruded themselves into my little exercise in futility—the grade placement for the items, which is both insoluble and open to endless and usually pointless arguments, and the controversial nature of some items. I'm painfully aware that some works have been challenged in some communities; indeed, some have a history of such follies. A less obvious, but very real, problem is that most of the world's great literature and virtually all the long works that follow are serious—some young people have thought them deadly serious and, quite possibly, they're right. Little that's truly amusing endures for long without requiring either considerable scholarship or the help of glossaries to read, possibly to enjoy. It's true that Aristophanes and Menander, especially the former, work well on stage, but reading either author is for most people something less immediately enjoyable. Woody Allen's books are delightful for many adults and some students. Much that is truly funny for young people deserves time in class but not as common, required reading. Most of what is heightened wit for adults, for example P. G. Wodehouse, simply isn't translatably funny to young people. That's sad, but it's true, and it's something good English teachers know.

Herewith, then, is my canon of works, ninth through twelfth grade, chosen because they work with young adults, because they are first-rate literature, and because they introduce the young to authors and fictional worlds and problems worth talking about.

Ninth Grade

Shakespeare
Romeo and Juliet (whole play, not the emasculated versions)

Novels
Garfield's *The Sound of Coaches* (undeservedly neglected in America)
Sillitoe's *The Loneliness of the Long Distance Runner*

Plays
Gibson's *The Miracle Worker*
Rose's *Twelve Angry Men*

Short Stories
Connell's "The Most Dangerous Game"
Benét's "The Devil and Daniel Webster"
Agee's "A Mother's Tale"
Jacobs' "The Monkey's Paw"
Poe's "The Cask of Amontillado"
Tolstoy's "How Much Land Does a Man Need?"
Bryan's "So Much Unfairness of Things"
Doyle's "The Red Headed League"

Tenth Grade

Shakespeare
Julius Caesar

Novels
Twain's *The Adventures of Huckleberry Finn*

Steinbeck's *Of Mice and Men*

Plays
Ibsen's *An Enemy of the People*
Clark's *Whose Life Is It Anyway?*

Short Stories
Jackson's "The Lottery"
Steinbeck's "Flight"
Lawrence's "The Rocking-Horse Winner"
Anderson's "I'm a Fool"
Bierce's "An Occurrence at Owl Creek Bridge"
Whitehill's "The Day of the Last Rock Fight"
Lardner's "Haircut"
Clark's "The Portable Phonograph"

Eleventh Grade

Shakespeare
Macbeth

Novels
Melville's *Billy Budd*
Malamud's *The Assistant*

Plays
Miller's *Death of a Salesman*
Sophocles' *Oedipus Rex* and *Antigone*

Short Stories
Updike's "A & P"
Hawthorne's "The Birthmark"
Thurber's "The Greatest Man in the World"
Shaw's "The Eighty-Yard Run"
Crane's "The Open Boat"
Faulkner's "A Rose for Emily"
Porter's "The Jilting of Granny Weatherall"
Wright's "Almos' a Man"

Twelfth Grade

Shakespeare
Hamlet

Novels
Hughes' *A High Wind in Jamaica* (aka, *The Innocent Voyage*)
Joyce's *A Portrait of the Artist as a Young Man*

Plays
Everyman and *The Second Shepherd's Play*

Rostand's *Cyrano de Bergerac*

Short Stories
Conrad's "The Secret Sharer"
James' "The Real Thing"
Melville's "Bartleby the Scrivener"
Mérimé's "Mateo Falcone"
Kafka's "The Metamorphosis"
Tolstoy's "The Death of Ivan Ilyich"
Twain's "The Man That Corrupted Hadleyburg"
Akutagawa's "In a Grove" and "Rashomon"

The problem with this list, or any canonical list, is that it is doomed to leave out many favorite, great books, and I had to delete Dostoevsky's *Crime and Punishment*, Turgenev's *First Love*, Austen's *Persuasion*, Ellison's *Invisible Man*, Faulkner's *The Sound and the Fury*, Wilder's *Heaven's My Destination*, Storey's *This Sporting Life*, Kawabata's *Snow Country*, Fast's *April Morning*, Beckett's *Waiting for Godot*, Cormier's *The Chocolate War*, Dickens' *Hard Times*, Childress' *A Hero Ain't Nothin' but a Sandwich*, and Greene's *The Heart of the Matter*, all of them first-rate, all eminently teachable in some schools to some students.

My little exercise in pointlessness proved to be both fun and frustrating, fun because I enjoyed considering what works I would require had I the power to do so, frustrating because even though it was an exercise I was forced to leave out literature I am committed to teaching, books and short stories and plays that I love and some of my students seem to have enjoyed.

And that is what matters in the classroom, the teacher's satisfaction in teaching something he or she admires because particular students—this year's students in this school for reasons clear to a good teacher—need this work. Good teachers learn to sense that need. No one, Bennett or I or anyone else, can do that for a teacher of English. Besides, only a fool would think anyone but a teacher could make the classroom run effectively. That's why listmakers and would-be canon-makers are doomed to failure. They come with their canons, they shoot them off to loud noise and much applause, and then they disappear, and no one is the wiser for their brief appearance on stage.

> Every now and then, at a party, you meet someone who tells you about a book she has just read. She describes its tremendous reception and the growing fame of its author. Finally, in a tone of friendly authority, she says, 'You *must* read it. Do remember its title now, and don't forget. You *must* read it.'
>
> At once your stomach—assisted by the canapés—turns. You thank her civilly. You fix the name of the book in your memory. You resolve never, never on any account, to read it.
>
> Yet it might have been quite a good book. She explained how important it was. What made you feel it must be revolting? Was the evidence in its favor inadequate? No. The evidence was fairly sound. But you were biased against the book simply because someone told you that you *must* MUST read it.
>
> We have all felt this. It goes back to the days when we were in school, when we were told that we were obliged to read some books about which we usually knew nothing, nothing whatever, except that it was a *must*.
> —Gilbert Highet, "Compulsory Reading" in his *Talents and Geniuses*, New York: Oxford University Press, 1957, pp. 271–272.

Well, there you have it, my answer to Bennett's list, my little experiment in establishing a literature curriculum. A bit of work, there, but not all that hard. Why don't you do what I did so inadequately? List books that you think are essential for your students: devise your own literature curriculum. Good English teachers have been doing it for years. Go thou and do likewise.

For Further Thought

1. Examine Donelson's list. How many of these works have you read? How important is that? Then look at the process of choosing described in the article. What attitude does Donelson take toward the classics? Toward genres? Toward "enjoyment"? (Note his citation of Louise Pound in the headnote.) How would you characterize the resulting list?

2. Donelson's list is surprising in several respects, not the least of which is the failure to include many works by non-White, non-male, or non-European writers. What do you think of this kind of list? Is it legitimate to say that this is a "core" to which other kinds of works will be added? Or does that suggest a kind of traditional bias in the first place?

3. Consider the case of Shakespeare. Donelson assumes that a Shakespearean play should be taught in each of the four years of high school. Do you agree? Take a position on the value of including the works of Shakespeare in the secondary curriculum. Should we teach these plays? If so, how many? On what levels?

4. Donelson says the grade placement for his items is an "insoluble [problem] and open to endless and usually pointless arguments." He has a point. I have found Mary E. Wilkins Freeman's story "The Revolt of Mother" included in anthologies aimed at eighth, tenth, and eleventh grade, as well as college audiences. And yet one does have to place a work somewhere. Are there upper limits for any works on your list? (Would you assign a middle-level book like *Where the Lilies Bloom* in twelfth grade?) Are there lower limits? (Would you assign Conrad's "The Secret Sharer" in seventh grade?)

5. Make your own list of "must" reading for grades seven through twelve. Use Donelson's criteria as a guide, if you wish. Note that you need to include six grades, so you might wish to shorten the list. If you need guidelines, try these: two novels, two plays, and four short stories per grade level.

Application 3.1:
The Process of Choosing

A Scenario for Teaching American Literature

Imagine the following situation. You are about a month into the fall term of an eleventh-grade American literature course. Having chosen to add a unit on Native Americans at the start of the semester, you have fallen behind the schedule. You have only a week and a half (seven class days) before you begin a unit on the transcendentalists. "Not good," you say to yourself as you stare at the list of readings below. This is what is available in the textbook and the book room. It is clearly too much for the next seven days.

Washington Irving, "Rip Van Winkle" and "The Devil and Tom Walker"

James Fenimore Cooper, excerpt from *The Deerslayer*

William Cullen Bryant, "Thanatopsis"

Henry Wadsworth Longfellow, "The Children's Hour"

John Greenleaf Whittier, excerpt from "Snowbound"

Edgar Allan Poe, "The Black Cat," "Hop Frog," "The Raven," and "Annabel Lee"

James Russell Lowell, "Stanzas on Freedom"

James W. C. Pennington, excerpt from *The Fugitive Blacksmith* (slave narrative)

Harriet Jacobs, excerpt from *Incidents in the Life of a Slave Girl*

Spirituals: "Swing Low, Sweet Chariot" and "Follow the Drinking Gourd"

Audiotape: "The Legend of Sleepy Hollow" (abridged, thirty minutes)

Audiotape: "The Cask of Amontillado" (twenty-five minutes)

Videotape: "The Tell-Tale Heart" (twenty minutes)

Videotape: "The Fall of the House of Usher" (thirty minutes)

Videotape: "The Raven" (starring the Simpsons, fifteen minutes)

The situation is a bit extreme, but in its essentials it is one you will have to face throughout your teaching career. You have made a choice (beginning the course with a Native American unit), and that has consequences. You now have a limited amount of time to cover a fair-sized chunk of material. You are not free to dump this material completely, nor are you free to take three weeks to cover it, thus delaying the start of the next unit. Your colleagues expect you, at least by the semester break when students switch sections, to get to roughly the same place in the curriculum. You have exercised some flexibility, but now it's time to conform.

What will you want your students to read? And why? The canon question cannot be evaded, and behind it lies E. D. Hirsch's notion of cultural literacy. The very course title, "American Literature," suggests that it is a sort of cultural enterprise, though this cannot be our only consideration; we need also to think of student interest, the length and difficulty of texts, and the versions of those texts that are available to us. So we can ask: Should students be exposed to "The Legend of Sleepy Hollow"? Reasoning that this is an American classic, we might say yes, but is it more of a classic than "The Cask of Amontillado"? What makes a classic more important than either of the slave narratives, both "classics" in their own way? And what, in the end, does "exposure" mean—a thorough reading, just a skimming, a condensed film version, a few names and titles?

"Stop!" you want to say. "This is only a week stuck in between the colonial period and the transcendentalists! Give me a break! Maybe we should just watch some Poe movies and then start reading Walden." That is a natural impulse, one that every teacher has entertained. But it will not do. (You don't have enough Poe movies anyway.) You have to choose, and E. D. Hirsch is (figuratively) looking over your shoulder.

Some Things to Consider About the American Literature Situation

1. Consider the situation just described and make your choices. Which works will you assign, and why? Your answer should explain what you believe to be the goals of a course in American literature. You might need to find an American literature anthology to familiarize yourself with these works.

2. Look at the Poe and Irving materials on the list. What are the relative advantages or disadvantages of using audiotapes and films instead of reading the texts themselves? Do you satisfy the demands of cultural literacy by showing students a film of "The Legend of Sleepy Hollow"?

3. "Thanatopsis" has always appeared on lists of "must read" American poems. Find this poem and read it. Why is it so frequently anthologized? Would you assign it? Why or why not?

Creating a Unit: Initial Choices

Let's assume that you need to create a teaching unit for a body of literature—for, say, a month. (The applications in this chapter build toward such a unit assignment: see pp. 129–132). The grade level and the content will be up to you. Where do you begin? For organizing a literature unit, you have three basic choices. First, you might think of a body of literature with some cultural, historical, or geographical coherence. "American Literature" is an example, but you might also think of "African-American Literature," "Canadian Authors," "Seventeenth-Century British Literature," or "Literature of the Southwest." These have a kind of built-in coherence, but you'll want to think carefully about your goals and possible thematic connections among the various pieces. Indeed, one danger of selecting a body of material this way is that we are inclined to take goals for granted. It is not enough to say that students should read Jewish-American literature because "everyone should read Jewish-American literature." This might be true, but it's hardly self-evident. Moreover, historical or geographical connections are not always meaningful to students—so we sometimes have to work hard to get students to see what holds this kind of unit together.

Another possibility is the unit of study based on genre. A recent tenth-grade anthology, for example, includes sections on the short story, nonfiction essays, poetry, drama, and a mixed bag of mythology/folklore/legend. (Interestingly, there is no novel in this book, even though the novel is by far the most popular literary form among modern readers.) Thus, with the exception of drama, the emphasis of modern anthologies is clearly on short forms that can be readily assembled into coherent units of study. Although this is a very popular way of constructing units, it is important to remember that it privileges considerations of genre. There is no point in limiting oneself to short stories, for example, unless one has a genuine interest in having students learn something about the short story form—and, here again, it is clear that teachers are often more interested in such formal considerations than are students.

Thematic or topical units would thus seem to have a certain advantage: The content, what the literature is about, holds the course of study together. The connectedness of one text to the next is therefore more apparent and meaningful, at least in theory. In the textbook previously mentioned, for example, the poetry section is actually organized around four general themes: "Hard Choices," "Hearts that Love," "Exiles, Castaways, and Strangers," and "Breakthroughs." What these titles actually mean, of course, depends on the selections and the way they are ordered, but the point should be clear: The textbook writers understood that "poetry" was far too broad to mean much to students, so they superimposed on the genre section a more meaningful thematic principle.

There are, of course, other ways of organizing a literature unit: around a single author ("Shakespeare" or "Frost"), a literary element or technique

("Metaphor" or "Plot"), or even a skill ("Reading for Meaning" or "Analysis of Literature"). But the three I have mentioned—culture/history/geography, genre, and theme—are by far the most common, and other approaches tend to resolve themselves, in one way or another, into one of these. These categories are not necessarily distinct from each other: It is easy enough to put a thematic spin on a selection of American short stories written around the turn of the century. Still, as a starting point for this assignment, you will probably want to start with one of these principles. When in doubt, I'd advise working with a thematic unit. Naturally, there is some danger in boring students with works that are too narrowly focused ("What! *Another* growing up story!"), but on the whole, the thematic unit has the double advantage of fixing attention on the meaning of texts and making you choose from the broadest variety of texts. That's good, for this is, after all, an exercise in choice.

Some Things to Consider About Literature Units
(see pp. 129–132 for a unit writing assignment)

1. Choose a grade level for your literature unit. What do you know about students at that level? To explore possibilities, do some free writing in which you (a) remember what you studied in that grade, (b) remember what you enjoyed reading when you were that age, (c) think of the reading abilities of students at that level.
2. Refer to the preceding description and consider the kind of unit you will write. Explain your choice.
3. List possible texts for your unit. If you are working with the same genre, how will you mix things up to maintain interest? If you are working with a theme or some other principle, be sure to include a variety of genres.
4. Find a literature textbook for your chosen grade level and analyze its contents. What do the editors seem to assume about students of that age? Are there works that might fit your unit?

Academic Guidelines for Selecting Multiethnic and Multicultural Literature

Sandra Stotsky

In the previous article, Ken Donelson began the process of curriculum building by asking us to consider what great works we would consider to be essential reading in secondary schools. The result of that exercise was a list which, though it has some unusual features, would be consid- *ered very traditional in some quarters. Now Sandra Stotsky examines the value of a multiethnic and multicultural curriculum. Confining herself to American literature, Stotsky begins with the basics—that is, with definitions and goals—and then proceeds to examine some of the more difficult as-*

pects of the canon debate: how various stereotypes get represented, often unconsciously, in the curriculum; whose traditions should be included; how regionalism becomes a factor; and how the selection of texts relates to censorship.

This essay appeared in English Journal, *Vol. 83, No. 2 (February 1994); copyright 1994 by the National Council of Teachers of English. It is reprinted with permission.*

English teachers face an extraordinary challenge in attempting to reshape school literature programs for twenty-first century America. Today's students need to become familiar with three broad groups of literary work: (1) the literature that contributes to our common civic culture (for example, *The Federalist Papers*, Benjamin Franklin's autobiography, Thoreau's and Emerson's essays, or Walt Whitman's poems), (2) the remarkable diversity of ethnic literature that is part of this country's national literature, and (3) literary texts from a broad range of cross-cultural literary traditions—from those that served as the foundation for our own national literature, to those of other countries and regions of the world from which our citizens have come, either in the past or today. Although the exact proportions and priorities for these three groups of works will vary from school to school, few teachers or parents would disagree that all our students deserve as broad a liberal education as possible.

Nevertheless, while exposure to all three broad groups of works would appear to be reasonable if not desirable, any educational program designated as multicultural seems to generate enormous controversy today. Further, there seems to be an inordinate amount of confusion about just what constitutes multiethnic and multicultural literature for American students. I have col-

lected many lists of suggested titles for multiethnic/multicultural literature programs as well as descriptions of suggested curriculum units and teaching practices from schools and teachers around the country (for example, Blair 1991; Gonzalez 1990; Ripley 1991; Robinson and Gingrich 1991; Savage and Savage 1991). These lists and descriptions reveal many inconsistent if not contradictory organizing principles at work. Perhaps a chief source of this confusion and inconsistency is the failure of scholars, curriculum developers, and other educators to offer a clear and consistent definition of the terms "multiethnic" and "multicultural" themselves; they appear to mean all things to all educators (Fullinwider 1991).

My purpose is to offer unambiguous definitions of these terms, to elaborate on what seem to be the two major principles in selecting multiethnic and multicultural literature for our public schools, and to spell out specific criteria for teachers and curriculum developers to consider in constructing or evaluating school literature programs. I conclude by suggesting how we might diminish some of the discord surrounding the use of multiethnic and multicultural literature in the curriculum.

MATTERS OF DEFINITION

"Ethnic" is probably the most accurate term to use for all the non-indigenous groups in this country, such as Japanese Americans, Italian Americans, Greek Americans, African Americans, Cuban Americans, German Americans, or Mexican Americans. In a major work on ethnicity, Werner Sollars (1986) refers to the "polyethnic character of America" and includes as ethnic both those groups whose members migrated or fled to this country and those groups whose members were brought here as slaves or servants. Unlike their ethnic relatives in their countries of origin, members of these groups are not part of organically distinct cultures in this country because most of their members speak and write English after the second generation (even though some remain bilingual) and participate in our political and popular culture, although at varying rates. The literature in English about members of these groups should, for the sake of accuracy, be referred to as American ethnic literature rather than multicultural literature. This literature should be seen as a prominent part of our national literature.

Those peoples who under some circumstances might be considered members of organically distinct cultures in this country are the descendants of the indigenous peoples of this country, including the various Indian tribes (who, according to Kruse, 1992, prefer the term Indian or their tribal name to the term "Native American") and the Eskimos, Aleuts, and other groups in the Pacific Islands, whose current members are situated (or can still situate themselves if they choose) within the original geographical boundaries and within some of the original social context that shaped their ancestors' lives. But because the literature about members of these groups is almost always written in English and because most members of most of these groups participate legally, occupationally, and socially within our national framework, this literature, too, is best seen as part of our national ethnic literature.

In order to differentiate the term "multicultural" from "multiethnic" and to realize its apparent meaning, "multicultural" should encompass works that arise in the context of other cultures or peoples geographically separate from the fifty states of the United States of America. Other terms that might be considered synonymous are "international" or "cross-cultural."

INCLUSIVENESS AND AVOIDANCE OF STEREOTYPE-FORMATION

There are two major purposes for including multiethnic and multicultural literature in our school literature programs: to develop our students' knowledge of and respect for the extraordinary religious, racial, and ethnic diversity of American citizens, and to enhance their familiarity with and appreciation of the literary traditions of other peoples in countries around the world. To accomplish these purposes, our literature programs need to reflect two major principles—inclusiveness and the avoidance of stereotype-formation.

With respect to ethnicity, inclusiveness refers to the curriculum's acknowledgment of the existence of all self-identified ethnic/racial/religious groups in this country through the assignment of literary works by or about members of these groups. When designers of self-described multicultural programs choose to extend the meaning of "culture" to social groups defined by gender, sexual orientation, or physical or mental disability, then inclusiveness refers to the curriculum's acknowledgment of the existence of these groups as well. As a matter of practice, curricular inclusiveness almost always refers to works by and about females today.

In contrast, stereotypes refer to the consistent characterization of people from any ethnic, racial, religious, or gender group in a way that is either unflattering, demeaning, or limited. An unflattering stereotype of members of specific ethnic or religious groups is created when works regularly show, for example, Italians as members of the Mafia, such as Don Corleone in *The Godfather*, or Jews as greedy or unscrupulous businessmen, such as Shylock in the *Merchant of Venice*, or Fagin in *Oliver Twist*. Characterizations now considered demeaning or insulting by some (though not all) people are, for example, those of black Americans as only passive slaves (before the Civil War), as in *Uncle Tom's Cabin*, or simply as passive victims of their society today, as in *Sounder* (see Trousdale, 1990); or those of young American males as chiefly loners, confused social misfits, or morally depraved, as in *The Catcher in the Rye, A Separate Peace, The Pigman, The Outsiders*, and *The Chocolate War* (see Nelms 1989). Stereotypes of members of particular groups in a restricted range of activities (although the activities are not negative in themselves) are created when works portray women, for example, primarily in nurturing roles, as in *Mary Poppins* and *Little Women*, or black Americans as only gifted athletes, as in *The Jackie Robinson Story*, or civil rights activists or ministers, as in *The Autobiography of Malcolm X*. Stereotypes are thus created either by consistent negative portraits of people in particular social groups, or by consistent portraits of people in particular social groups engaging in a restricted range of activities and achievements.

GUIDELINES FOR AMERICAN LITERATURE

There are at least nine ways in which American literature programs for our public schools can demonstrate inclusiveness and avoid the formation of what may be considered undesirable stereotypes of any group of human beings, regardless of race, gender, religion, or ethnicity.

1. Introduce students over the course of their school years to literature by and/or about members of all ethnic and other socially defined groups in this country. (See Gates 1991 for the best discussion of the difficulties in using "authenticity" of authorship as a criticism.)

2. Offer some literature each year about a few different ethnic groups; these should include such religious groups as the Amish (for example, the tales of Elsie Singmaster), the Shakers (for example, *A Day No Pigs Would Die*), or the Chasidim (for example, *The Chosen*).

3. Show how indigenous cultures differed with respect to how well they got along with their neighbors as well as how they were oriented to their environment. Some were usually peaceful (for example, the Hopi), while others were quite warlike (for example, the Cherokee and the Sioux). Some even had slaves (for example the Aleuts). Avoid romanticizing them (see Shore 1991 for a discussion of this issue) or engaging in overkill. Literary texts by and/or about members of indigenous groups in this country deserve a regular place in our curriculum, but not necessarily at every grade level and not to the exclusion of works about the various European ethnic groups, whose members constitute a far larger number of people in this country.

4. Cover a range of groups, some religious, some secular, some based on gender, such as Thomas Merton's *Seven Storey Mountain*, an autobiography about life in a Trappist monastery; Mary McCarthy's *Memoirs of a Catholic Girlhood*, an autobiographical novel of life in a Catholic girls' school; *Mr. Roberts*, a play about life on board a ship during wartime; and *Little Women*, a novel about a group of sisters growing up in the latter part of the nineteenth century. Older as well as newer works with different kinds of gender groups merit inclusion.

5. Include literary works about the immigrant experience in this country that, across works, feature characters responding in a variety of ways to their experiences. For example, the Italian female protagonist of *The Fortunate Pilgrim* and the Jewish female protagonist of *Bread Givers* are to a large extent liberated by their experiences in the America of the early decades of this century. Works like *Everything But Money* and *The Education of H*Y*M*A*N K*A*P*L*A*N* portray the ethnic immigrant experience with great humor. Younghill Kang, a Korean immigrant, expresses the classic tensions between positive and negative experiences in his autobiography, *East Meets West*. On the other hand, the Italian male protagonist of *Christ in Concrete* and the Jewish male protagonist of *Jews Without Money* are alienated by their experiences as immigrants.

6. Feature literary works with male characters (regardless of race or ethnicity) who demonstrate such positive qualities as adventurousness, risk-taking, compassion, principled thinking, love of family, love of country, and heroism, as well as such negative qualities as greed, brutality, cynicism, immoral behavior, and moral confusion (for example, *The Story of Johnny Appleseed, Growing Up, To Kill a Mockingbird,* and *Twenty One Balloons* as well as *Bartleby, the Scrivener* and *The Great Gatsby*). Similarly, feature female characters across works who demonstrate both negative qualities, such as greed, spite, amorality, and irresponsibility, and such positive qualities as principled thinking, ambition, love of family, love of country, and professional achievement, in addition to victimization by males (for example, *The Little Foxes* and *The Bad Seed* as well as *The Miracle Worker, Harriet Tubman: Conductor of the Underground Railroad,* and *The Awakening*). Neither gender has the corner on virtue or vice (see Vitz, 1991, for a discussion of these related issues as they have been played out in recent elementary school textbooks).

7. Include literary works that feature, across works, both negative and positive characters who are members of particular ethnic, religious, or racial groups, not just one kind of character. For example, *Maggie's American Dream*, a story about a strong-minded black mother in a two-parent family whose four children all became successful professionals despite racial discrimination, counterbalances *The Women of Brewster Place*, a bleak novel about mainly single mothers and their children in a housing project; while the biography of Colin Powell or Samuel B. Fuller (an extraordinarily successful entrepreneur) counterbalances the negative image of black males in *The Color Purple*. Or, as another example, the characterization of Shylock or of Fagin in British literature can be balanced by the characterization of Isaac of York in *Ivanhoe* or of Daniel Deronda in George Eliot's novel. Historical truthfulness is served by showing that all groups have people who can be admired or criticized, and that different authors in a country's mainstream literary tradition have held different points of view about members of particular religious or ethnic minority groups.

8. Include literary works in which "white" America is portrayed as containing decent, civic-minded people as well as prejudiced or mean-spirited people. An overdose of "white guilt" literature in the curriculum (like *Ceremony, Farewell to Manzanar,* and *The Bluest Eye*) may cause students to associate "multicultural" literature with white-guilt literature and to develop a negative reaction either to "white" America or to the authors and the groups featured in them, depending on the social group in which they may see themselves as a member. (See Stotsky 1991a for further discussion.) Many literary works by and about members of minority groups are realistic yet do not portray all white Americans as bigoted, for example, *Nisei Daughter*, by Monica Sone, or *Journey to Topaz*, by

Yoshiko Uchida (stories based on the authors' experiences in internment camps for Japanese-Americans in California during World War II), and *In the Year of the Boar and Jackie Robinson*, by Bette Bao Lord (a story about a young Chinese girl as an immigrant to Brooklyn in the 1940s).

9. Include literary works about members of ethnic or social groups that feature a range of themes, not just those focusing chiefly on contemporary social and political issues. For example, works like *My Antonia, All in the Family*, or *A Tree Grows in Brooklyn* show members of ethnic groups coping with the kind of problems or situations that may arise in the private lives of many human beings and that have little to do with their ethnicity.

CONSIDERATIONS FOR CROSS-CULTURAL (OR MULTICULTURAL) LITERATURE

Several other guidelines warrant consideration in the selection of cross-cultural works. Clearly, a well-conceived literature program needs to reflect a literary history of the English language. This means familiarizing all students with some of the choice works that were significant in the evolution of British literary culture through the nineteenth century. These are the works that inform the development of contemporary American language and literature.

In addition, educators will want to include works beyond those that are part of British literary culture from countries that have supplied large numbers of immigrants to this country over the past two-hundred years. Works from Irish literary culture as well as well-translated works from, for example, German, French, Polish, Yiddish, Czech, Italian, Hungarian, Scandinavian, Armenian, and Greek literary culture deserve a substantial place in

the curriculum at all grade levels because of the extremely large numbers of Americans who trace their ancestry to these peoples (and in some cases still come from the original country, such as contemporary Irish and Polish immigrants). According to the 1990 census, at least 75% of Americans trace their ancestry to Europe.

Works originating in Spanish-speaking countries, or in Japan, China, Korea, or other Asian countries, or in former colonies of the British, French, Spanish, or Portuguese empires in the West Indies, Africa, or South and Central America belong as will in the curriculum but to no greater extent than works originating in countries in Central, Southern, and Eastern Europe. Even if relatively new groups of immigrants are increasing at a faster rate than earlier immigrant groups, cross-cultural works from Central, Southern, and Eastern Europe have been as neglected in previous decades in our K-12 curriculum as cross-cultural works from the parts of the world from which newer groups of immigrants are coming. In some ways, works from Central and Eastern Europe (especially twentieth-century works) have been more neglected than works from other areas of the world (or about native Indian groups) because of the status of Central and Eastern European countries during the "Cold War" and because, today, they are frequently classified with, and overshadowed by, Western European countries in multicultural literature programs. There is no academic rationale for considering continents rather than individual foreign cultures as the basic unit of representation. And although some educators seem to believe otherwise, the notion that each continent reflects a unique race and a unique set of cultural features has no empirical support whatsoever.

Cultural sensitivity also suggests consideration of the range of themes to be found in the literature of other countries. Selected works about a non-Western country are likely to convey a distorted picture of its culture if they focus only on the country's contact with the West and exclude other themes in its literature. For example, works about India might include *Azadi*, by Chaman Nahal, which deals with the deadly conflicts among Hindus, Moslems, and Sikhs in the years after independence from Great Britain. Or, works about Korea might include Sook Nyul Choi's two well-reviewed autobiographical novels for young adolescents, *Year of Impossible Goodbyes*, which focuses on the author's experience as a Roman Catholic in North Korea after the separation of Korea into two countries, and *Echoes of the White Giraffe*, which deals with Japan's brutal treatment of the Koreans during World War II.

Similarly, selected works from a Western country are more informative about its culture if they deal with more than its social problems or its effect on a non-Western people, especially since a Western country's literature almost always deals with many other themes in addition to those. For example, *Kon-Tiki* (a true adventure story) and *A Doll's House* (a work with social significance) together can begin to give students a better picture of Norwegians than either one alone can. It is a disservice to the humanity of any people to romanticize them as victims or to reduce them simplistically to the role of oppressors.

DECIDING WHAT TO INCLUDE AND WHAT TO ELIMINATE

In order to integrate multiethnic and multicultural literature into a school curriculum, three questions need to be addressed at the local level. (1) Who should decide what ethnic groups and what cultures should be presented in a multiethnic and multicultural literature curriculum? (2) On what basis might currently studied works be removed from the curriculum in order to make room for newer or different works? (3) What local considerations should be kept in mind? The answers to these questions matter a great deal because they affect the breadth, quality, and integrity of our students' literary learning.

Clearly, it seems wise at the K–12 level for educators to solicit the advice of a committee representing a broad spectrum of parents and teachers and, possibly, representative of various civic and political organizations in order to decide on the ethnic and other social groups to be presented in the curriculum. Such a committee should reflect a range of ethnic groups and a range of opinions within these various groups, as no groups contain monolithic thinking. Decisions about the ethnic and cross-cultural composition of school literature programs are likely to be more widely accepted if they reflect a broad consensus of agreement among committee members. Selection of specific works should remain in the hands of the literature teacher. It does not seem professionally appropriate to give to any group the authority to approve or "veto" specific literary texts, whether or not they focus on the particular group.

In order to make room for classroom study of newer or different works, the following three guidelines can help determine what works presently in the curriculum could be eliminated.

1. Replace more contemporary works (those published since the 1970s) than older works, since there seem to be fewer pre-twentieth-century works than twentieth-century works in most literature curricula today, as suggested by recent research (Stotsky, 1991b). A reasonable balance between pre-twentieth-century and twentieth-century works is necessary for encouraging interdisciplinary curricula with history departments, for familiarizing students with our literary past, and for helping them understand the evolution of contemporary literature.

2. Replace recent works flagged by respected English educators as having clear didactic intent and little literary merit with works of more obvious literary merit (see, for example, the discussion by Smagorinsky, 1992, of "Chee's Daughter," a frequently anthologized short story by Platero and Miller).

3. Reduce the number of works about those groups that may happen to be overrepresented in the curriculum, as may be the case with Eastern European Jewish Americans, African Americans, or Native Indians, and replace them with works reflecting a broader range of groups.

Individual teacher interests, local community characteristics, or regional distinctiveness should, of course, continue to play a role in shaping a particular school's literature curriculum, just as they always have. For example, students in the state of Vermont have usually studied Vermont writers (writers who wrote about Vermont or lived in Vermont while they wrote), students in New England have traditionally studied the nineteenth-century literature written in New England, while students in the South have usually read more by writers identified with the South than students in other areas of the country. Similarly, if a community contains a large number of members of a particular ethnic group, as does, for example, the state of Alaska with respect to several Indian groups and the Inuit people, then it would seem reasonable for more works about or by members of those groups to appear in the curriculum. Educators simply need to take care that any local emphases do not command such a proportion of the curriculum that the students who are from these local or regional groups are thereby deprived of exposure to the range of religious and ethnic diversity in this country and to those works that form our common civic culture.

QUESTIONS OF CENSORSHIP

As some readers may have noticed, I have not suggested that teachers, parents, or others apply the criteria I have spelled out for achieving inclusiveness and avoiding stereotypes to works currently in the curriculum. These criteria were designed to guide the choice of only new works for the curriculum. I have limited their application deliberately because it is unlikely that most older works or even many recent works now in the curriculum would survive the use of these criteria. For example, *The Pigman, The Outsiders*, and *West Side Story* may evoke a negative stereotype of young males, while *The Color Purple* and *The Women of Brewster Place* may create very negative stereotypes of black males in particular. Similarly, for some, the language of *Huckleberry Finn* may be offensive, while the defense of a black man by a white lawyer in *To Kill a Mockingbird* may now be perceived as demeaning. These works are in many school curricula today, and to eliminate them on the grounds that they offend specific groups of people would clearly constitute censorship. (And when teachers, who are public employees, eliminate particular literary works from the curriculum on the grounds that they offend some people in some way, that clearly constitutes censorship.) In fact, works like *Huckleberry Finn* and *To Kill a Mockingbird* may be especially important to keep because they are among the very few works in the secondary curriculum showing white characters acting with moral principles in their relations with non-white characters. Balancing works that vary in their characterizations of different groups of people, as described earlier, is a far healthier way to counter what some might consider negative stereotyping or demeaning characterization than outright banishing of specific works from the curriculum—and arousing parental anger and the activities of civil libertarians once it is discovered. Indeed, a case can often be made for teaching a work that has some stereotyped characterizations.

However, it is important to keep in mind that the very act of selecting works automatically excludes as well as includes. Thus, any criteria for selecting works need to be applied judiciously and can, with care, be modified. English teachers and English departments who would prefer a smaller number of guidelines to consider when incorporating multiethnic literature into their literature programs might wish to consult those recently published by the American Library Association (Hayden 1992, vi). It recommends five broad criteria which are similar in spirit and content to my own: (1) "Look for a quality of reality that gives the reader a chance to experience something," (2) "Try to determine the author's commitment to portray cultural groups accurately," (3) "Avoid materials that sensationalize, enumerate unusual customs, or practice reversed stereotyping," (4) "Be sensitive to emphasis on cultural differences at the expense of similarities," and (5) "Whenever possible, use the same critical criteria appropriate for all types of literature—distinctive language and appropriate dialogue, style, relevance and potential interest, clearcut plots, and believable characterizations."

At present, anything labeled "multicultural" seems fraught with controversy. It may be possible to diminish much of the discord on multicultural

education if works by writers who live and write in English in any of the fifty states of the United States of America (or its territories), regardless of religion, gender, and ethnicity, are judged primarily on the basis of their merit as literature and integrated within the framework of our national literature without authorial ethnic, gender, or religious distinction. (This does not, of course, exclude discussion of an author's gender or ethnic background if it is relevant to his or her work.) If a school's American literature curriculum were so designed, local variation could still take care of local characteristics so that this feature would not be lost. But in addition to avoiding the marginalization of many authors, a label-free curriculum could also mean that every single ethnic group would not have to be represented at every grade level so long as students could be exposed over a period of years to a rough balance between works about Americans as members of ethnic groups and works about Americans as individual Americans.

Discord may also be reduced if a majority of the works our students read are works expressing the "American imagination," whatever their racial or ethnic background may be and whatever the racial or ethnic background of the writers. And if we want to develop our students' civic identity and, hence, the basic bond supporting their sense of social responsibility to each other despite racial, ethnic, and religious differences, we need to make sure that the American-centered literature curriculum it has taken us several centuries to achieve in this country does not disintegrate into a superficial cultural smorgasbord with no strong and meaningful core to develop our students' civic identity as Americans. (See Stotsky 1989, 1991b, 1991–2, and in press for further discussion.) The "American experience" is what all

Americans share, regardless of background, and literary interpretations of that experience, historical and contemporary, would seem to be the proper focus for our literature programs.

WORKS CITED

Blair, Linda. 1991. "Developing Student Voices with Multicultural Literature." *English Journal* 80.8 (Dec.): 24–28.

Fullinwider, Robert. 1991. "Multicultural Education." *The University of Chicago Legal Forum.* 75–99.

Gates, Henry Louis, Jr. 1991. "Authenticity, or the Lesson of Little Tree." *The New York Times Book Review* November 24, 1 ff.

Gonzalez, Roseann Duenas. 1990. "When Minority Becomes Majority: The Changing Face of English Classrooms." *English Journal* 79.1 (Jan.): 16–23.

Hayden, Carla D., ed. 1992. *Venture into Cultures: A Resource Book of Multicultural Materials and Programs.* Chicago: American Library Association.

Kruse, Ginny Moore. 1992. "No Single Season: Multicultural Literature for All Children." *Wilson Library Bulletin* 66.6 (Feb.): 30–34.

Nelms, Ben. 1989. "Holden's Reading." *English Journal* 78.4 (Apr.): 13.

Platero, Juanita, and Sijowin Miller. 1991. "Chee's Daughter." In *Literature & Language*, Grade 10. Evanston, IL: McDougal.

Ripley, Nonie. 1991. "Red and Yellow, Black and White and Brown: Minds across Five Cultures." Unpublished handout. NCTE Spring Conference. Indianapolis, Indiana, March 14–16.

Robinson, Connie and Gingrich, Randy. 1991. "Multicultural Literacy." Unpublished handout. NCTE Fall Conference. Seattle, Washington, November 20–24.

Savage, Marcia and Savage, Tom. 1991. "Exploring Ethnic Diversity through Children's Literature." Unpublished handout. NCTE Fall Conference. Seattle, Washington, November 20–24.

Shore, Debra. 1991. "Our Captors, Our Selves." *The University of Chicago Magazine* 83.5: 28–32.

Smagorinsky, Peter. 1992. "Towards a Civic Education in a Multicultural Society." *English Education* 24.4 (Dec.): 212–228.

Stotsky, Sandra. 1989. "Literature Programs and the Development of Civic Identity." *The Leaflet* 88.1 (Winter): 17–21.

Stotsky, Sandra with Barbara Hardy Beierl. 1991a. "Teaching Contemporary American Literature: A Professional Dilemma." *Connecting Civic Education and Language Education: The Contemporary Challenge.* New York: Teachers College P.

Stotsky, Sandra. 1991b. "Does a Literary Canon Exist in our Secondary Schools? Or How Many Students Need to Read the Same Body of Works Before It Can Be Called a Literary Canon?" Paper presented at the American Educational Research Association, Chicago, Illinois. ERIC 326 877.

Stotsky, Sandra. 1991-92. "Whose Literature? America's!" *Educational Leadership* 49.4 (Dec./Jan.): 53–56.

Stotsky, Sandra. In press. "Multicultural Literature and Civic Education: A Problematic Relationship with Possibilities." *Public Education in a Multicultural Society.* New York: Cambridge UP.

Trousdale, Ann. 1990. "A Submission Theology for Black Americans: Religion and Social Action in Prize-Winning Children's Books about the Black Experience in America." *Research in the Teaching of English* 24.2 (May): 117–141.

For Further Thought

1. Consider Stotsky's distinction between multiethnic and multicultural literature. What rationale does she offer for including each type? What kind of balance would you strike between the drive to represent various kinds of American authors and the need to foster global or cross-cultural understandings?

2. In her discussion of stereotyping, Stotsky offers some familiar and some surprising examples of the way literature can reinforce prejudicial views of certain groups. What do you think of her discussion of young American males or the reference to works like *Sounder* or *The Color Purple*? Think of two texts that might be taught together to achieve some balance in the way groups are characterized.

3. Another unusual feature of Stotsky's analysis is the attention she pays to local and regional factors. What might be the benefit of using literature that has a local flavor? Is there a tension between Stotsky's recommendation in this

regard and her Hirsch-like insistence on an American "core" to the curriculum (see her final paragraph). Do you find her overall argument to be convincing, or is she trying to cover all bases in an unrealistic manner?

4. Consider Stotsky's discussion of censorship. Do you accept her position that eliminating works that are currently enshrined in the curriculum would amount to censorship? Again, there seems to be a tension between this position and her recognition that "the very act of selecting works automatically excludes as well as includes." What do you think of the guidelines she offers in this regard?

5. Think of a school in your region, one that you know pretty well. In addition to the kinds of works that Donelson lists in his article, what kinds of literature would you consider to be especially important reading for students in that school? Assuming that you would add some texts to achieve diversity, how might you avoid having them stand out as the "minority" texts?

Application 3.2:
Dealing With Diversity

A Look at Textbooks

For the first edition of this book, I analyzed the contents of a 1989 American literature anthology and discovered the following: Of 224 separate titles in the table of contents, 59 (26%) were by women, 25 (11%) by African Americans, 13 (6%) by Native Americans, 4 (1.7%) by Hispanic or Hispanic-American writers, and 2 (less than 1%) by Asian Americans. These figures, though not impressive in the sense of fostering multiethnic awareness, were a distinct advance of an earlier (1963) edition of the same text.

For this edition, I looked at a sampling of five American lit texts, all published between 1994 and 1997. My research was informal, but the results are fairly consistent and they jibe with what I have encountered as I look through textbooks in nearby schools. On the American lit front, it seems that things have reached a plateau. The combined contents break down this way: 24% by women, 12% by African Americans, 3.8% by Native Americans, 3.7% by Hispanic or Hispanic-American writers, and 1.8% by Asian Americans. One very up-to-date text with a distinct multicultural/multiethnic stance in its background and critical reading sections offers the following: Of 207 separate selections, 26% are by women, 11% by African Americans, 4% by Native Americans, 5% by Hispanic or Hispanic-American writers, and 5 (2.5%) by Asian Americans. Clearly, there are advances on some fronts, but the overall picture is not so very different today from the way it was in 1989.

My point is not to cast blame but to register something about the complexity of the problem of finding a "representative" sampling of literature. As Sandra Stotsky points out (p. 98), there are many good reasons for seeking diversity in the English curriculum, but for those very reasons, the choices one makes can be quite complicated. Regional considerations and the ethnic background of one's students are of course important, but equally significant is the way individuals and groups are represented within a work. So it is not a question of simply "adding some minority authors" to the curriculum. That kind of thoughtless approach can cause more problems than it solves. Here, as with all educational decisions, it makes sense to begin with goals for learning and a consideration of the actual students with whom we are working. Then more political concerns, local, national, and global, can come into play.

Stotsky's point of view, though favorable to diversity, is thoughtful and relatively balanced. For that reason, it might be difficult to argue with her. Yet even if we agree that the goal of achieving diversity in the curriculum is good, it is not always easy to achieve. The canon is not endlessly expandable. Time, resources, and the teacher's knowledge constrain what can really be taught. No one knows this better than the textbook publisher, who must somehow manage to deal with many different views—not just political attitudes, but concerns about regional representation, urban versus rural material, varying ability levels, "inappropriate material," and so on. There are also problems of copyright, availability, and length. These are real problems for the textbook publisher, who wants to please everyone and offend no one.

But before we start to pity the poor textbook companies, let's recognize, too, that this is an enormously profitable business. The sale of a seven-through-twelve literature series to a single school district (to say nothing of the adoption of a series by a whole state) can be very profitable. No wonder, then, that companies like to play it safe, including works that offend the least number of people. In the past this led to a certain sameness and blandness in the material, but nowadays there is more pressure to include other voices. Hence the change in American literature texts described in the opening of this section, a trend that can be interpreted as a success story, a record of continued failure, or a sign of the disintegration of the culture. The fact that a trend can be interpreted in such conflicting ways suggests that the canon is still very much in flux, which is perhaps appropriate. But given the powerful shaping force that textbooks exert on the curriculum, the situation makes it doubly important that teachers make thoughtful choices, of textbooks themselves and of materials to teach from a particular book.

Some Things to Consider About Textbooks

1. Comment on the data about American literature textbooks. How do you view the trends? Does the inclusion of more diverse materials indicate progress, or is it a mistake? How far should textbooks go in this direction?

2. Choose a literature anthology used in a local school and analyze its contents with an eye to diversity. You can use the categories of writers that I used: women, African-American, Native American, Hispanic or Hispanic-American, Asian-American writers. A category like "international" or "multicultural" can be added, or (as I did) collapsed into the others. Using whatever categories seem appropriate to you, show a breakdown of the contents of the book. Then, considering the book as a whole, comment on the diversity of the readings.

3. What was your education like? Were you asked to read works that reflect the diversity of American literature, or of world literature? Using your own experience as a guide, consider the pros and cons of a broader versus a more concentrated approach to the canon.

4. Comment on the way gender works in the curriculum. What difference does it make if women writers are represented in the curriculum? What about works

with interesting female characters, although they might have been written by men (*Island of the Blue Dolphins*, for example, or many of Shakespeare's plays)? And how do you react to what Stotsky says about the way young men are frequently characterized in literature?

Creating a Unit: Using Textbook Materials

The individual teacher, of course, does not usually choose a textbook. Such choices are normally made in committee, frequently on a district-wide basis. So when you begin teaching, it is likely that the textbook will be a given, and unlike Mrs. Martinez (see chapter 2), who keeps hers on the shelves in the classroom, you will probably feel some pressure to use it. Certainly, without a well-stocked book room full of paperbacks (or a classroom library if you use the workshop approach), your textbook will play an important role in the choices you make.

Textbooks come in all shapes and sizes, but those that are published as a multigrade series have some common features. Normally these are six-volume sets (grades seven through twelve), although the inclusion of a seventh volume is becoming more common as school districts reconfigure into middle schools that include sixth grade. Most books include a mixture of genres, with a decided preference for shorter pieces, many of them excerpts from longer works. Hence the preference for the novella over the full-length novel. As previously noted, some of the older pieces that are not protected by copyright will have been bowdlerized—that is, edited to eliminate "offensive" material. And, as noted elsewhere, textbooks for grades seven through ten likely to be arranged by genre, with some thematic subgroups.

If you are unfamiliar with a secondary textbook series, you might need a little guidance with their structure and with the accompanying teaching materials, which can be quite elaborate. If you need to determine the grade level, look for the list of series volumes, which will appear somewhere before the title page. For some mysterious reason, textbook publishers seldom call a book, in title or subtitle, by its grade level. Instead you will see "Level 5" (usually eleventh grade) or something like "Gold Level" or "Laurel Level." When in doubt, identify the American literature volume; that will be the junior year and count down (or up) from there.

For the unit assignment at hand (see pp. 129–132), you have more than one book to choose from, so you'll need to skim the tables of contents and peruse selections that seem to fit your unit, looking for variety of all kinds—not just cultural diversity, but also different genres and points of view. No matter how your unit is organized, its success will depend, to some degree, on your ability to avoid a boring repetition of literary types and classroom activities. As you review the text, pay some attention to its format and any supplementary materials included in the text itself—historical and biographical background, literary theory, vocabulary, writing assignments, comprehension questions, and so forth. Although in the end you might choose not to use much of this material, it is foolish to disregard it; at the very least it can enrich your understanding of the contexts that surround texts, and something like a suggested writing assignment might stimulate your thinking in useful ways. The same advice applies to the teaching packets that come with many texts. You might not wish to use the prefab quizzes and tests provided by the publisher, but it doesn't hurt to look at them; sometimes valuable things are hidden within the folds of these large packets—supplementary readings, for example, or audiotapes, overhead transparencies, and sample activities. With textbooks, as with every kind of teacher material, your guiding philosophy should be, "Look at everything; adapt everything to your own ends."

Some Things to Consider When Reviewing a Textbook

1. Choose a textbook on the grade level you have chosen for your unit. If it is the book you reviewed in the previous application, then you already have an idea of its range and the diversity of cultures it represents. If it is different, then review it for diversity.

2. Check the date of the textbook, asking yourself in what ways it might reflect the dominant ideas of its time, especially in regard to the canon. If possible, compare and contrast its contents with another text on the same grade level but with a different copyright date. Ask yourself if the more recent text is necessarily an improvement.

3. What principles lie behind the organization of the text? Is it organized around genre? Theme? History? Cultural group? How does this arrangement suit your own decisions about the unit? Although the actual selections might be useful regardless of the organizational principle, the accompanying study questions or teaching materials might assume teaching goals different from your own.

4. If possible, find the teaching materials that accompany the text. If you have borrowed it from a teacher, that might not be difficult. If it is from a library, ask if the materials are available.

It's the THAT, Teacher

Ted Hipple

Ted Hipple is one of the foremost experts in the field of young adult literature. He has served as Executive Director of the Adolescent Literature Assembly of NCTE (ALAN) and has written widely on the subject. His main point here is about reading: Teachers should be more concerned THAT students read than worried about WHAT they read. Because young adult novels spark student interest, they are more likely to help us achieve that goal. It's a familiar line of reasoning, though it needs to be supported by Hipple's other argument about the intrinsic value of young adult literature.

This essay appeared in English Journal, *Vol. 86, No. 3 (March 1997); copyright 1997 by the National Council of Teachers of English. It is reprinted with permission.*

Curious, isn't it, how some expressions capture attention and linger awhile in our language, even as others, no doubt equally worthy, are forgotten within seconds of their utterance? Think on these: As Dorothy, a young Judy Garland reminded us and Toto that "We're not in Kansas anymore." Television's most inept spy, Maxwell Smart, was "Sorry about that." Yogi Berra entered Bartlett's with "It's deja vu all over again." More recently James Carville of the 1992 Clinton presidential campaign kept workers on task by constantly telling them "It's the economy, stupid."

I'd like to modify that last line to open this admittedly biased piece about the value of adolescent literature in secondary school (grades six through twelve) English classes by suggesting that "It's the THAT, teacher." Said a bit differently but with the same intent: "The THAT of teenagers' reading is vastly more important than the WHAT." Pure and simple: I want kids to be readers, a goal I think I share with most English teachers. I worry, however, about whether the common schoolhouse preoccupation with the classics—*belles lettres*—helps achieve this goal or, as I believe, runs counterproductive to it.

CLASSICS IN THE CURRICULUM

Readers of this journal need but a brief recounting of the pedagogical imperatives that sustain classic literature as a major part of the English curriculum. It has, after all, "stood the test of time." Classic literature also plays well in Peoria, with principals and school board members pleased that today's kids are getting the right stuff. It's relatively safe from the censors: even if Dimmesdale and the married-to-someone-else Hester do the nasty, how can one censor an author like Hawthorne? Classics are traditional, they've been around, with teachers able to use last year's (if not last decade's) teaching tools: lesson plans, tests, even bulletin boards. (My favorite bulletin board was one I saw a few years ago, entitled "A Choo-Choo Train in New England Literature Land." A train cut out of laminated cardboard wound its way over an outline map of the New England states,

with boxcars labeled Hawthorne, Emerson, Thoreau, Longfellow, and so on.)

And I agree fully that classic literature is good. I'd be elated if students adored *Hamlet*, shared my belief that Jane Austen has benefited humankind in significant ways, returned every so often to Twain or Dickens just for the sheer pleasure of doing so. But that seems not to be the case. We have too much evidence, from our own observation, from excellent scholarship like *Beyond the Classroom* by Laurence Steinberg (1996, New York: Simon and Schuster) and *Horace's Hope* by Theodore Sizer (1996, Boston: Houghton Mifflin), from anecdotal and incidental learnings, that today's secondary school students are not doing much reading. A bookstore manager recently told me that her store moves Cliffs Notes "by the bushel." Bestsellers include the usual suspects—any Shakespeare play that schools require, *The Scarlet Letter, Moby Dick*, and so forth. She went on to say that the buyers are secondary school students, some of whom, she pointed out with bemusement, bought the required book at the same time they bought the Cliffs Notes about that book. Ugh.

The question thus becomes an easy one to ask—and, as it happens, in my judgment at least, an easy one to answer. The query: how do we get kids to read, not simply their assignments but just to read for the sake of reading? The response: use young adult literature.

YA LITERATURE

Much of what I said about classic literature above applies to young adult literature. Viewed one way, it has stood the test of time. If you think of the life span of adolescence as about four or five years—eleven or twelve to about sixteen or seventeen—then a work like, say, *The Outsiders*, which has been widely read for almost 30 years has, in effect, been around for six or seven generations of readers, as long relatively as late nineteenth-century adult literature.

Adolescent literature can play well in Peoria, too. We do need to be patient, give it the same chances that the Bard has had, repeated exposure, continued support from teachers and librarians, but ultimately we will be rewarded with favorable community reactions.

I must acknowledge the potential censorship difficulties inherent in much adolescent fiction, but these, too, can be dealt with, I think, by a frank admission that adolescent literature typically focuses on adolescents' problems and in their language, a language that often features epithets stronger than "oh my goodness" or "shucks." All anyone, censors included, has to do is to listen to adolescents talk to each other to discover that the problems and language of the literature often mirror the problems and language of life.

Adolescent literature permits the same pedagogical tools classic literature affords: analyses of character, theme, language. Tests. Response-based classes. Small group discussions. All sorts of writing activities. Even bulletin boards. (I'll return in a minute to this topic.)

CLASSICS IN YA LITERATURE

And YA literature is good literature. There's even the beginnings of a canon of sorts. A couple of surveys I did a few years ago suggest such a "classics" (for want of a better word) list among adolescent novels. My first survey of some university-based professors of young adult literature, secondary school teachers, librarians, and publishers asked about the best adolescent novels of all time. These eight were the most commonly mentioned (the full survey can be found in *English Journal*, December 1989):

The Chocolate War by Robert Cormier
The Outsiders by S. E. Hinton
The Pigman by Paul Zindel
Home Before Dark by Sue Ellen Bridgers
A Day No Pigs Would Die by Robert Newton Peck
All Together Now by Sue Ellen Bridgers
The Moves Make the Man by Bruce Brooks
Jacob Have I Loved by Katherine Paterson

A second survey asked about the best novels of the 1980s and yielded these results (see *English Journal*, November 1992):

Hatchet by Gary Paulsen
Fallen Angels by Walter Dean Myers
Permanent Connections by Sue Ellen Bridgers
Jacob Have I Loved by Katherine Paterson
The Goats by Brock Cole
The Moves Make the Man by Bruce Brooks
Dicey's Song by Cynthia Voigt

Provided I make it, I plan a year-2000 survey about the best of the 1990s, and I'll bet you a milkshake that these novels get considerable support:

The Giver by Lois Lowry
Make Lemonade by Virginia Euwer Wolff
The Toll Bridge by Aidan Chambers
Tunes for Bears to Dance To by Robert Cormier
The Drowning of Stephan Jones by Bette Greene
Ironman by Chris Crutcher

Can any teacher doubt the quality of these books, their importance, their usefulness with young adults? I hope not.

STUDENTS READ YA LITERATURE

Thus, there are lots of good reasons to use adolescent literature in the schools, but I've saved the best to last: students will read it. Get a kid 30 pages into a Paterson or a Crutcher, a Bridgers or a Brooks, and she'll finish it. If you share my judgment that the THAT of teenaged reading is more important than the WHAT, then I think you will also agree that young adult literature belongs in the curriculum in a central, not a peripheral, place, as readings in common, not just as books on a list of supplementary materials.

TEACHING LITERATURE

But I must return to pedagogy, both as culprit and as savior. Part of the problem of students' dislike of classic literature may—I'm hedging here—lie in outmoded and uninspiring methods of teaching that literature, an overweening focus on literary history and biography, for example; hunts for obscure symbols; lit crit kinds of activities that tease out tensions and ironies but make the book an intellectual artifact and not a living, breathing, meaningful, powerful, and potentially life-changing force for its readers. One is reminded of the pregnant warning from writer Flannery O'Connor:

> If teachers are in the habit of approaching a story as if it were a research problem for which any answer is believable so long as it is not obvious, then I think students will never learn to enjoy fiction.

And enjoyment, I think, is what we're after, at least at the secondary school level, where our students are going to grow up to be pediatricians and politicians, carpenters and car mechanics, bookkeepers and beekeepers, but only very rarely English majors who need this early lit crit training. What we want is to excite them about reading while they are in school, help them share our love of it, so that they will remain readers when they are adults, readers at least of Michener if not of Melville. And they will be readers to their children, too, so that the cycle of enjoyment of print will continue.

READERS' RIGHTS

To that end teachers would find useful a marvelous little book by French author Daniel Pennac: *Better Than Life* (1994, Toronto: Coach House Press). In a series of short, pithy, and pointed chapters Pennac traces the reading habits of youth, from the pre-school delights of being read to, to the nervousness at school, where one MUST READ and, worse, MUST UNDERSTAND, and do both very quickly. And the longer the kid stays in school, for many youngsters, the worse it gets, with greater and greater pressures to read and understand. The joy of reading is gone. One of Pennac's chapters summarizes his concerns about the state of affairs in more than a few schools today:

> To each his loneliness. The boy with his contraband notes on his unread book. The parents faced with the shame of his failure. The English teacher with his spurned subject matter. Where does reading fit in? (79)

Pennac ends this important book with his Reader's Bill of Rights, some ten principles worth the attention of all teachers. Though not all will agree with every one of them, just thinking about these rights can change teaching habits and student attitudes and, I think, make reading the winner for both teacher and student. Here they are:

The right to not read.
The right to skip pages.
The right to not finish.
The right to reread.
The right to read anything.
The right to escapism.
The right to read anywhere.
The right to browse.
The right to read out loud.
The right to not defend your tastes.
(175–207)

Pause for a moment over these rights. How might the implementation of one or more of them change literature classrooms? And would the change be for the better? Would it result possibly in the goal I am seeking, a focus on the THAT of students' reading, a lessening of the emphasis on the WHAT? I believe Pennac is right, that we must return to the joys found in the printed page, to that magic pre-school threesome—Mom (or Granpa), the kid on her (or his) knee, and Dr. Seuss, all of them worrying about whether the cat in the hat will get the house cleaned before Mom comes home.

This, then, is my hope, as I concurrently thank you for reading all of this, that teachers of secondary school English take to heart my Carville paraphrase: it's the THAT, teacher. And if they do, I am confident that they will find in young adult literature a THAT well worth classroom time and attention.

For Further Thought

1. Consider Hipple's argument that our main concern should be getting students to read. What are the limits to that argument? How might it be answered by the proponents of cultural literacy?

2. Hipple cites twenty titles, nominations of the "canon" of young adult literature. Which of these have you read? What kinds of gaps are there in your knowledge of the field? How do you account for those gaps? What titles would you add to the list?

3. Think about the kinds of books that do not appear on the list. There is nothing here by Stephen King, V. C. Andrews, Mary Higgins Clark, or R. L. Stine. Yet these are very popular authors among adolescent readers. Why are these works not canonical? Is there a place in the curriculum for them? If you were conducting a reading workshop, how would you respond to students who chose the works of these or similar authors?

4. A follow-up to the previous question: Hipple cites Daniel Pennac's "Reader's Bill of Rights." With how many of these do you agree? How far would you go in offering students free choice of what they read for school credit?

Application 3.3:
Working With Young Adult Literature

It is important that beginning teachers should realize clearly that their interests in literature are not a teenager's interests. They need constantly to be reminded of their own reactions to books when they themselves were in the seventh or ninth or eleventh grades . . . of what things were significant for them at those particular times. (G. Robert Carlsen, "What Beginning English Teachers Need to Know about Adolescent Literature." English Education, Vol. 10 No. 4 [May 1979]: 200-201)

G. Robert Carlsen was one of the first scholars to take young adult literature seriously. In *Books and the Teenage Reader* (1967, 1980) and other works, he argued persuasively that literature of this sort serves the developmental needs of teenagers. Young adult novels suit early adolescents' concerns with "ego" and "status," middle teens' need to "test their own normality," and later adolescents' emerging concern with "the dilemmas of human life" ("What Beginning English Teachers Need to Know about Adolescent Literature," pp. 198–199). Generalizations, of course, have a limited value, and we can all think of exceptions—the twelve-year-old who loves *1984* and the seventeen-year-old who is still hooked on animal stories or adventures. Yet Carlsen's main idea has the ring of truth, as does his assertion that young adult literature typically develops around some kind of rite of passage: "A simplified explanation suggests that there are three stages of passage: (1) *separation from childhood*; (2) *testing and initiation*; and (3) *incorporation*" (p. 200). What is important in Carlsen's remarks is not so much the terms that he applies to young adult literature but his insistence on seeing these works as worthwhile in educational and social terms, that is, in terms of what they do to promote the well being of young readers.

As critics have frequently pointed out, young adult literature ranges from the excellent to the mediocre to the truly wretched. In this sense, it is like any other form of literature. Our concern here is with the best in the field, which is why lists are so useful. Ted Hipple (p. 111) has provided us with a starter list, and Ken Donelson's offers a longer list of 92 titles in "Honoring the Best YA Books of the Year: 1964–1995" (*English Journal*, March 1997, pp. 41–47). Among the more recent titles mentioned by Donelson, and not included by Hipple, are the following:

> Paula Fox, *The Moonlight Man* (1986)
> Bruce Clement, *The Treasure of Plunderell Manor* (1987)
> Ron Koertge, *The Arizona Kid* (1988)
> Brock Cole, *Celine* (1989)
> Avi, *The Confessions of Charlotte Doyle* (1990)
> Robert Cormier, *We All Fall Down* (1991)
> Berlie Doherty, *Dear Nobody* (1992)
> Peter Dickinson, *A Bone from a Dry Sea* (1993)
> Frances Temple, *The Ramsay Scallop* (1994)
> James Bennett, *The Squared Circle* (1995)

Just as Carlsen's ideas give a starting point for understanding the special nature of YA lit, the judgments of Donelson and Hipple can help us gain a foothold in a field that is rapidly growing too large to handle through unguided reading. Even with booklists to narrow the field, there is a lot to read, although fortunately the books themselves are enjoyable and often quite short. And in the end we are often faced with the prospect of choosing among books, all of them fine works in their own way, which seem to serve a similar educational end.

Thus, a seventh-grade teacher, putting together a unit on death and dying, might be faced with a choice of Robert Newton Peck's *A Day No Pigs Would Die*, Sharon Creech's *Walk Two Moons*, or Katherine Paterson's *Bridge to Terabithia*. Assuming all three texts were available, the choice poses some interesting problems, some having to do with age level, others with gender. So too, a ninth-grade teacher fashioning a unit on peer pressure might have to choose between Robert Cormier's *The Chocolate War* and an abridgement of Dickens's *Great Expectations*. Another tough choice, although some teachers might immediately opt for Dickens—and indeed, *Great Expectations* may well be the best choice. But the likelihood that most ninth graders will find Cormier easier to read and more immediately relevant than Dickens is not a negligible consideration. Or think of a tenth-grade teacher who wishes students to read about race relations in America. *To Kill a Mockingbird* is right there on the shelf, but there is also the classroom set of Mildred Taylor's *Roll of Thunder, Hear My Cry*, and the possibility of introducing Bruce Brooks's *The Moves Make the Man*. Again, these books are not "equivalent," but they are all worthy choices that move, more or less, in the same thematic direction.

Some Things to Consider About Young Adult Literature

1. React to Carlsen's comments on adolescent development and the value of young adult literature. Is there any reason why these needs cannot be served by older, more traditional texts? *The Call of the Wild* is an adventure story; *Jane Eyre* and *Huckleberry Finn* are about growing up and initiation; and *1984* is as chilling a picture of the future as *The Giver*. Comment on the special value of young adult novels.

2. Some of the pairings mentioned in item 1 suggest that the classics and newer YA texts often move in the same thematic direction. Consider the idea of teaching works like these together, especially if one mixes genres (poems about death and dying to go with *A Day No Pigs Would Die*, short stories about peer pressure to accompany *The Chocolate War*, or *A Raisin in the Sun* for a unit on race relations that includes *Roll of Thunder, Hear My Cry*). Suggest some pairings of your own, especially those that mix genres or match a contemporary YA novel with a classic.

3. Recall your own experience as a reader during junior and senior high school. Which were your favorite books? Were they assigned in school? How has your taste in reading changed over the years?

4. Find Donelson's article in the March 1997 issue of *English Journal*. Read it and react to the full list. How many of these books have you read or even heard of? Which would you choose to read first?

5. Choose three YA books from any list, books that you have not read. Look them up in Donelson and Nilsen's *Literature for Today's Young Adults*, one of the NCTE booklists mentioned at the end of this chapter, or another book on the subject. Then choose one and read it. Explain why you might suggest that students read it, or why not.

6. If you are working on a unit plan, find a work of young adult literature that suits your developing draft of the unit plan. Write a page or two in which you describe the work and explain how it might fit into your unit. Be sure to consider forms of literature other than the strictly literary forms that we have discussed so far. Are there magazine or newspaper articles that might complement your developing reading list? Pamphlets or advertisements? Other forms of nonfiction? Add to your list.

Protecting Holden Caulfield and His Friends From the Censors

Edward B. Jenkinson

*Of the many articles and books writ-
ten on the subject of censorship,
Jenkinson's essay, though it was written in 1985, remains one of the most
useful. He not only gives some background on debates like the famous
Kanawha County book battle but also
examines the variety of censorship
targets, the rationale behind the (still
common) charges of "secular humanism," and the way textbook adoptions
have been contested ground in many
states. Jenkinson ends with some
sound advice on how teachers might
deal with would-be censors.*

This essay appeared in English
Journal, *Vol. 74, No. 1 (January
1985); copyright 1985 by the National
Council of Teachers of English. It is reprinted with permission.*

When Holden Caulfield checked into
public school classrooms and libraries
across America in the early fifties, he
inadvertently brought trouble with
him. In cities and towns, in so-called
liberal communities as well as "conservative backwaters,"[1] individuals and
groups occasionally protested Holden's
presence in schools. In a few communities, teachers were fired for teaching
Salinger's novel. In others, teachers
were admonished never to bring that
"kind of trash" into their classrooms
again, and their future literary selections were carefully monitored. In the
majority of instances, however, those
teachers who "were brave enough" to
teach *The Catcher in the Rye* because
they thought it was a very fine novel did
so without protest, without negative
comment, without any interference.[2]

Such is the nature of schoolbook
protest in America. No one can predict
how any one community will respond
to any novel, textbook, short story,
poem, or play. No one can foretell what
will precipitate the next censorship incident or how explosive it will be. No
one can outguess the self-appointed
guardians of the young who have
formed hundreds of organizations that
want to rid the schools of all they deem
to be "anti-God, anti-moral, anti-family, anti-free enterprise, and anti-
American."[3]

When I began teaching in the early
fifties, I was neither concerned with,
nor heard much about, censorship.
The class sets of novels and plays I was
required to teach had been selected
several years before I began teaching,
and the only protests I ever heard came
from those students who thought *Silas
Marner* was boring. For outside reading, my students read, and discussed
in class, a variety of novels—including,
occasionally, *The Catcher*. On rare occasions my colleagues and I would hear
about a teacher who was in trouble for
teaching a "questionable" book, but the
incident always seemed to be far away.
We alternately laughed at, and were
embarrassed by, the state senator who
introduced legislation to rid Indiana of
that Communist menace, "Little Red
Riding Hood." But censorship was
something that happened somewhere
else. It was never a threat.

Like hundreds of teachers, I thought
that censorship—if I ever thought
about it at all—was concerned with
four-letter words, with explicit descriptions of sex, and with restrictions on
what could be printed in newspapers in
wartime. Censorship did occur in the
schools, but it certainly did not excite
many teachers because so few seemed

affected by it. The 1974 textbook war changed that.

KANAWHA COUNTY'S BOOK BATTLE

The "battle of the books" began when a first-term school board member and wife of a sclf-ordained minister launched a vigorous campaign against English textbooks submitted for adoption in Kanawha County, West Virginia.[4] To show their displeasure with the books, coal miners went on strike. Twenty-seven ministers denounced the books from their pulpits and in public meetings and rallies; ten ministers supported the school board members who voted for the books. Snipers fired at school buses, and, on one occasion, bullets struck a state police car that was escorting a bus filled with children. Gunmen wounded at least two persons and shot at others. Teachers repeatedly received threats on their lives. Textbook protesters firebombed an elementary school. Angry citizens dynamited at least three cars, vandalized school buses, and blasted windows in the board of education building with shotguns.[5] And the nation's most prominent schoolbook critics—Norma and Mel Gabler of Longview, Texas—flew to Charleston for "a whirlwind six-day speaking campaign"[6] against the 325 English language arts textbooks tentatively approved by the Kanawha County school board.

A free-lance writer who reported on the nine-month dispute called it

> in part a class war, a cultural war, a religious war. It is a struggle for power and authority that has sundered a peaceful community into rigid and fearful factions. And it is a complex and profoundly disturbing reflection of the deep fissures that crisscross American society.[7]

Since 1974, hundreds of less violent skirmishes over textbooks, trade-books, films, courses and teaching methods used in the schools have "sundered peaceful communities." Disputes over classroom and library materials have erupted in every state, in rural as well as metropolitan school districts, in inner-city as well as suburban neighborhoods. The battles have left long-lasting scars and, in many instances, wounds that will never heal.

About three years before the Kanawha County book war, I began studying attempts to censor schoolbooks because several teachers who were using the books in the Indiana University English Curriculum Study Series told me they were having difficulty teaching some novels explicated in that series. They reported some opposition to such classics as *The Scarlet Letter, The Red Badge of Courage, Huckleberry Finn, Heart of Darkness,* and *Siddhartha.* So I began reading about schoolbook protests, started collecting press clippings, and initiated conversations and correspondence with the handful of people in America who, at that time, knew a great deal about school censorship: NCTE members Ken Donelson and Lee Burress, Judith Krug of the American Library Association, and Dorothy Massie of NEA. What started out to be a brief study developed into a 10-year investigation that will probably continue for another decade at least.

THE SCHOOLBOOK PROTESTERS

Lee Burress encouraged me to study censorship incidents firsthand whenever possible and to talk with censors. During the last ten years, I have debated or have talked with most of the major schoolbook protesters in this country. I have also talked with many people in both big cities and small towns who were unhappy with certain books or courses. From those conversations and confrontations, I began drawing some conclusions about people who would remove books from libraries and classrooms.

Schoolbook protesters usually fall into one of three categories. The first consists of those parents who read—or hear about—something in their children's schoolbooks that trouble them. Parents have every right to be concerned about what their children read in school, and teachers make a serious mistake when they do not listen attentively to the concerns of parents. Hundreds of teachers throughout the nation have told me that if they have the opportunity to talk freely and calmly with such parents, the disputes are usually settled amicably in one or two meetings. In many instances, parents withdrew their objections to a book after they discovered why the teacher assigned it and how it was being treated in the classroom.

In the second category are persons who have not read the "objectionable" book, may not even know the exact title, but are convinced that the book is evil and must be removed from the school library or classroom. Unfortunately, in the censorship incidents I have studied, all too frequently such literary ignorance is rewarded with the removal of the book by a school official or school board member who also does not know the book.

A third category consists of persons who are motivated by one of the hundreds of local, state, and national organizations that protest textbooks. Such protesters frequently begin their attacks on the schools with just one book or one course—like values clarification, sex education, or global education. But the first target may not be the major one. If the protesters win the first battle, they will undoubtedly turn to the school board or to an administrator with more targets—most of which have been identified by Norma and Mel Gabler of Educational Re-

search Analysts or by some other organization.

Nearly a decade ago, Ken Donelson wrote the following description of the censor which, I think, aptly describes the schoolbook protesters in categories two and three above:

> The censor, however good and decent and sincere and religious and dedicated and patriotic, is usually supremely confident of his or her own rightness. The censor seems certain while the teacher can never be. The censor knows truth while the teacher is only trying to perceive it. The censor sometimes claims to have a direct pipeline to God and truth and right while the teacher can make no such sacrilegious assertion. The censor may claim that he knows what is good for every person while the teacher knows only that each of us must take a personal trip through this world searching for the good. The censor can afford the luxury of arrogance and omniscience while the teacher can not so pretend.[8]

Who attempts to have materials removed from classrooms and libraries? According to the results of surveys conducted by Lee Burress, parents file the majority of complaints. Then come administrators, teachers, clergymen, librarians, English department chairpersons, school board members, and students.[9] An emerging group consists of "concerned citizens" who may or may not have children in school but who belong to organizations that plan to "clean up" the schools.

FREQUENCY OF INCIDENTS AND TARGETS

During the early seventies, approximately one hundred censorship incidents were reported to the ALA's Office for Intellectual Freedom each year. By 1976, the number had risen to slightly less than two hundred and climbed to nearly three hundred in 1977.[10] Shortly after the 1980 Presidential election, Judy Krug of the ALA reported a five-fold increase in censorship incidents reported to her office. She later revised her estimate to a threefold increase, which would mean roughly nine hundred reported incidents a year.[11]

But reported incidents, I believe, are only a small part of the censorship attempts each year. Very early in my study of censorship, I read an article by a librarian in Wisconsin who estimated that for every incident reported in the newspapers or to a professional organization at least twenty-five go unreported. After talking with teachers, librarians, and administrators in meetings in 33 states, I believe that for every reported incident of censorship at least fifty go unreported.

What excites the schoolbook protesters? During the last ten years, I've examined thousands of pages of criticism of schoolbooks, and I have concluded that there are at least two hundred targets of censors who belong to organizations. Not all of the groups have the same targets. For example, Norma and Mel Gabler provide their reviewers with a three-page outline of "objectionable" content to oppose. I have included only a few of the Gablers' targets among the twenty-five that most directly affect teachers of English:

1. Novels, stories, poems, or plays that portray conflicts between children and their parents or between children and persons in authority. Also, literary works in which children question the decisions or wisdom of their elders.

2. Literary works that contain profanity or any "questionable" language.

3. Literary works that contain characters who do not speak standard English. Such characters, it is alleged, are designed by the authors to teach students "bad English."

4. Black literature and black dialect.

5. Literary works and textbooks that portray women in non-traditional roles (anything other than housewife and mother). On the other hand, some feminist groups object to illustrations in basal readers and other textbooks that show women in the so-called traditional roles.

6. Mythology—particularly if the myths include stories of creation.

7. Stories about any pagan cultures and lifestyles.

8. Stories about the supernatural, the occult, magic, witchcraft, Halloween, etc.

9. Ethnic studies. (One protesting organization calls ethnic studies "un-American.")

10. Violence.

11. Passages that describe sexual acts explicitly, or passages that refer to the sex act.

12. Invasions of privacy. Any questions, theme assignments, or homework that asks students to examine their personal backgrounds—family, education, religion, childhood experiences, etc.

13. An abundance of pictures, cartoons, drawings, and songs in basal readers or in any textbooks.

14. Literature written by homosexuals; literature written about homosexuals; any favorable treatment of homosexuals.

15. Books and stories that do not champion the work ethic.

16. Books and stories that do not promote patriotism.

17. Negative statements about parents, about persons in authority, about the United States, about American traditions.

18. Science fiction.

19. Works of "questionable writers," such as Langston Hughes, Dick Gregory, Richard Wright, Malcolm X, Eldridge Cleaver, Joan Baez, and Ogden Nash.

20. "Trash." Examples: *The Catcher in the Rye, Go Ask Alice, Flowers for Algernon, Black Boy, Native Son, Manchild in the Promised Land, The Learning Tree, Black Like Me, Daddy Was a Numbers Runner*, and *Soul on Ice*.

21. Any books or stories that do not portray the family unit as the basis of American life.

22. Assignments that lead the students to self-awareness and self-understanding.

23. Critical thinking skills.

24. Books and stories that are perceived to be unfavorable to blacks.

25. The use of masculine pronouns to refer to both male and female.

SECULAR HUMANISM

At least five of those targets can be placed under the umbrella of secular humanism—the so-called religion of the public schools. New Right critics of the public schools use the terms *secular humanism* and *humanism* interchangeably, and such critics are convinced that the schools are destroying America's youth by indoctrinating them with the religion of humanism, which has become the number one target of the schoolbook protesters.

The Rev. Tim LaHaye, a California minister and a founder of the Moral Majority, attacks the religion of secular humanism in his best-selling books, sermons, speeches, and television appearances. In *The Battle for the Mind*, he declared: "Most of the evils of the world today can be traced to humanism, which has taken over the government, the UN, education, TV, and most of the other influential things of life."[12] In *The Battle for the Public Schools*, the Rev. LaHaye charged that humanists have invaded public classrooms, brainwashing children with ideas about evolution, sex, death, socialism, internationalism, and situation ethics.

Humanists, according to the writer of the "battle" series, are "secular educators who no longer make learning their primary objective. Instead our public schools have become conduits to the minds of youth, training them to be anti-God, anti-moral, anti-family, anti-free enterprise, and anti-American."[13]

What is this "religion" that enrages the Moral Majority and that has led to numerous attacks on the nation's public schools, their libraries, their teachers, and their textbooks? Definitions abound. But one of the most common is distributed by Norma and Mel Gabler through their Educational Research Analysts, which they call the nation's largest textbook review clearinghouse.[14] Part of that definition follows:

Humanism is faith in man instead of faith in God. Humanism was officially ruled a religion by the U.S. Supreme Court. Humanism promotes: (1) situation ethics, (2) evolution, (3) sexual freedom, including public sex education courses, and (4) internationalism. Humanism centers on "self" because it recognizes no higher being to which man is responsible. Thus there is much emphasis in public education on each child having a "positive self-concept." The child must see a good picture of himself. This eliminates coming to Christ for forgiveness of sin. It eliminates the Christian attributes of meekness and humility. Where does self-esteem end and arrogance begin?[15]

That definition has been expanded several times to include more targets of the schoolbook protesters. For example, the Rev. LaHaye devotes 27 pages of his *The Battle for the Public Schools* to prove that secular humanism has all "the markings" of a religion.[16] In that chapter and others, he attacks these "hallmarks" of secular humanism: the look-say method of reading, values clarification, death education, global

education, evolution, sex education, total reading freedom, the "negation" of
Christianity in the schools, and socialism—among others.[17]

But regardless of how much is written about secular humanism and how
many definitions are circulated, few
censors can define the religion of secular humanism even though they believe
it is corrupting youth. One organizer of
parent protest groups defined the religion on a national television program
as "the philosophy of anything goes."[18]
Another school critic told a school
board that humanism is the "belief that
if something feels good, do it." Others
believe that the Supreme Court established secular humanism as the religion of the public schools when it "removed God" from classrooms in the
case of *Abington v. Schempp*. That belief is supported by Senator Jesse
Helms, who wrote:

> When the U.S. Supreme Court pro-
> hibited children from participating in
> voluntary prayers in public schools,
> the conclusion is inescapable that the
> Supreme Court not only violated the
> right of free exercise of religion of all
> Americans; it also established a na-
> tional religion in the United States—
> the religion of secular humanism.[19]

REFUTING THE SECULAR HUMANISM CHARGE

Does it follow, then, that if "voluntary"
prayer were restored to classrooms,
the religion of secular humanism
would be abolished from the schools—
if it could ever be conclusively proved
that it was there in the first place? The
New Right has brought the secular humanism charge to Federal courts twice,
and on both occasions the Federal
judges dismissed the cases without a
trial.

In the first case, *Grove v. Mead*,[20]
Michael Farris, the former president of

the Moral Majority in the State of
Washington, sued a school district for
refusing to remove Gordon Parks' *The
Learning Tree* from the curriculum.
Farris, who is also an attorney,
charged that when the school system
refused to remove the book that it violated students' First Amendment rights
by imposing upon them the religion of
secular humanism. The judge dismissed the suit on the grounds that the
plaintiffs had not presented sufficient
evidence to support their allegations.

In the second case, *Mozert et al. v.
Hawkins County Public Schools*,[21] Michael Farris, acting as legal counsel for
Beverly LaHaye's Concerned Women
for America, filed the brief for this case
in Church Hill, Tennessee. Parents of
children in elementary and junior high
schools in Church Hill alleged that the
First Amendment rights of their children were violated when they were
forced to study secular humanism as
presented in the Holt, Rinehart &
Winston basal readers. The Federal
judge dismissed the case without trial
on the grounds of insufficient evidence
to substantiate the charges. The case
will probably be appealed.

Essentially the same argument is repeated in the literature of New Right organizations opposed to humanism and
in the more than twenty books they use
to support the allegation that secular
humanism is the religion of the public
schools. John Dewey and thirty-three
other "liberal humanists" signed *Humanist Manifesto I* in 1933. B. F. Skinner signed *Humanist Manifesto II* in
1973. Since those two prominent educators, among others, signed the documents, it follows—so goes the argument—that all educators subscribe to
the tenets of the manifestos, which
members of the New Right call the bi-
bles of public school teachers. Since
there is an American Humanist Association (AHA) that publishes articles
about secular humanism and its goals,

it follows—again, so goes the argument—that America's public school teachers belong to the organization and read its journals. Finally, since the Supreme Court declared secular humanism to be a religion, the spreading of the doctrine of humanism in the public schools—the argument continues—is in direct violation of the First Amendment.

There are at least four flaws in the argument. First, probably no more than three percent of the public school teachers and administrators in this nation even know about—let alone have read—either *Humanist Manifesto*.[22] Second, hundreds of today's teachers know little—if anything—about John Dewey and his philosophy of education. Simply because a prominent educator called himself a secular humanist, it does not follow that all who enter the teaching profession are secular humanists.

Third, the Moral Majority and other New Right organizations attribute great influence over education to the AHA, the publisher of the manifestos. But AHA has fewer than four thousand members, and only a relative handful of the nation's two million teachers and administrators even know about AHA—let alone call themselves members. Fourth, the Supreme Court did not *declare* secular humanism to be a religion. In the frequently cited case of *Torcaso v. Watkins*, this footnote is included:

> Among religions in this country which do not teach what would generally be considered a belief in the existence of God are Buddhism, Taoism, Ethical Culture, Secular Humanism and others. . . .[23]

In a second case that is often cited,[24] there is a footnote referring to *Torcaso*. Two footnotes hardly constitute a Supreme Court *declaration*.

But the battle over secular humanism has only begun. Last summer [1984] Congress passed a math-science bill with an amendment on magnet schools assistance that was introduced by Senator Jeremiah Denton. Section 509 of that amendment reads:

> Grants under this title may not be used for consultants, for transportation, or for any activity which does not augment academic improvement, or for courses of instruction the substance of which is secular humanism.[25]

THE GABLERS AND THE TEXAS TEXTBOOK ADOPTIONS

Since 1961, Norma and Mel Gabler have dedicated themselves to "cleaning up" the nation's textbooks because they are convinced that textbooks exert tremendous influence on children. That belief is reflected in these two statements that seem to be the creed of the non-profit, tax-exempt organization they call Educational Research Analysts.

> UNTIL TEXTBOOKS ARE CHANGED, there is no possibility that crime, violence, VD, and abortion rates will do anything but continue to climb.

> TEXTBOOKS mold NATIONS because textbooks largely determine HOW a nation votes, WHAT It becomes and WHERE It goes![26]

Since the Gablers started reviewing textbooks and protesting what they consider to be objectionable content, their efforts have paid dividends. In one of the printed sheets they distributed to their followers in 1977, they noted that

> last year God gave parents a number of victories. In Texas alone, the State Textbook Committee did a good job of selecting the best of the available

books. Then, the State Commissioner of Education removed 10 books, including the dictionaries with vulgar language and unreasonable definitions.[27]

One year later the Gablers sent this report to their followers:

> We submitted 659 pages in our Bills of Particulars against twenty-eight textbooks, including Supplemental Readers, Literatures, and American Histories. All of the Readers and Literature books were either oriented toward violence, cruelty, death and despair, or they were trivial. The history texts were distorted and biased against traditional American values. God saw fit to direct the State Textbook Committee to remove eighteen of these objectionable textbooks in the first stage. *Many* others should have been eliminated.[28]

In that same report the Gablers noted that the Texas State Board of Education directed the removal of Shirley Jackson's "The Lottery" from three textbooks, and it eliminated "Mateo Falcone" and "A Summer Tragedy" from one text. The Gablers had objected to all three stories.

The Texas textbook adoption process affects the entire nation. Texas does not accept textbooks as they are published; rather, the Texas State Board of Education directs publishers to remove "objectional content" from textbooks before they can be distributed in Texas. Once such content is removed, it is not profitable for publishers to restore it in editions sold in other states.

Until 1983, the Texas board permitted only those persons objecting to textbooks to testify at public hearings. But last year, Barbara Parker, Director of the Freedom to Learn Project of People for the American Way, and Michael Hudson, director of PFAW's Texas office, lobbied for a review of the adoption process. The Texas board conducted a public hearing In May during which at least thirty speakers spoke for and against the process. (I had the privilege of speaking for NCTE against the system.) As a result of that hearing and many other meetings orchestrated by PFAW, the adoption process has been changed so that people who support certain textbooks may speak at the hearings. Other changes have also occurred. The elected state board will be abolished and an appointed board will take its place next January. And the Texas Attorney General has declared unconstitutional the adoption plank that calls for the origins of humankind to be balanced between evolution and creationism.

Since 1961, the Gablers have been granted an increasing amount of time each year for their testimony against textbooks submitted for adoption. In 1981, for example, they were allotted more than eight hours of the week-long hearings. But in 1983, after the process was changed, the Gablers were allotted only six minutes—just as everyone else.

Nevertheless, the Gabler influence on textbooks is still immeasurable. In a 1980 interview on the *Phil Donahue Show*, the Gablers said their reviews of textbooks were used in all fifty states and in twenty-five foreign countries. On that program, they admitted that they review textbooks line by line, searching for material that does not coincide with their religious and political points of view. Some of us who study censorship are also convinced that the Gablers also search for anything that does not coincide perfectly with their particular view of reality or with their perception of any subject matter.

As I read about and study schoolbook protest incidents, I frequently find that the local protesters have been guided by the Gablers' reviews and strategies. And in four censorship incidents in Indiana that I investigated, the Gablers' reviews, strategies, and attack on secular humanism were used in every one.

More than 95 percent of the schoolbook protests that I have studied were precipitated by persons who would be classified as being on the right. But protests come from the left, as well. Only three months ago, two school librarians in Indiana reported to me incidents that merit mentioning here. The first involved a directive from a school administrator ordering the librarian to search the shelves for any books unfavorable to blacks and to remove them. Her carefully drafted response to the directive pointed out that if she searched the shelves for books that might be construed to have statements offensive to any group that the library's shelves would be decimated, at least. She then pointed out that teachers can teach young people how to handle their books, and that such handling is the hallmark of an educated person.

In the second incident, a local group requested that the librarian remove all the "Little House" books since they contained sexist stereotypes. She refused to comply.

The principal of the Mark Twain Junior High School in Fairfax County, Virginia, removed *The Adventures of Huckleberry Finn* from the school because he charged that it was racist. He had done the same thing when he worked in a school in Illinois. But the school board in Virginia restored the Mark Twain classic to the school that bears his name.

Individuals and groups have protested such works as *To Kill a Mockingbird, Daddy Was a Numbers Runner, Mary Poppins, Back to School with Betsy*, and the Harlequin romances. They have also protested plays, such as *Show Boat* and *The Merchant of Venice*, which they charge are offensive to one group or another.

PROTECTING HOLDEN AND HIS FRIENDS

Parents have the right—even the duty—to be concerned with what their children learn in school. Parents—as well as all citizens—have the right to protest. But that does not mean that because one parent objects to a book or story that the school must remove that book or story. What it does mean is that all school systems must have established policies for selecting classrooms and library materials and must have procedures for handling complaints.

During the last eighteen months I have examined 222 sets of policies and procedures for school systems in Indiana. I believe that my findings are applicable for all states. I discovered that less than 15 percent of the school systems had both policies and procedures that protected intellectual freedom and, at the same time, guaranteed a fair hearing to all who might protest. In many instances, school systems had edited documents such as the Library Bill of Rights or NCTE's procedures for handling complaints so that they would not be controversial or strong. In a few cases, the school systems had simply removed any statement that might be considered controversial. As a result, what was left almost guaranteed success for the protester.

My ten-year study of schoolbook protest and my reading of the articles of Lee Burress, Ken Donelson, Dorothy Massie, Barbara Parker, and Diane Shugert have helped me draw some guidelines for teachers who want to protect Holden's friends—Harper Lee's Scout, Judy Blume's Margaret, Paul Zindel's Pigman, Carson McCullers's F. Jasmine Addams, Stephen Crane's Henry Fleming, Mark Twain's Huck and Tom, Shakespeare's Romeo and Juliet, and Swift's Gulliver—among hundreds of others. Here are ten steps that I think every teacher must take:

1. Make certain that every book selected for classroom study or for supplementary reading lists meets solid educational objectives. Make certain you know every book on your reading list so that you can talk about it intelligently if you're challenged. Also, make certain that you have previewed every film you show and that you have sound objectives for using the film.

2. Review the materials selection policies for your school system and play the devil's advocate as you do so. Challenge every statement as if you were trying to find some excuse for removing books from classrooms and libraries. Then work with your colleagues to strengthen the policies.

3. Review procedures for handling complaints against teaching materials. Make certain that the procedures do not give anyone the authority to remove a book without the full action and recommendation of a reconsideration committee. Also, make certain that the procedures call for that very important, informal first step in which the person lodging the complaint has the opportunity to talk with the person—librarian or teacher—responsible for the "objectionable" work.

4. Make certain that the school system has adequately informed citizens of its educational philosophy, of its curriculum, of its goals and objectives, of its policies and procedures, etc.

5. Make certain that anyone who has a complaint about a book or a teaching method is given a fair hearing. (One of the largest protesting groups in the nation was formed by a person who was "put down" by a teacher when the parent asked about a book.)

6. Insist on a public hearing when a citizen insists that a book be removed from a classroom or library.

7. Help to form a group of citizens who are supportive of the schools, of intellectual freedom, and of first-rate education. (Such informal groups have proved to be invaluable in censorship

incidents. Ministers who support intellectual freedom are invaluable assets to such a group.)

8. Become acquainted with the publications of protest groups. Learn their "buzz words" and be prepared to refute their charges.

9. Be prepared to help the administration refute unfounded charges about classroom activities and the school system's indoctrination of students in the religion of secular humanism.

10. Do the best job possible. That does not mean that you will never be the victim of schoolbook protest, but it may cut the percentage of possible trouble in half. It will also help you acquire friends among students and parents who will rally around you in the time of need.

NOTES

1. On at least five occasions, teachers on both the East and West coasts have indicated that I probably became interested in censorship because I live in that "conservative backwater" where censorship occurs daily. No community is immune. And some of the so-called liberal communities have experienced more censorship activity than the "conservative backwaters."

2. As I talk with teachers throughout the nation, I meet some in every community who have taught *The Catcher* and other controversial books for years without protest.

3. Tim LaHaye, *The Battle for the Public Schools* (Old Tappan, New Jersey: Fleming Revell, 1983), p. 13.

4. Part of my report on Kanawha County is based on an article by John Egerton and a Phi Delta Kappa Fastback by Franklin Parker, both of which bear the title, "The Battle of the Books." See notes 5 and 7.

5. Franklin Parker, *The Battle of the Books: Kanawha County* (Bloomington, Indiana: Phi Delta Kappa Educational Foundation, 1975).

6. James C. Hefley, *Textbooks on Trial* (Wheaton, Illinois: Victor Books, 1976), p. 166.

7. John Egerton, "The Battle of the Books." *The Progressive* (June 1975): 13.

8. Ken Donelson, "Censorship: Some Issues and Problems," *Theory into Practice* (June 1975): p. 193.

9. Lee Burress' nationwide surveys of censorship have been published periodically by NCTE. His surveys are also referred to in *The Student's Right to Know*, a 1982 NCTE publication by Lee Burress and Edward Jenkinson.

10. *Indianapolis Star*, December 31, 1978, p. 1; *Los Angeles Times*, June 3, 1978, p. 1.

11. Speech at University of Minnesota conference, January 26, 1983.

12. Tim LaHaye, *The Battle for the Mind* (Old Tappan, New Jersey: Fleming Revell, 1980), p. 9.

13. LaHaye, *The Battle for the Public Schools*, p. 13.

14. Printed sheet entitled "The Mel Gablers Educational Research Analysts," November 1977.

15. Mimeographed sheet included in a packet sent to a concerned parent by Educational Research Analysts.

16. LaHaye, *The Battle for the Public Schools*, pp. 71–97.

17. *Ibid.* pp. 36–42, 173–202, 227–238, 71–97, 203–226.

18. Janet Egan of Parents of Minnesota, Inc., on the MacNeil-Lehrer Report, February 20, 1980.

19. From the Introduction to Homer Duncan's *Secular Humanism: the Most Dangerous Religion in America* (Lubbock, Texas: Missionary Crusader, 1979), p. 4.

20. From a mimeographed transcript of the decision in *Grove v. Mead*, United States District Court, Eastern District of Washington.

21. From the brief filed by Michael Farris in the United States District Court, Eastern District of Tennessee.

22. This figure is based on informal summaries I have conducted in speeches to teachers and administrators in 33 states.

23. *Torcaso v. Watkins*, 367 U.S. 488 (1961).

24. *United States v. Seeger*, 380 U.S. 163 (1965).

25. *Congressional Record—Senate*, June 6, 1984, S6674.

26. Mimeographed sheet distributed by the Gablers and entitled "FOR YOUR CONSIDERATION. . . ."

27. Mimeographed sheet distributed by the Gablers and entitled "1978 Report," mailed in November of 1978, p. 2.

28. Mimeographed sheet distributed by the Gablers in 1979.

For Further Thought

1. Jenkinson holds strong views on censorship. Do you think they are justified or one-sided? For example, there are only two brief instances in which he entertains the possibility that people might object to books in the curriculum for legitimate reasons. Comment on the emphasis in the essay.

2. Does Jenkinson's advice to teachers seem realistic? Find out about the book review policies in your local school district. How are those policies like or unlike those recommended by Jenkinson?

3. Think of a book that shocked you. For me it was James Baldwin's *Giovanni's Room*, which I read when I was about fourteen (a long time ago). This was my first encounter with homo-eroticism in literature; I was surprised, shocked, and fascinated. Describe your reaction to a book that shocked you. Was it a beneficial or harmful experience? Assuming it was beneficial, would you assign this book in school? If it was harmful, how does this experience relate to your views on censorship?

4. If you had an experience with censorship, describe the situation. It need not have involved you directly. What makes you think of this as "censorship," as opposed to exercising good judgment? Whether you can recall such an experience or not, consider the idea of "hidden censorship"—the way a teacher's own values or fear of criticism can cut off certain possibilities for students.

5. Read more about censorship. You might begin with one of the following: *Censorship: A Threat to Reading, Learning, Thinking*, a collection of interesting essays on many aspects of the problem; *Opposing Censorship in the Public Schools: Religion, Morality, and Literature*, a book that offers arguments and strategies for defending particular texts; or *Caught off Guard:*

Teachers Rethinking Censorship and Controversy, a book that provides thoughtful discussion of censorship and other controversies in education.

Application 3.4:
Thinking About Censorship

In "Protecting Holden Caulfield and His Friends from the Censors," Edward Jenkinson makes a strong case for teacher control of the curriculum and the need to be prepared to fight those who would limit that control and students' right to read a range of literary materials. But by virtue of his main examples (the Kanawha County battle, the Gablers' textbook initiative, and other high-profile censorship fights), Jenkinson might lend the impression that the teacher's greatest concern is the action of an organized group that might lead to legal action. These are legitimate concerns, to be sure, but my own experience is that the actions of individual parents are equally important. The issues, I believe, are difficult and complex. As a point of entry into the discussion, let's consider the following situation, which is based on a real-life incident.

> *A well-respected teacher had been accustomed to assigning Judith Guest's* Ordinary People *in her senior English course. One day the father of a boy in the class showed up at school and asked to speak with her. The teacher was on good terms with him and the conversation was casual at first. Before she realized it, however, the teacher was involved in a conversation about the curriculum. The man asked, politely but firmly, that she stop teaching* Ordinary People, *on the grounds that it set a bad example for young people.*
>
> Ordinary People, *he suggested, was a bleak, secular book that might lead young readers to despair. In the novel, Conrad's family offers no positive set of values; indeed, Conrad gets help only from his girlfriend and the heroic psychiatrist. Sex and psychiatry, the parent insisted, are offered as the only sources of comfort and moral values. He did not want his son reading this book, nor did he think any students should be reading it. Surely, he went on, there were better books than this to be offering students.*
>
> *The teacher listened and said she would think about it. A few days later, however, the man returned and a second conversation ensued. Now the parent was emphasizing the sex in the novel (there is one sex scene), implying that the teacher would not want to be dragged into a public controversy. At this point the teacher asked that the conversation cease.*
>
> *After these two conversations, the teacher considered many factors. A fairly conservative, churchgoing person herself, she did not wish to spark a controversy, but neither did she want to be intimidated. She had often expressed a desire for more parental involvement in education, and here she was complaining if the involvement wasn't on her own terms. Moreover, as she listened to the man speak, she realized that this was a parent who had read the novel carefully and was making a legitimate point. Conrad does live in a world largely devoid of values, so the parent's point of view was neither ex-*

treme nor silly. On the other hand, the teacher knew, and had tried to convey to the parent, that this was a subject of discussion in class. She and the parent did not disagree that much about the book; however, they did seem to disagree about its function (how literature works on young minds) and about the educational purpose for making the assignment (how discussion can lead students to explore moral issues).

Furthermore, the teacher recognized that she had no particular investment in Ordinary People. *It was a good book, she thought, worth teaching, but she did not feel the need to defend it to the same degree that she might defend* Huckleberry Finn *or* The Catcher in the Rye *(both of which she taught in other courses). So she felt ambivalent. There were other books to teach. Did she really want to go to the barricades for a Judith Guest novel? Perhaps not, but neither did she like the tone of the second conversation. Could she allow herself to be bullied into changing the curriculum because one parent found a book offensive?*

She also thought about the administrative angles, considering some of the things Jenkinson mentions. She had written general objectives for the course, but they did not specifically mention Ordinary People. *She had considered the sex issue and found it to be unimportant but had not previously thought about the other objections raised by this parent. The district had a book selection policy and a procedure for referring challenges to a review committee. That seemed helpful, but the district's overall educational mission and its other policies were so general that any side of any controversy could invoke to support any position. The school administration had a history of supporting faculty, but the school board was very sensitive to parental complaints; the general tendency was to steer a middle course, seeking to protect teachers while placating parents. So if the situation escalated, it could go either way. Finally, the teacher judged that she was not personally vulnerable, having taught in this school for over twenty years and having developed a reputation for solid, responsible teaching. With these thoughts in mind, she went to see her principal.*

Like all real events, this situation is complex. So before reaching a conclusion and determining a course of action, we need to consider a number of factors. The first has to do with the rights of students. According to one line of reasoning, students should not be prevented from reading *Ordinary People* because of one man's objections. But perhaps they also have the right not to be forced to read a book, any book. A teacher might feel that a certain reading experience is good for them, but that is not the same as possessing a right. Rights usually depend on choices, so we might ask what choices students have in a case like this.

Then there is the issue of parental rights. What are this man's rights in this situation? It is generally accepted that he has some say over what his children read in school, but does that extend to the reading of other students? Practically speaking, would he be satisfied if his son were given the option of reading another novel? Should the teacher extend that option to other students in the class? How far should the teacher go in offering choices?

Finally, there are the professional rights and responsibilities of the teacher. Even the complaining parent recognized that the teacher is the prime authority in this situation. What are his rights? Surely the parent was out of line with the threat of adverse publicity, but otherwise he seems not to have directly violated the teacher's academic freedom. Is pressure a violation of rights or is it simply the way things get done in the world?

There is a lot to think about here: the rights of students, the rights of parents, and the rights of teachers. Moreover, there are responsibilities attached to every right. It is within this web of rights and responsibilities that the teacher must make a decision.

Some Things to Consider in the Ordinary People Situation

1. Review Jenkinson's article, especially his advice to teachers. How does this situation differ from some that Jenkinson described? How would you describe this teacher's situation: Is she in a good position to stand up to the parent or not?

2. What course of action would you take if you were in this situation? Describe what you would do and explain why. Be sure to weigh the different rights and responsibilities outlined earlier.

3. As a teacher, what will you do to stay in touch with parents? Some teachers send home minischedules and others use newsletters or conferences to let parents know what their children are reading. What are some of the advantages and risks of doing this?

4. Think about textbooks for a moment. Many literature anthologies contain "cut" versions of *Romeo and Juliet*, in which the nurse's more salty remarks are removed. (Interestingly, the recent "contemporary" version of the play has made many students aware of what they were missing.) And there is the case of "Leinengen Versus the Ants." This popular story appears in many anthologies, but certain passages, in which Indians are described as savages, have been removed. How legitimate are these practices? How would you handle texts like these?

5. Ted Hipple suggests that young adult literature might lend itself to more challenges from would-be censors (p. 111). Consider the following titles from Hipple's YA "canon": *The Chocolate War*, *The Giver*, and *Ironman*. Find out about these three books. What about each might cause a parent (or interested party) to object to the book? How might you answer those objections?

6. Review your list of texts that you are collecting for your unit and identify any that might be considered controversial for students at that grade level. Consult a teacher for advice. Then consider your reasons for assigning the text. Write a rationale for any text that concerns you.

Writing Assignment: Building a Unit

The articles in this chapter all deal with the teacher's choice of literary texts for students to read. But what does this mean in practical terms? How do teachers go about choosing texts and then shaping them into units of instruction?

When you are actually teaching, you will discover that your choices are limited by three factors: the age and ability of your students, the availability of books and other resources, and the expectations of your fellow teachers and the school district. The kids, the books, the curriculum. These factors are partly under your control; that is, you can seek to change the kids (teaching is all about change), you can order new books and develop new materials, and you can try to alter the curriculum. And yet these three factors will always remain, to a degree, beyond your immediate control. As we saw in chapter 2, they are some of the things upon which "it all depends."

In the assignment that follows, you are asked to think about texts and materials you might use in teaching a month-long literature unit. The constraints on your choice are built into the basic scenario described below. My goal has been to strike a balance between offering you totally free choice (which is unrealistic) and tying you up in a straitjacket (which means no choice at all).

A Scenario

It is the summer after college graduation, and you find yourself relocated and without work. Then you get a call from the principal of Washington (Junior or Senior) High, asking if you would like to substitute teach for the first month of the school year, while Mr. Boyer takes paternity leave. This is surprising: Months ago, you sent your credentials and a letter of application to Washington, and have heard nothing until now. But you jump at the chance to earn some money, gain some experience, and get your foot in the door at Washington.

You are offered a contract to teach three sections of literature and two of math. (It turns out that you were offered the position because, like Mr. Bayer, you are certified in both English and math.) When you visit with Mr. Boyer at the beginning of August, he tells you that the three lit classes are heterogeneous groups, with a wide range of ability levels and roughly the same number of boys as girls. There are about twenty-five students in each class. You will teach all three in Room 108, Mr. Boyer's room, at 8:30, 9:30, and 1:00. (See the following schedule.) Fortunately, you have no extracurriculars because Mr. Boyer's speech team does not begin meeting until November, after you are gone.

Mr. Boyer says that you can do "whatever you like," which seems like a mixed blessing to you. On the one hand, it feels good to be given some freedom and to be treated like a professional. You can organize the material however you like and integrate a lot of writing into the lit classes. On the other hand, it is frightening to have to create a curriculum all by yourself. Nor is there much to work with: When you look in the book room, you find only the literature textbooks and class sets of several novels. Moreover, you are not certain that Mr. Boyer is totally serious when he says that you can do whatever you like. As the conversation progresses it becomes clear that he expects you to use the textbook. He doesn't care where you begin and isn't fussy about how much you cover, but he does build his year-long curriculum around the selections in the book, and he reminds you a few times that, upon his return at the end of September, he will be "picking up where you leave off."

You therefore resolve to use some selections from the book but to supplement them with readings of your own and (perhaps) one of the novels. You also resolve to keep the kids writing. You're not sure what this means yet, but you believe strongly that reading and writ-

*ing should be integrated. With Mr. Boyer's blessing, you take home a
copy of the textbook and begin browsing. . . .*

Your Schedule at Washington

Period 1	8:30–9:20	Literature
Period 2	9:25–10:15	Literature
Period 3	10:20–11:10	Math
Period 4a	11:10–11:40	Lunch
Period 4b	11:40–12:30	Math
Period 5	12:35–1:25	Planning
Period 6	1:30–2:20	Literature
Period 7	2:25–3:15	Hall duty

Yes, I know that you probably won't be certified in math. And yes, I know that the whole scenario might seem like an unlikely "fit" to your circumstances. Indeed, your instructor might well wish to alter it or simply scrap the idea. But when you need to do some planning and you have not taught before, there is a certain advantage in working from a concrete situation. Even a fictional situation is a bit more "real" than the idea of teaching in a vacuum, and at the very least there are fewer choices to make. Like all assignments, then, the scenario offers a balance of freedom and constraint. You are limited to four weeks (a constraint); it is the beginning of the school year (not constrained by prior activities); you are a sub (constrained by Mr. Boyer's wishes); you have only one English prep (free to concentrate on that); you have to use the textbook (constraint); and so forth. The whole idea is to make you focus on one problem at a time, in this case the problem of finding four weeks worth of readings on a given grade level, as well as appropriate activities to accompany them.

Your job is to create a four-week course of study for students on a grade level of your choice, using a textbook and other materials. Unless your instructor indicates otherwise, you should not limit yourself to a single work or even a single genre. For example, a ninth-grade unit on Romeo and Juliet *might turn out to be very practical, but only under certain circumstances. A short-story unit for seventh grade is broader, but even so, it's usually better to get some practice with different genres. The actual product, the unit plan, should have the following sections:*

1. *An introduction in which you refer to the scenario (if it's being used); tell the story of your planning, explaining why you chose the works you did; describe the principles you worked from in creating the unit; and state what you hope students will learn*

2. *A list of materials—that is, everything you will give to students (texts and activity materials), with the source for anything you did not create yourself*

3. *A schedule of some kind, perhaps a four-week grid that indicates briefly what will happen on a given day*

4. *A set of miniplans—that is, brief descriptions of what will happen each day (perhaps two or three per page)*

5. *Sample assignments or activities: at least one writing assignment described in some detail and one fairly detailed description of a classroom activity*

6. *A conclusion, in which you evaluate the unit's strengths and weaknesses and comment on the process of creating it*

For Further Reading

Applebee, Arthur N. *Tradition and Reform in the Teaching of English: A History.* Urbana, IL: NCTE, 1974. A history of the discipline from the 1880s to the 1960s, with a focus on the teaching of literature.

Applebee, Arthur N. *Literature in the Secondary School: Studies of Curriculum and Instruction in the United States.* NCTE Research Report #25. Urbana, IL: NCTE, 1993. Not a book that you will necessarily need to read, but a good resource for facts and figures on the curriculum, especially what textbooks include and English teachers assign.

Bishop, Rudine Sims, and the Multicultural Booklist Committee, eds. *Kaleidoscope: A Multicultural Booklist for Grades K-8.* Urbana, IL: NCTE, 1994. A useful annotated bibliography that lists nonfiction by topic and genres by grade level.

Brinkley, Ellen Henson. *Caught off Guard: Teachers Rethinking Censorship and Controversy.* Boston: Allyn and Bacon, 1999. A broad-based and thoughtful discussion of censorship, focusing on the English classroom but including chapters on science, sexuality education, religion, and values.

Donelson, Kenneth L., and Aileen Pace Nilsen. *Literature for Today's Young Adults,* 4th edition. Glenview, IL: Scott, Foresman, 1993. The authoritative textbook on young adult literature, this book describes the history of the genre, discusses categories of young adult literature, and provides ideas for teaching.

Edwards, June. *Opposing Censorship in the Public Schools: Religion, Morality, and Literature.* Mahwah, NJ: Lawrence Erlbaum Associates, 1998. Offers arguments and strategies for defending particular texts using the morality and logic to counter the ideas of censors.

English Journal. Periodically, *English Journal* devotes part of an issue to a particular aspect of the teaching of English. Note the following: "New Voices: The Canon of the Future" (December 1997), "Multicultural Literature" (March 1995), "Censorship" (February 1997), and "Young Adult Literature" (March 1997).

Hirsch, E. D., Jr. *Cultural Literacy: What Every American Needs to Know.* Boston: Houghton Mifflin, 1987. This book has become famous for its list of cultural literacy terms, but there is more to it than that. Hirsch makes the best "conservative" case for a curriculum based on "the classics." Better than the book is the essay, "Cultural Literacy," published in *The American Scholar* (Spring 1983).

Kaywell, Joan F. *Adolescent Literature as a Complement to the Classics,* Volumes I and II. Norwood, MA: Christopher Gordon Publishers, 1993, 1995. A collection of essays, each of which focuses on a frequently taught work (e.g., *Great Expectations* or *The Odyssey*) and explores the uses of adolescent literature in the context of teaching the "classic" work.

Phelan, Pamela, et al., eds. *High Interest—Easy Reading: An Annotated Booklist for Middle School and Senior High School,* 7th edition. Urbana, IL: NCTE, 1996. An annotated list of easy-to-read books with high interest elements: "exciting story, suspenseful action, likable characters, and effective handling of topics, mirroring your everyday concerns." Twenty-three categories, by topic and genre.

Simmons, John S., ed. *Censorship: A Threat to Reading, Learning, Thinking*. Newark, DE: International Reading Association, 1994. A collection of very practical essays on the complexity of censorship.

Webb, C. Anne, and the Committee on the Junior High and Middle School Booklist, eds. *Your Reading: A Booklist for Junior High and Middle School*, 9th edition. Urbana, IL: NCTE, 1993. An annotated booklist for the junior high/middle school level, including fiction and nonfiction, arranged thematically and topically.

Wurth, Shirley, and the Committee on the Senior High Booklist, eds. *Books for You: A Booklist for Senior High Students*, 11th edition. Urbana, IL: NCTE, 1992. An annotated booklist for the senior high level; thirty-two categories, most of them topical.

4

Teaching Writing

Introduction

I have trouble remembering the way writing was taught when I was in school. Teachers gave assignments and we tried to satisfy them. At the due date, we handed in the papers; later, the teacher handed them back with the grammatical errors marked and a letter grade penciled in at the end. The better teachers wrote some comments below the grade. By the time we saw these papers, the class had moved on to something else, so few of us paid much attention to anything besides the grade. That had been recorded in the grade book: the assignment was over.

All that seemed very natural at the time, though now—looking back on it as a teacher of writing—I find it to be rather odd. Why did my teachers seem to look on writing assignments more as tests than as opportunities to learn something? Why was I left so much on my own, cudgeling my brain for things to write about? And why was I never (not until my dissertation!) asked to rewrite anything? Although I had good English teachers in high school, I have to conclude that teaching writing was not their greatest strength.

The Writing Process

Nowadays, when I look around at English teachers whom I admire, I see something quite different going on. They are teaching another way, looking on students as real writers, alert to students' purposes and needs. There are essential differences between this "process approach" and what my teachers did. For one, the teacher does not so much assign topics as construct occasions for writing. This may seem nebulous, more a question of attitude than method, but that is what we are talking about—a shift in attitude toward the writer. And this suggests another shift—away from judging and toward helping. Of course, the two roles are related; in seeking our help, students want to know what we think of their work. In most schools teachers do have to evaluate their students' work eventually. But, as Peter Elbow points out in his essay in this chapter, it makes a profound difference in teaching to think of yourself first as a helper and then as a judge.

There are some very definite and practical consequences to taking a process approach to writing. For example, deadlines need to be pushed back to allow time to live with an assignment for a while: time to think before drafting, time to have the students' work read by someone else, time to revise, time to edit. If you allow time for all this, you probably will not have students write a theme per week. Coverage, or getting a certain number of papers written, becomes less important than the learning that takes place in the process.

It is common, too, for teachers to talk about the stages in the writing process: prewriting, drafting, revising, editing, and publishing. Although this linear way of looking at the process is not without its problems, it does provide a useful way to talk about how we write. Moreover, most teachers work within a framework that calls for some deadlines and, perhaps, a regularization of the writing process. In any case, because we want to examine the process more carefully and analytically, it helps to think of it in stages.

Prewriting, or invention, is the time of discovery and exploration. Ideally, the writer considers several topics before deciding on one, taking time with each to think and write about it. Perhaps the best form of prewriting is writing itself, either the sort of "free writing" popularized by Elbow or just tentatively starting on a piece to see where it might go. Writers can also do more formal invention exercises—organized procedures that raise the relevant questions about a topic. These range from simple lists such as those used by journalists (5 $Ws + H$), to visual maps like clustering, to more elaborate networks of questions (heuristics). But whatever approach is taken, be it formal or informal, our goal is to help writers overcome what Donald Murray, in "Write before Writing" (pp. 139–145), calls our natural resistance to writing.

While writers are *drafting*, the teacher's role is that of coach. This is the time for one-on-one help. I visit many classes in which students are at work while the teacher roams about, ready to help, on the lookout for a raised hand (or raised heads or raised eyebrows). This is the way writing is taught. Or sometimes the teacher is hard at work writing something. That's fine too, though he or she needs to allow for interruptions. As Nancie Atwell pointed out in "Making Time" (chapter 2, pp. 55–66), the crucial thing is to value the act of writing—not just as homework, but as the "main event," worthy of class time.

Revising means, literally, "seeing again," which suggests that when a person rewrites he or she is returning to the invention stage, thinking things through once more. This is difficult for writers and it also takes time—time to test out a draft on readers, time to think, time to put the piece aside for a while, time to create the next draft. Above all, teachers need to convince students of two things: Thorough revision is worth the risk, and they can indeed help each other with revision. Nancy Sommers discusses the former in "Responding to Student Writing" (pp. 148–156). Because writing is essentially a form of thinking, Sommers argues, drafting and revising are really extensions of the thinking and exploring that began in prewriting. What we write on student papers, then, takes on a crucial importance, for in our comments we tell students not just what we think of their ideas and style but what we believe about writing itself. According to Sommers, our comments should take the writer's intention into account and should be geared to help the writer think more thoroughly about his or her subject. Moreover, we need to help students do this for each other, that is, teach them how to comment productively on each other's work.

Editing is the cleaning-up stage, what writers do if their work is to be published. This is where grammar, usage, spelling, and punctuation, all the things we mean when we use the term *mechanics*, figure in the teaching of writing. They are important, but they come relatively late in the process. From the students' point of view, of course, the purpose for editing is primarily the grade—a problem that Peter Elbow explores in "Ranking, Evaluating, and Liking" (pp. 160–175). Elbow's discussion of evaluating is complex and challenging, but it is worth considering the various ways in which we make judgments about student writing and the techniques we can use to clarify our purposes to students. As Elbow says, "Much of what we do in the classroom is determined by the assessment structures we work under" (p. 160).

The writing process reaches fruition in *publishing*, by which I mean anything that can be done to extend the writing beyond the teacher and, if possible, beyond the classroom. Posting work on the bulletin board is a time-honored way of publishing, but students can also publish their work in a class magazine or newsletter. Or they can write for another audience: students in another class or grade level, students in another school, the local newspaper, organizations that sponsor contests, businesses, civic groups, and political bodies—anyone who might be interested in what they have to say. It is not always easy to arrange this kind of publishing and it sometimes feels artificial, but efforts in this direction, even if it only means reading some work aloud in class, are important in showing that writing can go somewhere besides the teacher's desk.

Freedom and Constraint

The writing process can be put on a time line, but as I suggested earlier, this linear approach is not without problems. To begin with, who benefits? Is this approach helpful to students, or is it merely convenient for the teacher? For it *is* convenient. If we think of prewriting activities as taking place first and in roughly the same way, and if we think of drafting as something that occupies a certain period of time, then we can schedule the process with fixed activities and due dates, and this in turn facilitates whole-group instruction. On the other hand, the writing process can be thought of in a more individualized way, with students working in different ways and at different rates. In this case, the linear approach might look more like a straitjacket for writers than a helpful agenda. Thus, in Nancie Atwell's workshop approach (chapter 2, pp. 55–66), the same principles that characterized reading workshop (time, ownership, and response) are applied to writing workshop.

This entire question of scheduling is important, although it does not lend itself to easy solutions. There are two things to consider: Students do write in different ways, but they are writing in school, in the company of others. So the analogy of school writing to "natural" or individualized writing is imperfect. For example, if students are to work on one another's drafts, they need to have something ready on a particular day. Seen this way, as part of a social situation, the writing process is obviously complex—neither totally individual nor totally automated to suit the need of the larger group. This is one of the issues that underlies Barbara Carney's description of her own writing classroom, in "Process Writing and the Secondary School Reality: A Compromise" (pp. 177–187). Carney's decision to treat the writing process in a fairly linear manner is quite different from Nancie Atwell's writing workshop, but both reveal teachers negotiating the delicate balance between the individual writer's needs and the dynamics of the group.

One can also see a creative tension between freedom and constraint in Joseph Tsujimoto's "Teaching Poetry Writing to Adolescents: Models and Teaching Designs" (pp. 191–204). Tsujimoto, a middle school teacher in Honolulu, is a master at getting young people to write good poetry, and he is unabashed in adopting the assignment approach. In one sense, his assumption of the leadership role is constraining, even demanding, but in another sense, his approach is liberating for students. The kinds of constraints vary from assignment to assignment, allowing for freedom of choice in each case. More importantly, Tsujimoto introduces his students to major traditions in poetry and helps students establish their own poetic traditions. In so doing, he embraces the very paradox or tension that characterizes so much of the writing process: "In the end, freedom of choice really means freedom to select one's limitations. That is, in the act of choosing for oneself, one simultaneously imposes limitations upon oneself. Though, at first, the teacher imposes the larger limitation . . . , the student later imposes the specific ones" (p. 192).

Why Write?

But first, we need to consider an even more basic question: Why write? Both students and teachers accept the value of writing, but they tend to differ in their views of what writing ability can do for a person. Students generally think of extrinsic values (the way skills help you in the "real" or working world), whereas teachers tend to adopt an intrinsic set of values (what writing, in and of itself, can accomplish for a person). These two value schemes appear to be in tension with each other.

The students' view, of course, is valid: There is a sense in which writing ability helps a person "get ahead" in the world. But ironically, appeals to such extrinsic rewards seldom motivate students. Those rewards will arrive so far in the adult future that they have little effect on student behavior. We can tell students about the material rewards of literacy and quote columns of figures about how much writing is done by the successful engineer or doctor, but unless we manage to capitalize on the intrinsic rewards of writing, we are not likely to make much headway with students.

In the end, those intrinsic rewards come down to one concept: Writing is a way of learning. This way of thinking about writing is perhaps most evident to students when they are asked to do expository assignments that involve research, but even then they tend, in their minds, to split off the research (where the "real learning" takes place) from the writing (which is seen as a technology for recording facts on the page). Our goal, I think, should be to show students that all aspects of writing involve selecting and shaping ideas through the creative use of language—that is, thinking and learning. If this takes place even in library research, it is certainly true of the way ideas take shape through successive drafts. And what is true of expository writing is even more true of other forms: Self-expressive writing is a way of learning about oneself, persuasive writing is a way of learning by testing one's ideas against another's, and aesthetic writing is a way of exploring ideas and emotions through the interaction of form and content.

In using these four terms (expository, self-expressive, persuasive, and aesthetic), I have tried to cover the basic forms of discourse with terminology that is familiar to most teachers. Others employ slightly different terms: expressive, transactional, and poetic or expressive, referential, persuasive, and aesthetic. We need not quibble over terms, but it is important to understand that different forms of writing, for all their common elements, have their own functions and aims. At the very least, we will not want to create a writing curriculum that limits students unduly—with constant literary analysis papers (exposition), for example, or personal narratives (self-expression). But whatever forms we require of students, it is even more essential that we keep our eye on the main goal: to help them use writing to become better learners. Writing may (or may not) bring them a career advancement or an extra car in the garage, but it can certainly be a lifelong means of learning.

Write Before Writing

Donald Murray

Donald Murray is a pioneer of the writing process movement. A practicing writer himself, he has consistently argued that school writing is not essentially different from writing outside of school. Thus, when Murray describes the writing process he tends to talk in very practical terms about what writers need to advance the process. The goal is to bring a piece of work to fruition, but that process begins, as he argues here, with the writing we do in our heads before pen meets paper.

This essay appeared in College Composition and Communication, *Vol. 29 (December 1978); copyright 1978 by the National Council of Teachers of English. It is reprinted with permission.*

We command our students to write and grow frustrated when our "bad" students hesitate, stare out the window, dawdle over blank paper, give up and say, "I can't write," while the "good" students smugly pass their papers in before the end of the period.

When publishing writers visit such classrooms, however, they are astonished at students who can write on command, ejaculating correct little essays without thought, for writers have to write before writing.

The writers were the students who dawdled, stared out windows, and, more often than we like to admit, didn't do well in English—or in school.

One reason may be that few teachers have ever allowed adequate time for prewriting, that essential stage in the writing process which precedes a completed first draft. And even the curricula plans and textbooks which attempt to deal with prewriting usually pass over it rather quickly, referring only to the techniques of outlining, note-taking, or journal-making, not revealing the complicated process writers work through to get to the first draft.

Writing teachers, however, should give careful attention to what happens between the moment the writer receives an idea or an assignment and the moment the first completed draft is begun. We need to understand, as well as we can, the complicated and intertwining processes of perception and conception through language.

In actual practice, of course, these stages overlap and interact with one another, but to understand what goes on we must separate them and look at them artificially, the way we break down any skill to study it.

First of all, we must get out of the stands where we observe the process of writing from a distance—and after the fact—and get on the field where we can understand the pressures under which the writer operates. On the field, we will discover there is one principal negative force which keeps the writer from writing and four positive forces which help the writer move forward to a completed draft.

RESISTANCE TO WRITING

The negative force is *resistance* to writing, one of the great natural forces of nature. It may be called The Law of Delay: that writing which can be delayed, will be. Teachers and writers too often consider resistance to writing evil, when, in fact, it is necessary.

When I get an idea for a poem or an article or a talk or a short story, I feel myself consciously drawn away from it. I seek procrastination and delay. There must be time for the seed of the idea to be nurtured in the mind. Far better writers than I have felt the same way. Over his writing desk Franz Kafka had one word, "Wait." William Wordsworth talked of the writer's "wise passiveness." Naturalist Annie Dillard recently said, "I'm waiting. I usually get my ideas in November, and I start writing in January. I'm waiting." Denise Levertov says, "If . . . somewhere in the vicinity there is a poem then, no, I don't do anything about it, I wait."

Even the most productive writers are expert dawdlers, doers of unnecessary errands, seekers of interruptions—trials to their wives or husbands, friends, associates, and themselves. They sharpen well-pointed pencils and go out to buy more blank paper, rearrange offices, wander through libraries and bookstores, chop wood, walk, drive, make unnecessary calls, nap, daydream, and try not "consciously" to think about what they are going to write so they can think subconsciously about it.

Writers fear this delay, for they can name colleagues who have made a career of delay, whose great unwritten books will never be written, but, somehow, those writers who write must have the faith to sustain themselves through the necessity of delay.

FORCES FOR WRITING

In addition to that faith, writers feel four pressures that move them forward towards the first draft.

The first is *increasing information* about the subject. Once a writer decides on a subject or accepts an assignment, information about the subject seems to attach itself to the writer. The writer's perception apparatus finds significance in what the writer observes or overhears or reads or thinks or remembers. The writer becomes a magnet for specific details, insights, anecdotes, statistics, connecting thoughts, references. The subject itself seems to take hold of the writer's experience, turning everything that happens to the writer into material. And this inventory of information creates pressure that moves the writer forward towards the first draft.

Usually the writer feels an *increasing concern* for the subject. The more a writer knows about the subject, the more the writer begins to feel about the subject. The writer cares that the subject be ordered and shared. The concern, which at first is a vague interest in the writer's mind, often becomes an obsession until it is communicated. Winston Churchill said, "Writing a book was an adventure. To begin with, it was a toy, and amusement; then it became a mistress, and then a master. And then a tyrant."

The writer becomes aware of a *waiting audience*, potential readers who want or need to know what the writer has to say. Writing is an act of arrogance and communication. The writer rarely writes just for himself or herself, but for others who may be informed, entertained, or persuaded by what the writer has to say.

And perhaps most important of all, is the *approaching deadline*, which moves closer day by day at a terrifying and accelerating rate. Few writers publish without deadlines, which are imposed by others or by themselves. The deadline is real, absolute, stern, and commanding.

REHEARSAL FOR WRITING

What the writer does under the pressure not to write and the four countervailing pressures to write is best described by the word *rehearsal*, which I first heard used by Dr. Donald Graves of the University of New Hampshire to describe what he saw young children doing as they began to write. He watched them draw what they would write and heard them, as we all have, speaking aloud what they might say on the page before they wrote. If you walk through editorial offices or a newspaper city room you will see lips moving and hear expert professionals muttering and whispering to themselves as they write. Rehearsal is a normal part of the writing process, but it took a trained observer, such as Dr. Graves, to identify its significance.

Rehearsal covers much more than the muttering of struggling writers. As Dr. Graves points out, productive writers are "in a state of rehearsal all the time." Rehearsal usually begins with an unwritten dialogue within the writer's mind. "All of a sudden I discover what I have been thinking about a play," says Edward Albee. "This is usually between six months and a year before I actually sit down and begin typing it out." The writer thinks about characters or arguments, about plot or structure, about words and lines. The writer usually hears something which is similar to what Wallace Stevens must have heard as he walked through his insurance office working out poems in his head.

What the writer hears in his or her head usually evolves into note-taking. This may be simple brainstorming, the jotting down of random bits of information which may connect themselves into a pattern later on, or it may be journal-writing, a written dialogue between the writer and the subject. It may even become research recorded in a formal structure of note-taking.

Sometimes the writer not only talks to himself or herself, but to others—collaborators, editors, teachers, friends—working out the piece of writ-ing in oral language with someone else who can enter into the process of discovery with the writer.

For most writers, the informal notes turn into lists, outlines, titles, leads, ordered fragments, all sketches of what later may be written, devices to catch a possible order that exists in the chaos of the subject.

In the final stage of rehearsal, the writer produces test drafts, written or unwritten. Sometimes they are called discovery drafts or trial runs or false starts that the writer doesn't think will be false. All writing is experimental, and the writer must come to the point where drafts are attempted in the writer's head and on paper.

Some writers seem to work more in their head, and others more on paper. Susan Sowars, a researcher at the University of New Hampshire, examining the writing processes of a group of graduate students found

> a division . . . between those who make most discoveries during prewriting and those who make most discoveries during the writing and revision. The discoveries include the whole range from insights into personal issues to task-related organizational and content insight. The earlier the stage at which insights occur, the greater the drudgery associated with the writing-rewriting tasks. It may be that we resemble the young reflective and reactive writers. The less developmentally mature reactive writers enjoy writing more than reflective writers. They may use writing as a rehearsal for thinking just as young, reactive writers draw to rehearse writing. The younger and older reflective writers do not need to rehearse by drawing to write or by writing to think clearly or to discover new relationships and significant content.

This concept deserves more investigation. We need to know about both the reflective and reactive prewriting mode. We need to see if there are developmental changes in students, if they move from one mode to another as they mature, and we need to see if one mode is more important in certain writing tasks than others. We must, in every way possible, explore the significant writing stage of rehearsal which has rarely been described in the literature on the writing process.

THE SIGNALS WHICH SAY "WRITE"

During the rehearsal process, the experienced writer sees signals which tell the writer how to control the subject and produce a working first draft. The writer, Rebecca Rule, points out that in some cases when the subject is found, the way to deal with it is inherent in the subject. The subject itself is the signal. Most writers have experienced this quick passing through of the prewriting process. The line is given and the poem is clear; a character gets up and walks the writer through the story; the newspaperman attends a press conference, hears a quote, sees the lead and the entire structure of the article instantly. But many times the process is far less clear. The writer is assigned a subject or chooses one and then is lost.

E. B. White testifies, "I never knew in the morning how the day was going to develop. I was like a hunter, hoping to catch sight of a rabbit." Denise Levertov says, "You can smell the poem before you see it." Most writers know these feelings, but students who have never seen a rabbit dart across their writing desks or smelled a poem need to know the signals which tell them that a piece of writing is near.

What does the writer recognize which gives a sense of closure, a way of handling a diffuse and overwhelming subject? There seem to be eight principal signals to which writers respond.

One signal is *genre*. Most writers view the world as a fiction writer, a re-porter, a poet, or an historian. The writer sees experience as a plot or a lyric poem or a news story or a chronicle. The writer uses such literary traditions to see and understand life.

"Ideas come to a writer because he has trained his mind to seek them out," says Brian Garfield. "Thus when he observes or reads or is exposed to a character or event, his mind sees the story possibilities in it and he begins to compose a dramatic structure in his mind. This process is incessant. Now and then it leads to something that will become a novel. But it's mainly an attitude: a way of looking at things; a habit of examining everything one perceives as potential material for a story."

Genre is a powerful but dangerous lens. It both clarifies and limits. The writer and the student must be careful not to see life merely in the stereotype form with which he or she is most familiar but to look at life with all of the possibilities of the genre in mind and to attempt to look at life through different genres.

Another signal the writer looks for is a *point of view*. This can be an opinion towards the subject or a position from which the writer—and the reader—studies the subject.

A tenement fire could inspire the writer to speak out against tenements, dangerous space-heating systems, a fire-department budget cut. The fire might also be seen from the point of view of the people who were the victims or who escaped or who came home to find their home gone. It may be told from the point of view of a fireman, an arsonist, an insurance investigator, a fire-safety engineer, a real-estate planner, a housing inspector, a landlord, a spectator, as well as the victim. The list could go on.

Still another way the writer sees the subject is through *voice*. As the writer rehearses, in the writer's head and on paper, the writer listens to the sound of the language as a clue to the meaning in the subject and the writer's attitude toward that meaning. Voice is often the force which drives a piece of writing forward, which illuminates the subject for the writer and the reader.

A writer may, for example, start to write a test draft with detached unconcern and find that the language appearing on the page reveals anger or passionate concern. The writer who starts to write a solemn report of a meeting may hear a smile and then a laugh in his own words and go on to produce a humorous column.

News is an important signal for many writers who ask what the reader needs to know or would like to know. Those prolific authors of nature books, Lorus and Margery Milne, organize their books and each chapter in the books around what is new in the field. Between assignment and draft they are constantly looking for the latest news they can pass along to their readers. When they find what is new, then they know how to organize their writing.

Writers constantly wait for the *line* which is given. For most writers, there is an enormous difference between a thesis or an idea or a concept and an actual line, for the line itself has resonance. A single line can imply a voice, a tone, a pace, a whole way of treating a subject. Joseph Heller tells about the signal which produced his novel *Something Happened*:

> I begin with a first sentence that is independent of any conscious preparation. Most often nothing comes out of it: a sentence will come to mind that doesn't lead to a second sentence. Sometimes it will lead to thirty sentences which then come to a dead end. I was alone on the deck. As I sat there worrying and wondering what to do, one of those first lines suddenly came to mind: "In the office in which I work, there are four people of whom I am afraid. Each of these four people

is afraid of five people." Immediately, the lines presented a whole explosion of possibilities and choices—characters (working in a corporation), a tone, a mood of anxiety, or of insecurity. In that first hour (before someone came along and asked me to go to the beach) I knew the beginning, the ending, most of the middle, the whole scene of that particular "something" that was going to happen; I knew about the braindamaged child, and especially, of course, about Bob Slocum, my protagonist, and what frightened him, that he wanted to be liked, that his immediate hope was to be allowed to make a three-minute speech at the company convention. Many of the actual lines throughout the book came to me—the entire "something happened" scene with those solar plexus lines (beginning with the doctor's statement and ending with "Don't tell my wife" and the rest of them) all coming to me in that first hour on that Fire Island deck. Eventually I found a different opening chapter with a different first line ("I get the willies when I see closed doors") but I kept the original, which had spurred everything, to start off the second section.

Newspapermen are able to write quickly and effectively under pressure because they become skillful at identifying a lead, that first line—or two or three—which will inform and entice the reader and which, of course, also gives the writer control over the subject. As an editorial writer, I found that finding the title first gave me control over the subject. Each title became, in effect, a pre-draft, so that in listing potential titles I would come to one which would be a signal as to how the whole editorial could be written.

Poets and fiction writers often receive their signals in terms of an *image*. Sometimes this image is static; other times it is a moving picture in the writer's mind. When Gabriel Garcia Marquez was asked what the starting point of his novels was, he answered, "A completely visual image ... the starting point of *Leaf Storm* is an old man taking his grandson to a funeral, in *No One Writes to the Colonel*, it's an old man waiting, and in *One Hundred Years*, an old man taking his grandson to the fair to find out what ice is." William Faulkner was quoted as saying, "It begins with a character, usually, and once he stands up on his feet and begins to move, all I do is trot along behind him with a paper and pencil trying to keep up long enough to put down what he says and does." It's a comment which seems facetious—if you're not a fiction writer. Joyce Carol Oates adds, "I visualize the characters completely; I have heard their dialogue. I know how they speak, what they want, who they are, nearly everything about them."

Although image has been testified to mostly by imaginative writers, where it is obviously most appropriate, I think research would show that nonfiction writers often see an image as the signal. The person, for example, writing a memo about a manufacturing procedure may see the assembly line in his or her mind. The politician arguing for a pension law may see a person robbed of a pension, and by seeing that person know how to organize a speech or the draft of a new law.

Many writers know they are ready to write when they see a *pattern* in a subject. This pattern is usually quite different from what we think of as an outline, which is linear and goes from beginning to end. Usually the writer sees something which might be called a gestalt, which is, in the words of the dictionary, "a unified physical, psychological, or symbolic configuration having properties that cannot be derived from its parts." The writer usually in a moment sees the entire piece of writing as a shape, a form, something that is more than all of its parts, something that is entire and is represented in his

or her mind, and probably on paper, by a shape.

Marge Piercy says, "I think that the beginning of fiction, of the story, has to do with the perception of pattern in event." Leonard Gardner, in talking of his fine novel *Fat City*, said, "I had a definite design in mind. I had a sense of circle ... of closing the circle at the end." John Updike says, "I really begin with some kind of solid, coherent image, some notion of the shape of the book and even of its texture. The *Poorhouse Fair* was meant to have a sort of wide shape. *Rabbit, Run* was kind of zigzag. *The Centaur* was sort of a sandwich."

We have interviews with imaginative writers about the writing process, but rarely interviews with science writers, business writers, political writers, journalists, ghost writers, legal writers, medical writers—examples of effective writers who use language to inform and persuade. I am convinced that such research would reveal that they also see patterns or gestalts which carry them from idea to draft.

"It's not the answer that enlightens but the question," says Ionesco. This insight into what the writer is looking for is one of the most significant considerations in trying to understand the freewriting process. A most significant book based on more than ten years of study of art students, *The Creative Vision, A Longitudinal Study of Problem-Finding in Art*, by Jacob W. Getzels and Mihaly Csikszentmihalyi, has documented how the most creative students are those who come up with the *problem* to be solved rather than a quick answer. The signal to the creative person may well be the problem, which will be solved through the writing.

We need to take all the concepts of invention from classical rhetoric and combine them with what we know from modern psychology, from studies of creativity, from writers' testimony about the prewriting process. Most of all, we need to observe successful students and writers during the prewriting process, and to debrief them to find out what they do when they move effectively from assignment or idea to completed first draft. Most of all, we need to move from failure-centered research to research which defines what happens when the writing goes well, just what is the process followed by effective student and professional writers. We know far too little about the writing process.

IMPLICATIONS FOR TEACHING WRITING

Our speculations make it clear that there are significant implications for the teaching of writing in a close examination of what happens between receiving an assignment or finding a subject and beginning a completed first draft. We may need, for example, to reconsider our attitude towards those who delay writing. We may, in fact, need to force many of our glib, hair-trigger stu-

dent writers to slow down, to daydream, to waste time, but not to avoid a reasonable deadline.

We certainly should allow time within the curriculum for prewriting, and we should work with our students to help them understand the process of rehearsal, to allow them the experience of rehearsing what they will write in their minds, on the paper, and with collaborators.

We should also make our students familiar with the signals they may see during the rehearsal process which will tell them that they are ready to write, that they have a way of dealing with their subject.

The prewriting process is largely invisible; it takes place within the writer's head or on scraps of paper that are rarely published. But we must understand that such a process takes place, that it is significant, and that it can be made clear to our students. Students who are not writing, or not writing well, may have a second chance if they are able to experience the writers' counsel to write before writing.

For Further Thought

1. Comment on your own practice as a writer. Do Murray's descriptions of writers' practice hit home? Describe in detail what you do at the prewriting stage. What kinds of classroom techniques would be most helpful to students who take your approach to prewriting?

2. Think about the related ideas of resistance and delay. Some might say that Murray is simply rationalizing—trying to make a problem seem like a good thing. Or is there a more creative aspect to the tension between the urge to delay and the need to write? In any case, how could a teacher use the "Law of Delay" constructively in the classroom?

3. The idea of rehearsal seems central to any idea of prewriting. Look at what Murray says about rehearsal and then consider the following standard prewriting activities as forms of rehearsing for writing: conversation with another writer, listing ideas, clustering, outlining, freewriting. How are these like or unlike what Murray means by rehearsal?

4. Murray's idea of waiting for "signals" seems to apply to students who have an idea but are not yet ready to put pen to paper. But how do we help a student find that beginning, germinal idea upon which the awaited signal would be based? Which of the ideas mentioned in question 3 would be helpful in this respect? What else might you do to help students at this very early stage?

5. Freewriting has been mentioned several times, and later in this chapter Peter Elbow alludes to the practice. Freewriting can be defined as informal writing that is neither collected nor evaluated by the teacher and that is intended to help students use language to generate ideas. Thus, in a sense, freewriting seems to proceed in a manner quite different from Murray's idea of waiting for signals to write: It involves putting pen to paper at the earliest stages of writing. What do you think?

Application 4.1:
Finding and Exploring a Topic

> *Resistance to writing [is] one of the great natural forces of nature. It may be called the Law of Delay: that writing which can be delayed, will be. Teachers and writers too often consider resistance to writing evil, when, in fact, it is necessary. (Donald Murray, "Write before Writing")*

Does anyone doubt that Murray is correct? Is there anyone, even the person who enjoys writing, who is not familiar with the Law of Delay? As Murray suggests, we can fret forever about resistance and delay, but in the end it is best to recognize them as inevitable features of the writing process.

Sometimes the delay comes at the very beginning of the process ("I don't have anything to write about") and sometimes it comes a bit later ("I know what I want to say, but I can't seem to get started"), but it is almost always something students experience. It is here, at the invention stage, that teachers can help students, not so much by forcing them to make progress—although sometimes a firm reminder or an enforced deadline is exactly what is needed—but by helping them make this delay time productive.

Hence the value of the prewriting activities described in composition textbooks. These range from free writing (writing about a topic as a process of discovery, without attention to correctness) to lists of questions (the journalist's 5 Ws + H or more formal lists with particular goals) to mapping techniques like clustering (see Figure 4.1). These are all ways of using the delay time, of exploring a topic before what Murray calls "the signals which say 'write.' "

But there is a problem with these teaching techniques—or, rather, another of those tensions that we have noticed in the teaching of English. We can begin to see it by looking at the examples of clustering in Figure 4.1. One is an idealized version created by a teacher: The circles are even, the categories are logical, and the whole thing is fairly complete, with no loose ends. The other is what an eighth grader actually wrote: The page is messy, the categories are inexact, and the resulting diagram is only marginally comprehensible to anyone but the writer. This student benefited from clustering (he told me that and I believe him), but what he did looks different from what a teacher might have envisioned. Moreover, there were probably students in that same classroom who did not benefit from the activity, perhaps because they had not arrived at a topic. Maybe they had already heard a signal to write, or maybe the kind of classifying encouraged by clustering did not fit their topics or styles of learning.

There is a moral here. When we make an assignment, we are often working from a generalization about what most students will need to do to get

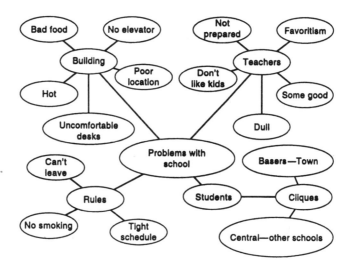

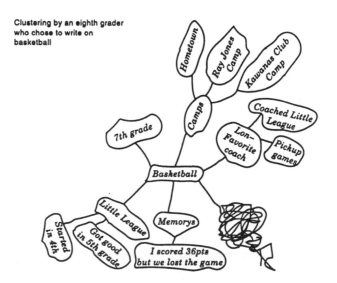

FIGURE 4.1. Examples of Clustering

the job done. This is inevitable. But just as inevitable is variation from that norm, the different ways students will work out the process in their real lives. And this disparity between the teacher's agenda and the students' individual needs applies everywhere: in the kinds of topics students choose, in the ways they explore those topics, in whether they find a particular prewriting activity useful or a waste of time, in the time needed to meet deadlines—in everything.

So there is a difference between the process suggested by the classroom situation and the real process of writing. There is no ideal solution to the problem: It is, in one way or another, part of every writing situation. But we can be sensitive to the way it causes problems for students, and the best way to ensure that sensitivity is to write along with students. True, considering the busy lives of teachers, it is unreasonable to expect that we will write every assignment we give students, and yet there is something equally unreasonable in asking students to write something that we, as teachers, have never even tried to write ourselves. That is why it is so useful for teachers to know the process from the inside. How else can we really know what it is like to do the assignment? How else can we appreciate students' resistance to the act of writing? How else can we be helpful coaches, true teachers of writing?

Some Things to Consider About Prewriting

1. Consider the possibility of having students do some topic exploration activities together: answering a list of questions, for example, or clustering. What do you think of these formal approaches to prewriting? How did you respond to them when you were in school? If you don't take this route, what will you do to ensure that students have indeed thought about their subject?

2. Look again at the eighth-grade student's clustering (p. 147). The theory behind this form of invention is that it asks the writer to use "the right side of the brain"—in this case, visual ways of learning. What do you think of that theory? Why should it help? Can you think of other techniques that help writers explore ideas in nonverbal or extraverbal ways?

3. Choose a kind of writing and create an assignment suitable for a given grade level, for example, personal narrative for ninth grade, or a persuasive essay for twelfth. What would you say to a student who said, "I don't know what to do. What should I write about?" What kinds of activities would be helpful to that student?

4. If your instructor has asked you to write "The Assignment Assignment" at the end of this chapter (pp. 211–213), begin to write that assignment for yourself; that is, begin to do what you intend to ask students to do. What will you do at the beginning, at the resistance stage? Explain how you got started on fulfilling the assignment.

Responding to Student Writing

Nancy Sommers

Since this article appeared in 1982, a great deal has been written about teacher response to student writing. But no one, to my knowledge, has commented on the issues as clearly and incisively as Nancy Sommers does here. Those issues are many, but as Sommers explains, they can be summed up in three concerns: the primacy of the writer's intention, the expectation of meaningful revision, and the teacher's role as reader/responder.

This essay appeared in College Composition and Communication, *Vol. 33, No. 2 (May 1982); copyright 1982 by the National Council of Teachers of English. It is reprinted with permission.*

More than any other enterprise in the teaching of writing, responding to and commenting on student writing consumes the largest proportion of our time. Most teachers estimate that it takes them at least 20 to 40 minutes to comment on an individual student paper, and those 20 to 40 minutes times 20 students per class, times 8 papers, more or less, during the course of a semester add up to an enormous amount of time. With so much time and energy directed to a single activity, it is important for us to understand the nature of the enterprise. For it seems, paradoxically enough, that although commenting on student writing is the most widely used method for responding to student writing, it is the least understood. We do not know in any definitive way what constitutes thoughtful commentary or what effect, if any, our comments have on helping our students become more effective writers.

Theoretically, at least, we know that we comment on our students' writing for the same reasons professional editors comment on the work of professional writers or for the same reasons we ask our colleagues to read and respond to our own writing. As writers we need and want thoughtful commentary to show us when we have communicated our ideas and when not, raising questions from a reader's point of view that may not have occurred to us as writers. We want to know if our writing has communicated our intended meaning and, if not, what questions or discrepancies our reader sees that we, as writers, are blind to.

In commenting on our students' writing, however, we have an additional pedagogical purpose. As teachers, we know that most students find it difficult to imagine a reader's response in advance, and to use such responses as a guide in composing. Thus, we comment on student writing to dramatize the presence of a reader, to help our students to become that questioning reader themselves, because, ultimately, we believe that becoming such a reader will help them to evaluate what they have written and develop control over their writing.[1]

Even more specifically, however, we comment on student writing because we believe that it is necessary for us to offer assistance to student writers when they are in the process of composing a text, rather than after the text has been completed. Comments create the motive for doing something different in the next draft; thoughtful comments create the motive for revising. Without comments from their teachers or from their peers, student writers will revise in a consistently narrow and predictable way. Without comments from readers, students assume that their writing has communicated their meaning and perceive no need for revising the substance of their text.[2]

Yet as much as we as informed professionals believe in the soundness of this approach to responding to student writing, we also realize that we don't know how our theory squares with teachers' actual practice—do teachers comment and students revise as the theory predicts they should? For the past year my colleagues, Lil Brannon, Cyril Knoblach, and I have been researching this problem, attempting to discover not only what messages teachers give their students through their comments, but also what determines which of these comments the students choose to use or to ignore when revising. Our research has been entirely focused on comments teachers write to motivate revisions. We have studied the commenting styles of thirty-five teachers at New York University and the University of Oklahoma, studying the comments these teachers wrote on first and second drafts, and interviewing a representative number of these teachers and their students. All teachers also commented on the same set of three student essays. As an additional reference point, one of the student essays was typed into the computer that had been programmed with the "Writer's Workbench," a package of twenty-three programs developed by Bell Laboratories to help computers and writers work together to improve a text rapidly. Within a few minutes, the computer delivered editorial comments on the student's text, identifying all spelling and punctuation errors, isolating problems with wordy or misused phrases, and suggesting alternatives, offering a stylistic analysis of sentence types, sentence beginnings, and sentence lengths, and finally, giving our freshman essay a Kincaid readability score of 8th grade which, as the computer program informed us, "is a low score for this type of document." The sharp contrast between the teachers' comments and those of the computer highlighted how arbitrary and idiosyncratic most of our teachers' comments are. Besides, the calm, reasonable language of the computer provided quite a contrast to the hostility and meanspiritedness of most of the teachers' comments.

The first finding from our research on styles of commenting is that *teachers' comments can take students' attention away from their own purposes in writing a particular text and focus that attention on the teachers' purpose in commenting*. The teacher appropriates the text from the student by confusing the student's purpose in writing the text with her own purpose in commenting. Students make the changes the teacher wants rather than those that the student perceives are necessary, since the teacher's concerns imposed on the text create the reasons for the subsequent changes. We have all heard our perplexed students say to us when confused by our comments: "I don't understand how you want me to change this" or "Tell me what you want me to do." In the beginning of the process there was the writer, her words, and her desire to communicate her ideas. But after the comments of the teacher are imposed on the first or second draft, the student's attention dramatically shifts from "This is what I want to say," to "This is what you the teacher are asking me to do."

This appropriation of the text by the teacher happens particularly when teachers identify errors in usage, diction, and style in a first draft and ask students to correct these errors when they revise; such comments give the student an impression of the importance of these errors that is all out of proportion to how they should view these errors at this point in the process. The comments create the concern that these "accidents of discourse" need to be attended to before the meaning of the text is attended to.

It would not be so bad if students were only commanded to correct errors, but, more often than not, students are given contradictory messages; they are commanded to edit a sentence to avoid an error or to condense a sentence to achieve greater brevity of style, and then told in the margins that the particular paragraph needs to be more specific or to be developed more. An example of this problem can be seen in the student paragraph on p. 151.

In commenting on this draft, the teacher has shown the student how to edit the sentences, but then commands the student to expand the paragraph in order to make it more interesting to a reader. The interlinear comments and the marginal comments represent two separate tasks for this student: the interlinear comments encourage the student to see the text as a fixed piece, frozen in time, that just needs some editing. The marginal comments, however, suggest that the meaning of the text is not fixed, but rather that the student still needs to develop the meaning by doing some more research. Students are commanded to edit and develop at the same time; the remarkable contradiction of developing a para-

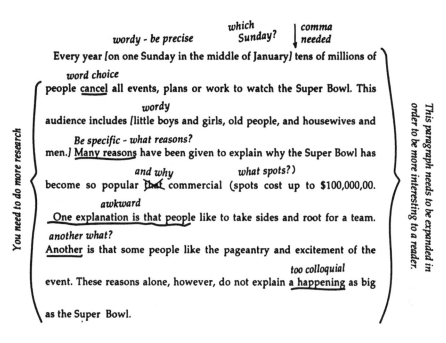

You need to do more research

wordy - be precise   which | comma
                            Sunday? | needed

Every year [on one Sunday in the middle of January] tens of millions of

word choice

people <u>cancel</u> all events, plans or work to watch the Super Bowl. This

wordy

audience includes [little boys and girls, old people, and housewives and

Be specific - what reasons?

men.] <u>Many reasons</u> have been given to explain why the Super Bowl has

and why   *what spots?)*

become so popular ~~that~~ commercial (spots cost up to $100,000,00.

awkward

<u>One explanation is that people</u> like to take sides and root for a team.

another what?

<u>Another</u> is that some people like the pageantry and excitement of the

too colloquial

event. These reasons alone, however, do not explain a <u>happening</u> as big

as the Super Bowl.

This paragraph needs to be expanded in order to be more interesting to a reader.

graph after editing the sentences in it represents the confusion we encountered in our teachers' commenting styles. These different signals given to students, to edit and develop, to condense and elaborate, represent also the failure of teachers' comments to direct genuine revision of the text as a whole.

Moreover, the comments are worded in such a way that it is difficult for students to know what is the most important problem in the text and what problems are of lesser importance. No scale of concerns is offered to a student, with the result that a comment about spelling or a comment about an awkward sentence is given weight equal to a comment about organization or logic. The comment that seemed to represent this problem best was one teacher's command to his student: "Check your commas and semicolons and think more about what you are thinking about." The language of the comments makes it difficult for a student to sort out and decide what is most important and what is least important.

When the teacher appropriates the text for the student in this way, stu-

dents are encouraged to see their writing as a series of parts—words, sentences, paragraphs—and not as a whole discourse. The comments encourage students to believe that their first drafts are finished drafts, not invention drafts, and that all they need to do is patch and polish their writing. That is, teachers' comments do not provide their students with an inherent reason for revising the structure and meaning of their texts, since the comments suggest to students that the meaning of their text is already there, finished, produced, and all that is necessary is a better word or phrase. The processes of revising, editing, and proofreading are collapsed and reduced to a single trivial activity, and the students' misunderstanding of the revision process as a rewording activity is reinforced by their teachers' comments.

It is possible, and it quite often happens, that students follow every comment and fix their texts appropriately as requested, but their texts are not improved substantially, or, even worse, their revised drafts are inferior to their previous drafts. Since the teachers' comments take the students' attention away from their own original purposes, students concentrate more, as I have noted, on what the teachers commanded them to do than on what they are trying to say. Sometimes students do not understand the purpose behind their teachers' comments and take these comments very literally. At other times students understand the comments, but the teacher has misread the text, and the comments, unfortunately, are not applicable. For instance, we repeatedly saw comments in which teachers commanded students to reduce and condense what was written, when in fact what the text really needed at this stage was to be expanded in conception and scope.

The process of revising always involves a risk. But, too often revision becomes a balancing act for students in which they make the changes that are requested but do not take the risk of changing anything that was not commented on, even if the students sense that other changes are needed. A more effective text does not often evolve from such changes alone, yet the student does not want to take the chance of reducing a finished, albeit inadequate, paragraph to chaos—to fragments—in order to rebuild it, if such changes have not been requested by the teacher.

The second finding from our study is that *most teachers' comments are not text-specific and could be interchanged, rubber-stamped, from text to text*. The comments are not anchored in the particulars of the students' texts, but rather are a series of vague directives that are not text-specific. Students are commanded to "Think more about [their] audience, avoid colloquial language, avoid the passive, avoid prepositions at the end of sentences or conjunctions at the beginning of sentences, be clear, be specific, be precise, but above all, think

more about what [they] are thinking about." The comments on the following student paragraph illustrate this problem. One could easily remove all the comments from this paragraph and rubberstamp them on another student text, and they would make as much or as little sense on the second text as they do here.

We have observed an overwhelming similarity in the generalities and abstract commands given to students. There seems to be among teachers an accepted, albeit unwritten canon for commenting on student texts. This uniform code of commands, requests, and pleadings demonstrates that the teacher holds a license for vagueness while the student is commanded to be specific. The students we interviewed admitted to having great difficulty with these vague directives. The students stated that when a teacher writes in the margins or as an end comment, "choose precise language," or "think more about your audience," revising becomes a guessing game. In effect, the teacher is saying to the student, "Somewhere in this paper is imprecise language or lack of awareness of an audience and you must find it." The problem presented by these vague commands is compounded for the students when they are not offered any strategies for carrying out these commands. Students are told that they have done something wrong and that there is something in their text that needs to be fixed before the text is acceptable. But to tell students that they have done something wrong is not to tell them what to do about it. In order to offer a useful revision strategy to a student, the teacher must anchor that strategy in the specifics of the student's text. For instance, to tell our student, the author of the following paragraph, "to be specific," or "to elaborate," does not show our student what questions the reader has about the meaning of

*Begin by telling your reader
what you are going to write about*

In the sixties it was drugs, in the seventies it was rock and roll. Now in

avoid - "one of the"
the eighties, one of the most controversial subjects is nuclear power. The

elaborate
United States is in great need of its own source of power. Because of

environmentalists, coal is not an acceptable source of energy. [Solar and

be specific
wind power have not yet received the technology necessary to use them.]

avoid - "it seems"
It seems that nuclear power is the only feasible means right now for ob-

taining self-sufficient power. However, too large a percentage of the

be precise
population are against nuclear power claiming it is unsafe. With as many

problems as the United States is having concerning energy it seems a

Think more about your reader

shame that the public is so quick to "can" a very feasible means of power.

Nuclear energy should not be given up on, but rather, more nuclear

plants should be built.

Thesis sentence needed

the text, or what breaks in logic exist, that could be resolved if the writer supplied specific information; nor is the student shown how to achieve the desired specificity.

Instead of offering strategies, the teachers offer what is interpreted by students as rules for composing; the comments suggest to students that writing is just a matter of following the rules. Indeed, the teachers seem to impose a series of abstract rules about written products even when some of them are not appropriate for the specific text the student is creating.[3] For instance, the student author of our sample paragraph presented above is commanded to follow the conventional rules for writing a five paragraph essay—to begin the introductory paragraph by telling his reader what he is going to say and to end the paragraph

with a thesis sentence. Somehow these abstract rules about what five-paragraph products should look like do not seem applicable to the problems this student must confront when revising, nor are the rules specific strategies he could use when revising. There are many inchoate ideas ready to be exploited in this paragraph, but the rules do not help the student to take stock of his (or her) ideas and use the opportunity he has, during revision, to develop those ideas.

The problem here is a confusion of process and product: what one has to say about the process is different from what one has to say about the product. Teachers who use this method of commenting are formulating their comments as if these drafts were finished drafts and were not going to be revised. Their commenting vocabularies have not been adapted to revision and they comment on first drafts as if they were justifying a grade or as if the first draft were the final draft.

Our summary finding, therefore, from this research on styles of commenting is that the news from the classroom is not good. For the most part, teachers do not respond to student writing with the kind of thoughtful commentary which will help students to engage with the issues they are writing about or which will help them think about their purposes and goals in writing a specific text. In defense of our teachers, however, they told us that responding to student writing was rarely stressed in their teacher-training or in writing workshops; they had been trained in various prewriting techniques, in constructing assignments, and in evaluating papers for grades, but rarely in the process of reading a student text for meaning or in offering commentary to motivate revision. The problem is that most of us as teachers of writing have been trained to read and interpret literary texts for meaning, but, unfortunately, we have not been trained to act upon the same set of assumptions in reading student texts as we follow in reading literary texts.[4] Thus, we read student texts with biases about what the writer should have said or about what he or she should have written, and our biases determine how we will comprehend the text. We read with our preconceptions and preoccupations, expecting to find errors, and the result is that we find errors and misread our students' texts.[5] We find what we look for; instead of reading and responding to the meaning of a text, we correct our students' writing. We need to reverse this approach. Instead of finding errors or showing students how to patch up parts of their texts, we need to sabotage our students' conviction that the drafts they have written are complete and coher-

ent. Our comments need to offer students revision tasks of a different order of complexity and sophistication from the ones that they themselves identify, by forcing students back into the chaos, back to the point where they are shaping and restructuring their meaning.[6]

For if the content of a student text is lacking in substance and meaning, if the order of the parts must be rearranged significantly in the next draft, if paragraphs must be restructured for logic and clarity, then many sentences are likely to be changed or deleted anyway. There seems to be no point in having students correct usage errors or condense sentences that are likely to disappear before the next draft is completed. In fact, to identify such problems in a text at this early first draft stage, when such problems are likely to abound, can give a student a disproportionate sense of their importance at this stage in the writing process.[7] In responding to our students' writing, we should be guided by the recognition that it is not spelling or usage problems that we as writers first worry about when drafting and revising our texts.

We need to develop an appropriate level of response for commenting on a first draft, and to differentiate that from the level suitable to a second or third draft. Our comments need to be suited to the draft we are reading. In a first or second draft, we need to respond as any reader would, registering questions, reflecting befuddlement, and noting places where we are puzzled about the meaning of the text. Comments should point to breaks in logic, disruptions in meaning, or missing information. Our goal in commenting on early drafts should be to engage students with the issues they are considering and help them clarify their purposes and reasons in writing their specific text.

For instance, the major rhetorical problem of the essay written by the student who wrote the first paragraph (the paragraph on nuclear power) quoted above was that the student had two principal arguments running through his text, each of which brought the other into question. On the one hand, he argued that we must use nuclear power, unpleasant as it is, because we have nothing else to use; though nuclear energy is a problematic source of energy, it is the best of a bad lot. On the other hand, he also argued that nuclear energy is really quite safe and therefore should be our primary resource. Comments on this student's first draft need to point out this break in logic and show the student that if we accept his first argument, then his second argument sounds fishy. But if we accept his second argument, his first argument sounds contradictory. The teacher's comments need to engage this student writer with this basic rhetorical and conceptual problem in his first draft rather than impose a series of abstract commands and rules upon his text.

Written comments need to be viewed not as an end in themselves—a way for teachers to satisfy themselves that they have done their jobs—but rather as a means for helping students to become more effective writers. As a means for helping students, they have limitations; they are, in fact, disembodied remarks—one absent writer responding to another absent writer. The key to successful commenting is to have what is said in the comments and what is done in the classroom mutually reinforce and enrich each other. Commenting on papers assists the writing course in achieving its purpose; classroom activities and the comments we write to our students need to be connected. Written comments need to be an extension of the teacher's voice—an extension of the teacher as reader. Exercises in such activities as revising a whole text or individual paragraphs together in class, noting how the sense of

the whole dictates the smaller changes, looking at options, evaluating actual choices, and then discussing the effect of these changes on revised drafts—such exercises need to be designed to take students through the cycles of revising and to help them overcome their anxiety about revising: that anxiety we all feel at reducing what looks like a finished draft into fragments and chaos.

The challenge we face as teachers is to develop comments which will provide an inherent reason for students to revise; it is a sense of revision as discovery, as a repeated process of beginning again, as starting out new, that our students have not learned. We need to show our students how to seek, in the possibility of revision, the dissonances of discovery—to show them through our comments why new choices would positively change their texts, and thus to show them the potential for development implicit in their own writing.

NOTES

1. C. H. Knoblach and Lil Brannon, "Teacher Commentary on Student Writing: The State of the Art," *Freshman English News*, 10 (Fall, 1981), 1–3.

2. For an extended discussion of revision strategies of student writers see Nancy Sommers, "Revision Strategies of Student Writers and Experienced Adult Writers," *College Composition and Communication*, 31 (December, 1980), 378–388.

3. Nancy Sommers and Ronald Schleifer, "Means and Ends: Some Assumptions of Student Writers," *Composition and Teaching*, 2 (December, 1980), 69–76.

4. Janet Emig and Robert P. Parker, Jr., "Responding to Student Writing: Building a Theory of the Evaluating Process," unpublished papers, Rutgers University.

5. For an extended discussion of this problem see Joseph Williams, "The Phenomenology of Error," *College Composition and Communication*, 32 (May, 1981), 152—168.

6. Ann Berthoff, *The Making of Meaning* (Montclair, NJ: Boynton/Cook Publishers, 1981).

7. W. U. McDonald, "The Revising Process and the Marking of Student Papers," *College*   *Composition and Communication*, 24 (May, 1978), 167–170.

For Further Thought

1. Think about your own schooling. How did your teachers respond to your work? Did you feel that teachers "appropriated" your texts? Were you expected to rewrite? In general, how helpful were teachers' comments, and in what ways did they help you?

2. One of the most striking passages in this essay is Sommers's characterization of many teachers' comments as "mean-spirited." Do you think this is accurate? If so, to what would you attribute this attitude on the part of a teacher (what causes this behavior)? Or if you think Sommers is misinterpreting, what kinds of attitudes do you think teachers are expressing?

3. Many teachers, including Nancie Atwell in *In the Middle*, talk about student ownership of a text, and this idea seems to figure in Sommers's warnings about teachers appropriating the text. What does it mean to "own" a text? If the idea is legitimate, then the teacher has certain responsibilities. What might those be?

4. Sommers clearly assumes a process approach to teaching—that is, she takes it for granted that students will revise these drafts. But there comes a time when the process is over. How might a teacher's comments on a final draft differ from those on an earlier draft?

5. Later in this chapter, you will be referred to some student papers and will have a chance to respond to them. For now, take a look at the paragraphs that Sommers provides, written by first-year college students. Write a comment to each of these students based on your reading of these paragraphs. What would you say to them to help them improve their work?

Application 4.2:
Working With Student Drafts

At the earliest stage . . .

If you were to compare our school with different high schools, you would see its a pretty decent school. We don't have a big drug problem here and there's not a bunch of tough guys pushing everyone around. Sure there's some but nothing like the big cities.

Like all schools ours has its disadvantages too. I think it would be a neat idea if the elevator was opened up for use [by all students]. And another one built on the opposite end of the hall. It would save a lot of time for getting to class on time and all. The stairs can be a real headache when you have class on the south end of the first floor and your next one is on the north end of the third floor.

One big problem with having the elevators running would be the over crowding. Everyone would want to go on the elevator, instead of the stairs. There could be someone standing by the elevators to make sure only a certain amount gets on. There might be hassling, but I think it would work.

> *Also there are risks of the elevators getting stuck. Would everyone suffocate from lack of oxygen? Just think of all the man hours it would take to put in another elevator. Would the job be too costly? And even if the school could afford it, would it be really worth it?*
>
> *I feel it would take the strain off our feet, but I don't think its really going to hurt us to walk three flights of stairs everyday. Maybe if we had an elevator, there would disadvantages in that too. We all should be happy that our feet can take us that far. But I still think it sure would be relaxing to have one.*

On the first day of school, this tenth grader was given the assignment to write about "one thing you would like to see changed in school" (see Appendix 1). He began writing in class and had until the next day to hand in a draft of the paper. The result was this journey through his thinking about the elevator.

At first glance it looks like a mistake—the kind of paper that needs to be aborted. The student had an idea and then seems to have talked himself out of that idea. No idea, no paper. And yet there is something here. At the very least we can treat the draft as a record of this student's intention: He wanted to say something about the elevator.

In short, this paper is a *rough* draft. It is useless to complain about its roughness: That is part of the writing game, the writing process. It is better, I think, to consider roughness as a necessary stage for the student writer. Perhaps he has talked (or written) himself out of his own topic. If so, then he has learned something. Or perhaps there is yet something to say. If so, then he needed to write this draft to discover his own purpose.

Rough drafts are like that—rough. They often take the form of a dumping ground, wherein the student throws everything he or she knows about the topic. In teacher language, these are the ones that "lack focus." Perhaps the student has given us a narrative of discovery—telling the reader each step in his or her learning process ("where I found this, where I found that"), as if that were the main thing a reader wants to know. Or maybe the prose is cryptic, full of loaded terms and assumptions about what the reader already knows. In the terms used by Linda Flower (see "For Further Reading" at the end of this chapter), the prose is *writer-based* rather than *reader-based*: It seems to be written for the author and needs to be made more intelligible for readers.

But no matter how rough the draft might be, it still represents some kind of thought. Can we doubt that about the elevator paper? Surely this student could not have written this draft without thinking—about the needs of students, the layout of the building, the inflexibility of the time schedule, and the practicality of change. To be sure, those thoughts are not yet organized and the draft lacks focus, but at this stage it is not appropriate to make too many judgments about the student's (lack of) success. Our job is to help him clarify what he wants to say and help him achieve his goal.

Some Things to Consider About Early Drafts

1. Write a response to the elevator draft. What would you say to this student? Can you offer some specific strategies for revising the paper?

2. Read the drafts in Appendix 1. What do they have in common; that is, what traits seem to be characteristic of early drafts? Do you think these are rougher than usual because of the sketchiness of the assignment, or are they pretty much what you might expect?

3. Write a response to each of the drafts in Appendix 1. Bear in mind Nancy Sommers's advice: Comments should be specific to each particular paper; they should set some reasonable priorities for the student; and they should suggest some constructive strategy for revision.

4. Consider the possibility of using peer response for early drafts. What are the pros and cons of that choice? If you were to use peer response, how would you proceed? Pairs or groups? Reading aloud or written copies? Directing students about what to look for or leaving them free to respond in different ways?

At a later stage . . .

By now you might have read some of the student papers contained in the appendixes of this book, all of them (except for those in Appendix 1) second drafts. If so, you will have noticed that there is considerable variation in performance: Some papers are excellent, some are in the middle range, and some are very poorly done. Indeed, they were chosen to reflect that kind of variation. (I hasten to add that opinions about particular papers will also vary, but that's the subject of the next application, on evaluation.) The variation in quality is due in part to the different ability levels of students: They do not, after all, come to us with equal experience in writing and equal literacy skills. But another way to look at the variation is to say that, even with their second drafts, students are at different stages of the writing process.

Examples of this variation can be found in every set of papers, but let me illustrate with two pairs of papers from two different sets. In Appendix 5, we have a set of tenth-grade comparison-contrast papers. Most readers, I think, would agree that Leanne's paper is superior to Eddie's. In the teacher's opinion, Leanne has fulfilled the assignment: She has found something significant to say, she has discovered a voice and rhetorical mode for saying it, and she has worked on her style so that it is smooth and clean. There is, of course, room for improvement, but realistically, it's time for Leanne to stop. She is at the end of the writing process, because the teacher's judgment and Leanne's own sense of satisfaction with her work are congruent.

Eddie, on the other hand, is at an earlier stage. It's not that his writing is particularly prone to mechanical error. Compared to a paper like Jeff's, Eddie's work is smooth and correct. But he still seems to be grappling with the implications of his subject. His views on "Mexicans," for example, need more thought—not just because they seem unfair, but also because they are not well integrated into a paper about two high schools. (Indeed, if he tried to connect his feelings about Mexican Americans to how *he* feels about school, what he wants school to do for him, Eddie might arrive at a less prejudicial position.) For this reason, and because his categories for comparison are not well focused, Eddie needs to work on a third draft. He, of course, might disagree, but that's where teaching comes into play. Our job is to demonstrate to Eddie how he can benefit from further revision.

It would seem, then, that one could simply say, "The good writers can stop, but the poorer writers need to keep writing." A simple plan, but it doesn't really work that way. For one thing, there are different kinds of "goodness" and "badness." Jeff's paper is no better than Eddie's, but in a sense Jeff is further along in the process; though there are serious stylistic and mechanical problems with his paper, he seems ready for (very intense) editing. Indeed, to say that Leanne's work is better than Eddie's, or that Eddie's is better than Jeff's, is to speak the language of assessment. In Peter Elbow's terms, it is to engage in ranking, which is legitimate enough but irrelevant to the issue at hand. The question is not, "which is better?" but "where is this writer in the process?" and "what does he or she need?"

This point can be further illustrated by looking at the seventh graders' short stories in Appendix 2. Brad's story on "Mr. Linden's Library" is clearly "better" than Claire's or Diane's on "The Magic Harp." Like Leanne, Brad is at the end of the process. But, in a way, the same might be true of Claire and Diane—for it turns out that Claire has a pretty serious learning disability (spelling is extremely difficult for her) and Diane is a highly resistant writer (for her to have written this much is a major triumph). So when is it time to stop? Do we really want to do battle with Diane over another draft? And what are the limits to Claire's patience in her constant struggle with words? Maybe it's time for both of these students to celebrate their own efforts and move on to another project.

"Oh great," you might say, echoing Debbie in chapter 1 (p. 19). "You want us to respond to all these papers and probably grade some, but it turns out that 'it all depends' on who these particular students are—and we don't even know them!" Yes, this is a fair criticism and, yes, I do think you should evaluate some of these papers. But it's not as impossible as it might seem. For one thing, what students need is often apparent in the writing itself. Though we might want to know a little more about his racial attitudes, we don't need to know Eddie intimately to find a way to help him revise. Moreover, it is legitimate to make a distinction between the writer and the work: Diane's *paper* needs revision, even though, "in real life," it might be unproductive to require her to revise it. I'll grant, then, the artificiality of responding papers by anonymous writers; it will be very different when you are dealing with the work of your own students. But you have to start practicing sometime, and these papers are real. This is what students wrote; it awaits your response.

Some Things to Consider About Responding to Second Drafts

1. Read a set of papers from the appendixes (except 1), and then choose three: one that seems fairly "finished," one that needs editing, and one that needs more substantive revision. Explain what about each paper led you to this conclusion.

2. Choose another set of papers and respond to them. Write a note to each student, bearing in mind Nancy Sommers's advice: Comments should be specific to this particular paper; they should set some reasonable priorities for the student; and they should suggest some constructive strategy for revising.

3. Many of the drafts are full of small errors—what Barbara Carney calls low-order concerns (misspellings, punctuation errors, grammatical mistakes). If you decide to respond to these, how will you get students to see the relative importance of these concerns in the writing process? If you decide not to respond to them, when would you ask students to address these problems?

Ranking, Evaluating, and Liking: Sorting Out Three Forms of Judgment

Peter Elbow

Ever since the publication of Writing without Teachers *(1973), Peter Elbow has been one of the most insightful critics and analyzers of writing pedagogy. His style is informal and personal—deceptively so, for what he does best is examine teaching practice to unearth its underlying complexities and paradoxes. In this essay, he takes on the issue of assessment, using his own teaching practice as the prime example. Elbow is a college teacher, but what he says is equally applicable to the secondary classroom.*

This essay appeared in College English, *Vol. 55, No. 3 (February 1993); copyright 1993 by the National Council of Teachers of English. It is reprinted with permission.*

This essay is my attempt to sort out different acts we call assessment—some different ways in which we express or frame our judgments of value. I have been working on this tangle not just because it is interesting and important in itself but because assessment tends so much to drive and control *teaching.* Much of what we do in the classroom is determined by the assessment structures we work under.

Assessment is a large and technical area and I'm not a professional. But my main premise or subtext in this essay is that we nonprofessionals can and should work on it because professionals have not reached definitive conclusions about the problem of how to assess writing (or anything else, I'd say). Also, decisions about assessment are often made by people even less professional than we, namely legislators. Pat Belanoff and I realized that the field of assessment was open when we saw the harmful effects of a writing proficiency exam at Stony Brook and worked out a collaborative portfolio assessment system in its place (Belanoff and Elbow; Elbow and Belanoff). Professionals keep changing their minds about large-scale testing and assessment. And as for classroom grading, psychometricians provide little support or defense of it.

THE PROBLEMS WITH RANKING AND THE BENEFITS OF EVALUATING

By ranking I mean the act of summing up one's judgment of a performance or person into a single, holistic number or score. We rank every time we give a grade or holistic score. Ranking implies a single scale or continuum or dimension along which all performances are hung.

By evaluating I mean the act of expressing one's judgment of a performance or person by pointing out the strengths and weaknesses of different features or dimensions. We evaluate every time we write a comment on a paper or have a conversation about its value. Evaluation implies the recognition of different criteria or dimensions—and by implication different contexts and audiences for the same performance. Evaluation requires going *beyond* a first response that may be nothing but a kind of ranking ("I like it" or "This is better than that"), and instead looking carefully enough at the performance or person to make distinctions between parts or features or criteria.

It's obvious, thus, that I am troubled by ranking. But I will resist any temptation to argue that we can get rid of all ranking—or even should. Instead I will try to show how we can have *less* ranking and *more* evaluation in its place.

I see three distinct problems with ranking: it is inaccurate or unreliable; it gives no substantive feedback; and it is harmful to the atmosphere for teaching and learning.

(1) First the unreliability. To rank reliably means to give a *fair* number, to find the single quantitative score that readers will agree on. But readers don't agree.

This is not news—this unavailability of agreement. We have long seen it on many fronts. For example, research in evaluation has shown many times that if we give a paper to a set of readers, those readers tend to give it the full range of grades (Diederich). I've recently come across new research to this effect—new to me because it was published in 1912. The investigators carefully showed how high school English teachers gave different grades to the same paper. In response to criticism that this was a local problem in English, they went on the next year to discover an even greater variation among grades given by high school geometry teachers and history teachers to papers in their subjects. (See the summary of Daniel Starch and Edward Elliott's 1913 *School Review* articles in Kirschenbaum, Simon, and Napier 258–59.)

We know the same thing from literary criticism and theory. If the best critics can't agree about what a text means, how can we be surprised that they disagree even more about the quality or value of texts? And we know that nothing in literary or philosophical theory gives us any agreed-upon rules for settling such disputes.

Students have shown us the same inconsistency with their own controlled experiments of handing the same paper to different teachers and getting different grades. This helps explain why

we hate it so when students ask us their favorite question, "What do you want for an A?": it rubs our noses in the unreliability of our grades.

Of course champions of holistic scoring argue that they get *can* get agreement among readers—and they often do (White). But they get that agreement by "training" the readers before and during the scoring sessions. What "training" means is getting those scorers to stop reading the way they normally read—getting them to stop using the conflicting criteria and standards they normally use outside the scoring sessions. (In an impressive and powerful book, Barbara Herrnstein Smith argues that whenever we have widespread inter-reader reliability, we have reason to suspect that difference has been suppressed and homogeneity imposed—almost always at the expense of certain groups.) In short, the reliability in holistic scoring is not a measure of how texts are valued by real readers in natural settings, but only of how they are valued in artificial settings with imposed agreements.

Defenders of holistic scoring might reply (as one anonymous reviewer did), that holistic scores are not perfect or absolutely objective readings but just "judgments that most readers will agree are the appropriate ones given the purpose of the assessment and the system of communication." But I have been in and even conducted enough holistic scoring sessions to know that even that degree of agreement doesn't occur unless "purpose" and "appropriateness" are defined to mean acceptance of the single set of standards imposed on that session. We know too much about the differences among readers and the highly variable nature of the reading process. Supposing we get readings only from academics, or only from people in English, or only from respected critics, or only from respected writing programs, or only from feminists, or only from sound readers of my tribe (white, male, middle-class, full professors between the ages of fifty and sixty). We *still* don't get agreement. We can sometimes get agreement among readers from some subset, a particular community that has developed a strong set of common values, perhaps *one* English department or *one* writing program. But what is the value of such a rare agreement? It tells us nothing about how readers from other English departments or writing programs will judge—much less how readers from other domains will judge.

(From the opposite ideological direction, some skeptics might object to my skeptical train of thought: "So what else is new?" they might reply. "Of *course* my grades are biased, 'interested' or 'situated'—always partial to my interests or the values of my community or culture. There's no other possibility." But how can people consent to give grades if they feel that way? A single teacher's grade for a student is liable to have substantial consequences—for example on eligibility for a scholarship or a job or entrance into professional school. In grading, surely we must not take anything less than genuine fairness as our goal.)

It won't be long before we see these issues argued in a court of law, when a student who has been disqualified from playing on a team or rejected from a professional school sues, charging that the basis for his plight—teacher grades—is not reliable. I wonder if lawyers will be able to make our grades stick.

(2) Ranking or grading is woefully uncommunicative. Grades and holistic scores are nothing but points on a continuum from "yea" to "boo"—with no information or clues about the criteria behind these noises. They are 100 percent evaluation and 0 percent description or information. They quantify the degree of approval or disapproval in

readers but tell nothing at all about what the readers actually approve or disapprove of. They say nothing that couldn't be said with gold stars or black marks or smiley-faces. Of course our first reactions are often nothing but global holistic feelings of approval or disapproval, but we need a system for communicating our judgments that nudges us to move beyond these holistic feelings and to articulate the basis of our feeling—a process that often leads us to change our feeling. (Holistic scoring sessions sometimes use rubrics that explain the criteria—though these are rarely passed along to students—and even in these situations, the rubrics fail to fit many papers.) As C. S. Lewis says, "People are obviously far more anxious to express their approval and disapproval of things than to describe them" (7).

(3) Ranking leads students to get so hung up on these oversimple quantitative verdicts that they care more about scores than about learning—more about the grade we put on the paper than about the comment we have written on it. Have you noticed how grading often forces us to write comments to justify our grades?—and how these are often *not* the comment we would make if we were just trying to help the student write better? ("Just try writing several favorable comments on a paper and then giving it a grade of D" [Diederich 21].)

Grades and holistic scores give too much encouragement to those students who score high—making them too apt to think they are already fine—and too little encouragement to those students who do badly. Unsuccessful students often come to doubt their intelligence. But oddly enough, many "A" students also end up doubting their true ability and feeling like frauds—because they have sold out on their own judgment and simply given teachers whatever yields an A. They have too often been rewarded for what they don't really believe in. (Notice that there's more cheating by students who get high grades than by those who get low ones. There would be less incentive to cheat if there were no ranking.)

We might be tempted to put up with the inaccuracy or unfairness of grades if they gave good diagnostic feedback or helped the learning climate; or we might put up with the damage they do to the learning climate if they gave a fair or reliable measure of how skilled or knowledgeable students are. But since they fail dismally on both counts, we are faced with the striking question of why grading has persisted so long.

There must be many reasons. It is obviously easier and quicker to express a global feeling with a single number than to figure out what the strengths and weaknesses are and what one's criteria are. (Though I'm heartened to discover, as I pursue this issue, how troubled teachers are by grading and how difficult they find it.) But perhaps more important, we see around us a deep *hunger to rank*—to create pecking orders: to see who we can look down on and who we must look up to, or in the military metaphor, who we can kick and who we must salute. Psychologists tell us that this taste for pecking orders or ranking is associated with the authoritarian personality. We see this hunger graphically in the case of IQ scores. It is plain that IQ scoring does not represent a commitment to looking carefully at people's intelligence; when we do that, we see different and frequently uncorrelated *kinds* or *dimensions* of intelligence (Gardner). The persistent use of IQ scores represents the hunger to have a number so that everyone can have a rank. ("Ten!" mutter the guys when they see a pretty woman.)

Because ranking or grading has caused so much discomfort to so many students and teachers, I think we see a lot of confusion about the process. It is hard to think clearly about something that has given so many of us such anxiety and distress. The most notable confusion I notice is the tendency to think that if we renounce ranking or grading, we are renouncing the very possibility of judgment and discrimination—that we are embracing the idea that there is no way to distinguish or talk about the difference between what works well and what works badly.

So the most important point, then, is that *I am not arguing against judgment or evaluation*. I'm just arguing against that crude, oversimple way of *representing* judgment—distorting it, really—into a single number, which means ranking people and performances along a single continuum.

In fact I am arguing *for evaluation*. Evaluation means looking hard and thoughtfully at a piece of writing in order to make distinctions as to the quality of different features or dimensions. For example, the process of evaluation permits us to make the following kinds of statements about a piece of writing:

- The thinking and ideas seem interesting and creative.
- The overall structure or sequence seems confusing.
- The writing is perfectly clear at the level of individual sentences and even paragraphs.
- There is an odd, angry tone of voice that seems unrelated or inappropriate to what the writer is saying.
- Yet this same voice is strong and memorable and makes one listen even if one is irritated.
- There are a fair number of mistakes in grammar or spelling: more than "a sprinkling" but less than "riddled with."

To rank, on the other hand, is to be forced to translate those discriminations into a single number. What grade or holistic score do these judgments add up to? It's likely, by the way, that more readers would agree with those separate, "analytic" statements than would agree on a holistic score.

I've conducted many assessment sessions where we were not trying to impose a set of standards but rather to find out how experienced teachers read and evaluate, and I've had many opportunities to see that good readers give grades or scores right down through the range of possibilities. Of course good readers sometimes agree—especially on papers that are strikingly good or bad or conventional, but I think I see difference more frequently than agreement when readers really speak up.

The process of evaluation, because it invites us to articulate our criteria and to make distinctions among parts or features or dimensions of a performance, thereby invites us further to acknowledge the main fact about evaluation: that different readers have different priorities, values, and standards.

The conclusion I am drawing, then, in this first train of thought is that we should do less ranking and more evaluation. Instead of using grades or holistic scores—single number verdicts that try to sum up complex performances along only one scale—we should give some kind of written or spoken evaluation that discriminates among criteria and dimensions of the writing—and if possible that takes account of the complex context for writing: who the writer is, what the writer's audience and goals are, who we are as readers and how we read, and how we might differ in our reading from other readers the writer might be addressing.

But how can we put this principle into practice? The pressure for ranking seems implacable. Evaluation takes more time, effort, and money. It seems as though we couldn't get along without scores on writing exams. Most teachers are obliged to give grades at the end of

each course. And many students— given that they have become conditioned or even addicted to ranking over the years and must continue to inhabit a ranking culture in most of their courses—will object if we don't put grades on papers. Some students, in the absence of that crude gold star or black mark, may not try hard enough (though how hard is "enough"—and is it really our job to stimulate motivation artificially with grades—and is grading the best source of motivation?).

It is important to note that there are certain schools and colleges that do *not* use single-number grades or scores, and they function successfully. I taught for nine years at Evergreen State College, which uses only written evaluations. This system works fine, even down to getting students accepted into high quality graduate and professional schools.

Nevertheless we have an intractable dilemma: that grading is unfair and counterproductive but that students and institutions tend to want grades. In the face of this dilemma there is a need for creativity and pragmatism. Here are some ways in which I and others use *less ranking* and *more evaluation* in teaching—and they suggest some adjustments in how we score large-scale assessments. What follows is an assortment of experimental compromises—sometimes crude, seldom ideal or utopian—but they help.

(a) Portfolios. Just because conventional institutions oblige us to turn in a single quantitative course grade at the end of every marking period, it doesn't follow that we need to grade individual papers. Course grades are more trustworthy and less damaging because they are based on so many performances over so many weeks. By avoiding frequent ranking or grading, we make it *somewhat* less likely for students to become addicted to oversimple numerical rankings—to think that evaluation always translates into a simple number—in short, to mistake ranking for evaluation. (I'm not trying to defend conventional course grades since they are still uncommunicative and they still feed the hunger for ranking.) Portfolios permit me to refrain from grading individual papers and limit myself to writerly evaluative comments—and help students see this as a positive rather than a negative thing, a chance to be graded on a body of their best work that can be judged more fairly. Portfolios have many other advantages as well. They are particularly valuable as occasions for asking students to write extensive and thoughtful explorations of their own strengths and weaknesses.

A midsemester portfolio is usually an informal affair, but it is a good occasion for giving anxious students a ballpark estimate of how well they are doing in the course so far. I find it helpful to tell students that I'm perfectly willing to tell them my best estimate of their course grade—but only if they come to me in conference and only during the second half of the semester. This serves somewhat to quiet their anxiety while they go through seven weeks of drying out from grades. By midsemester, most of them have come to enjoy not getting those numbers and thus being able to think better about more writerly comments from me and their classmates.

Portfolios are now used extensively and productively in larger assessments, and there is constant experimentation with new applications (Belanoff and Dickson; *Portfolio Assessment Newsletter, Portfolio News*).

(b) Another useful option is to make a strategic retreat from a wholly negative position. That is, I sometimes do a *bit* of ranking even on individual papers, using two "bottom-line" grades: H and U for "Honors" and "Unsatisfactory." I tell students that these

translate to about A or A– and D or F. This practice may seem theoretically inconsistent with all the arguments I've just made, but (at the moment, anyway) I justify it for the following reasons.

First, I sympathize with a *part* of the students' anxiety about not getting grades: their fear that they might be failing and not know about it—or doing an excellent job and not get any recognition. Second, I'm not giving *many* grades; only a small proportion of papers get these H's or U's. The system creates a "non-bottom-line" or "non-quantified" atmosphere. Third, these holistic judgments about best and worst do not seem as arbitrary and questionable as most grades. There is usually a *bit* more agreement among readers about the best and worst papers. What seems most dubious is the process of trying to rank that whole middle range of papers—papers that have a mixture of better and worse qualities so that the numerical grade depends enormously on a reader's priorities or mood or temperament. My willingness to give these few grades goes a long way toward helping my students forgo most bottom-line grading.

I'm not trying to pretend that these minimal "grades" are truly reliable. But they represent a very small amount of ranking. Yes, someone could insist that I'm really ranking every single paper (and indeed if it seemed politically necessary, I could put an OK or S [for satisfactory] on all those middle range papers and brag, "Yes, I grade everything.") But the fact is that I am doing *much less sorting* since I don't have to sort them into five or even twelve piles. Thus there is a huge reduction in the total amount of unreliability I produce.

(It might seem that if I use only these few minimal grades I have no good way for figuring out a final grade for the course—since that requires a more fine-grained set of ranks. But I don't find that to be the case. For I also give these same minimal grades to the many other important parts of my course such as attendance, meeting deadlines, peer responding, and journal writing. If I want a mathematically computed grade on a scale of six or A through E, I can easily compute it when I have such a large number of grades to work from—even though they are only along a three-point scale.)

This same practice of crude or minimal ranking is a big help on larger assessments outside classrooms, and needs to be applied to the process of assessment in general. There are two important principles to emphasize. On the one hand we must be prudent or accommodating enough to admit that despite all the arguments against ranking, there *are* situations when we need that bottom-line verdict along one scale: which student has not done satisfactory work and should be denied credit for the course? which student gets the scholarship? which candidate to hire or fire? We often operate with scarce resources. But on the other hand we must be bold enough to insist that we do far more ranking than is really needed. We can get along not only with fewer occasions for assessment but also with fewer gradations in scoring. If we decide what the *real* bottom-line is on a given occasion—perhaps just "failing" or perhaps "honors" too—then the reading of papers or portfolios is enormously quick and cheap. It leaves time and money for evaluation—perhaps for analytic scoring or some comment.

At Stony Brook we worked out a portfolio system where multiple readers had only to make a binary decision: acceptable or not. Then individual teachers could decide the actual course grade and give comments for their own students—so long as those students passed in the eyes of an independent rater (Elbow and Belanoff; Belanoff

and Elbow). The best way to begin to wean our society from its addiction to ranking may be to permit a tiny bit of it (which also means less unreliability)—rather than trying to go "cold turkey."

(c) Sometimes I use an analytic grid for evaluating and commenting on student papers. An example is given in Figure 1. I often vary the criteria in my grid (e.g. "connecting with readers" or "investment") depending on the assignment or the point in the semester.

Grids are a way I can satisfy the students' hunger for ranking but still not give in to conventional grades on individual papers. Sometimes I provide nothing but a grid (especially on final drafts), and this is a very quick way to provide a response. Or on midprocess drafts I sometimes use a grid in addition to a comment: a more readerly comment that often doesn't so much tell them what's wrong or right or how to improve things but rather tries to give them an account of what is *happening to me* as I read their words. I think this kind of comment is really the most useful thing of all for students, but it frustrates some students for a while. The grid can help these students feel less anxious and thus pay better attention to my comment.

I find grids extremely helpful at the end of the semester for telling students their strengths and weaknesses in the course—or what they've done well and not so well. Besides categories like the ones above, I use categories like these: "skill in giving feedback to others," "ability to meet deadlines," "effort," and "improvement." This practice makes my final grade much more communicative.

(d) I also help make up for the absence of ranking—gold stars and black marks—by having students share their writing with each other a great deal both orally and through frequent publication in class magazines. Also, where possible, I try to get students to give or

Strong OK Weak

			CONTENT, INSIGHTS, THINKING, GRAPPLING WITH TOPIC
			GENUINE REVISION, SUBSTANTIVE CHANGES, NOT JUST EDITING
			ORGANIZATION, STRUCTURE, GUIDING THE READER
			LANGUAGE: SYNTAX, SENTENCES, WORDING, VOICE
			MECHANICS: SPELLING, GRAMMAR, PUNCTUATION, PROOFREADING
			OVERALL [Note: this is not a sum of the other scores.]

Figure 1

send writing to audiences outside the class. At the University of Massachusetts at Amherst, freshmen pay a ten dollar lab fee for the writing course, and every teacher publishes four or five class magazines of final drafts a semester. The effects are striking. Sharing, peer feedback, and publication give the best reward and motivation for writing, namely, getting your words out to many readers.

(e) I sometimes use a kind of modified *contract grading*. That is, at the start of the course I pass out a long list of all the things that I most want students to do—the concrete activities that I think most lead to learning—and I promise students that if they do them *all* they are guaranteed a certain final grade. Currently, I say it's a B—it could be lower or higher. My list includes these items: not missing more than a week's worth of classes; not having more than one late major assignment; *substantive* revising on all major revisions; good copy editing on all final revisions; good effort on peer feedback work; keeping up the journal; and substantial effort and investment on each draft.

I like the way this system changes the "bottom-line" for a course: the intersection where my authority crosses their self-interest. I can tell them, "You have to work very hard in this course, but you can stop worrying about grades." The crux is no longer that commodity

I've always hated and never trusted: a numerical ranking of the quality of their writing along a single continuum. Instead the crux becomes what I care about most: the *concrete behaviors* that I most want students to engage in because they produce more learning and help me teach better. Admittedly, effort and investment are not concrete observable behaviors, but they are no harder to judge than overall quality of writing. And since I care about effort and investment, I don't mind the few arguments I get into about them; they seem fruitful. ("Let's try and figure out why it looked to me as though you didn't put any effort in here.") In contrast, I hate discussions about grades on a paper and find such arguments fruitless. Besides, I'm not making fine distinctions about effort and investment— just letting a bell go off when they fall palpably low.

It's crucial to note that I am *not* fighting evaluation with this system. I am just fighting ranking or grading. I still write evaluative comments and often use an evaluative grid to tell my students what I see as strengths and weaknesses in their papers. My goal is not to get rid of evaluation but in fact to emphasize it, enhance it. I'm trying to get students to listen *better* to my evaluations—by uncoupling them from a grade. In effect, I'm doing this because I'm so fed up with students *following* or *obeying* my evaluations too blindly—making whatever changes my comments suggest but doing it for the sake of a grade; not really taking the time to make up their own minds about whether they think my judgments or suggestions really make sense to them. The worst part of grades is that they make students obey us without carefully thinking about the merits of what we say. I love the situation this system so often puts students in: I make a criticism or suggestion about their paper, but it doesn't matter to their grade whether they go along with me or not (so long as they genuinely revise in some fashion). They have to think; to decide.

Admittedly this system is crude and impure. Some of the really skilled students who are used to getting A's and desperate to get one in this course remain unhelpfully hung up about getting those H's on their papers. But a good number of these students discover that they can't get them, and they soon settle down to accepting a B and having less anxiety and more of a learning voyage.

THE LIMITATIONS OF EVALUATION AND THE BENEFITS OF EVALUATION-FREE ZONES

Everything I've said so far has been in praise of evaluation as a substitute for ranking. But I need to turn a corner here and speak about the *limits* or *problems* of evaluation. Evaluating may be better than ranking, but it still carries some of the same problems. That is, even though I've praised evaluation for inviting us to acknowledge that readers and contexts are different, nevertheless the very word *evaluation* tends to imply fairness or reliability or getting beyond personal or subjective preferences. Also, of course, evaluation takes a lot more time and work. To rank you just have to put down a number; holistic scoring of exams is cheaper than analytic scoring.

Most important of all, evaluation harms the climate for learning and teaching—or rather *too much* evaluation has this effect. That is, if we evaluate *everything* students write, they tend to remain tangled up in the assumption that their whole job in school is to give teachers "what they want." Constant evaluation makes students worry more about psyching out the teacher than about what they are really learning. Students fall into a kind of defensive or on-guard stance toward the teacher: a desire to hide what they don't understand and try to impress. This stance gets in the way of learning. (Think of the patient trying to hide symptoms from the doctor.) Most of all, constant evaluation by someone in authority makes students reluctant to take the risks that are needed for good learning—to try out hunches and trust their own judgment. Face it: if our goal is to get students to exercise their own judgment, that means exercising an immature and undeveloped judgment and making choices that are obviously wrong to us.

We see around us a widespread hunger to be evaluated that is often just as strong as the hunger to rank. Countless conditions make many of us walk around in the world wanting to ask others (especially those in authority), "How am I doing, did I do OK?" I don't think the hunger to be evaluated is as harmful as the hunger to rank, but it can get in the way of learning. For I find that the greatest and most powerful breakthroughs in learning occur when I can get myself and others to *put aside* this nagging, self-doubting question ("How am I doing? How am I doing?")—and instead to take some chances, trust our instincts or hungers. When everything is evaluated, everything counts. Often the most powerful arena for deep learning is a kind of "time out" zone from the pressures of normal evaluated reality: make-believe, play, dreams—in effect, the Shake-spearian forest.

In my attempts to get away from too much evaluation (not from all evalua-tion, just from too much of it), I have drifted into a set of teaching practices which now feel to me like the *best* part of my teaching. I realize now what I've been unconsciously doing for a num-ber of years: creating "evaluation-free zones."

(a) The paradigm evaluation-free zone is the ten minute, nonstop free-write. When I get students to freewrite, I am using my authority to create un-usual conditions in order to contradict or interrupt our pervasive habit of al-ways evaluating our writing. What is es-sential here are the two central features of freewriting: that it be private (thus I don't collect it or have students share it with anyone else); and that it be non-stop (thus there isn't time for planning, and control is usually diminished). Students quickly catch on and enter into the spirit. At the end of the course, they often tell me that freewriting is the most useful thing I've taught them (see Belanoff, Elbow, and Fontaine).

(b) A larger evaluation-free zone is the single unevaluated assignment—what people sometimes call the "quick-write" or sketch. This is a piece of writ-ing that I ask students to do—either in class or for homework—without any or much revising. It is meant to be low stakes writing. There is a bit of pres-sure, nevertheless, since I usually ask them to share it with others and *I* usu-ally collect it and read it. But I don't write any comments at all—except per-haps to put straight lines along some passages I like or to write a phrase of appreciation at the end. And I ask stu-dents to refrain from giving evaluative feedback to each other—and instead just to say "thank you" or mention a couple of phrases or ideas that stick in mind. (However, this writing-without-feedback can be a good occasion for

students to discuss the *topic* they have written about—and thus serve as an ex-cellent kick-off for discussions of what I am teaching.)

(c) These experiments have led me to my next and largest evaluation-free zone—what I sometimes call a "jump start" for my whole course. For the last few semesters I've been devoting the first three weeks *entirely* to the two evaluation-free activities I've just de-scribed: freewriting (and also more lei-surely private writing in a journal) and quickwrites or sketches. Since the stakes are low and I'm not asking for much revising, I ask for *much more* writing homework per week than usual. And every day we write in class: various exercises or games. The em-phasis is on getting rolling, getting flu-ent, taking risks. And every day all stu-dents read out loud something they've written—sometimes a short passage even to the whole class. So despite the absence of feedback, it is a very audi-ence-filled and sociable three weeks.

At first I only dared do this for two weeks, but when I discovered how fast the writing improves, how good it is for building community, and what a pleas-ure this period is for me, I went to three weeks. I'm curious to try an ex-periment with teaching a whole course this way. I wonder, that is, whether all that evaluation we work so hard to give really does any more good than the constant writing and sharing (Zak).

I need to pause here to address an obvious rejoinder: "But withholding evaluation is not normal!" Indeed, it is *not* normal—certainly not normal in school. We normally tend to emphasize evaluations—even bottom-line ranking kinds of evaluations. But I resist the ar-gument that if it's not normal we shouldn't do it.

The best argument for evaluation-free zones is from experience. If you try them, I suspect you'll discover that they are satisfying and bring out good writing. Students have a better time writing these unevaluated pieces; they enjoy hearing and appreciating these pieces when they don't have to evaluate. And *I* have a much better time when I engage in this astonishing activity: reading student work when I don't have to evaluate and respond. And yet the writing improves. I see students investing and risking more, writing more fluently, and using livelier, more interesting voices. This writing gives me and them a higher standard of clarity and voice for when we move on to more careful and revised writing tasks that involve more intellectual pushing—tasks that sometimes make their writing go tangled or sodden.

THE BENEFITS AND FEASIBILITY OF LIKING

Liking and disliking seem like unpromising topics in an exploration of assessment. They seem to represent the worst kind of subjectivity, the merest accident of personal taste. But I've recently come to think that the phenomenon of liking is perhaps the most important evaluative response for writers and teachers to think about. In effect, I'm turning another corner in my argument. In the first section I argued against ranking—with evaluating being the solution. Next I argued not *against* evaluating—but for no-evaluation zones in *addition* to evaluating. Now I will argue neither against evaluating nor against no-evaluation zones, but for something very different in addition, or perhaps underneath, as a foundation: liking.

Let me start with the germ story. I was in a workshop and we were going around the circle with everyone telling a piece of good news about their writing in the last six months. It got to Wendy Bishop, a good poet (who has also written two good books about the teaching of writing), and she said, "In the last six months, I've learned to *like* everything I write." Our jaws dropped; we were startled—in a way scandalized. But I've been chewing on her words ever since, and they have led me into a retelling of the story of how people learn to write better.

The old story goes like this: We write something. We read it over and we say, "This is terrible. I *hate* it. I've got to work on it and improve it." And we do, and it gets better, and this happens again and again, and before long we have become a wonderful writer. But that's not really what happens. Yes, we vow to work on it—but we don't. And next time we have the impulse to write, we're just a *bit* less likely to start.

What really happens when people learn to write better is more like this: We write something. We read it over and we say, "This is terrible. . . . But I *like* it. Damn it, I'm going to get it good enough so that others will like it too." And this time we don't just put it in a drawer, we actually work hard on it. And we try it out on other people too—not just to get feedback and advice but, perhaps more important, to find someone else who will like it.

Notice the two stories here—two hypotheses. (a) "First you improve the faults and then you like it." (b) "First you like it and then you improve faults." The second story may sound odd when stated so baldly, but really it's common sense. Only if we like something will we get involved enough to work and struggle with it. Only if we like what we write will we write again and again by choice—which is the only way we get better.

This hypothesis sheds light on the process of how people get to be published writers. Conventional wisdom assumes a Darwinian model: poor writers are unread; then they get better; as a result, they get a wider audience; finally they turn into Norman Mailer. But now I'd say the process is more complicated. People who get better and get published really tend to be driven by how much *they* care about their writing. Yes, they have a small audience at first—after all, they're not very good. But they try reader after reader until finally they can find people who like and appreciate their writing. I certainly did this. If someone doesn't like her writing enough to be pushy and hungry about finding a few people who also like it, she probably won't get better.

It may sound so far as though all the effort and drive comes from the lonely driven writer—and sometimes it does (Norman Mailer is no joke). But, often enough, readers play the crucially active role in this story of how writers get better. That is, the way writers *learn* to like their writing is by the grace of having a reader or two who likes it—even though it's not good. Having at least a few appreciative readers is probably indispensable to getting better.

When I apply this story to our situation as teachers I come up with this interesting hypothesis: *good writing teachers like student writing* (and like students). I think I see this borne out—and it is really nothing but common sense. Teachers who hate student writing and hate students are grouchy all the time. How could we stand our work and do a decent job if we hated their writing? Good teachers see what is only *potentially* good, they get a kick out of mere possibility—and they encourage it. When I manage to do this, I teach well.

Thus, I've begun to notice a turning point in my courses—two or three weeks into the semester: "Am I going to like these folks or is this going to be a battle, a struggle?" When I like them everything seems to go better—and it seems to me they learn more by the end. When I don't and we stay tangled up in struggle, we all suffer—and they seem to learn less.

So what am I saying? That we should like bad writing? How can we see all the weaknesses and criticize student writing if we just like it? But here's the interesting point: if I *like* someone's writing it's *easier* to criticize it.

I first noticed this when I was trying to gather essays for the book on freewriting that Pat Belanoff and Sheryl Fontaine and I edited. I would read an essay someone had written, I would want it for the book, but I had some serious criticism. I'd get excited and write, "I really like this, and I hope we can use it in our book, but you've got to get rid of this and change that, and I got really mad at this other thing." I usually find it hard to criticize, but I began to notice that I was a much more critical and pushy reader when I liked something. It's even fun to criticize in those conditions.

It's the same with student writing. If I like a piece, I don't have to pussyfoot around with my criticism. It's when I don't like their writing that I find myself tiptoeing: trying to soften my criticism, trying to find something nice to say—and usually sounding fake, often unclear. I see the same thing with my own writing. If I like it, I can criticize it better. I have faith that there'll still be something good left, even if I train my full critical guns on it.

In short—and to highlight how this section relates to the other two sections of this essay—liking is not the same as ranking or evaluating. Naturally, people get them mixed up: when they like something, they assume it's good; when they hate it, they assume it's bad. But it's helpful to uncouple the two domains and realize that it makes perfectly good sense to say, "This is terrible, but I like it." Or, "This is good, but I hate it." In short, I am not arguing here *against* criticizing or evaluating. I'm merely arguing *for* liking.

Let me sum up my clump of hypotheses so far:

- It's not improvement that leads to liking, but rather liking that leads to improvement.
- It's the mark of good writers to like their writing.
- Liking is not the same as evaluating. We can often criticize something better when we like it.
- We learn to like our writing when we have a respected reader who likes it.
- Therefore, it's the mark of good teachers to like students and their writing.

If this set of hypotheses is true, what practical consequences follow from it? How can we be better at liking? It feels as though we have no choice—as though liking and not-liking just happen to us. I don't really understand this business. I'd love to hear discussion about the mystery of liking—the phenomenology of liking. I sense it's some kind of putting oneself out—or holding oneself open—but I can't see it clearly. I have a hunch, however, that we're not so helpless about liking as we tend to feel.

For in fact I can suggest some practical concrete activities that I have found fairly reliable at increasing the chances of liking student writing:

(a) I ask for lots of private writing and merely shared writing, that is, writing that I don't read at all, and writing that I read but don't comment on. This makes me more cheerful because it's so much easier. Students get *better* without me. Having to evaluate writing—especially bad writing—makes me more likely to hate it. This throws light on grading: it's hard to like something if we know we have to give it a D.

(b) I have students share lots of writing with each other—and after a while respond to each other. It's easier to like their writing when I don't feel myself as the only reader and judge. And so it

helps to build community in general: it takes pressure off me. Thus I try to use peer groups not only for feedback, but for other activities too, such as collaborative writing, brainstorming, putting class magazines together, and working out other decisions.

(c) I increase the chances of my liking their writing when I get better at finding what *is* good—or *potentially* good—and learn to praise it. This is a skill. It requires a good eye, a good nose. We tend—especially in the academic world—to assume that a good eye or fine discrimination means *criticizing*. Academics are sometimes proud of their tendency to be bothered by what is bad. Thus I find I am sometimes looked down on as dumb and undiscriminating: "He likes bad writing. He must have no taste, no discrimination." But I've finally become angry rather than defensive. It's an act of discrimination to see what's good in bad writing. Maybe, in fact, this is the secret of the mystery of liking: to be able to see potential goodness underneath badness.

Put it this way. We tend to stereotype liking as a "soft" and sentimental activity. Mr. Rogers is our model. Fine. There's nothing wrong with softness and sentiment—and I love Mr. Rogers. But liking can also be hard-assed. Let me suggest an alternative to Mr. Rogers: B. F. Skinner. Skinner taught pigeons to play ping-pong. How did he do it? Not by moaning, "Pigeon standards are falling. The pigeons they send us these days are no good. When I was a pigeon . . ." He did it by a careful, disciplined method that involved close analytic observation. He put pigeons on a ping-pong table with a ball, and every time a pigeon turned his head 30 degrees toward the ball, he gave a reward (see my "Danger of Softness").

What would this approach require in the teaching of writing? It's very simple . . . but not easy. Imagine that we want to teach students an ability they badly lack, for example how to organize their writing or how to make their sentences clearer. Skinner's insight is that we get nowhere in this task by just telling them how much they lack this skill: "It's disorganized. Organize it!" "It's unclear. Make it clear!"

No, what we must learn to do is to read closely and carefully enough to show the student little bits of *proto*-organization or *sort of* clarity in what they've already written. We don't have to pretend the writing is wonderful. We could even say, "This is a terrible paper and the worst part about it is the lack of organization. But I will teach you how to organize. Look here at this little organizational move you made in this sentence. Read it out loud and try to feel how it pulls together this stuff here and distinguishes it from that stuff there. Try to remember what it felt like writing that sentence—creating that piece of organization. Do it some more." Notice how much more helpful it is if we can say, "Do *more* of what you've done here," than if we say, "Do something *different* from anything you've done in the whole paper."

When academics criticize behaviorism as crude it often means that they aren't willing to do the close careful reading of student writing that is required. They'd rather give a cursory reading and turn up their nose and give a low grade and complain about falling standards. No one has undermined behaviorism's main principle of learning: that reward produces learning more effectively than punishment.

(d) I improve my chances of liking student writing when I take steps to get to know them a bit as people. I do this partly through the assignments I give. That is, I always ask them to write a letter or two to me and to each other (for example about their history with writing). I base at least a couple of assignments on their own experiences, memories, or histories. And I make sure some of the assignments are free choice pieces—which also helps me know them.

In addition, I make sure to have at least three conferences with each student each semester—the first one very early. I often call off some classes in order to keep conferences from being too onerous (insisting nevertheless that students meet with their partner or small group when class is called off). Some teachers have mini-conferences with students during class—while students are engaged in writing or peer group meetings. I've found that when I deal only with my classes as a whole—as a large group—I sometimes experience them as a herd or lump—as stereotyped "adolescents"; I fail to experience them as individuals. For me, personally, this is disastrous since it often leads me to experience them as that scary tribe that I felt rejected by when *I* was an eighteen-year-old—and thus, at times, as "the enemy." But when I sit down with them face to face, they are not so stereotyped or alien or threatening—they are just eighteen-year-olds.

Getting a glimpse of them as individual people is particularly helpful in cases where their writing is not just bad, but somehow offensive—perhaps violent or cruelly racist or homophobic or sexist—or frighteningly vacuous. When I know them just a bit I can often see behind their awful attitude to the person and the life situation that spawned it, and not hate their writing so much. When I know students I can see that they are smart behind that dumb behavior; they are doing the best they can behind that bad behavior. Conditions are keeping them from acting decently; something is holding them back.

(e) It's odd, but the more I let myself show, the easier it is to like them and their writing. I need to share some of my own writing—show some of my own feelings. I need to write the letter to them that they write to me—about my past experiences and what I want and don't want to happen.

(f) It helps to work on my own writing—and work on learning to *like* it. Teachers who are most critical and sour about student writing are often having trouble with their own writing. They are bitter or unforgiving or hurting toward their own work. (I think I've noticed that failed PhDs are often the most severe and difficult with students.) When we are stuck or sour in our own writing, what helps us most is to find spaces free from evaluation such as those provided by freewriting and journal writing. Also, activities like reading out loud and finding a supportive reader or two. I would insist, then, that if only for the sake of our teaching, we need to learn to be charitable and to like our own writing.

A final word. I fear that this sermon about liking might seem an invitation to guilt. There is enough pressure on us as teachers that we don't need someone coming along and calling us inadequate if we don't *like* our students and their writing. That is, even though I think I am right to make this foray into the realm of feeling, I also acknowledge that it is dangerous—and paradoxical. It strikes me that we also need to have permission to hate the dirty bastards and their stupid writing.

After all, the conditions under which they go to school bring out some awful behavior on their part, and the conditions under which we teach sometimes make it difficult for us to like them and their writing. Writing wasn't meant to be read in stacks of twenty-five, fifty, or seventy-five. And we are handicapped as teachers when students are in our classes against their will. (Thus high school teachers have the worst problem here, since their students tend to be the most sour and resentful about school.)

Indeed, one of the best aids to liking students and their writing is to be somewhat charitable toward ourselves about the opposite feelings that we inevitably have. I used to think it was terrible for teachers to tell those sarcastic stories and hostile jokes about their students: "teacher room talk." But now I've come to think that people who spend their lives teaching *need* an arena to let off this unhappy steam. And certainly it's better to vent this sarcasm and hostility with our buddies than on the students themselves. The question, then, becomes this: do we help this behavior function as a venting so that we can move past it and not be trapped in our inevitable resentment of students? Or do we tell these stories and jokes as a way of staying stuck in the hurt, hostile, or bitter feelings—year after year— as so many sad teachers do?

In short I'm not trying to invite guilt, I'm trying to invite hope. I'm trying to suggest that if we do a sophisticated analysis of the difference between liking and evaluating, we will see that it's possible (if not always easy) to like students and their writing—without having to give up our intelligence, sophistication, or judgment.

Let me sum up the points I'm trying to make about ranking, evaluating, and liking:

- Let's do as little ranking and grading as we can. They are never fair and they undermine learning and teaching.
- Let's use evaluation instead—a more careful, more discriminating, fairer mode of assessment.
- But because evaluating is harder than ranking, and because too much evaluating also undermines learning, let's establish small but important evaluation-free zones.
- And underneath it all—suffusing the whole evaluative enterprise— let's learn to be better likers: liking

our own and our students' writing, and realizing that liking need not get in the way of clear-eyed evaluation.

WORKS CITED

Diederich, Paul. *Measuring Growth in English.* Urbana: NCTE, 1974.

Belanoff, Pat, and Peter Elbow. "Using Portfolios to Increase Collaboration and Community in a Writing Program." *WPA: Journal of Writing Program Administration* 9.3 (Spring 1986): 27–40. (Also in *Portfolios: Process and Product.* Ed. Pat Belanoff and Marcia Dickson. Portsmouth, NH: Boynton/Cook-Heinemann, 1991.)

Belanoff, Pat, Peter Elbow, and Sheryl Fontaine, eds. *Nothing Begins with N: New Investigations of Freewriting.* Carbondale: Southern Illinois UP, 1991.

Bishop, Wendy. *Something Old, Something New: College Writing Teachers and Classroom Change.* Carbondale: Southern Illinois UP, 1990.

———. *Released into Language: Options for Teaching Creative Writing.* Urbana: NCTE, 1990.

Elbow, Peter. "The Danger of Softness." *What Is English?* New York: MLA, 1990. 197–210.

Elbow, Peter, and Pat Belanoff. "State University of New York: Portfolio-Based Evaluation Program." *New Methods in College Writing Programs: Theory into Practice.* Ed. Paul Connolly and Teresa Vilardi. New York: MLA, 1986. 95–105. (Also in *Portfolios: Process and Product.* Ed. Pat Belanoff and Marcia Dickson. Portsmouth, NH: Boynton/Cook-Heinemann, 1991.)

Gardner, Howard. *Frames of Mind: The Theory of Multiple Intelligences.* New York: Basic, 1983.

Kirschenbaum, Howard, Simon Sidney, and Rodney Napier. *Wad-Ja-Get? The Grading Game in American Education.* New York: Hart Publishing, 1971.

Lewis, C. S. *Studies in Words.* 2d ed. London: Cambridge UP, 1967.

Portfolio Assessment Newsletter. Five Centerpointe Drive, Suite 100, Lake Oswego, Oregon 97035.

Portfolio News. c/o San Dieguito Union High School District, 710 Encinitas Boulevard, Encinitas, CA 92024.

Smith, Barbara Herrnstein. *Contingencies of Value: Alternative Perspectives for Critical Theory.* Cambridge: Harvard UP, 1988.

White, Edward M. *Teaching and Assessing Writing.* San Francisco: Jossey-Bass, 1985.

Zak, Frances. "Exclusively Positive Responses to Student Writing." *Journal of Basic Writing* 9.2 (1990): 40–53.

For Further Thought

1. How does Elbow define ranking? (It's broader than the usual meaning of the term.) Do you agree with his negative view of this form of assessment? Comment on Elbow's idea that our society has a "hunger to rank."

2. In your own experience, how did it feel to have your writing ranked? (If you aspire to teach English, it is possible that your work was always ranked high. How might it have felt to a less capable writer?) What form of assessment seemed to help you most? Why?

3. Comment on Elbow's willingness to compromise with minimal forms of ranking or an analytic grid. What kind of compromises could you see yourself making? At this stage in your career, what kind of grading system do you think you would use for student writing?

4. Elbow is famous for stating things that many teachers believe but don't want to admit. Take his idea of "liking." Discuss his premise: "It's not improvement that leads to liking, but rather liking that leads to improvement." How convincing is his case for using this idea in the classroom?

Application 4.3:
Evaluating Student Writing

I have been working on this tangle [of assessment] not just because it is interesting and important in itself but because assessment tends so much to drive and control teaching. *Much of what we do in the classroom is determined by the assessment structures we work under. (Peter Elbow, "Ranking, Evaluating, and Liking")*

Can anyone doubt that Elbow is correct? We have only to consult our own behavior as students, recalling how important grades were to us and how much we worked "for the grade," to understand how thoroughly all teaching is colored by the inevitability of assessment. "The grade is *there*," say my students; "you can't just wish it away." They are right. And so it is doubly ironic that Elbow, in his essay on grading, spends so much time and energy evading the prospect of grading. It's fascinating to watch him duck, dodge, and weave, but one wants to yell, "It's there, Peter! Grading is *really* there. Give it up!"

Of course, to yell that is to miss Elbow's two main points: that there is more to assessment than just grading, and that (even if grading is inevitable) how and when one does it can make a lot of difference. Still, it's pretty obvious that Elbow is highly ambivalent about any kind of assessment. In this he is like many (I almost wrote "all") writing teachers. As we sit there with a set of papers to assess, we sense an inner conflict, one of the tensions that we have encountered so frequently in this book. We want to help students, so we call ourselves coaches or facilitators. But the act of judging seems out of keeping with that role. It is a different hat for us, and we frequently feel uncomfortable wearing it. But, as students themselves remind us, wear it we must.

Elbow's article, then, mirrors the struggle that many of us go through. We are looking for ways to assess writing that do not undermine (or that only minimally damage) the other understandings about writing that we have fostered in our classes. If we grade each paper as it comes along, will we shut down the writing process prematurely? If we don't grade each piece of work, will we give students an accurate picture of how well they are doing? How do we act as judge and yet encourage students to keep on writing—yes, even if they are likely to end up with a C or a D? Remember that, as teachers, we are thinking of the intrinsic rewards of writing. Students, on the other hand, think of extrinsic things, especially the grade (and the perks that a good grade brings with it). No wonder, then, that grading so often seems like a game, with students and teachers playing key roles according to different sets of rules.

It is a complicated issue but not a hopeless one. The essential thing is to communicate your judgments to students in a manner that they can understand and respect. As Elbow points out, there are many ways to assess student writing; by this stage in your academic career, you have probably experienced three or four of them. If you think about your own reactions to these "assessment structures," my guess is that you responded most favorably to teachers who told you what they were doing, and why. To the extent that you were in on the game, you were more likely to accept the judgments and maybe even learn something from them. Moreover, Elbow's article is a kind of lesson in teaching. Notice how often he comes upon a problem with assessment and then seeks to solve it through some teaching practice. In other words, the connection of assessment to teaching and learning does not have to be negative. As we gain practice with assessment, we confront many of the core issues in teaching.

Some Things to Consider About Evaluating Student Writing

1. What did grades mean to you when you were in junior or senior high? Did they motivate you to achieve more, or did they set caps on your learning? In particular, how did you react to the grade on a piece of your writing?

2. Go back and read Elbow's comments on liking, especially what he says about looking for what is potentially good in a piece of work (pp. 172–173). Then look at the 100-year birthday papers in Appendix 4. What is there to like about each paper? Write a comment to each student and an overall comment in which you discuss this form of judgment.

3. Reread Elbow's comments on evaluation, especially the use of the evaluation grid (p. 167). Then look at the comparison-contrast papers in Appendix 5. Using Elbow's categories (minus the one on revision) or a modification of them, create a grid for this assignment, and evaluate each paper. Attach to each grid a brief comment to the student.

4. Reread Elbow's comments on ranking (pp. 160–163). Then, in the face of all his criticism, grade the literary analysis papers found in Appendix 6. You might follow this procedure: (1) read the papers through, to get a sense of the whole set; (2) write your criteria, keeping the sheet handy as you grade; (3) read each paper and put a letter grade at the end, in pencil. Then write a brief comment to each student in which you explain the strengths and weaknesses of the paper.

5. Consider the three sets of papers that you evaluated. How did your criteria differ from one set to the other? Which were the hardest to evaluate? Which the easiest? Think about the seventh graders' short stories. How would you evaluate them?

Process Writing and the Secondary School Reality: A Compromise

Barbara Carney

In the general introduction to this chapter, I alluded to the tension teachers frequently feel between serving the needs of the individual writer and working with the whole group. Barbara Carney uses slightly different terms (she sees a conflict between the process approach and the de-mands of the rest of the curriculum), but the tension is similar. Even as we recognize that the writing process is different for each student, the school seems to demand a regularization of work and behavior. Thus, theory and practice are always in a dynamic tension with each other—as we see in

Carney's case, where the effort to work out conflicting demands becomes a way to improve as a teacher.

This essay appeared in English Journal, *Vol. 85, No. 6 (October 1996); copyright 1996 by the National Council of Teachers of English. It is reprinted with permission.*

Incorporating the process approach to writing into my English classroom has been the biggest challenge of my 20-year teaching career. I first had the opportunity to experiment with the process approach about 15 years ago in a one-semester composition elective. Students could choose to take this course in addition to their required English class, which already involved a significant amount of writing. The elective offered practice in a variety of different types of writing and, because it was usually a smaller group, more individualized attention.

I felt success with the process approach in the elective almost immediately, but when I attempted to adapt it to writing in my 11th-grade English classroom, where literature, vocabulary, and grammar units had to be covered in addition to composition, I found that the constraints of time and curriculum made the change much more difficult. I felt strongly that I wanted to make it work because of the consistent positive reaction of my elective students to the difference that the elements of the process had made in their writing. Over the years, their comments have served as the impetus for the change to process in my English classroom.

EXPERIMENTING IN THE COMPOSITION ELECTIVE

When I started teaching composition, students were accustomed to being assigned specific topics, hearing a lecture involving the best approaches to writing certain types of papers, reading models, creating an outline for approval, and doing most of the actual writing for homework. Most of the papers required by the English curriculum at that time were formal, multiparagraph papers, so more informal, personal writing was offered in the elective. I began to give these students more of a voice in choosing their topics. I encouraged them to write and revise during class. Over the first few semesters, I developed a writing workshop approach similar to that described by Stephen Zemelman and Harvey Daniels (1988, *A Community of Writers*, Portsmouth, NH: Heinemann, 89–99). After a general assignment was discussed, most students were motivated to choose their own topics and work at their own pace. At the beginning of the period, they would come into the classroom, find their writing portfolios, and get started. I held conferences at a table in the classroom with individuals while the rest of the class wrote. Only the final drafts of each paper were graded, and I always had a sense of how close everyone was to finishing, so I could set the due date for the final draft at a comfortable time. The atmosphere was relaxed and positive.

The number of students taking the elective grew larger each year, and it became difficult to meet with them individually as often as I wanted. I also realized that their insights could help each other. I did some research on training peer tutors and became aware of the benefits to everyone that writing response groups can produce. After working with a group for the first time, Laura, who had seemed reluctant to share, wrote about the experience: "It was very helpful reading our papers aloud in discussion groups because we could hear our mistakes and spot each other's weak paragraphs or sentences."

The most dramatic outcome of using process for me was that my role changed from director to facilitator. The students, mostly seniors, saw the class as an opportunity to express their opinions and to receive input as they were writing rather than waiting for my evaluation of their final draft. They actually showed appreciation for my responses, rather than being threatened by them. Even more surprising, many students indicated that being expected to write multiple drafts was the most beneficial part of the course. Tim, a senior, wrote in his final evaluation:

> The most helpful aspect I felt was the numerous revisions of the papers. This allowed me to see what I was doing wrong and correct it before receiving a final grade. It was also helpful to have other students read my papers and comment on them.

I know now that many teachers of writing have found success with a similar approach in their classrooms.

ADAPTING TO THE REQUIRED ENGLISH COURSE

I became more and more aware that this interaction and flexibility was possible because the elective composition course was devoted entirely to writing. I was excited to have developed such a positive situation in this one course, but for the rest of each day in my required 11th-grade English classes I faced the dilemma confronted by secondary English teachers. How can we fit the process approach into our large and regimented classrooms? Is it possible to allow the time-consuming activities for writing, revising, and conferencing with all of the other constraints demanded by our curriculum, not to mention the interruptions by activities, testing, and guidance? What about the students who are not motivated; can they be expected to work at their own pace, be interested enough to come up with ideas, or complete a paper with-

out a deadline? If they don't enjoy writing one draft, how can we expect them to revise?

The unwieldy nature of the writing process seems impossible to conform to a regimented English environment where literature, research, vocabulary, communication skills, and grammar are demanded in addition to writing. Yet, today, the process approach is commonly accepted by the secondary community and is expected in writing instruction, even though its inherent spontaneity continues to appear incongruous with the short daily chunks of time and the demands implicit in the secondary classroom.

What has evolved in my 11th-grade English class is a compromise. I felt so strongly about the benefits of the process approach to my students that I decided to attempt to force this abstractly shaped peg into the square hole of a classroom period. I listened to my students to determine the most important elements of the writing workshop approach, and although I have had to make some sacrifices to make it work, I feel that the strengths remain.

THE NECESSARY COMPROMISES

Student Ownership

The first compromise is that of total student ownership of the assignment. Our strong, sequential curriculum requires certain types of writing at each level 9–12. It does allow for some flexibility, however, and I try to give students as much choice as possible within its parameters. For example, a character analysis might be required, but students may choose the character and determine an appropriate thesis for analysis. Writers might choose a person or place to describe for a descriptive piece or a precept from *Poor Richard's Almanac* they would like to relate to their own lives. I think it is very important to give writers the experience of choosing a topic not only so they feel some ownership, but because deciding what to write about is a big part of the writing process: if we assign topics, we are not teaching what the process is all about. I believe that the process of selecting a topic, narrowing and refining it, should be the responsibility of the writer as far as the curriculum will allow. Although they do not "discover a subject" (Donald Murray, 1968, *A Teacher Teaches Writing*, Boston: Houghton Mifflin, 27) in the purest sense, my students do experience a wide range of subjects, approaches, and audiences.

Spontaneous Writing

The second major compromise involves the spontaneity of the process. Writing during class time that continues from one day to the next isn't possible because of time constraints, but I wanted my English students to learn the value of meaningful revision. Their reticence to write and revise led me to consider setting required deadlines for each draft. Spontaneity is destroyed by this approach, but I feel it is worth the sacrifice. Before I required the process, I had the strong feeling that when I collected final drafts, I was actually collecting first drafts in a pretty disguise, mostly because students did not allow the time they needed to develop a paper before the final draft was due.

I realize that setting deadlines flies in the face of process theory because it does not allow for individual writers to work at their own pace. It is, however, an answer for teachers who wish to more efficiently monitor the progress of their students, and it requires the writer who might otherwise be reluctant to do so to revise. Forcing the process allows writers to see what they are capable of through revision. As unbelievable as this may sound, my students continued to point to multiple

drafts as the main reason for their success as writers. "The thing most helpful in this class was writing so many rough drafts before our final copy. Doing this helped me realize how important it is to not only write one copy of a paper," Heather wrote. For many it meant a change in attitude about writing. When asked about whether his attitude about writing had changed after taking the elective course, Nick said, "Yes, my attitude has changed. I found out that writing was not as bad and as hard as I always thought it was. There is always room for improvement and so I keep writing. I hope I keep getting better."

RETAINING THE BEST OF THE WRITING PROCESS

Despite these compromises to the writing process' spontaneity and student ownership, my new plan for English contained the elements that my writing students consistently found to be the most helpful: writing multiple drafts and receiving a response at each stage of the process. Another important technique that is implied by the process approach is waiting until the end to deal with mechanics and grammar.

Ironically, critics of the process approach see postponing error correction as a shift in the emphasis on correctness; they believe that student writers are learning to write using poor grammar and incorrect mechanics. This does not need to be the case. Teaching students that editing is the final stage in the process should not lessen its significance. Postponing error correction does not mean putting it off altogether. If students are told that they are responsible for the editing process, then they must be held accountable in the final evaluation.

I first learned about emphasizing the editing stage from Lucy Calkins, who describes a special editing table in her 2nd grade classroom where students go to edit when their papers are ready

(1986, *The Art of Teaching Writing*, Portsmouth, NH: Heinemann, 206). I try to maintain this same separation in a figurative way by asking students to wait until the editing stage to address grammar and mechanics.

The success I have felt with this approach is a result of my students focusing more on development of their content in the earlier stages of writing. They have learned that revision is not just error-correction. As they begin to write and revise, they look more carefully at what they are saying without the constraints of how they are saying it.

When asked if waiting to think about editing until later in the process had changed her writing, Karen said, "Yes, I just think about development, paragraphing, and support and later change wording and punctuation. It makes me feel more organized while writing papers and helps me concentrate on one thing at a time." A number of students said that this approach helped to reduce their anxiety about writing. Chris responded, "I am more relaxed when starting a paper." Jen said, "Yes, I think my writing has improved since I concentrate on only the important things first." Thinking about what type of writing happens at which stage created an entirely different way of thinking and talking about writing in my classroom.

TRAINING STUDENTS TO UNDERSTAND THE PROCESS: HOCs AND LOCs

Now I begin each school year training all of my students using a framework from the NCTE TRIP booklet by Thomas Reigstad and Donald McAndrew (1984, *Training Tutors for Writing Conferences*, Urbana, IL: ERIC, 11–19). I ordered the booklet as part of my research on training peer tutors but have found it invaluable when talking about the type of writing that is done in each stage of the process. Reigstad and McAndrew provide a hierarchy of writing concerns and when they should be addressed. The High Order Concerns (thesis or focus, appropriate voice or tone, organization, and development) are dealt with first and in this sequence. If a writer's focus in a draft is unclear, organization confusing, or tone inappropriate, these weaknesses must be addressed before any discussion of spelling or word choice can take place. The Low Order Concerns (problems with sentence structure and variety, punctuation, spelling, and usage) are dealt with simultaneously, near the end of the process. Usually, we emphasize the HOCs when looking at the first two drafts; punctuation, spelling, and usage at the editing stage; and sentence structure and variety somewhere in the middle. It's especially rewarding when awkward language dissolves because the writer hears it while reading during a peer conference.

Labeling writing priorities helps to demystify the composing process and allows student writers to focus on one concern at a time instead of trying to do everything at once. *High* and *low* may

---

HOCs and LOCs

High Order Concerns

1. focus/thesis
2. appropriate tone
3. organization
4. development

Low Order Concerns

1. sentence structure
2. variety
3. punctuation
4. spelling
5. usage

Reigstad, Thomas J. and Donald A. McAndrew. 1984. *Training Tutors for Writing Conferences*. Urbana: NCTE. 11–18.

not be the most appropriate terms, but they do emphasize the idea that good writing is much more than correct writing. When I first read about waiting to edit, I didn't think it would make much difference, but retraining students to look at the priorities in their writing first continues to have the single biggest impact on my teaching of writing.

HOW IT WORKS: THE WRITING PROCESS IN MY ENGLISH CLASSROOM

My attempt to develop the process approach comfortably in my English classroom has evolved into a predictable framework of activities at each stage of the process: prewriting, drafting, revising, editing, and publishing. Although the type of assignment may change the approach, my students know what type of class session a writing workshop day will be. Each activity is designed to take a class period of 45 minutes or less; these periods are usually a few days apart to allow time for the writing outside of class that is needed for the next stage. These days add an enjoyable diversity to our more structured literature and vocabulary classes which usually involve more teacher-centered activities.

PREWRITING: THE VERY BEGINNING

The idea behind the general assignment, a character analysis, for example, is introduced before prewriting begins. When reviewing our agenda for the next week, I might say:

> You'll see that on Friday we are beginning a piece of writing in response to a character in *The Crucible*. Choose one character from the play that interests you. Your homework for Friday is to know the character you will write about. You will be answering ques-

tions about the character in class on that day.

Prewriting is done during class on the same day the written assignment is given, requiring students to write immediately. The goals of the final paper are described in detail on the sheet so students can return to them later, but on this first day I discuss the general focus needed to begin prewriting. For clarification, the assignment can be written in stages, and I delineate requirements for each stage of the process.

Prewriting is completed on the assignment sheet so that the writer has everything needed to begin on a single page. My goal is to have my students leave class with a sufficient start so that determining a specific focus on their own is not so difficult. A series of general prompts initiate prewriting. Using about five prompts is best and easier to look at quickly in a class period. For example, in the character assignment, students might be asked to list the character they have chosen, character traits and motivation, something puzzling that the character does, a physical trait that is significant, a conflict that is important or confusing, or an interesting relationship with another character.

I always do prewriting with the class as a whole, reading each prompt aloud and pausing, circling their desks, checking to see that they are writing, answering individual questions, encouraging them to do more. Everyone writes quietly, and I can sense from the beginning those who may be having difficulty with the assignment. Sometimes I collect this sheet, but usually I prefer the students keep it to use for determining a focus for their paper.

If I sense that students are ready by the end of the period, the exercise can be concluded by asking them to write an idea for a preliminary (topic or thesis) sentence stating the focus of the paper. This may also be due in the next day or two. Either way, asking students to write during class provides a concrete start that makes beginning a first draft a more palatable experience.

HOW EACH STAGE IS USUALLY HANDLED

Managing Process Activities in the Classroom

1.	Prewriting-	class as a whole or individual brainstorming topic slips responded to by teacher & revised
2.	1st Draft-	response by writer
3.	2nd Draft-	response by writing partner
4.	3rd Draft-	response by teacher
5.	Editing Draft-	response by teacher or partner or both
6.	Final Draft-	response by writer evaluation by teacher

DETERMINING A SPECIFIC FOCUS

Before beginning their first draft, student writers need to create a focus. Invariably, prewriting has led some to wonderful, original topics that I would not have offered had I assigned them. However, I have learned from experience that some guidance is necessary to avoid problems that result from a focus that is too general or inadequate.

Depending on the assignment, I may ask students to write their ideas in a formal thesis statement form, or in a sentence that simply states the focus, such as, "I will be describing my grandfather reading as he sits on the back porch." I always collect these on a form that facilitates my reading and grading them. These sheets are completed before the student comes to class and collected at the beginning of the period.

The process of drafting and revising actually begins with these topic slips. I try to return them as soon as possible with my responses. Often, a large percentage will be returned with my re-

quest to revise, and writers will not receive full credit for this stage until their attempts at revision are successful. Student writers often begin with a topic idea that is incomplete or too shallow to culminate in a meaningful analysis. Sometimes a grueling process of revision occurs as a result of my demanding an acceptable topic. I will not tell students what to write, but I do encourage them to be more specific or in- depth.

STARTING: THE FIRST DRAFT

Once a focus has been established and goals for the assignment are clear, the students begin the drafting process on their own time. With the guidelines on the written assignment and my responses on their topic sheet, they should be ready to start. The first draft is due in class in a reasonable amount of time after I have returned the focus sheets. (Longer assignments may be broken up at this point. First draft of the introduction could be due.) I emphasize that this draft is *first* and not *rough* and although there may be mechanical errors, it must be legible. The first draft is responded to during class, but not by me. I initially used student peer responders with the first draft, but found that many papers were not ready for someone else's perusal, so now I have the writer look carefully at the first draft before anyone else does.

I may address the class as a whole and ask them to look for certain things in their own drafts, but usually I ask each writer to analyze his or her text at this stage by answering a few questions in writing, such as: Why did you choose this subject? What is the mood that you hope to create? This allows individuals to read and answer the questions at their own pace. It also gives me time to circulate and check to see that each student has a draft.

Giving credit for completed drafts is tricky in a large class without collecting them, but I am able to check quickly as I circulate the room, making note of who has nothing and who has only a partial draft. I do feel it is important to give credit for completing drafts as well as the final piece of writing in order to place value on the process as well as the product.

Questions for the writer at this early stage should reflect the High Order Concerns only: focus, tone, organization, and development. The questions should guide students' careful rereading of their own draft and often reinforce assignment priorities. We often conclude this activity by writing goals for what will be changed to improve the second draft. The vehicle for answering these questions could be a writing journal, or part of a portfolio, or on a sheet of paper that the student can keep. The responses and drafts may be collected, but the student will need both to continue with the paper. Allowing writers to use these written thoughts to continue their work reinforces the idea that the activity is designed to help them and is not done for the teacher. Both the first draft (labeled D1) and the question sheets are saved and turned in with the final draft, so the students know the teacher will be seeing them eventually.

I have learned to limit my involvement in the early stages of the paper. In fact, teachers who "correct" drafts are missing the benefits of waiting and also are encouraging more dependence on their input. Reading every draft of each student creates an unhealthy dependence on the teacher's comments. Writers need to learn to see ideas that need to be developed or confusing passages without the approval of the teacher. My students appreciate that they should make some effort before I see their work and know that they will have the opportunity to react to my responses before the final paper is evaluated.

One final note: there is always the concern that students may not take this stage seriously and come to class with a paper that is carelessly written, knowing that it will not be carefully scrutinized. The benefits of getting this fresh start outweigh my concern for the unmotivated at this point. It reinforces the idea that the students are writing for themselves and planning to revise—two key elements of the process approach. It is also less threatening; many students who are intimidated by writing find this approach more relaxing, and many need the time to put the basics down on paper and then add to them in a second draft.

REVISING: THE SECOND DRAFT

The second draft always involves some type of collaboration. Students are assigned a due date soon after the first draft is due and the same procedure of credit is applied. This time another student—a writing partner—will respond to the draft, as I circulate and check that they have completed both drafts. They must, of course, have both their first draft (labeled D1) and their second draft (D2) with them. Partnering can provide an opportunity for a varied audience, and questions may be raised that might not be otherwise. Writing groups can also be effective, but the variety of responses takes much longer. My goal is to have each writer get a complete response by the end of one class period, so using partners has proven to be the most efficient approach.

TRAINING PEER TUTORS

Over the years I have experimented with training students and pairing them, I have found the most success with pairing students with similar ability levels. I also sometimes allow the students to choose their own partners. This adds to their comfort level when sharing their writing, and it may make for a more pleasurable experience. On the other hand, if I am less concerned about student comfort and more about writing focus, I choose opposite-sex partners of similar ability. Pairing can vary with assignment as well. It can be beneficial for students to be paired with another writer with a similar topic, or one who holds a contrasting point of view. Students who do not have a draft completed on this day forfeit the advantage of working with a partner and are asked to write quietly on their draft during conferences.

A variety of methods may be used to conduct the conference, but students must be trained in some general guidelines before these will be effective:

Peer Conference Guidelines

1. Writer reads out loud as partner reads silently.
2. Partners sit beside each other with paper between them.
3. The writer holds the pen.
4. The tone of the conference should be respectful and positive.

The first rule that I feel strongly about is reading the paper out loud. The writer should read the paper aloud while the responder reads silently, with the paper in between them. In order to facilitate this, students need to sit next to each other, not across from each other. Sometimes getting students to move and to read aloud is the most difficult part of the training. Asking students to read their work to someone else requires them to make a commitment that handing a paper over does not make. Also, they frequently hear their words in a different way when they are read out loud, and more meaningful revision occurs as a result of what they hear.

Another priority is that we show respect to the writer. The tone of each conference should be thoughtful and positive. Students can be very critical, so sensitivity must be encouraged. Looking for the good qualities in a piece can reinforce what students know about good writing. Also, the writer has ownership; as a result, I ask partners not to mark anything on the writer's paper during a conference, and I don't either. Only the writer has the right to make changes. The writer should listen carefully to suggestions and write them down, but the writer may choose to disagree with what was suggested. I feel this writer-centered approach has a real psychological advantage. Young writers see their papers as their own work, not what they have been told to do. Ultimately, the writer alone has the responsibility.

Once partners are assigned and students understand the general rules, I try to determine how directive I need to be to lead the partners through a successful conference. Possibilities include specific questions for the partner to answer about the writer's paper or an open discussion of each of the four HOCs followed by the writer listing what was learned from the conference and what will be revised as a result. Another approach I sometimes use to facilitate meaningful discussion is to ask the writer to write down three questions before the conference to guide the partner's listening. (*Does the second paragraph make sense? How can I make the beginning more interesting? Do I give enough examples?*) This technique enables the writer to *direct* the conference.

While the partners are meeting, my role is to see that the rules of the writer-centered conference are being followed and to oversee everyone's progress. I listen to what is being said and try to get around to all partnerships. Student conferences can give the teacher meaningful feedback as to the progress of the assignment. Clarifications can be made to the class as a whole based on questions that arise in the partnerships.

Teachers who question the value of students' responses to each other can have students answer questions about the draft they have listened to, collect the drafts and question sheets, and evaluate the partner's written responses. I have found that students do well with this exercise, and I believe they make more of an effort with their writing knowing that a peer is going to be listening. Although it takes preparation, the single period that a partner conference takes is well worth the time. The training can be a benefit all year.

THE THIRD DRAFT: TEACHER RESPONSE

In order for the process to be given the proper emphasis, the teacher should respond to a draft at least once before it is turned in for final evaluation. By waiting until a later draft, I feel I am giving validity to the students' responses and encouraging less dependence on what I say. I usually collect the third draft, where there is still need for meaningful revision, and my role is not seen only as error-checker.

With a shorter assignment, I comment on HOCs and identify LOCs in the third draft. (An ideal approach is to respond to HOCs separately, then focus on LOCs in a later editing draft, but there is only time for this on major papers.) By giving helpful suggestions before evaluating the paper, I believe I have changed my students' perception of my role in the process—from critic to helper. While the teacher who spends hours writing on a final evaluation is also trying to help students become better writers, this approach is perceived as being less helpful because the grade has already been given.

If I am dealing with editing on this draft, too, I also identify any errors by underlining or circling (never correcting) them. The writer is responsible for correcting any errors in the paper.

Sometimes I put a check in the margin by a line that contains an error so the writer can identify it. These drafts are especially helpful to peruse when giving a paper a final evaluation, especially if problems were noted and ignored.

EDITING: A SEPARATE DRAFT

As mentioned earlier, separating the editing stage is crucial for students' understanding of writing as a process. A separate draft, preferably done on a computer, should be labeled as the editing draft. The draft can be collected by the teacher and returned on a day when there is time for clarification during class. Another effective method is to have students meet for an editing conference with the same writing partner. The paper still is read out loud by the writer, but both should scrutinize the paper for errors only (LOCs). If the writer misses a correction, the partner can interrupt to point it out. If I have indicated a problem on the draft that students do not recognize, they can work together to determine what the problem is or use the resource materials in the room to help them. For anyone who has attempted to teach traditional grammar or spelling and seen little transference to writing, this class session can be a rewarding experience. Students who have a context for concern about mechanics will discuss them meaningfully.

PUBLISHING: THE FINAL STAGE

The final draft should reflect the sum of effort that is made in the stages of the process before it. Students should feel pride in their end result. Publishing parties, where a celebration takes place on the day the paper is due and writers share their final products, can reinforce this pride. If time does not allow for taking another class period on the due date, I ask students to answer a few questions on a cover sheet (see this page). These may reflect on the content of the paper as well as their revision process and frequently add insight to the paper itself.

When I collect the final drafts, my students turn in everything for my perusal—all the question sheets and drafts—so these must be arranged carefully. I evaluate the final copy with the use of a rubric with categories that emphasize the HOCs and LOCs and our goals for the assignment. Then everything is placed in each student's Working Portfolio where they will record further reactions. Taking time to look back and reflect on their work from the beginning enables students to see their own thinking process and to learn from it. Another meaningful technique is to have students revise the final copy after it has been graded so that they have a clean copy for their final portfolios. This reinforces the idea that writing continues to be an on-going process even after the so-called last draft has been completed. If students are interested, these revised final copies can be used in a class publication.

CONCLUSION

The use of the process approach can be intimidating at first, but it is possible to incorporate it successfully within a demanding secondary English curriculum. With preparation, workshop techniques like peer conferencing, reading out loud, and self reflection can occur meaningfully within a single period. While addressing the different stages during class does take more time than assigning a paper and collecting it two weeks later, there can be time for this work within traditional curricula. For instance, our high school's English curriculum has fewer literature requirements than it did 20 years ago because of the increased emphasis on composition. In addition, we probably finalize

fewer papers in a year as a result of requiring the process, although my students do much more writing. As Jeff commented, "The one thing I found the most helpful in my writing was the time we spent on each paper. Instead of just going from one paper to another quickly, we spent time on each paper, which made it more helpful."

As for my role, I don't believe I have to spend more time with the papers outside of class than I did before, and I feel the time that I spend with the drafts is much more meaningful. I do collect and respond to at least two drafts instead of just the final one. However, I see more immediate results from my comments in the earlier drafts, and the writing has improved so much by the final draft that there are fewer weaknesses to identify, so grading papers is more rewarding than frustrating. I cannot imagine ever returning to the traditional method of teaching writing after experiencing what the process approach to writing has done for me and for my students.

**FINAL CHARACTER ANALYSIS
COVER SHEET**

Your Name _____

Your Character _____

Your Writing Partner(s)_____

Read all of the questions first. Consider your answers carefully. Answer concisely in complete sentences.

1. What conflict or dilemma (involving your character) interested you the most? Why?
2. What insight into the character did you gain from writing this paper? Did any of your attitudes change?
3. Describe your organization (the order of discussion and paragraphing). Did this change as you revised?
4. How did responses of others affect your writing? Explain.
5. If you could continue working on this piece, what would you do?

For Further Thought

1. Contrast Carney's attitude of compromise with Nancie Atwell's attitude in "Making Time" (chapter 2, pp. 55–66). For example, they seem to see the allocation of time for writing in very different terms. What other differences do you see?

2. What do you think of Carney's schedule for writing? Is it realistic? Familiar? What kinds of compromises has she made in having her students adhere to this schedule?

3. Consider the HOCs and LOCs that Carney describes in the essay. Match up this scheme with what Nancy Sommers says about priorities for the teacher responding to student writing. Think, too, about the prospect of training students to become good responders to each other's work. What does Carney say on this subject? Are Sommers's principles for responding equally applicable to student responders?

4. Think of some of the contrasts or dichotomies that Carney mentions in her essay—individual needs/group needs, theory/practice, teacher-centered/student-centered, regimentation/spontaneity. Choose one of these and write about it, paying special attention to the idea of compromise.

5. Carney is a practicing high school teacher. The other authors in this chapter are (or were) college teachers. Do you think that makes a difference? Does she have more or less authority to speak on the subject? What, if any, do you think are the essential differences between teaching writing on the high school and college levels?

Application 4.4:
Adapting the Writing Workshop

> . . . today, the process approach is commonly accepted by the secondary community and is expected in writing instruction, even though its inherent spontaneity continues to appear incongruous with the short daily chunks of time and the demands implicit in the secondary classroom. (Barbara Carney, p. 179)

Barbara Carney recognizes the tension between the process of writing as it is practiced by individual students and what she calls the "realities" of secondary teaching: a segmented school day that leaves only one period for English, the demands of the rest of the English curriculum, the intrusion of the rest of the school culture on one's classroom, the number of students one has in a class, and the widely differing abilities of those students. Carney's response to this tension is to "compromise"—that is, to strike a balance between the demands of the individual (spontaneity, free choice) and those of the school regime (predictability, constraints on options).

At first glance, Carney's approach seems very different from that of Nancie Atwell. In "Making Time" (pp. 55–66), Atwell clearly favors spontaneity and choice:

> Writers need choices. They need to take responsibility for their writing: their own materials, subjects, audiences, genres, pacing, purposes, number of drafts, and kinds of changes to be made, if any. When we invite student writers to choose, they write for all the reasons literate people anywhere engage as writers—to recreate happy

> *times, work through sad times, discover what they know about a sub-*
> *ject and learn more, convey and request information, apply for jobs,*
> *parody, petition, play, argue, apologize, advise, make money. (p. 59)*

Choices like these, when left to the student, seem to preclude assignments in the traditional sense. With this level of freedom, the constraints imposed by an assignment have dropped away, and students need to reimpose them through the choices they make on their own. In theory, then, genre and subject, once chosen, have their own built-in constraints, as do situational factors like audience. But the workshop offers students more than just the freedom to choose what they write. Deadlines are also under the student's control, as are other aspects of the process, like the decision to revise. Thus, it appears that Atwell relies heavily on students' willingness to accept the intrinsic rewards of writing, without the extrinsic pressure of an assignment. They write, she says, "for all the reasons literate people anywhere engage as writers."

At first glance, it looks like a free-for-all, although a second glance and a thorough reading of *In the Middle* dispel that idea. Workshop sessions have a definite structure, and behavioral expectations are quite clear, laid out in a series of rules and procedures. Indeed, these structural features of the workshop provide the conditions that enable student choice. In this respect, it is not so different from the more traditional assignment approach that has been presented in the preceding applications. What differs is the level of choice and the degree to which the writing process is treated in an individualized manner. And because there are different kinds of workshops, some more restrictive than the model that Atwell first posed nearly a decade ago, the phrase "writing workshop" can mean many things nowadays. If it helps, you can think of a line, or scale of relativity, with a highly constrained assignment approach on one left and a write-whatever-you-like-on-your-own-schedule approach on the right. Practices start to look like a "workshop" as they move toward the right.

Constrained Assignments ------------------------ "Free" Writing Workshop

This suggests that the writing workshop does not have to be an all-or-nothing proposition, any more than reading workshop does—that, in fact, any approach is an attempt to deal with the tension that Carney described at the start of this application. Recall, for example, the modifications of reading workshop described in chapter 2. In regard to writing workshop, Teresa Tande (whom you met on pp. 70–71) adopts an approach that is very reminiscent of Nancie Atwell, but she does so for only part of the school year. Teresa actually begins the school year with a more traditional assignment approach and then introduces the freer workshop setting when she knows her eighth graders better and when she feels they are ready for it. Betty Van Vugt, whom you also met in chapter 2, uses a modified assignment approach with her sixth and seventh graders, though there are workshop-like features to her system: the rearranged classroom, lots of writing time in class, and individualized help. On our scale, Teresa would be on the right, though not all the time; Betty would be toward the left but moving toward the right. Barbara Carney would be to the left of Betty, whereas Atwell herself would be to the right of Teresa.

Right and *left*, of course, have no political connotations here. Nor should they carry with them any special sense of approval. All these teachers have made choices based on what they see as the needs and capabilities of their students. All can legitimately call their work "process" oriented, for there is a heavy emphasis on drafting and revising. And all are experimenters, teachers who are always adapting as students and situations change. Perhaps more importantly, they themselves are on a journey of change. They read, they think, they try new things. Where they wind up on our scale is less important than the fact they are continually fashioning and refashioning their teaching practice. This is not to deny the real differences between the assignment and workshop approaches, but it does suggest that the best model for a beginning teacher is not this or that teacher, but instead the teacher who is alert to new ideas and who is ready to change for the good of students.

Some Things to Consider About the Workshop and Assignment Approaches

1. Think about your English teachers, as you did in chapter 1. Which of them used an approach that was most like the workshop (farthest to the right on the scale)? Which was farthest to the left? How would you rate their effectiveness?

2. Learn more about writing workshop. The best source is the second edition of Atwell's *In the Middle*. See "For Further Reading" at the end of chapter 1 (p. 80). Pay close attention to the structure of writing workshop. Do you think all these rules are necessary? Why or why not?

3. Timing seems to be a big issue. Atwell begins both reading and writing workshop on the first day of school, but Teresa and Betty disagree. They want to wait until they know students better and can judge if students are "ready." What do you think?

4. What is the essence of writing workshop? If the sliding scale idea has any validity, the term *workshop* could be rather amorphous—it could denote a classroom that uses any (or all) of a group of related classroom procedures. Atwell would probably object. What do you think? What makes an approach a legitimate workshop?

5. Evaluate the assignment and workshop approaches. What are their strengths and weaknesses? Which do you think you, as a beginning teacher, will adopt? Or would you favor a compromise between the two approaches?

6. If you have been asked by your instructor to write "The Assignment Assignment" at the end of this chapter (pp. 210–213), evaluate your own assignment according to the principles of the workshop approach. Where on the sliding scale would you locate your own work?

Teaching Poetry Writing to Adolescents: Models and Teaching Designs

Joseph Tsujimoto

Joseph Tsujimoto teaches middle school students at the Punahou School in Honolulu. Working in the tradition of Kenneth Koch, a pioneer in the teaching of poetry writing, Tsujimoto wrote Teaching Poetry Writing to Adolescents *(1988) in which he presents the work of his seventh and eighth graders and then elaborates on his teaching practice. Basically, he works from two principles: that students should be exposed to a wide range of good poetry, and that they can then be expected, with the aid of a sequence of demanding assignments, to join the tradition by writing good poetry of their own. What is striking about Tsujimoto is how demanding he is, how he expects (even assumes) that his middle school kids can write excellent verse. And, as you will see, they live up to his expectations.*

"Models and Teaching Designs" is the second chapter of Teaching Poetry Writing to Adolescents *(Urbana, IL: NCTE/ERIC, 1988). It is reprinted with permission.*

The Potter

The poet is like a potter
shaping and molding words onto
paper
He spins the wheel,
pressing detail and action
into crevices of phrases
and baking feeling into every line.
　　　　　—Tracie Tsukano (grade 8)

Nothing deadens a work quicker than weak feelings. Strong feelings, on the other hand, enhance a work, even if we were to read it in a foreign tongue. For example, my friend Larry Traynor, who used to moonlight singing at weddings and funerals, played for me a recording of his reading of Wallace Stevens's "River of Rivers in Connecticut." Although I didn't understand the poem at the time (it was intellectually foreign to me), I was nonetheless moved by the rhythm of the lines, the sounds of the words, the powerful feelings in Larry's voice, and I came to love the work almost as much as Larry did. So it happens with our students. Because we are moved, they will be moved—they who are experts in reading us.

CHOOSING EXAMPLES

Much depends, then, on what we choose to read as examples. I use the following three student poems, as well as others, to teach extended metaphor and to introduce the tradition of writing poems about poems, poetry, and the poet.

Vulture in a Poet

The poet sits and waits for an idea
　　like a vulture in a dead tree
waiting for a fair chance

His gripped hands nervously tapping
　　the desk like a vulture pacing the sky

At last an idea strikes as he grasps
　　his paper
like a vulture diving for his feast his
　　mouth opened wide
　　　　　—Brandy Spoehr (grade 7)

The Poem in the River

As a river flows
so flows a poem

into every
crack and crevice

rearranging soil
inventing a new geography

it changes the
face of the Earth

—Kale Braden (grade 8)

hands

He creates
with a mind from above
taking others beyond
the present world
with his brush
and his pen

The rainbow falls from his hands
splashing unending color
shattering reality—
a rock thrown through a picture window

in his mind
in his painting
in his hands
    The sun explodes

—unknown student (grade 10)

In presenting this assignment—in presenting every assignment, in fact—I read numerous student examples: many that demonstrate the rules for extended metaphor and many, like "hands," that break or change the rules in wonderful ways.

Student poems often make the best examples; their impact is large. Mention to the class a poet's grade level and name, and you will spark immediate interest, rousing curiosity, attuning (it seems evident now) the listeners critical ears. Not only do the students share with the poet similar experiences and sensibilities, but more importantly, the young poet shows other students the potential quality of work that *they* themselves can produce. On the other hand, if students know that a work is authored by an adult (because they have been told or because it is evident through sophistication of the language or ideas), the work will appear beyond the students' reach. Often, what makes the adult work inaccessible is not so much its language or ideas (which we can lead them to understand), as it is

the impossibility of their "duplicating" such work. Skills aside, they have little interest in wanting to. (This is not to say I don't use any adult examples at all. I do. The point is, they are not my primary examples.)

Finally, as we accumulate more and more examples of the students' best work, we help them establish for themselves their own literary tradition, to be used in helping them teach themselves and to become a standard for evaluating new student work.

OPTIONS AND LIMITATIONS

Paradoxically, giving students *many* examples, by both students and adults, can encourage the writing of original poetry. Originality can best be realized through freedom of choice, which becomes meaningful only when one is aware of many options. So I give students as many examples as I can, not just to fire their imaginations with good works, but to increase their awareness of options as well.

First, the sheer number of examples makes students feel like emotional kaleidoscopes. Second, the redundancy illustrates the rules for extended metaphor and, especially, the exceptions to the rules—creating more options.

In the end, freedom of choice really means freedom to select one's limitations. That is, in the act of choosing for oneself, one simultaneously imposes limitations upon oneself. Though, at first, the teacher imposes the larger limitation ("Write an Extended Metaphor poem on poetry, poems, or the poet"), the student later imposes the specific ones. Allison Higa (grade 8) said, "I think I'll describe the poet as a circus clown, remembering what he looks like and how he acts," and wrote the following:

Clown

Clowns are supposed to be happy.
They're always funny, so they must be happy,
at least most of the time.

A poet's words are like a clown's makeup.
A wide mouth painted to smile, a stark white
face, stars for eyes.
His clothing is hilarious: gigantic, floppy saddle
shoes, bum suits or polka dots. A fake burning
building, a net without a center, a midget car.
These are the things he's based his act on.
Some sad, mostly humorous.
He leaves a feeling behind, a feeling you can
remember for a long time.

Gina Pagliaro (grade 8) stated, "I think I'll make a poem describing poetry as technology, using three similes—a technician, an operator, and a machine—rolled into one," before she wrote this poem:

Technical Similarities

The poet is like a technician
Mending and repairing
Words that are used
Omitting the trite.

The poet is attached to his work
As the telephone operator is
   often entangled.

The poem is like a machine
Walking, talking, showing action.

Do you know what I mean?

As Ann E. Berthoff (1981) says, it is precisely the choosing of limits—amalgamating, differentiating, classifying, comparing, discarding, and so forth—that constitutes the composing process. And as Rollo May (1975) comments, it is the struggle with limits that is actually the source of creative production. Sam Onaga (grade 8) struggles directly with the limits of his own experience as a writer who wants to make fine things, conscious of what works against him as well as for him.

The Writer

He sits
In front of a typewriter
Typing about:
Plot

Flow
Conflict
Character
Drama
Style
Effect
Doing his job.

Other times he is writing about
John Doe
His dark past
His great future
His tears
His smiles
His good and evil
About John's inside.

It is John's inside
That so moves us,
That dazzles
And shines.
And takes out of the dark
A part of his maker
A part of *his* story.

More important than students' knowing extended metaphor is their grasping, more strongly with each assignment, the pivotal notion of originality. For one thing, they know that originality ultimately precludes their imitating the poetry already created. Now they must discover for themselves that it *can be*. In a sense, we confine the students in a prison whose walls they must shatter. In this way they emancipate their own minds, realizing further the enormous creative power within their hands.

DERIVATIONS

Every original work, in one way or another, is derived from other works. T. S. Eliot (1950) makes this clear in his essay "Tradition and the Individual Talent." The writer speaks not only with the voice of his own age but also with the voices of his eminent predecessors. Eliot's "April is the cruellest month" recalls Chaucer's "Whan that Aprill with his shoures soote," which also "begot" the springtimes of Nashe, Herrick, and Hopkins; and as the structuralists point out, Chaucer's spring also begot the winter in Hardy's "The Darkling Thrush," as well as the fall in Keats's "To Autumn." A seminal work implies not only its opposite but also every other possible variant to which the seminal work can be transformed. Thereafter, each derivative work itself can become a seminal work, spawning its own variations. In this way, Eliot says, the past directs the present, while the present, the truly original derivation, alters, ever so slightly, the entire tradition, which at any moment in time is complete.

Traditions abound, from rock music to stamps to textbooks. This book, for example, is derived in part from Kenneth Koch's *Wishes, Lies, and Dreams* (1980) and *Rose, Where Did You Get That Red?* (1974). In both, Koch demonstrates the dramatic effectiveness of modeling as a tool in teaching elementary school children to write poetry. As a derivative work, this book differs from Koch's in its assumptions, offering theoretical underpinnings—alternative opinions and strategies—geared to the teaching of adolescents.

Now let me make a promise beforehand.

Most teachers, as you know, are always on the lookout for new ideas in order to improve their teaching. In so doing, they collect ideas found in publications (which often report the ideas found in other publications); they borrow ideas from other teachers (who in turn have borrowed ideas from still others); and, of course, they invent and share their own ideas—equally without thought to attribution.

This is especially true when teachers hunt for, find, or invent writing assignments. I think many teachers instinctively view assignments as anonymous ballads that have been passed from town to town, passed down through generations by word of mouth, modified over and again by the many voices that sing them. Like ballads, assignments are sources that belong to the community, practiced and perpetuated by its experts for the benefit of its people. The teachers' concern is: Does it work for me? Will it work now? If not now, when? How? All that I can promise is that I will note derivative sources where I can.

All the poems in this book are also derivations. Of these, there are three kinds. First is the derivation "born" of a specific poem. For example, the Self Portrait poem (or definition poem) springs from Wallace Stevens's "Thirteen Ways of Looking at a Blackbird." However, instead of an animal as its subject (as in Stevens's work) or instead of an object as its subject (as Koch directs his children to choose), the students are asked to turn Stevens's strategy on themselves. Like Stevens's blackbird, the presence of the self is manifest in each stanza, which can be "seen" as a unique sketch on a transparency. Like Stevens's blackbird, the self is defined by the total number of stanzas, which can be "seen" as the total number of transparencies laid one atop another, resulting in a complex symbol. Red-haired Eric Meyer (grade 7) shows us how he sees himself.

Self Portrait

A dark snowy day.
The pine trees whisper
As he looks up at them.
He catches a word about loneliness,
He tramples back to his house.

He peers at an ant
Crawling on a flower
He tries to decipher
The pattern of its dance.

He whistles as he walks.
The wind
Rises around
Him

Telling him
To be quiet.
It wonders
How he could dare
Interrupt
The song
The crickets play
At this hour.

The birds fly past him
Looking at him
Up in the magnolia tree
And wonder if he's one
Of their kind.

He runs into his room
To play with his kitten
He leaves as soon as he comes,
He looks back
And sees it licking itself
With a confused face.

Snow
Covered, as far as can be seen.
There are two things moving
A red bird
A small figure
Kicking the snow.

He is such a brainy
Pest, he hears his sister
Say to his mom.

He sees himself
Through the gates of clocks
A careful one
Stepping through time stones
Cautiously.

As he studies
He is of five minds
Combined in one.

He stays still
As he holds up
A can of seed
A bird comes
And feeds
From his hands
As if he were a statue.

In a telescope
He sees stars being born
And dying . . .
He wonders if it is
The stars' way
of telling him

What his life
Will be.

Second is the derivation "born" of a traditional type of poetry (e.g., poems that embody a traditional form or that address traditional topics or themes). For example, Chris Peters (grade 7) talks about love, using the sonnet form.

Love, a Feeling

Love is a feeling between a mixed pair
Upon first sight or after a long, long
    time
It creates a spirit, a world to share
Like a silent person, speaking in
    mime
Love, like wine, must age to taste just
    right
The vines of both bear fruit of varied
    hue.
While wine makes its choice, either
    red or white
Love cannot be limited to so few.
Love, like an orchestra, brings
    together
People of many different sections
It ties all voices one to another
Through the emotion of shared affection
Let love of two or more be justly
    earned
And not diminished by other things
    yearned.

Third is the derivation "born" of the unique literary traditions that the individual has consciously or unconsciously assimilated. For example, the following surrealistic poem (by an unknown eighth grader) was no doubt founded on his or her understanding of fairy tales, fantasies, science fiction, comics, the drug culture, cartoons, music, and movies.

Penguin

The skunk opened the door to the sewing
machine and got out.
He was pink.
He flew to the attendant, took the gas hose
and emptied his tank with ethyl lipstick.
He spilled it on his shabby purple socks,

which got dizzy and spaced out.
He looked down just as they burst into flames.
Immediately he took out his radio to block himself
from the smoke, so that he wouldn't turn into an
Infection.
Desperate for air, he took a sniff of fumes.
He got sick on an orange Arab standing
Next to him.
It had the license plate GLUE.
The ethyl stopped flowing so he pumped it back
into the attendant.
Out of his pocket aquarium, he took his
Fur credit cards. He gave them to the Blue-Gray
Shirt,
Who burned and then snorted them.
He wheeled around and said "Crazy Tuna."
The skunk then inked the shirt's face,
Jumped on his sewing machine,
And trucked back to the Sears Indian Reservation.

In general, there are only two kinds of writing: derivations, which draw on traditions, and imitations, which are bland copies. Sadly, most of the time our students submit the latter to us in bulk.

MAKING ASSIGNMENTS

In another approach aimed at getting students to write, three simple characteristics of all poems are identified.

1. They have a subject.
2. They have some kind of emotional impact.
3. They are constructed of verbal strategies to which we can give meanings.

If we turn the above statements into questions, they act as a rubric that can help us generate any number of possible writing assignments.

1. What, to you, is the poem about?
2. What is the poem's impact on you?
3. What strategies in the poem allow you to give meanings to it?

Simply take any poem that you truly admire, and identify one or two of its outstanding characteristics according to the rubric. I never apply more than two questions to the poem when making an assignment. Often I apply only one.

For example, I have always admired Whitman's "The Compost." Among other things, I like the idea that life is born of dead things. In answering the first question—what is the poem about?—I discovered this was my "seminal" poem for a category called Paradox Poems (or poems about apparent contradictions). Then I hunted up Robinson Jeffers's "The Great Explosion" (where, oddly, the root of all things is "faceless violence"); Blake's "The Tiger" (why did God, who made the lamb, also make the ferocious tiger?); and my friend Paul Wood's unpublished poem "Attraction" (where "Love is a great garlic sandwich"). Here was the beginning of my repertoire. Soon after, these poems became secondary examples, read after the poems written by students. The following example was written by Keli Sato (grade 7).

Behind Her Eyes

Though girls do say that they
hate boys,
we know that isn't so.
For every time the boy goes by
we see their red cheeks glow.

Still yet the boys confront her,
and look her in the eyes,
and ask her, "You do like him,"
and she says, "No." and lies.

But yet when girls confront her
she shares her secrets dear,
and at a slumber party
they're spread for all to hear.

She told them to keep a secret
this was her happy dream,
but telling them *this* secret
insures they'll spill the beans.

The news shot out like wildfire
as fast as beans will grow

but she actually wanted this to
  happen,
she wanted him to know.

So what's the whole big secret?
Why did she wait days?
Why not get it over with—
a woman has her ways.

Often we work the other way around when making assignments. Starting off with a literary concept that we would like our students to know, we then hunt about for examples. Making assignments this way is often more difficult than making assignments from poems we already love. Sometimes we can't find the examples that fulfill our purpose, especially if what we want them to know is a verbal strategy. We are always looking for the ideal example that will do its job with ruthless speed, where a point of literary understanding is the preeminent point the poem must demonstrate. So we find ourselves talking about parts of poems or secondary issues. Let me explain.

I wanted my students to understand that poems often operate according to various sorts of logic other than chronology or linearity, when moving from one set of words to another. In hunting for examples, I encountered two seemingly insurmountable problems. First, poets move between words in innumerable ways; second, the most striking aspects of the poems I found were the subjects and the emotional impact, not the poets' way of advancing their ideas. These problems, though, would foil my intentions, deflecting my students' attention from what I wanted them to know, or would suggest to them that my first concern was not the poem itself. The only solution to these particular problems was to invent my own poem "Snow Tracks" (the Circle Poem assignment), from which students derived their own poems.

My point is *not* that we write our own poetry examples for the verbal strategies we want to teach. I am saying

instead that it is easier making assignments with poems we already know and enjoy, many having dominant verbal strategies that we can lead students to appreciate.

ORGANIZING ASSIGNMENTS

The three characteristics common to all poems suggest categories under which we can organize poetry assignments. I organized the following assignments under the characteristic that seemed to dominate the students' attention.

1. *Subject*
   Change Poem
   List of Twelve
   Animal Poem
   Visual Response Poem
   Form Poem
   Self Portrait
   Invitation Poem

2. *Emotional Impact*
   Memory Poem
   Bitterness Poem
   Paradox Poem
   Awe Poem
   Teacher Poem
   End Poem

3. *Verbal Strategies*
   Found Poem
   Two-Word Poem
   Circle Poem
   Transformation Poem
   Extended Metaphor

Organizing assignments in this manner can help in planning a unit, a quarter, or a semester of teaching. Depending on the time we have and what our students already know, we can choose and order our assignments easily for our own ends. My goal is to teach the students as much as I can within a quarter, so that they have at least twenty poems to make into poetry books. My students do little more than listen to poetry, write poetry, and read poetry to the class. (Actually, they write a total of twenty-six poems. I have excluded from this text nine of the more conventional assignments, like the haiku, sonnets, and poems written in response to music.)

Another approach to organizing poetry assignments suggests incremental teaching: the Found Poem can come first because it focuses on lining, spacing, and other fundamental conventions; the Two-Word Poem follows, focusing on similitude; next come the Circle Poem, based on associative progression, the Change Poem, employing chronological leaping, and the Transformation Poem, using diction as a means of expressing the transmutation of one thing into another. That is, one could rationalize various logical progressions for the assignments—as I do, and intend, for the teaching of craft. Yet, I know, too, that learning an art, as opposed to a craft, transcends block-by-block learning.

To be honest, I am not sure that my students fully see the connections among the techniques that they initially practice. What I do know, however, is that they are wonderfully befuddled, disoriented, puzzled, and bemused by the singularity of the assignments and the peculiarity of their teacher. They know from the outset that they are embarking on something new—a trip whose each step can never be anticipated, like the trip we ideally take when experiencing the finest poems.

As when students read a fine poem, and we gain satisfaction in their discovering an original meaning for a single part—we are satisfied with the understanding that they do manifest when they are deeply engaged in writing their own poetry. More important, then, than ordering assignments like building blocks is maintaining that heightened sense of wonder, oddness, beauty, challenge, and excitement that will empower them to step over the edge.

PRESENTING ASSIGNMENTS

For many teachers the presentation of an assignment amounts to little more than announcing its directives. If they do not also provide guidance during revision, the writing assignment becomes a test, whether the test is overnight, over the weekend, or over the semester.

At the very minimum, as I pointed out earlier, we must expose the students to as many examples as possible, to make them aware of their options. There are times when reading examples alone is sufficient preparation, as with assignments that focus on feelings or on the subject of the poem. For Bitterness Poems, the examples, the angry reading I sometimes give the class, and the comments I make aloud to myself (about insensitivity, cruelty, and so forth) make the assignment clear. For other assignments, it is often necessary to provide additional preparation as well. These instances, obviously, are determined by the nature of the assignment. For Two-Word Poems, which focus on unusual similarities, students first play a word association game, exercising their associative skills.

Discussion is of great importance. This involves more than fielding questions about the assignment and forewarning students of the difficulties others have experienced before them. It should also involve leading them to discover the strategy you want them to exploit, and sharing ideas and opinions, anecdotes and stories, which are often the most interesting parts of the presentation.

The following illustrates the kind of thinking I exercised—the preparatory thought necessary for me—when preparing the presentation for the Awe Poem assignment. Let me say, right away, that the assignment did not succeed as well as I hoped, I think because I was overconfident about my stories and examples and so did not follow through with student brainstorming and freewriting (for homework) and in-class defining, which I initially intended them to do (see below).

> First, I will give the students a copy of Keats's "On First Looking into Chapman's Homer" and lead them to what Keats had felt. Then I think I'll tell them my experience in seeing a scene from *Lawrence of Arabia* or *Amadeus* (maybe show them a tape?). Or maybe I will recount the first time I went to Yankee Stadium, when I saw Mickey Mantle hit a home run in the bottom of the ninth with a man on first. (He hit the ball on an ascending line, striking the fancy iron facade of the overhanging eaves of the top deck, which circled three-quarters of the ballpark—and I will tell them what I felt when the ball struck and the whole stadium rang like a gong with the vibrating iron. Bong!) On the subject of awesome power, I will then read W. S. Merwin's "Leviathan" and follow up with Ishmael's meditation on the mysterious head of the sperm whale. (I put that head before you. Read it if you can.) Or perhaps I should leap over that to Macbeth's "tomorrow" speech, first telling them the story in short (preparing them nicely for the play when we study it in the third quarter). Do I then dare read them the opening of *Paradise Lost*, ending with Milton's awesome promise: to "justify the ways of God to men"? I'm tempted. In any case, I'll have God appear out of the whirlwind, reading parts of Job, who not only heard God speak, but *saw*!
>
> For homework, they will brainstorm all the instances in which they ever felt awe, freewriting a half-page on three of these experiences. The next day in class they will freewrite a definition for *awe*, which they can share with each other without my input.
>
> Then I will tell them to write an Awe Poem (assignment number 13) based on one of their freewritings. After they revise their "final" drafts, I can have the poems copied and use them as my primary examples.

REVISION

> Revision means re-seeing, re-visioning, hence re-thinking one's thoughts, over and again, to discover and clarify final meaning: the What-to-write and the How-to-write-it.
> —Joseph I. Tsujimoto (1984, 52)

Most student writings are egregiously flawed because students, never having been taught, do not know how to revise their work. Revision, for most students, is nothing more than tedious recopying, the penalty exacted for incorrect spelling, punctuation, and grammar. Revision, in this sense, yields little or no real improvement in their writing.

The game the students try to play is Get-it-right-the-first-time-through. The way they do that is to get, first of all, a good idea, as though *getting* good ideas means plucking them out of a tree. But (often at the last moment) pluck them they do—out of the proverbial Tree of Superficiality. With this as their modus operandi, is it any wonder that their writing lacks originality? That their writing fails to improve from one week to the next or throughout a semester?

The way we can help students become better writers is to cultivate in them the *capacity to suspend closure on the selection of a problem*. We can do this by showing them the workable options—the various revisionary operations—that allow for genuine reseeing, that will lead them to problems worth addressing, problems that they themselves have discovered. Obviously, then and only then are the problems worth solving, worthy of the commitment that good writing demands.

The following revisionary options are variations on three of the eleven strategies I listed in "Re-Visioning the Whole" (Tsujimoto 1984).

Partner Revision

As Peter Elbow points out in *Writing with Power*, revision is most easily learned by working on someone else's writing. Free of the writer's preconceptions and biases for the poem, the reviser has an easier time making changes in the poem. That is, revising other people's work nurtures in the reviser the cold calculation necessary when reseeing, judging, and recasting their own work.

After exchanging drafts, parners revise the poems, on a separate page, as if the drafts were their own. What students want in return, I suggest, is not necessarily a second draft superior to the original, but a second draft that is markedly different from the original, that allows them to resee their work meaningfully. For it is in acknowledging, comparing, judging, and choosing among alternatives that the students learn how to improve their work.

In order to ensure second drafts that are markedly different from originals, I often assign partner revision in combination with revising by varying the audience, the speaker, the purpose, or the form of discourse. Or, if a particular area of concern arises, I will tell the students to revise their partners' work by focusing their attention on, perhaps, lining, spacing, and making stanzas, or on their suggesting new directions that the poem can take.

Students benefit not only from revising others' work and from the feedback gained through their partners' revisions, but also, as they have told me in their journals, from their partners' original drafts. They learn new vocabulary, new strategies of organization and possibilities of style, and bold new attitudes of tone and voice.

Revising by Group Feedback

The following approach is a modification of Elbow's revision groups. Students read their poetry twice to their group of four or five students. After the first reading, listeners write, on a scrap of paper, sentences in response to the following two questions: What do you think is the poem's central idea? What emotion, if any, does the poem arouse in you? After the second reading, the listeners write in response to two further questions: What words and phrases stuck in your mind because of their effectiveness? What would you work on if the poem were yours? Then the listeners give the author feedback orally before handing him or her their written responses. Since the responses are not threatening, emphasizing their subjectivity and demanding no esoteric knowledge of criticism, both the writer and listeners are disarmed by the positive nature of the comments.

Later, the authors can focus the group's attention by asking their own questions. By this time they know the kind of feedback that is needed, and suspect or sense where the poem may be weak.

Circle Revision

First, writers number their lines and attach a blank page to their original poem. Second, seated in a circle, they pass their originals to the reader on the left, who responds by choosing lines, by number, to revise on the attached page. Third, since everyone will not complete the work simultaneously, readers who finish early are to exchange papers with other students who have also completed their first revisions. The process continues in this manner, with each student working at a comfortable pace, until the class has produced multiple feedback for each poem.

After the initial exchange, subsequent readers also have the responsibility of responding to the alternative lines suggested by previous readers. If readers agree with the alternatives, they write "Yes." If they disagree, they can write "Keep Original," or they can write another alternative line.

Guidelines for Revision

I focus the students' attention on three areas of concern, sometimes separately, sometimes in combination. In the first area, *diction*, I suggest that students make verbs more vivid and forceful, make nouns more specific or precise, replace clichés and trite statements with statements that express the unique experience conveyed in the poem, and change dull, abstract statements into sensual "pictures," using imagery or tropes.

Regarding the second area, *compression*, I instruct students to delete redundant or ineffective words, to delete words that do not contribute information or that overload lines, to delete irrelevancies that dilute emotional impact, and to replace word groups with shorter expressions that do the same job with greater economy.

In the third area of revision, *development and extension*, students are to add words that supply the *who, where, when, how, why, whose,* or *which* where necessary for clarity and in places where ambiguity seems counterproductive to the poem's overall scheme; to add words at important points that seem to beg elaboration; and to add words or stanzas to the end of the poem, extending its possibilities and perhaps making the poem more original.

As with other feedback used for revision, none of the alternatives need be adopted. It is more important that writers be directed to areas that they themselves can improve, areas, for example, that inspire unanimous or controversial responses.

EVALUATION

> I wonder if you wanted to address the subject of poetry evaluation. Too subjective? Too banal?!!
> —Richelle Fujioka (teacher, high school)

> Would you consider touching this tough problem? How much does the teacher advise, suggest to the poet about "lining"? . . . In short, how much does the teacher "tamper" with the poems through pointed questions? . . . Indeed, 'tis a ticklish question.
> —Nellie McGloughlin (teacher, grades 5–8)

The teachers' questions are these: *How* should the teacher evaluate student poetry? *How much* should the teacher advise the students? As I imply throughout this book, I can only volunteer how one teacher goes about this work. Let me answer the questions this way.

First, the image of poetry, when it is thought of at all, tends to be perverted in two ways: through the belief that it is less than what it is and through the belief that it is more than what it is. At the first extreme, poetry (like art in general) is shoved into the "creativity corner" by many administrators who pretend to champion its importance at awards assemblies and parent-teacher meetings. In general, it is deemed (again like the other arts) a divine gift given to the few, an idiosyncratic endeavor, or a frivolous waste of time. In English, not to mention the other disciplines, thinking that poetry writing is exclusively, and pejoratively, a creative endeavor can lead to the belief that the "more scholarly" endeavor of essay writing requires no creativity, as if creativity were not the chief cause of the first-rate essay or first-rate thinking. This negatively affects the way the essay is perceived by students and taught by teachers.

At the other extreme, where the perversion of poetry may be equally damaging, is the belief that poetry is somehow more precious than the other arts, more precious than music and painting, more precious than dance and drama, more precious than its cousins the short story, the personal narrative, and the essay. For some reason—according to some students, some parents, and even some teachers—criticizing a student's poem is tantamount to sacrilege, for by doing so, we dampen the poet's enthusiasm and inhibit budding creativity; worse, we condition the student to our understanding of excellence. To tamper with the poet's work is taboo. And to pronounce it shoddily done is justification to bear the umbrage and wrath of the poet's offended parents, who are not infrequently college graduates and professors.

Such consequences are rare, however, where the instructor corrects the beginning pianist, criticizes the novice ballerina, or gives advice to the fledgling painter, architect, or essayist. Like poetry, these arts are a craft to be mastered; they must be practiced, corrected, refined.

Part of the reason, I think, that poetry seems something exceptional compared to the other arts is that originally it was divinely inspired. Holy. The poet, then, was priest, seer, prophet, wise man, shaman—the mystic voice that enunciated the words of God. Such an age with such conviction, of course, has passed, and with its passing, the purity and holiness . . . became, through time, attached to group and then to individual identity. Therefore, to comment on another's poetry is to comment on the poet's identity or personality, which is an unfortunate misunderstanding.

The corollary is this: in order to preserve and sustain selfhood, the poet must always work alone, independent of and beholden to no one, which is patently absurd because it is impossible. Not discounting Ezra Pound's advice to T. S. Eliot and other poets in their youth; Maxwell Perkin's advice to Hemingway, Fitzgerald, and Thomas Wolfe; or Ford Maddox Ford's advice to Conrad over *Heart of Darkness*—poets, whether or not influenced directly, are never alone, keeping their visions all to themselves.

Hamlet said, "there is nothing either good or bad, but thinking makes it so." That is, to answer the first teacher's questions—no, evaluation is not banal. It is a fact of life. Rather than moral relativity, Hamlet refers to the judgment born of thinking, defining the basically moral nature of humanity (however much Hamlet himself often wishes not to think).

Student poetry is good or bad insofar as it measures up to the best of the literary tradition that the students themselves have established, and insofar as it measures up to the best work a student has done to date, demonstrating growth or the lack thereof. More specifically, if the work shows growth, the poem demands comment (even if the work is graded a 2 in a 4-point system). "Getting stronger" is not an uncommon accompaniment to a grade. Otherwise, I say nothing about the work in general, speaking instead, in shorthand, about specific words, lines, and stanzas.

In answering the second teacher's question, I give the student as much advice as I can. What I mean by advice is for the teacher to suggest changes; to offer alternative words and means, asking the student to compare them with what the student has written; to ask the student to expand or compress, deepen or extend thoughts and feelings—that is, the teacher does exactly what the student revisers do. The difference between the teacher's subjective responses and those of the students (as well as those of lay adults) is that the teacher's subjectivity is born of specialized experience and training, which makes a great difference. Were I to withhold from my students my expertise—my critical opinion—I would have to call myself to account as a teacher who believes that by my actions, my students come to share, in part, my reverence for writing and literature.

POETRY BOOKS

It wasn't until the pages had covers on them that I knew I had written a book. Me! Sure, you feel kind of proud when the teacher puts your poem up for a week or reads it to the class but that's nothing like holding your own book in your hands. It's like holding all your clay sculptures in your hands at one time and saying this is what I did.

—unknown student

Three things come to mind when I think of another favorite teacher, Professor Kriegel. The first is his shoot-from-the-hip responses to my short story characters, who, for the most part, tended toward loud, ignorant pronouncements on famous writers. ("One would wonder why that ass Fitzgerald bothered to write in the first place!")

A number of good things resulted from Kriegel's heavy-handed forthrightness. For one, my "vision" improved; I began to "see" more honestly. For another, I eventually published two works that had taken seed in his class. (One story, which was not published, was about him—only my hero was a heroine, a tyrannical virtuoso singer confined to a wheelchair. Her correspondence to Kriegel was uncanny and obvious, so obvious that I didn't recognize it until twelve years later.)

Second, and more important, I remember Kriegel's intolerance of mediocrity. This was evidenced not so much in his words as it was in his voice, in his street-fighter's grimace (which was his smile), and in his thick upper body that challenged you and hoped that you would do your best—that to do otherwise was dishonesty. His passion was infectious.

The third thing that comes to mind when I think of Kriegel is this: after setting his battered briefcase on the desk at the head of the class and propping his crutches against the chalk rail be-hind him, he bent to shift his steel-braced legs beneath the desk. On this particular day, he withdrew a book from his briefcase—his book, which had been published. He remarked, without raising his eyes, that there were a number of sentences or passages that he didn't recall writing. In any case, his talk was short, and we turned to our own work, though I'm sure others, like myself, watched him, fascinated. Oblivious to us, he seemed to fondle the book with his large powerful hands, feeling the spine, tracing its edges, testing the thickness and quality of the paper. Cradling the book in one hand, he flipped through the pages with the other, his eyes glazed with a fiercely possessive, fiercely proud light.

And so, after writing twenty-six poems, after arranging them in book form, after magically receiving them, spiral-bound, from the school's production center, my students have their own books to feel in their palms, to hold between their fingers. Yes, the books are real—the record of a whole quarter's effort, the proud product of what one student called "Mission Impossible, day after day."

As I return the books to them, in a very businesslike manner, I watch the students out of the corner of my eye. A few, as show, flip their books casually on their desks; others quickly glance at the pages, perhaps for publishing errors, while others want to see the books of their friends: "Let me see, let me see"; "Wow, this is thick"; "You sure wrote a lot"; "Boy, you write neatly." The room is filled with a loud, excited hum, which is colored, infused, and shaped by a sense of culmination, of having grown, of having arrived as expected. No big thing, really. Just a fact of life.

At the end of class, the books are hauled off to the closed reserve section of the library, where they are preserved fingerprint-free until Christmas vacation. At that time the books are returned to the students, who wrap them at home to give away as gifts to parents and grandparents. And how do *they* react? One common parent practice, according to my students (to my students' "chagrin"), is their having the book copied and sent, hither and yon, to the rest of the clan. Another practice is the parents telling me how surprised they are at the sophisticated level of their children's insight, their sensitivity, their emotional honesty—surprised, really, at the invisible, inner growth their children are experiencing, the growth of hearts and minds so close to their own yet never seen in this light before. And they are moved as only parents can be.

Each of the student books concludes with an End Poem. The following poem, modeled on Jack Spicer's "Five Words for Joe Dunn on His 22nd Birthday," was written by Sam Onaga (grade 8).

A Christmas Present

For Christmas day
I give you

What I have
Five names.

Breug and his bronzed arms
Which are like soft walls
To brace you
From falls
And weather your blows.
For you;

Trink and his wit of chimes
To entertain you
With rainbow leaps
And shiny tinklings
During your long moments;

Schnook
The cynic
And his curled lip
To keep you thinking
In idle times;

Unk and his stupidity
And stumbling clumsiness
To laugh at
In bad times;
There is always one worse;

And *Is-Was*
His twinkling eyes and reverent speech
To remind you
To make you look back and remember
When you can't look forward.

For Further Thought

1. Respond to the poetry of Tsujimoto's students. What, if anything, distinguishes them from the work of other seventh and eighth graders? In what ways are these poems typical of the work of young adolescents?

2. Tsujimoto argues that the writing of poetry cannot be separated from the reading of poetry, that is, from immersing students in what he calls "the traditions." What was your experience in school? Were poetry reading and poetry writing taught together? What are some of the pros and cons of this approach?

3. Tsujimoto takes a pretty hard-headed stance toward revision and evaluation. In this he differs from teachers who treat students' creative writing with kid gloves and back off from evaluation. What do you think? Is there any reason that student poems should not be revised? Any reason that they shouldn't be evaluated the way other writing is evaluated?

4. Consider Tsujimoto's way of presenting an assignment. The emphasis is clearly on reading, on the examples of student and professional poems. What might this tell us about the way we approach "regular" expository writing assignments? If you are doing the "The Assignment Assignment" (pp. 210–213), how might you change it, now that you have thought about Tsujimoto's approach?

5. Find Tsujimoto's book, *Teaching Poetry Writing to Adolescents*, and get a fuller sense of how he works. Write at least two poems, using two of his assignments.

Application 4.5:
Reading and Writing Poetry

Mrs. Hedden

You were so weird in fourth grade,
With your perfume and flouncy dresses
And curled hair. I imagined you
Hanging bat-like in the evenings,
Upside down in the cloakroom,
Above abandoned galoshes and torn notebooks.
You emerged in the morning with more
Homework: maps of South America
To trace and color and label
With "principal products," poems
And stories to read, family trees,
Spelling, and endless long division.

No doubt I wrong you in memory,
Having mistaken your intentions
And confused your lessons
With those of others. But
I still recall the smell of perfume
And more: a way of loving
Our maps and taking our stories
Seriously. You were, after all,
No bat-creature, just a middle-
Aged woman with grown children
Teaching out her years with fourth
Graders. Grown now, I am myself
Teaching out my years, like you.

It isn't the greatest poem in the world, I know, but I am mildly proud of it: It says something about Mrs. Hedden and teachers like her—and, after all, I wrote it. For someone who has been afraid of poetry for a long time, that is an accomplishment.

I am not alone in this fear. I know teachers who think nothing of assigning fairly difficult fiction but avoid poetry whenever possible. Like many of their students and like me until a few years ago, they have been victims of some of the myths about poetry: the belief that poems must be difficult (unlike a Faulkner story?), that they can be understood only by a select few (college professors?), and that they are somehow "sissified" (for girls, not boys?).

None of this true and it has the unfortunate effect of depriving both students and teachers of the rewards of reading and writing poetry.

The solution, I think, is to concentrate less on teaching poetry and more on experiencing it. I do not mean to disparage teaching or to imply that teacher talk about poetry is not important. The example of Joseph Tsujimoto argues otherwise. But as much as he talks about poetry to his students, Tsujimoto never forgets that the experience of the poem matters most. So he reads a great many poems to his students—many more than can be analyzed and discussed in great detail. In addition to being exposed to poetry, kids must *do* something with a poem, they must be active and not merely passive. Thus, lessons on poetry are successful to the degree that students and teacher are actively reading and rereading poems, writing response statements, tinkering with the language of the poem, or sharing interpretations. In lessons like these, the goal is not to search out the one "correct" interpretation of the poem, and if poetic devices and figures of speech are mentioned, the emphasis is not on terminology and definitions but on the practical uses of this kind of language to produce responses in readers.

Writing poetry is also a key feature of the poetic experience. At first, that might seem perverse—a little like telling people they need to confront their worst fears—but it actually works quite well. As the following examples suggest, it is not that difficult to get students to write poems. Once that is accomplished, nearly everything else about poetry starts to seem possible.

Poetry Writing in the Classroom

In two books on teaching poetry to young children—*Wishes, Lies and Dreams* (1970) and *Rose, Where Did You Get That Red?* (1974)—Kenneth Koch describes an approach whereby he gets kids to write poems. In the first book, he provides students with a "poetry idea" and a general poetic form and then encourages students to express themselves within that form. The emphasis is on positive reinforcement: What a child writes is accepted as a poem and cheerfully "published" in the classroom. According to the method of the second book, students read the work of great poets (among them Shakespeare, Herrick, Blake, Hopkins, Yeats, even Ashberry!) and write their own poems using the original as a model. The results are illuminating: Koch's elementary school students wrote poems that are fresh, readable, and insightful.

As poet Robert King has pointed out, the use of model poems has disadvantages as well as advantages: ". . . if one only has a couple of model poems in one's possession, the opportunities for poetic development will be extremely limited and students will soon be copying William Carlos Williams's 'The Red Wheelbarrow' or 'This is just to say' as mechanically as they now copy the form of the haiku" (King, p. 19). This word of caution is valuable, reminding us of the wisdom of Tsujimoto's practice of reading many poems to his students. Yet there is something to be said for close imitation, provided it is not carried too far and students move on to looser kinds of modeling. For example, Vickie Peake, an English teacher in Grand Forks,

North Dakota, uses Koch's approach with her seventh graders, presenting to them a variety of forms based on the work of professional poets: the ideo- gram of cardinal numbers (based on a poem by May Sarton), the poem in praise of an animal (e.g., Blake's "The Tyger" and other examples presented by Koch), and the extended metaphor or simile (used by both Koch and Tsujimoto). The examples that follow are fairly close, in the formal sense, to the models presented by Mrs. Peake, and yet they are not to be dismissed as slavish imitations. Like Koch's grade school kids, these seventh graders are on their way to thinking and writing as poets.

Cardinal Ideogram (by Jaci Ludwig)

0 A cordless clock, broken
1 A skinny book on a shelf
2 A fish swimming very fast
3 Bunny's ears, sideways
4 A one-legged woman wearing a skirt
5 A lady's nose, with her eyelash above
6 A piece of hair, just permed
7 A cliff that comes to an end
8 A half-done snowman, a pair of eyes
9 A light bulb with a string to turn it on
10 A cordless clock holding up a skinny book on a shelf.

The Magnificent Dragon (by Ryan Vorachek)

My dragon is as green as a lime.
He is as green as the summer grass.
My dragon has a ferocious roar like thunder.
His roar is like that of the biggest cannon.
My dragon breathes fire as hot as the blazing sun.
His fire is as bright as the most intense yellow.

My Parents Are Like Alarm Clocks (by Leonora Gershman)

My parents are like alarm clocks because if you set them up just right, they'll be sure to go off.
My parents are like alarm clocks because when they go off, it'll be sure to wake you up!
My parents are like alarm clocks because sometimes waking up to them isn't exactly something to look forward to.
My parents are like alarm clocks because when you really need something to count on . . . parents will always be there.

Which brings us back to Tsujimoto's poetry writing assignments. As he says, these are derived from Kenneth Koch's work. Because Tsujimoto lists the actual assignments only briefly in the piece you have read (pp. 191–205), let me remind you that there are eighteen in all: (1) *found poem*, in which the writer takes the words from another source and shapes them into a poem; (2) *two-word poem*, which shows surprising associations of things and ideas; (3) *circle poem*, in which a chain of words circles back to the idea expressed in the original word; (4) *change poem*, in which single-word lines record a temporal change of some kind; (5) *transformation poem*, in which someone or something is transformed in a surprising yet appropriate manner; (6) *list of twelve*, in which a poem is fashioned from a list of twelve evocative phrases; (7) *animal poem*; (8) *visual response poem*, in which the writer responds to something like a painting or photo; (9) *extended metaphor*; (10) *memory poem*; (11) *poem expressing bitterness*; (12) *paradox poem*; (13) *poem expressing awe*; (14) *teacher poem*; (15) *form poem*, in which the writer follows the form of something else, like a dictionary definition or menu item; (16) *self-portrait*, which gives different views of the author; (17) *invitation poem*, which introduces the student's personal collection of poems; and (18) *end poem*, which concludes the collection.

As you can see, each assignment focuses on one aspect of the poetic experience—a particular subject (animal, teacher), an emotion (bitterness, awe), a specified form (two words, circle), a verbal strategy (metaphor), or rhetorical function (invitation, end). One thing at a time in focus. Some of the earlier tasks are like finger exercises, more for practice than for publications, whereas the later assignments are quite complex, requiring previous practice and more discipline. All in all, Tsujimoto's students write twenty-six poems, quite an accomplishment for seventh or eighth graders, and perhaps a daunting challenge for the teacher. But this is not an all-or-nothing proposition. I have used a selection of these assignments, mixing in some others, with seventh graders and college students, and I think I can testify that there is no magic to this list of eighteen assignments or even to their order. Here are some examples of work done from Tsujimoto's earlier assignments, written by members of a college class:

Found Poem (Words from the *Grand Forks Herald,* Sunday, June 18, 1989)

Road House

Patrick Swayze
flexes both mind
and muscle
in this
totally
unbelievable action
film

   (R)
   Nudity
   violence
   language.

Two-Word Poems

#1 Mirror
    Doorway

#2 Tremble   Arrive

Circle Poem

Bicycle

Balance
Beam
Ceiling
Bats
Claws
Painted Lady
Bag Lady
Grocery Cart
Wheels

Transformation Poem

The Road Crew Worker

mounts his squisher
rolls, levels, planes,
obliterates potholes
in the hot July sun.

His pancake face
grows smoother and
more expressionless
as he rolls down
Interstate 29.

Some Things to Consider About Reading and Writing Poetry

1. Consider your own history as a reader and writer of poetry. Have you been poetry-phobic? If so, what in your experience caused the fear? If not, how did you manage to remain immune? Then look at the lesson plan on "in Just-spring" (p. 37). As a student, how might you have responded to that lesson?

2. Find several poems on a subject dear to the hearts of adolescents, such as sports, cars, food, appearance, sex, love, or parents. If you nose around the library, you should be able to find collections of poems on such popular subjects. Bring your chosen poems to class and read one of them aloud to your classmates.

3. Write a poem about a teacher from your past. You might structure it in two parts: "then" (the way you reacted as a student) and "now" (the view of the prospective teacher). My poem on Mrs. Hedden is put together this way.

4. Find Kenneth Koch's *Rose, Where Did You Get That Red?* and read several sections. What are the strengths and weaknesses of this approach? Write a poem following Koch's directions.

5. Find Joseph Tsujimoto's *Teaching Poetry Writing to Adolescents*, and read the rest of the book. It's not very long. Write a poem using one of Tsujimoto's assignments.

Writing Assignment:
Creating a Writing Assignment

> *To cap off a literature unit on the short story, a seventh-grade teacher asks his students to write a story of their own, using illustrations from a children's books as starters. An eighth-grade teacher asks students to write about a childhood toy, providing a definite format and fairly detailed instructions. A tenth-grade teacher begins the school year with a paper that asks students to imagine their one hundredth birthday and later asks students to compare/contrast a place they have lived or a time in their life, with another place or time. An eleventh-grade teacher assigns an interpretive essay on the literature students have read throughout the semester. (See Appendixes 2–6 for the teachers' assignments.)*

As these situations suggest, writing assignments are highly contextualized; they are created by particular teachers for particular students in particular situations. The seventh grade teacher wanted his students to come to grips with the short story form "from the inside," that is, by writing one themselves. His main focus was not exactly "creative writing"; he was more interested in reinforcing what students had learned in the literature unit. The eighth grade teacher had to consider what her thirteen-year-olds were capable of: How many rhetorical problems they could solve in one assignment. Feeling that she had a class of fairly inexperienced writers, she felt the need for a basic, beginning assignment. The tenth-grade teacher used the Hundred Year Birthday Paper as an introductory essay, whereas the comparison/contrast paper came much later in the school year. The eleventh-grade teacher felt the need to do some writing about literature, a form she had somewhat neglected lately, but she also wanted her students to review the semester's reading, possibly relating one text to another.

Out of situations like these, teachers devise writing assignments, that is, situations within which students must solve a range of rhetorical problems (what to write about, what mode or genre to adopt, what tone to use, and so forth). In making the assignment, teachers must try to strike a balance of freedom and constraint. On the one hand, students must be free to make choices if they are to grow as writers. Those choices will range from decisions about subject matter to rhetorical choices involving arrangement and style. In a very real sense, the success of a given assignment depends less on the quality of the finished products than it does on the learning that takes place through making rhetorical choices.

On the other hand, writers will have difficulty proceeding unless the choices are constrained in some way. A writing assignment that tells students to write something about anything they choose is no assignment at all. Because it offers students no limits or constraints, no writing situation develops, and without a situation from which to write, students are likely to feel paralyzed. Thus, the need for a writing situation is basic, even in the workshop approach, where no formal assignment is given. The teacher's example, the choices of other students, model papers, suggested readings, nudges in this direction or that—these allow students to impose upon themselves a set of constraints from which they can create a real writing situation.

These five assignments are described more fully in the appendixes to this book. As you analyze them, you will see that each teacher has struck a different kind of balance between freedom and constraint for students. As the tasks are spelled out for students, options are cut off, though this makes rhetorical choices easier to make. And as other things are left vague and undefined, students are called upon to "fill in the blanks." Of course students will frequently ask, "What is it, exactly, that you want?" But the wise teacher will not answer that question . . . at least not exactly. Instead, he or she will help with choices, which is a way of helping students exert some ownership over the assignment, of making it their own. Obviously, it is a situation filled with the kind of tensions we have been examining in this book, which is why creating a writing assignment is so challenging.

Some Things to Consider About Writing Assignments (Before Writing One of Your Own)

1. The seventh grade teacher works from a "story starter," in this case, illustrations from Chris Van Allsburg's *The Mysteries of Harris Burdick*. In certain ways it is very limiting, though of course a great deal depends on the pictures. Discuss the idea of using story starters, keeping the teacher's objectives in mind. To see the actual assignment and a sampling of what students wrote, see Appendix 2.
2. The eighth- and tenth-grade teachers include models for students, the former with a paper of her own, the latter with a newspaper article. What are some of the pros and cons of using models for students? Look at Appendixes 3 and 4 for the assignment and some sample student papers.
3. The eleventh-grade teacher's assignment is fairly traditional, in the sense that writing about literature is a standard approach to composition. How does the teacher manage to build in choices for students? What are the constraints of such an assignment? Look at Appendix 6 for the assignment and a sampling of student work.

The Assignment Assignment

Obviously, an assignment in this book is subject to the same general principles that apply to those that have just been presented. In other words, the assignment to create an assignment will present you with a balance of choices and constraints, which together constitute a rhetorical situation. As in chapter 3, with the Unit Assignment, I have decided to work from a scenario or fictional situation, this one having to do with student teaching:

It is early in the school year—about a month into the fall term. You are student teaching at Washington High School (or Middle School), on a grade level of your choice. Your cooperating teacher is Mrs.

Martinez, a wily veteran of twenty years, who has taught this grade level for nineteen of those years. You have been working with her, in her three English classes from the start of the school year, during which time she has asked students to read literature in a variety of genres, to do some informal writing, and to keep a journal with weekly entries. So, having read their writing and worked with them for four weeks, you know something about these students. Lately you have been teaching literature, first in one class and now in three; it has been going pretty well and your confidence is growing. You are about to finish a short novel you have assigned to all three classes.

"Starting Monday, there are two weeks," says Mrs. Martinez, "before we move on to the next piece of literature—just time enough to write something else." When you ask what kind of writing that should be, she says, "You're a professional now; you decide." This is frightening. You like Mrs. Martinez and have come to trust her, but you hadn't counted on this. When it came to literature, she gave you some choice, but actually a lot depended on what texts were available. Can it really be that she'll let you teach any kind of writing? "Yes," she says. "You're the boss; go for it." You walk off muttering to yourself, "Thanks a lot, Mrs. M."

Of course, you know what she is up to. She wants to wean you from dependence on her; she wants you to make, and live with, your own decisions. You know she is right, and you know she will help, but you still don't like it. And, anyway, what does it mean to "teach" a kind of writing? When you observed Mrs. Martinez last semester, she hardly seemed to be "teaching" at all. It seemed that all she did was give the assignment and then wander around helping kids, while they wrote and talked to each other about their writing. Upon reflection, however, you could see that there was indeed a structure here: she initiated the writing and set expectations; she helped kids find topics and think things through; she orchestrated those classroom conversations; she made herself available to kids for help; she kept to a timetable; she responded to their work; she evaluated the products; she arranged for them to read their work aloud in class. It wasn't exactly like those articles on teaching writing that you had read in college, but it was similar.

"OK," you say to yourself "it's not that scary. But what do I do next?" You need a kind of writing; you need a timetable for writing; and (this is still the scary part) you need to figure out what to do in class for those two weeks. For you know that although Mrs. Martinez makes things look easy and natural, there is nothing "natural" about it—at least not for you. You've got to plan.

A scenario like this does more than just create a situation with some concrete details. Contained within it are the main elements of the assignment: the "rules" that will influence the choices you make. For example, you can choose the grade level and the kind of writing, using whatever approach and whatever kinds of activities you like. This is the freedom side of the equation. On the other side, you note that students need to write some kind of paper (an extended piece of discourse), that the writing should be somewhat formal (not freewriting or journal writing), that you have two weeks for the entire process, and that you have three classes to consider—that is, three sets of papers to deal with somehow. Thus, the fictional situation leads to a series of practical and rhetorical problems that you need to solve to complete the assignment.

* * *

Write two weeks of plans for teaching a particular kind of writing on a particular grade level. Begin with a page or two of introduction in which you describe your initial decisions and objectives. Then map out your activities on a daily grid so your instructor can see the overview of the unit at a glance. Next, write ten mini–lesson plans in which you describe what you will do in each of the ten days, two or three per page. Then, in a page or two, describe how you will evaluate student work. Finally, write a short conclusion in which you reflect on your decisions and evaluate your unit. Attach any materials needed to understand the lessons (assignment sheets, readings, grading sheets, etc.).

For Further Reading

Elbow, Peter. *Writing without Teachers*. New York: Oxford, 1973. Elbow developed the idea of "free writing" and other techniques based on the premise that we learn to write by writing.

English Journal. *English Journal* has many articles devoted to the teaching of writing, but note especially the issue devoted to "Alternative Assessment" (January 1997).

Flower, Linda. "Writer-Based Prose: A Cognitive Basis for Problems in Writing." In *To Compose: Teaching Writing in High School and College*, 2nd edition, edited by Thomas Newkirk, 125–152. Portsmouth, NH: Heinemann, 1990. This frequently anthologized essay establishes the distinction between *writer-based prose*, which satisfies the needs of the writer, and *reader-based prose*, which is more audience directed.

King, Robert. "The Model Poem: A Structural Approach to Poetry Writing." *Writing Teacher*, April/May, 1989, 19–22. A brief, succinct discussion of Kenneth Koch's approach to poetry writing, with student examples based on a poem by Theodore Roethke.

Kirby, Dan, and Tom Liner, with Ruth Vinz. *Inside Out: Developmental Strategies for Teaching Writing*, 2nd edition. Portsmouth, NH: Boynton/Cook-Heinemann, 1988. A book full of good teaching ideas, all in the context of classroom situations.

Koch, Kenneth. *Rose, Where Did You Get That Red? Teaching Great Poetry to Children*. New York: Random House, 1974. A seminal text on poetry writing in the schools. Koch worked with elementary school students, but his approach is valid on all grade levels.

Macrorie, Ken. *The I-Search Paper* (Revised Edition of *Searching Writing*). Portsmouth, NH: Boynton/Cook-Heinemann, 1988. Macrorie has been one of the major proponents of expressive writing. His early work, especially *Telling Writing*, handles matters like "voice" in a powerful way. This book extends Macrorie's thinking to personal research projects in what he calls the "I-Search Paper."

National Council of Teachers of English (NCTE). *Motivating Writing in Middle School* (Standards Consensus Series). Urbana, IL: NCTE, 1996. An anthology of short pieces on teaching writing in the middle school, with sections on "Using Artifacts,"

"Self Exploration," "Real-World Writing," and "Peer Editing, Self Editing, and Student-Teacher Interaction."

———. *Teaching the Writing Process in High School*. Urbana, IL: NCTE, 1995. An anthology of short pieces on teaching writing in high school, with sections on "Audience and Purpose," "Prewriting and Drafting," and "Peer Editing, Self Editing, and Revision."

Newkirk, Thomas, ed. *To Compose: Teaching Writing in High School and College*, 2nd edition. Portsmouth, NH: Heinemann, 1990. A good collection of essays, useful on either the secondary or college level.

Proett, Jackie, and Kent Gill. *The Writing Process in Action: A Handbook for Teachers*. Urbana, IL: NCTE, 1986. A short practical book that covers the basics of using a process approach, with useful sections on prewriting, making rhetorical choices, and revising. An older book, but it holds up well.

Protherough, Robert. *Encouraging Writing*. London: Methuen, 1983. Another readable book on teaching writing in real school settings, this one from the British perspective. Protherough is particularly good at discussing questions of motivation (why kids write) and practical matters of teaching (when kids write disturbing things).

Routman, Regie. *Invitations: Changing as Teachers and Learners, K–12*, expanded edition. Portsmouth, NH: 1994. Routman covers a lot of ground, so there is much here that an individual teacher will not use. Still, *Invitations* is comprehensive, readable, and very practical. Includes a list of resources in the "blue pages" at the end.

Soven, Margot Iris. *Teaching Writing in Middle and Secondary Schools*. Boston: Allyn and Bacon, 1999. A comprehensive book, covering most of the major issues in the teaching of writing.

Tsujimoto, Joseph. *Teaching Poetry Writing to Adolescents*. Urbana, IL: NCTE/ERIC, 1988. A chapter is included in this book, as well as a discussion in Application 4.5.

Williams, James D. *Preparing to Teach Writing*. Mahwah, NJ: Lawrence Erlbaum Associates, 1996. A comprehensive book on the teaching of writing—particularly good at defining terms and laying out issues clearly.

Zemelman, Steven, and Harvey Daniels. *A Community of Writers: Teaching Writing in the Junior and Senior High School*. Portsmouth, NH: Heinemann, 1988. A comprehensive book that explores practical applications of "the process paradigm," including a version of the writing workshop.

5

Teaching About Language

Introduction

For some of us (and I include myself here) the idea of teaching about language is likely to produce some anxiety. We teach *English*, which ought to have something to do with the English *language*, but our training is really in the study of literature and (perhaps) rhetoric. So we frequently feel inadequate to work seriously with language. These fears seem to be well-founded when we look at a traditional breakdown of linguistics—the sort of list that usually begins with *phonology* and ends somewhere in the realm of *pragmatics*. Linguistics, as a scholarly field, often seems too technical and complicated to belong in the secondary classroom.

What are we English teachers to do? We can begin by setting priorities, asking what it is, after all, that students should understand about language. In this regard, two principles of language study can guide us: *variation* and *change*. One goal of language study is to encourage students to understand how the English language varies as they move from region to region, ethnic group to ethnic group, social class to social class, circumstance to circumstance. Although they may know this instinctively and may conduct themselves with great skill as they manage language variations in their own lives, they seldom really think about it. Schools often foster a monolithic view of language: A sameness of language has often been one of the goals of U.S. schooling. This makes it all the more important that we encourage students to confront the truth about English—that it exists in all the varieties that Caroline Adger, Donna Christian, and Walt Wolfram describe in "Language Variation in the United States" (pp. 220–233).

As many linguists suggest, a likely place to begin to teach about variation is with the study of dialects. We all speak a dialect, indeed several versions of a dialect, but such is the egocentrism of human-kind that we seldom recognize this fact. Thus, young people often feel that *their* English is *the* English language. Confronted with differences, they react with surprise (teenagers will often say that people from other parts of the country "speak funny") or defensiveness (in my town some students are angered when Hispanic students speak Spanish in the hallways) or intolerance (I know of a girl who told a teacher that she could not—and would not—read *Huckleberry Finn* because Huck's and Jim's speech was "different" from her own).

These attitudes are understandable, but they represent a view of language that we need to help students overcome. As Adger, Christian, and Wolfram suggest, our role is not so much to change the dialects of our students as it is to develop in them a respect for linguistic diversity. From dialects we can move to social registers of language and the various jargons that interest students (sports language, for instance, or computer jargon), broadening their view of how language works and helping them to see where their language fits into the larger construct called English.

For similar reasons, students need to understand the way language changes across time. This means more than just knowing that English has a history—though that is a good first step. More fundamentally, students need to understand that words are not static entities, frozen forever into dictionary meanings. We need to seize every opportunity to foster in our students a more dynamic view of language. In the study of vocabulary we can introduce students to the history of words, beginning with those that have colorful stories. As students learn and write about their surroundings and their families, they can investigate the names of persons and places to understand the ways in which language can carry on a culture and yet transform itself with cultural change. In the study of the older literary texts, we can have students transcribe Chaucer or Shakespeare into modern English and vice versa, extracting from their own translations some rules of language change. And in our work with writing, we can go beyond saying that *alot* is incorrect and point out that it, like *alright*, is on the way to becoming standard usage.

Exploring Language

As the foregoing examples suggest, a genuine understanding of language means much more than a grasp of abstract principles like *variation* and *change*. For language is not just a field of study—like ancient Greece—that can be understood without being lived. Rather, language is a human activity in which we all constantly engage, both in and out of school. We need to show students that language is not an abstraction but a way of defining ourselves, a way of exerting power, a way of thinking, and—ultimately—a way of living.

Our emphasis should be on the language of real life. For example, students need to see the connection between language and power. In this age of massive advertising campaigns, political sound bites, and "official language" movements, helping students to see the politics of language is practically a civic duty. But we cannot hope to impress on them that language makes a difference in the world—that it literally makes things happen—if we are always talking about someone else's words. Sooner or later we must come back to what is happening here and now in the students' own lives. How students are addressed and how they must address ethers (such as the teacher); how and when they are allowed to, and prohibited from, speaking; which words are permitted and which are forbidden, and in what contexts; what makes one use of language standard and therefore privileged whereas another is nonstandard and therefore less acceptable—these are subjects for exploration.

Not that language study always has to be terribly serious. Language is also an invitation to play, as students well know. I have yet to meet a teenager who did not enjoy playing games with words, whether it be in the private language of a group or in the prevailing lingo of teenagers nationwide. This is particularly true at the junior high/middle school level, where the legacy of more childlike language games is still quite strong. One of our goals should be to help students rediscover in the classroom that enjoyment of language that many seem to have lost.

Finally, we need to realize that language is not just a field for exploration—it is itself a means for conducting that exploration. We cannot explore language without using language. One implication is that language study has less to do with "book learning" than it does with activities—speaking and listening, writing and reading. Another implication is that we can trust students' natural language ability to appreciate the workings of language without a great deal of linguistic terminology. We teach about slang not by defining it but by showing examples and getting students to use slang—and the same applies to dialects, etymologies, puns, jokes, jargon, doublespeak, and so on. The learning takes place in the use.

This is the view taken by Larry Andrews in *Language Exploration and Awareness* (1998), in which he lists five criteria for effective exploratory activities: They emphasize meaning; they use authentic language found in genuine social circumstances; they are suited to students' level of development; they attend to several aspects of language; they are student centered and inquiry oriented; and they provide for reflection (Andrews, 1998, pp. 13–18). Andrews applies these principles to all kinds of language activities, for all kinds of students—even nonnative speakers, the "ESL students" who will inevitably be among the students we teach. In "When Some of Them Don't Speak English" (pp. 283–292), he argues for a mature approach to ESL students—that is, one that honors their social and cognitive maturity and asks them to learn English, with the help of their classmates and teacher, by actively using language in real learning situations.

The Grammar Argument

If few would dispute the idea that English teachers should help students understand language, when it comes to grammar everything suddenly becomes disputable. The controversy stems in part from differences in the way the word is used. As Russell Tabbert points out in "Parsing the Question: 'Why Teach Grammar?'" (pp. 244–249), there are at least three meanings to the term: grammar as working knowledge of the language (grammar-1), grammar as a descriptive system of language structures (grammar-2), and grammar as linguistic etiquette (grammar-3). The first is not really the concern of English teachers, not in the sense that it need be taught. The second has many variations, the most common of which are traditional (also called *classroom*, *Latinate*, or *eighteenth-century*) grammar and transformational (also called *transformational-generative*, *t-g*, or *modern*) grammar. The third is really correct usage, and that is what most of the fighting is about.

Later in this chapter you will be invited to participate in that debate, so my purpose here is only to clarify a bit. The question that Tabbert tries to "parse" is basically this: What, if anything, is the relationship between grammar-2 (systematic descriptive grammar) and the other two meanings of the term? For linguists, the primary question is the connection of grammar-2 to grammar-1. They want to know which grammatical system best describes the underlying structures of English, the internal grammar that native speakers use unconsciously. And so linguists will argue about the relative merits of transformational versus traditional grammar.

In the schools, however, the bigger controversy is the relationship of grammar-2, of whichever sort you adopt, to grammar-3, which is really a standard of correctness. Can the teaching of a grammatical system influence the way people actually use language, especially the way they write? If so, how and when should that grammar instruction take place? In "Teaching Grammar in the Context of Writing" (pp. 255–267), Constance Weaver reviews the research on the subject, which yields little real evidence that direct instruction in grammar-2 improves a person's ability to write. From this, Weaver does not conclude that grammar instruction is useless, but she does insist that it be taught in the context of students' own writing. Here again, the principle of *use* is at work: Grammatical concepts and rules seem to remain inaccessible to most students until these concepts and rules are shown to be useful in students' own writing.

Weaver's position on the teaching of grammar is neither pro nor con. Rather, she adopts a pragmatic stance that is shared, for the most part, by the teachers interviewed by Brenda Arnett Petruzella in "Grammar Instruction: What Teachers Say" (pp. 272–278). These are not teachers who thoughtlessly follow a "grammar curriculum"; nor are they picky "grammar nuts." But they do exercise their judgment about what students need—whether it be sentence combining exercises or minilessons on points of usage. Interestingly, they see the research establishment and "universities" as being antigrammar, a perspective we will explore later in this chapter. For the present, what matters most is that teaching grammar is not an all-or-nothing proposition. There are a variety of positions to consider here. My only advice is to keep an open mind and not to adopt a hard-line attitude—not yet. It seems silly to say, "Those kids need to know their grammar," before you are well acquainted with the kids themselves. Once you know how they read and write, once you get to know them as learners, then you can decide what they need. But it seems just as silly to say, "Grammar is a waste of time," before you have thought the matter through.

The Problem of Correctness

Underlying the grammar debate is a more basic concern about correctness in language use, especially when it comes to writing. What are we to do about the "lower order concerns" that Barbara Carney discusses—sentence structure, variety, punctuation, spelling, and usage? As Carney suggests, these are end-of-the-process concerns, but they have their own special importance: "Teaching students that editing is the final stage in the process should not lessen its significance. Postponing error correction does not mean putting it off altogether" (p. 181). Carney uses group editing procedures; Nancie Atwell holds editing conferences with students; both Atwell and Weaver focus on usage problems through minilessons.

Here again, we can see the principle of language use at work. We are much more likely to make progress with students if we concentrate our concern, not on correctness in the abstract, but on the value of correctness in *this* piece of writing, *this* piece of work in which the student has an investment. And if we want students to generalize to a rule—about subject–verb agreement, for example—we will be better able to do that if we first demonstrate, through examples from their own work, that the rule matters. The key principle is to work from genuine pieces of writing—that is, work that students have produced themselves or, when that is not possible, work in which they have some kind of investment. Connected to that is a principle of induction: If we want students to grasp a rule, it is best to provide lots of meaningful examples and then to ask students, as best they can, to search out the similarities and derive the rule. Conversely, grammar and usage rules, provided before the examples or illustrated with canned instances from a workbook, are not likely to affect student writing in any genuine fashion.

You will probably find that no one procedure works equally well for all editing problems with all students. So here again, it pays to remain flexible and to experiment. For in regard to correctness, the English teacher is (as usual) asked to perform a balancing act, which (as usual) can produce some tensions. On the one hand, we want students to avoid an undue concern for correctness, especially at the early stages of the process where inventiveness and risk taking are of primary importance. On the other hand, we do not want to foster the idea that correctness does not matter. It does. Errors in sentence structure, pronoun case, subject–verb agreement, spelling, and punctuation make a huge difference in the way a piece of writing is received. The trick is to address these concerns in the manner that best serves our students' interests.

Language Variation in the United States

Caroline Adger, Donna Christian, and Walt Wolfram

"Language Variation in the United States" is an excerpt from the first chapter of a book, Dialects in Schools and Communities *(Lawrence Erlbaum Associates, 1999). Adger, Christian, and Wolfram are linguists with a special interest in dialects—their social origins and their social effects. Although this excerpt does not address how we handle dialects or dialect study in schools, it does lay the groundwork for a discussion of those matters. As you read, think about how the various English dialects differ from each other and what they have in common. Also consider what the authors say about the deficit and difference approaches to language variation.*

Copyright 1999 by Lawrence Erlbaum Associates. This excerpt from Dialects in Schools and Communities *is used with permission.*

Kinds of Language Differences

Dialects may differ from each other at several levels in addition to pronunciation. One fairly obvious difference is in vocabulary items: for example, the use of a term like *tonic* in some regions of New England to refer to what in other regions is called *pop, soda pop,* or simply *soda.* The retention of the term *icebox* by members of older generations where the younger generation uses *refrigerator* also reflects this type of difference, as do the British forms *jumper, chemist,* and *boot* for American *sweater, drugstore,* and (car) *trunk,* respectively.

Dialects also contrast with each other in terms of the way words are

composed and words are combined in sentences—the grammatical patterns of the language system. For example, in some rural areas of the South (reflecting an affinity with dialects of the British Isles), the plural *-s* may be left off of nouns of measurement as in *four mile down the road* or *sixteen pound of fish.* Other dialect areas would use the *-s* plural in these phrases. With respect to the combinations of words in sentences, an indirect question may be expressed as *He asked me could he go to the movies,* or as *He asked me if he could go to the movies;* negative patterns may be expressed as *He didn't do anything,* or as *He didn't do nothing.* In some dialects, both alternatives are used; in others, only one. Similarly, alternate responses to the question *Have you read that book?* illustrate a grammatical difference between British and American English: *No, but I should have done,* (British) versus *No, but I should have* (American).

Variation extends even beyond differences in pronunciation, vocabulary, and grammatical structure. There is also variation in how members of a group use particular language forms in social interaction. Thus, a Northerner and a Southerner may both use the terms of respect *sir* and *ma'am* but in contrasting ways that reflect different social and cultural conventions governing respect and familiarity. One social group may feel that it is appropriate to ask people what they do for a living, whereas another group may consider that question invasive. Some of these rules are explicitly discussed as children are socialized, but many are part of our unconscious knowledge about how to get along in the world through talking. Such differences in language use, often related to social and cultural group differences, may be hard to pinpoint but they can be highly sensitive areas of difference between groups and readily lead to cross-cultural communication conflict.

Speech communities—groups of people who share basic expectations about language use (Hymes, 1974)— also differ in the ways that they carry on conversation. For example, in some speech communities speakers overlap each other's talk enthusiastically in a good, satisfying conversation, whereas in others, a speaker is likely to stop talking when another one starts. Even what makes for a good conversational contribution can vary from group to group (Tannen, 1984). Garrison Keillor often refers humorously to what a good Minnesotan or a good Lutheran would say. One of his stories included a conversation in which a new boat owner responds to compliments by talking about the expense and time involved in maintaining the boat—as a good Minnesotan should, said Keillor—rather than saying how much fun it is (National Public Radio broadcast, July 1986). Speakers of English from other backgrounds might find such a response to be inappropriate and even insulting.

SOURCES OF DIALECT DIFFERENCE

Language differences on all levels ultimately reflect basic, patterned behavior differences between groups of people. There may be diverse reasons underlying differences in language, but they all derive from this basic principle. When groups are physically or socially separated in some way, language differences can be expected. As a language changes—and languages are always changing—differences show up between dialects as groups of people follow different paths of language change (Wolfram & Schilling-Estes, 1998).

Physical, cultural, and social facts are responsible for the variation in U.S. English. Many of the regional differences can be traced to combinations of physical factors in the country's history and geography. Some patterns can be explained by looking at settlement history, which suggests the language patterns of the early settlers (Carver, 1987). The movement of the population, historically and currently, also has a bearing on the language of regions because people take their language practices with them when they move. Finally, characteristics of physical geography must be considered. Natural barriers such as mountains and rivers have historically cut people off from each other, creating a natural basis for differences to emerge and be maintained.

Social and cultural factors are also responsible for diversity in ways of speaking. Social status and ethnic distinctions in our society are often reflected in language differences, along with age and gender distinctions. We would certainly expect that the greater the social distance between groups, the greater the language differences. This principle does not always work exactly, but it is a reasonably accurate predictor of how language differences reflect group behavior differences (Labov, 1972; Wolfram & Schilling-Estes, 1998).

When we consider the general principle that behavioral differences between groups correlate with language differences, it seems reasonable enough to expect that a lawyer from Arkansas will speak differently from a Northern automobile factory worker, or a White Appalachian farmer in an isolated mountain area will speak differently from a Black California business executive, or a Native American artist in New Mexico will speak differently from an Italian police officer in New York. These characterizations include geographical, social, and cultural factors, all of which have been prominent in distinguishing groups of individuals from each other in American society. The same distinctions are important in understanding language differences.

Studies of various dialect groups generally indicate that regional dialects tend to be distinguished by pronunciation and vocabulary features, whereas social dialects show variation in these areas as well as in grammatical usage (Wolfram & Fasold, 1974; Wolfram & Schilling-Estes, 1998). We might guess that someone was from eastern Massachusetts if he or she pronounced the word spelled *idea* with an *r* sound at the end ("idear") in a phrase like *the idear of it* and dropped the *r* sound on a word like *car* ("cah"): *Take the car*.

Many pronunciation differences concern the vowel sounds in words. For instance, many Southern regional dialects vary from dialects in other parts of the country according to the way that speakers pronounce words with vowel glides, like *line* or *ride*. (A glide is a vowel quality that is attached to a main vowel. The vowel in *line* or *ride* consists of a main vowel, *a*, which flows into a vowel with the quality of *ee* or *y* [e.g., "layn," "rayd"].) People from Southern regional areas are likely to say something like "lahn" or "rahd," whereas people from Northern areas would pronounce these words with the glide as in "layn" or "rayd". Other pronunciation variants involve particular words rather than sets of words. For some people *route* rhymes with *boot*; for others, with *bout*. Similarly, *creek* is pronounced as "crick" in some Northern areas, but as "creek" elsewhere. These pronunciation differences are popularly referred to as accent.

Regional dialects also differ in vocabulary. Depending on what part of the country you were in, for instance, you would need to order a *sub* (or a *submarine*), a *hoagie*, *grinder*, *hero*,

and so forth, to get a particular type of sandwich. Water might be obtained through a *faucet*, a *tap*, or a *spigot*; and children would *favor* or *resemble* one of their parents. These alternative vocabulary items are readily noticed and commented on when speakers from different regions meet.

Social dialects not only show variation in vocabulary items and pronunciation features, they also have differences in grammatical structure. Some members of rural, working-class communities might say *You was right* and *I done it* whereas a middle-class office worker in a city might use *You were right* and *I did it* to mean the same thing. Variations in the verb are typical of grammatical differences between dialects. They affect the systems for relating subjects to verbs (i.e., agreement patterns) and for choosing a form of the verb for a particular tense.

People sometimes ask us how many dialects of English there are. Somewhat surprisingly, there is no agreed-on answer to this question, even after decades of research on differences in American English. We can discuss, as we have, the many differences in the speech patterns of different groups of people, but deciding where one dialect ends and another begins and then counting how many there are is a different matter. Dialects do not come in neat, self-contained packages; and many factors, of varying degrees of importance, must be considered in distinguishing them.

LANGUAGE STANDARDS

There are numerous dialects that make up the English language. The first section of this chapter primarily concerned English in the United States. Imagine the range of variation if we included England, Australia, Jamaica, and other countries where English is spoken! Yet there is no one correct way to speak English, in the sense that one set of language patterns is inherently better than all the others. Certain language patterns are preferred over others, according to social norms (which may vary as well). These are often referred to in terms of the correct use of English, but correctness involves decisions based on social, not linguistic, acceptability.

Correct is a judgment that we make, typically based on some objective set of information. For example, the result of an addition problem, like 7 plus 3, has one correct solution (10), and all others are incorrect (11, 9, etc.). To compare arithmetic and language use, we must look for a set of objective facts against which we might judge whether something in language is correct or incorrect.

One set of facts we might be able to depend on is our ability as proficient English speakers to decide what can and cannot count as English. So, for example, when we hear a sentence like "They will arrive tomorrow," we can observe that it is English and therefore in that sense correct. On the other hand, we would know that "Arrive will tomorrow they" or "Ils arriveront demain" are both incorrect as English sentences in that sense, although the latter would qualify for another language. Similarly, we would judge *pencil* to be a correct form of English but *tloshg* would not be accepted. In each case, we seem to be identifying things that speakers of English might say—as opposed to what they would not say—based on our knowledge of the English language. Here is one set of objective facts that we share as speakers of English.

When it comes to ways of saying things that are not shared by all speakers of English, however, the notion of correct becomes much more elusive and, at the same time, quite controversial. Consider two English sentences that may be used by native speakers of English: *I done it wrong* or *I can't see*

nothing. It is clear that these are both possible sentences of English: When someone says a sentence like this, we would not want to claim that they were not speaking English. In this sense, then, these are both linguistically patterned English sentences, in contrast with non-English. However, if you ask someone about them, you may be told that they aren't good, proper, or correct English. Here, correctness is determined by social acceptability, rather than accuracy or intrinsic worth. There is no single basis, in terms of objective facts, for determining whether *I did it wrong* or *I done it wrong* is a better way to convey information. It is not possible, then, to identify just one way of speaking English as the correct way. The socially unacceptable forms, like *I done it*, are often termed *nonstandard*, to contrast them with *standard* forms or those that conform to social norms. These norms are based on judgments of social acceptability rather than technical assessments of linguistic patterning.

The value placed on a certain way of saying something is very closely associated with the cultural identity or the social status of the people who say it that way. This valuing is not an individual decision; it is the society's evaluation of different groups, including their ways of speaking. As we are socialized, we learn these attitudes, sometimes unconsciously, sometimes through expressed regulations and rules, just as we learn eating behavior. As children, we learn to eat peas with a fork instead of with a spoon or our fingers. The nutritional content of peas is the same regardless of how we eat them, and all three ways succeed in getting the peas into our mouths, but our society socializes us into viewing one way as proper or correct, and the other ways as unacceptable. In a similar way, the communicative effectiveness of *I done it* or *I did it* is identical, but we have been socialized into considering only one alternative as correct or proper and the other as incorrect or bad. In terms of social evaluation, then, correctness does not involve real, intrinsic linguistic value or assessment by any objective standard. What is acceptable according to the standards of the dominant group in society is considered correct; what is not acceptable to them will be looked on as incorrect.

Beliefs about language correctness are actually shared by most members of our society. Speakers from groups whose dialects are not highly regarded generally feel that their language is not as good as other people's. Those from groups who speak the favored dialects are likely to be aware of only some of the differences between their language variety and others, but to feel that their way of speaking is self-evidently preferable.

The U.S. situation is in no way unique in this regard. General acceptance of a standard language variety accompanied by negative attitudes toward the other language varieties is an unavoidable product of the interaction of language and society (Fasold, 1984; Preston, 1996).

Language and Logic

Like the notion of correct language, the idea that some dialects are more logical than others results from the social attitudes that surround language. Believing that standard forms of English are inherently better than others, many people will go on to maintain that certain linguistic structures are more logical than others, more systematic, and even more advantageous for cognitive development. There is no evidence, however, to support the contention that any language variety will interfere with the development of reasoning ability, or the ability to express logical concepts. All dialects and all languages adequately provide for the conceptualiza-

tion and expression of logical propositions, but the particular manner of this expression may differ among language systems.

The use of so-called double negatives, or two negative forms in a single sentence, is often cited as evidence that a particular language variety is illogical. According to this argument, two negatives in a sentence like *They can't go nowhere* should cancel each other so that the meaning becomes positive (*They can go somewhere*). Because sentences like this are intended to have a negative interpretation, the claim is made that the structure is illogical. (According to this position, *Nobody can't go nowhere*, with three negatives, would have to be accepted as a negative sentence.) However, the natural logic of language users is not identical to formal mathematic logic, where for some operations (e.g., multiplication), two negatives do yield a positive. Natural logic allows both *They can't go anywhere* and *They can't go nowhere* to have a negative interpretation, depending on the language use conventions of the particular dialect community. Both are expressions of the logical concept of negation, but the singly negated form is socially acceptable whereas the doubly negated form is not.

It is interesting to note that multiple negation was an acceptable structure for English in the past. During the Old English and Middle English periods in the history of English, the only way certain negative sentences could be formed was through the use of double negatives (e.g., "There was no man nowhere so virtuous"; Pyles & Algeo, 1982). The change to favoring the use of a single negative in sentences like *They can't do anything* is a relatively recent development. Many other modern languages have extensive use of double negatives as a part of their standard grammar. In the French language, the use of two negative words (*ne . . .*

rien) is the current standard for making a negative utterance, as in *Je ne sais rien, I don't know nothing*. Similarly, in Spanish *no* and *nada*, as in *No hace nada, She or he isn't doing nothing*, is the standard form for making a negative utterance.

Another notion related to dialects with nonstandard features is the interpretation that these features simply reflect incomplete learning of the standard dialect. Common phrases used to describe certain language features reveal and reinforce this notion, such as "leaving off the endings of words," or "not using complete sentences." In some cases, the English speakers who are said to "leave off the endings of words" are really applying a pronunciation pattern that all English speakers use to a limited degree. For example, all speakers of English will, in casual speech, sometimes pronounce a word like *fast* as "fas'," leaving off the final *t* sound, as in "fas'break." If you listen carefully to the speech of those around you, you will probably notice this process in use to varying degrees. It is just one of the pronunciation rules of English that happens more often in casual speech.

This pronunciation rule of English is used somewhat differently in certain dialects, and it is often noticed by speakers of other dialects. One difference is that the rule is used more often in some dialects, and the higher frequency makes it noticeable. Another difference is in where the pronunciation rule applies. If *fast* is pronounced "fas'" in a phrase like "fas' or slow," speakers of other dialects notice the absence of the *t* sound before the vowel at the beginning of the next word. The practice of "leaving off endings of words" is really a case of an English language rule of pronunciation that is used with minor, but noticeable, differences by different groups, but this practice is not restricted to any one group.

Similarly, all speakers of English use incomplete sentences. The following dialogue shows that we do not need to repeat in conversation what can be easily assumed:

Eva: When are you going to lunch?
Tom: Oh, about 12.

In fact, if Tom used a complete sentence in response, saying for example, *I'm going to lunch at 12 o'clock*, Eva might think that he was being ponderous or that he was annoyed.

The differences between dialects do not show that dialects are simpler or more complex versions of the same language. The differences show only that dialects are contrasting versions. Some of these differences may involve extensions or retractions of shared structures, but others reveal unique language forms that mark subtle but important meaning differences. As we shall see, verb forms in sentences such as *I liketa died, I done took out the garbage*, and *I be doing my homework* all encode meaning differences that are unique to nonstandard dialects. Standard varieties of English would have to use alternative phrasing to capture the precise meaning of the nonstandard forms. For example, to capture the exact meaning of *I be doing my homework* in Standard English, one would have to frame the sentence as *I always do my homework*, or to capture the specific meaning of *I done took out the garbage*, one would have to say something like *I have already finished taking out the garbage*. The relationship between standard and nonstandard forms in English obviously cannot be reduced to a matter of incomplete learning or language complexity.

Standard English

There is really no single dialect of English that corresponds to a standard

English, although many believe that such a dialect exists in the speech of those who use so-called good English (Preston, 1993, 1996). This belief is actually close to the social truth: The speech of a certain social group of people does define what is considered standard in English. However, the norms for Standard English are not identical in all communities. Furthermore, there are two sets of norms—the informal standard and the formal standard.

The norms of language usage that members of a society consider to be acceptable constitute their informal language standard. This set of norms correlates to the way certain people actually speak and allows variation between speech communities in the society. It is fairly flexible and regionalized so that there is an *informal Standard American English* for the South, the Northeast, and so forth. It is also subjective in that different people may evaluate standards somewhat differently based on their background.

Formal Standard English, on the other hand, includes the norms prescribed in grammar books and is most typically reflected in the written language. For example, the formal standard dictates that certain distinctions should be made in the use of *lie* and *lay*, that one should avoid ending a sentence with a preposition, and so on. However, acceptable spoken language usage does not necessarily conform to these norms. Informal Standard English would allow sentences like *They're the ones you should depend on* with no stigma attached, despite the final preposition. In fact, an utterance like *They are the ones on whom you should depend* is probably less acceptable in social interaction in many circumstances because of its formality. Formal Standard English patterns that differ from the informal standard ones are often taught in English language arts.

If the formal standard is used as a reference point, it is unlikely that anyone speaks the standard language consistently. The formal standard is generally limited to the written language of educated people, and it is heard only in the most formal style of highly educated members of society. The informal standard is spoken, however, by those whose language usage sets the guidelines for what is acceptable in each community.

Two observations need to be made about the informal standard. First, because all speakers use a range of styles depending on the situation of speaking, someone who is considered a speaker of Standard English may at times use particular language patterns that are clearly not standard. For example, in an appropriate situation, a standard speaker might use *ain't* or double negatives. In fact, a president of the United States once said in a nationally televised address that *Washington ain't seen nothin' yet*. This usage did not indicate that the president had suddenly become a speaker of a vernacular dialect of English. Presumably, this nonstandard form was used to evoke a sense of toughness and resiliency, characteristic connotations of vernacular dialect forms.

Second, a number of different varieties qualify as informal Standard English. For example, a standard speaker from Maine and a standard speaker from Tennessee would have quite different pronunciation patterns and probably certain other differences as well. They would both be accepted as Standard English speakers in their own communities, however, and in most others as well, despite the fact that their accent might be noticed outside their home region. But although the informal standard for American English includes a range of language patterns, particularly in the area of pronunciation, there is a unified notion of what is not acceptable (unless used for effect as in the previous example).

The situation becomes quite a bit more complicated when we consider World Englishes—the varieties of English spoken in other countries. Just as in the United States, there are likely to be standard and vernacular English language varieties in countries that were colonized by English speakers, where English has become the mother tongue of most people (e.g., New Zealand) or a second language spoken by nearly everyone for certain purposes, like business and higher education (e.g., Nigeria). English is used for special purposes in many other countries as well, and local standards have developed. When English speakers travel abroad, they may find that speech considered standard in their own country may be considered difficult to understand, odd, even nonstandard according to the standards of the host country. Here again, Standard English is relative to the particular norms of the speech community. Standard Singapore English is very different from any version of Standard American English. Thus it is more accurate to speak of Standard Englishes.

In every society there are people whose position or social status makes their judgments about language use more influential than those of others, including, for example, teachers and employers. These people decide who will get what placement in school and who will be hired. Their judgments about what is acceptable and unacceptable in language enter into evaluations made ostensibly on other bases, such as people's experience and achievement. Such judgments have more weight and more consequence than casual remarks about others' language in the course of daily life. These influential people are often looked up to by other members of their community whose opinions about matters like language are also typically respected. The speech habits of this social core are often admired and serve as a model of acceptability.

Standard American English, then, is a composite of the real spoken language of this group, generally professionals and others in the educated middle-class. Because members of this group in Chicago might sound quite different from their counterparts in Charleston, South Carolina, we need to recognize the existence of a number of dialects of Standard American English. For the most part, there is more shared structure in the grammar of Standard English speakers across communities than in pronunciation, but there are still some regional grammar differences that keep us from concluding that a single set of standard grammatical features exists. Different communities may have slightly different norms, and this informal set of norms is the one that really counts in terms of social acceptance. It is important, for this reason, to carefully distinguish between those norms that make up the formal standard and the informal, yet highly influential, norms of social acceptability that govern most everyday, interactional evaluations of standardness.

We use the term *Standard English* as a proper noun with a capital *s* on *standard*, but we intend it as a collective noun. Standard English is a collection of the socially preferred dialects from various parts of the United States and other English-speaking countries.

DIALECTS AND UNDERSTANDING

Given the differences among English dialects, it stands to reason that communication among speakers of different dialects might be occasionally flawed. But although problems in comprehension and interpretation can arise, the severity of these problems and their precise source is not always clear.

Certainly, there are Standard English speakers who claim not to understand vernacular speakers. To put this in perspective, however, we have to realize that this is a claim that one may also hear when a person travels through another region, such as a Northerner traveling through the South or a person from the mainland visiting a historically isolated island area in the Chesapeake Bay or the Outer Banks off of the coast of North Carolina. In most cases, such reports are exaggerated, based on a few items that may legitimately prove troublesome for an outsider to comprehend. An outsider in Appalachia for the first time may have difficulty comprehending certain *ire* words such as *fire* (pronounced much like *far*) or *buyer* (pronounced much like *bar*), or the use of a vocabulary item like *garret* for *attic* or *vittles* for *food*, unless there is sufficient context to interpret these items.

But such isolated problems would not usually result in a total breakdown of conversation. Adjustments may have to be made to comprehend certain pronunciations, grammatical patterns, and distinct vocabulary uses, but most speakers of Standard English seem able to do this with ease. Certainly, most English speakers who interact with speakers of another dialect on a regular basis do not encounter severe comprehension problems.

One of the factors that makes objective assessment of comprehension difficult relates to language attitudes. If speakers of a dominant, mainstream dialect feel that the vernacular version of the language is simply an unworthy approximation of what they perceive as the real language, then problems in comprehension are attributed primarily to vernacular speakers' inability to make themselves understood. In this interpretation, speakers of the main-

stream variety may be unwilling to make the usual kind of language adjustments necessary to enhance comprehension across dialects. Studies of comprehension and social relations in other language contact settings have shown that the relative status of groups can play a very prominent role in the comprehension of language varieties (Fasold, 1984). Typically, the higher status group claims comprehension difficulties with the lower status groups, not the converse. In fact, the relative social status of groups may be a more important factor determining intelligibility than the actual language differences.

Vernacular speakers generally indicate less overall comprehension difficulty with standard varieties of English than Standard English speakers do with vernacular varieties. Vernacular speakers are typically exposed to Standard English varieties through educational and official institutions and the media, whereas Standard English speakers usually do not have comparable exposure to vernacular dialects. And, as we pointed out earlier, our society simply expects and assumes that vernacular speakers will comprehend standard varieties whereas the converse does not hold. Questions about comprehensibility have not been laid to rest, however, and additional research in this area would be helpful to educators.

The conclusion that vernacular speakers seem to comprehend standard varieties better than standard dialect speakers comprehend the vernacular does not, however, mean that comprehension of the standard dialect can be assumed to be equivalent for all speakers of English regardless of their dialectal background. In fact, people of different dialect and cultural backgrounds may comprehend particular constructions differently. For instance, there may be differences in literal or nonliteral interpretations of sentences: For example, *See you later* may be interpreted simply as a ritualistic way of taking leave or a commitment to return. Different inferences may be drawn from particular sentence constructions or word choices: Instructions in a testing situation to "repeat what I say" may be interpreted by students from some backgrounds as a request to paraphrase the test giver's words, and by those from other backgrounds as a request to repeat the utterance verbatim.

Subtle types of miscomprehension of standard language conventions by vernacular speakers can have an effect just as significant as more transparent cases of vocabulary comprehension difficulty. For example, standardized educational tests may assume that all students understand the Standard English directions for the task in exactly the same way. If, however, this is not the case, then the scoring of differential responses given by different groups of students as correct or incorrect may be called into question. Claims about Standard English comprehension by vernacular dialect speakers may have been overstated because of the preoccupation with obvious cases of literal word meaning. Only painstaking, detailed analysis of extended notions of comprehension can uncover such meaning loss, but these cases are extremely important in understanding the full range of potential miscomprehension across dialects.

DEFICIT VERSUS DIFFERENCE

We have been saying that in terms of how languages are organized, no variety of a language is inherently better than another. No speakers have a disadvantage in their fundamental ability to function cognitively and expressively as a result of the variety of the language that they acquire.

The realities of the social situation in this country cannot be denied, however. Members of some cultural and linguistic groups are at a disadvantage because of their less favored or stigmatized status in society. They are viewed as deficient in certain areas by members of the social groups that have more power and authority in our society's institutions and systems—education, government, health care, employment, and so on. Members of the powerful groups often believe that members of the stigmatized groups must change in order to be accepted. Success in school for children from these disenfranchised groups, for example, may depend on their changing aspects of their language and language use, and adapting to school norms—which are generally more like the norms of the powerful groups than those of the stigmatized groups. For members of a mainstream, powerful group, no change or adaptation is necessary. In this sense, children from some groups may be at risk for school failure although they are not intrinsically disadvantaged.

Two major schools of thought concerning groups that contrast linguistically and culturally with mainstream society have been referred to as the *deficit position* and the *difference position*. In terms of language, proponents of the deficit position believe that speakers of dialects with nonstandard forms have a handicap—socially and cognitively—because the dialects are illogical, or sloppy, or just bad grammar. Intelligence test scores and results of other standardized language measures may be cited as evidence for this position (Bereiter, 1965; Hernnstein & Murray, 1994) even though issues of test bias are typically not considered. On the basis of these test scores, recommendations may be made for remedial language and other educational services. The concept of compensatory programs evolved from this position. Educational programs were designed to fill in the gaps in language and other skills caused by the students' so-called linguistic and environmental disadvantages. According to this position, then, speakers of socially stigmatized dialects have a language deficit that can impede their cognitive and social development.

The contrasting perspective, and the one advocated here, is the difference position that views groups of speakers in terms of the differences among their language systems. Because no one linguistic system can be shown to be inherently better, there is no reason to assume that using a particular dialect can be associated with having any kind of inherent deficit or advantage. This perspective calls into question the evidence from test scores and school performance that is used to support the need for remediation. If educators assume that a particular dialect is best, if they formally accept and encourage only that dialect, and if they test ability and achievement only through the medium of that dialect, then it should not be surprising that students who enter school already speaking it fare better than those who use a different dialect. An understanding of the social attitudes and values concerning the dialects and their speakers is thus needed in order to deal with the differences.

From time to time, these contrasting positions, which have been discussed for decades now, produce acrimonious debate played out in a public arena. For example, in December, 1996, the Unified School Board of Oakland adopted a resolution that recognized Ebonics or African American Vernacular English as a language system to be taken into account in teaching school children Standard English. The resolution provoked wide comment, much of it scathing denunciation of vernacular dialect and the school system's acceptance of what was thought of as deficient language. Everyone had some-

thing to say—prominent persons in government, civil rights, entertainment, and education; ordinary citizens; national organizations concerned with linguistic research and language teaching (see Box 1.1); and many, many reporters and editorial writers. In fact, the debate even extended to a Senate subcommittee hearing on the topic. At the heart of the Ebonics controversy was the long-standing conflict between the deficit and the difference positions.

Taking the view that Ebonics, the language spoken by many of their African American students, is a legitimate linguistic system, different from the Standard English system, Oakland schools use students' knowledge of Ebonics in teaching Standard English. In this way, the schools respect and exploit students' linguistic competence as a resource for language development rather than a deficit. Their intention is neither to eradicate Ebonics nor to teach it, as some thought, but to help students add another language system.

Most educators are generally aware that dialect differences can interfere in education, but the Ebonics debate shows that the deficit position is still widely held, and that there is no consensus on how dialect differences ought to be accommodated.

Box 1.1.

The Linguistic Society of America Resolution on the Oakland Ebonics Issue

Whereas there has been a great deal of discussion in the media and among the American public about the 18 December 1996 decision of the Oakland School Board to recognize the language variety spoken by many African American students and to take it into account in teaching Standard English, the Linguistic Society of America, as a society of scholars engaged in the scientific study of language, hereby resolves to make it known that:

a. The variety known as "Ebonics," "African American Vernacular English" (AAVE), and "Vernacular Black English" and by other names is systematic and rule-governed like all natural speech varieties. In fact, all human linguistic systems—spoken, signed, and written—are fundamentally regular. The systematic and expressive nature of the grammar and pronunciation patterns of the African American vernacular has been established by numerous scientific studies over the past thirty years. Characterizations of Ebonics as "slang," "mutant," "lazy," "defective," "ungrammatical," or "broken English" are incorrect and demeaning.

b. The distinction between "languages" and "dialects" is usually made more on social and political grounds than on purely linguistic ones. For example, different varieties of Chinese are popularly regarded as "dialects," though their speakers cannot understand each other, but speakers of Swedish and Norwegian, which are regarded as separate "languages," generally understand each other. What is important from a linguistic and educational point of view is not whether AAVE is called a "language" or a "dialect" but rather that its systematicity be recognized.

c. As affirmed in the LSA Statement of Language Rights (June 1996), there are individual and group benefits to maintaining vernacular speech varieties and there are scientific and human advantages to linguistic diversity. For those living in the United States there are also benefits in acquiring Standard English and resources should be made available to all who aspire to mastery of Standard English. The Oakland School Board's commitment to helping students master Standard English is commendable.

d. There is evidence from Sweden, the U.S., and other countries that speakers of other varieties can be aided in their learning of the standard variety by pedagogical approaches which recognize the legitimacy of the other varieties of a language. From this perspective, the Oakland School Board's decision to recognize the vernacular of African American students in teaching them Standard English is linguistically and pedagogically sound.

Chicago, Illinois
January 1997
Reprinted with permission of the Linguistic Society of America.

Language Improvement at School

Some aspects of schooling explicitly concern developing language skills. There is an emphasis on developing reading and writing across the curriculum, and in that sense everyone is expected to learn how to use language better. Students also may increase their repertoire of language styles in school. They may learn to critique each others' performance in unoffensive ways, to ask questions suggested by texts, to explain their thinking. They may also increase their vocabulary and develop other aspects of academic language in the content areas. Although these activities are not all a question of learning to use language better, there is certainly some development of language skills for educational and social purposes.

It is important to bear in mind that not all groups start from the same base in terms of the language and social habits that have been developed in the home community. For some groups, language socialization differs from that which schools typically require for various socioeducational functions (Heath, 1983). From the basically middle-class perspective of schools, these children may be viewed as not yet ready to learn. As they progress through a school curriculum, members of these groups must often develop a facility with certain standard dialect forms and ways of interacting with language. Thus, these students have an extra hurdle to overcome simply because they do not have the same background as others and because the school does not value some of their strengths.

Dialect differences between groups of students can affect the quality of education in at least two ways, in spite of sincere efforts to ensure equality of opportunity. One area that has been widely discussed is the possibility that a child's dialect may interfere with the acquisition of various skills (such as reading) and concepts on which later success might depend. More subtle, and perhaps more crucial, are the social consequences of being a member of a different dialect group. The attitudes of teachers and other educators, as well as other students, can have a tremendous impact on the education process. Often people who hear a vernacular dialect make erroneous assumptions about a speaker's intelligence, motivation, and even morality. This kind of dialect-based stereotyping can affect even those who value cultural difference and who pride themselves on treating everyone with respect because dialect prejudice can be very subtle and can operate on an unconscious level.

When a teacher or other school official reacts negatively toward a student's dialect, the result can be detrimental to students from nonmainstream backgrounds. Studies have shown that there can be a self-fulfilling prophecy in teachers' beliefs about their students' abilities (Rosenthal & Jacobson, 1968). It is possible that if a teacher underestimates a child's ability because of dialect differences, perhaps as a direct result, the child will do less well in that class. In some cases, students are tracked with less able students or placed in classes for students

with disabilities largely because of their speech patterns. Obviously, children's self-concept may be injured if they encounter negative opinions about their dialect, and they may take up the negative stance toward their own dialect that they experience at school themselves. So educational and social equity may be directly affected by dialect differences.

FURTHER STUDY

Alvarez, L., & Kolker, A. (Producers). (1987). *American tongues*. New York: Center for New American Media.

This award-winning video (available in a 56-minute full-length version and a 40-minute secondary school version) is an invaluable supplement to any presentation of American English dialects. In a highly entertaining way, it presents a basic introduction to the nature of dialects and dialect prejudice. It can be used with a wide range of audiences representing quite different backgrounds (e.g., civic groups, professional development for educators, human relations seminars), and can be counted on to provoke a lively postviewing discussion.

American Speech. A publication of the American Dialect Society. Tuscaloosa: The University of Alabama Press.

This quarterly journal publishes articles on American dialects of all types, balancing more technical treatments with shorter, nontechnical observations.

Bauer, L., & Trudgill, P. (Eds.). (1998). *Language myths*. New York: Penguin.

The chapters in this book examine some strong and widely held beliefs about language use that are at odds with findings from research.

Carver, C. M. (1987). *American regional dialects: A word geography*. Ann Arbor: University of Michigan Press.

This work offers the most complete discussion available of all major regional dialects of the United States based on vocabulary differences, and includes summary maps of each region. Criteria for distinguishing regional varieties of English are also discussed. It is intended for dialectologists, but can be read by serious students in other fields as well.

Cassidy, F. G. (Chief Editor). (1985, 1991, 1996). *Dictionary of American regional English* (Vols. I–III). Cambridge, MA: Belknap Press of Harvard University Press.

Three volumes of this massive dictionary of American regionalisms are now available: Volume I, covering entries from A to C (Cassidy, 1985), Volume II, covering entries from D to H (Cassidy & Hall, 1991), and Volume III, covering entries from I to O (Cassidy & Hall, 1996). The front matter in the first volume presents important background information about American dialects that is well worth reading for its own sake.

Ferguson, C. A., & Heath, S. B. (Eds.). (1981). *Language in the USA*. New York: Cambridge University Press.

This anthology covers a broad range of issues relating to English and other languages in the United States. It is divided into sections on 1) American English, 2) Languages before English, 3) Languages after English, and 4) Language in Use.

Lippi-Green, R. (1997). *English with an accent: Language, ideology and discrimination in the United States*. London/New York: Routledge.

Social attitudes toward accents are institutionalized in courts and perpetuated in the media and at work, so that people whose accents are not considered prestigious may suffer discrimination and job loss.

McKay, S. L., & Hornberger, N. H. (Eds.). (1996). *Sociolinguistics and language teaching*. Cambridge, England: Cambridge University Press.

Teachers in culturally diverse schools will find important background information in this collection of chapters on Language and Society, Language and Variation, Language and Interaction, and Language and Culture.

Miller-Cleary, L., & Linn, M. D. (Eds.). (1986). *Linguistics for teachers*. New York: McGraw-Hill.

This collection of articles covers a wide range of themes, including articles covered in this and subsequent chapters of this book. Topical areas covered are: History of English and Acquisition of Language; Language and Culture; Language and the Teaching of Reading and Writing; The Nature of Language and its Classroom Applications; and Teaching English as a Second Language. Many of the authorities relied on extensively in this book have articles in this collection.

For Further Thought

1. What was new to you in the discussion of dialects? What made the information surprising (what did you previously think?) and how might it affect your attitudes toward other English speakers?

2. The authors advocate the *difference*, as opposed to the *deficit*, position in regard to dialects. How do they account for the common idea that some dialects are superior to others? How do they deal with the issue of standards of effective speech and writing?

3. When you were a secondary student, were you aware of dialect differences among your fellow students? If so, explain how you became so aware and what the teacher's attitude seemed to be. If not, what might that say about the community in which you were educated?

4. What do you think is the role of the English teacher in regard to speech? Should we try to change the way students talk? Discuss the pros and cons of the issue.

5. In arguing their position, Adger, Christian, and Wolfram seem to be saying that the *deficit* position is something "society" has superimposed on neutral linguistic *differences*. But school is itself an extension of society. How realistic is this value-neutral attitude toward dialects?

Application 5.1:
Four Aspects of Language

Dialects

I spent the first twenty years of my life in New York City, where I spoke the dialect of the borough of Queens. Now I live in northern Minnesota and, like a linguistic chameleon, I have adapted to my sur-

roundings. Still, the dialect of my nurture betrays me from time to time. The chief culprit is the r sound, usually at the end of words. I still add an r to words like parka *or* alfalfa *and drop the r's indiscriminately, as in* boiler *or* carpenter. *On the grammar/usage side, little of New York speech persists, probably because I am an English teacher. However, I do wait "on line" instead of "in line" (despite the confusion with computer-speak) and continue to use* over *in place of* to *(as in "come over my house for dinner"). And certain terms have stayed with me. I have learned to say* pop *instead of* soda, *but the steps in front of my house will always be the* stoop.

For the most part, Minnesota-speak, now famous from the movie Fargo, *has become second-nature to me, except in extreme cases. My vowels have become elongated, though not to the extent of pronouncing* boat *and* vote *with two syllables or my own name as* Dee-un. *And I firmly resist the tendency to use the simple past in place of the past participle: "I have went" or "Have you ate yet?" are anathema to me. I have to bite my tongue when I hear them. On the other hand, I have adopted other localisms ("go with" for "go along") and nearly all the local terms, including* berm *for the strip of grass between the sidewalk and the street.*

In one of the activities that follow, you will be asked to describe the features of your own dialect. I've found it to be a revealing exercise. For if we are to convince students that language variation is normal and acceptable, we need to come to terms with our own beliefs and attitudes. In particular, we teachers need to be clear about two things: first, that each of us does indeed speak a dialect (this despite the inner conviction that we each speak "broadcast" English) and, second, that a person does not have to be a professional linguist to talk intelligently about language.

Of course, describing the way you speak is only a beginning. There is much more to be learned about the dialects of English, much for students to encounter and discuss. Indeed, the study of language variation, like the study of anthropology, humanizes us precisely because it makes us more deeply aware of people who are *not* like ourselves in some important ways. But this does not change the fact that studying language can begin with oneself and thus become a route to self-understanding.

That is why I began this application with a bit of linguistic autobiography. As you can see from my examples, I am not trying to be very scientific, or even complete, in my description. This is what I would call a first pass at a dialect description—an early attempt to think like a linguist. If we as teachers can do that and encourage it in students, we will have taken the first major step in helping them understand language.

Some Things to Consider About Dialect Study

1. Describe the features of a dialect you have spoken or one that you have lived with for some time. Do not be afraid: This is a brief, nontechnical exercise, and it should be fun. All you need to do is identify one phonological, one grammatical, and one lexical feature of a dialect. (The grammatical feature

might pose some problems; think of word order and agreement of different parts of a sentence.)

2. Consider the proposition that language is never studied in a truly neutral way. For example, look at your description of a dialect in the previous question. Is it neutral, or do you betray judgments about dialects? Or take my description at the start of this section: Why do you think I resist some features of the local dialect; why do others irritate me?

3. Complete the following checklist of regional expressions. Note particularly any instances where your use of a term has changed. How do you account for the change? Indicate those items in which the speaker's age might be just as important as the region.

4. Create a lesson in which students explore a dialect—either their own or one that is quite different. How will you illustrate the features of a dialect? How will you guide students in their research about dialects?

A Checklist of Regional Expressions*

Linguists sometimes use questionnaires to learn about dialects. The following checklist contains a few items from a much longer list used for this purpose. The focus is on vocabulary. Make four columns on a sheet of paper. In column 1, for each number, jot down the words you ordinarily use; in column 2, write those that you have heard others use; in column 3, put those that you have never heard before; in column 4, write any other words for this thing that you have heard people use. Be prepared to compare your answers with the rest of the class.

1. Paper container for groceries: bag, poke, sack, toot
2. Large open metal container for scrub water: pail, bucket
3. Web hanging from the ceiling of a room: cobweb, dust web, spider's web, web
4. Immediate family: my family, my folks, my parents, my people, my relatives, my relations, my kin, my kinfolks
5. Grass strip in the center of a divided road: median, center strip, separator, divider, barrier, grass strip, boulevard
6. Place where packaged groceries can be purchased: grocery store, general store, supermarket, store, delicatessen, grocery, market, food market, food store, super mart
7. A carbonated drink: pop, soda, soda pop, tonic, soft drink
8. Large sandwich designed to be a meal in itself: hero, submarine, hoagy, grinder, poor-boy
9. To be absent from school: bag school, bolt, cook jack, lay out, lie out, play hookey, play truant, run out of school, skip class, skip school, slip off from school, ditch, flick, flake school, blow school
10. Become ill with a cold: catch a cold, catch cold, get a cold, take cold, take a cold, come down with cold

---

*Excerpted and condensed from *Language Works*, by Ronald T. Shephard and Alan C. Coman. Copyright 1975 by McDougal, Littell & Company, Evanston, IL 60204.

Slang

> *How many ways are there to say you are tired? In 1991, a methods
> class quickly came up with a list of eighteen: wasted, out of it, spaced,
> pooped, beat, bummed, crapped out, dead, spent, worn out, wiped,
> bushed, zoned, whacked, gone, done-in, finito, vegged. A more re-
> cent class did not recognize crapped out or finito, and felt that
> bummed and vegged meant other things. How many will be in fash-
> ion by the time you read this book?*

Slang is in the air teenagers breathe. From *daddio* and *dig* in the 1950s, to
bummed and *cool* in the 1960s, the demise of *awesome* in the 80s, and the
return of *cool* in the 90s, young people have developed their own special
language. It is natural, healthy, and amusing, although it can also be cruel.

As the foregoing illustrates, slang is as much the result of language
change as it is an example of language variation. All language is subject to
change—not just slang, but dialects themselves, even the language that is
considered standard. There are large and complex issues here: how and
when words can be said to "enter" and "leave" a language, how language
contact affects both languages, how literature provides a history of changes
in the language, whether schools should encourage or retard change—these
and many more, including the more formal history of the English language
itself. Some of these issues will be discussed in the next application, but for
now we only note that the study of slang is a ready way to introduce students to the idea that English is a dynamic thing, undergoing constant
change.

But slang also illustrates language variation. For individuals, it is but one
of several language codes that vary from situation to situation and allow us
to negotiate our business in the world. It is the least formal of many registers
of language—different, for example, from the language we use in church, in
job interviews, and (as many teachers hope) in formal writing situations.
And the social functions of slang go further. Obviously, slang terms help
young people differentiate themselves and their peers from an older generation, but in addition the various slangs that proliferate in schools divide students into social groups. Mallspeak, for example, is one way of identifying
the speaker by interest, values, and social class—and the same can be said of
rap-speak, jock-speak, skateboard-speak, goth-speak, etc. As recent incidents of violence and conflict suggest, American schools are highly organized cultures in which students make very refined distinctions about each
other. Speech is one way to make those differences apparent.

We should recognize, therefore, that entering the "real world" of student
talk poses some problems and tensions. Language is never neutral. It is a
way of doing things: of acting cool, of separating one group from another, of
making others feel good or bad. For example, I might have listed terms for
ugly or out-of-it kids instead of just words for being tired. Or what about
words for drinking, vomiting, or sexual intercourse? Students certainly have
a rich vocabulary for these activities, but how should teachers respond—by
avoidance, confrontation, acceptance? Can this kind of language be treated

neutrally in spite of the moral and social norms it challenges or reinforces? And what should we do about the social groups that exist in the class itself? Can we examine terms like *nerd, geek, loser,* or *goth* in the abstract, as if they were not being applied to kids in the class?

Slang can be an incredibly rich source of material in the study of language, but there is nothing abstract about this kind of language to the boy who has been called a *wuss* or a *geek,* or the girl who has heard herself referred to as a *skank* or *dog.* I do not mean that we should avoid discussions of slang because they are too dangerous, but I do mean that we should proceed with caution, with due regard for students' feelings.

Some Things to Consider About the Study of Slang

1. Interview some teenagers, asking them what words they use in these categories: adjectives for tired (*zoned*) or good looking (*studly*); nouns for people who don't pay attention (*space cadets*); actions like being treated unfairly (*getting screwed*); emotions like being depressed (*bummed out*). Focus on new words—those that were not current when you were this age. Then make a list of "your" words, matched to the new ones you have discovered. Before beginning, look ahead to question 2, which strikes a note of caution.

2. Consider the following categories of words: nouns that denote an ugly girl (*dog*) or a social misfit (*nerd, geek*); actions like vomiting (*ralphing*) or being drunk (*hammered*); nouns that reinforce sexism (*chicks*); words for sexual feelings or activities (*horny, doing the nasty*). What are some of the dangers of discussing these words? What might be some of the advantages?

3. Think of other areas in which language is likely to change in noticeable ways—with the introduction of new technology (computer speech), for example, or because of contact with new groups of people. What are the possibilities for teaching in these areas? Are there dangers, like those previously mentioned, that language might alienate or divide people, as well as unite them?

4. Look at the following two activities. They are taken from Larry Andrews's *Language Exploration and Awareness* (Lawrence Erlbaum Associates, 1998). Discuss each of them, indicating whether you would use them in the classroom and at what grade level.

Two Language Explorations on Slang*

EXPLORATION: Leave it to Beaver and Bart

DIRECTIONS: Watching television carefully can help us learn a great deal about language. Watch one episode of *Leave it to Beaver* and one episode of *The Simpsons.* How many specific differences in language use can you observe? For example, how does Beaver greet his father; how does Bart greet Homer?

1. What slang terms did you see in the episodes?
2. How do Beaver's conversations with his friends differ from the ways Bart talks to his friends?

---

*From *Language Exploration and Awareness: A Resource Book for Teachers,* 2nd edition, by Larry Andrews (Mahwah, NJ: Lawrence Erlbaum Associates, 1998), pp. 229–230.

3. How do the conversations between Beaver and Wally differ from those between Bart and Lisa?

4. How do the parents on the two programs talk to their children?

5. What are some of the reasons for the language differences you've observed in these programs?

EXPLORATION: Good, Bad, or Ugly?
DIRECTIONS: Visit with a grandparent or a person old enough to be a grandparent about changes they've observed in the way language is being used today. Do they think the changes are examples of progress? Of decay? You might talk about the following:

1. What about "taboo" words? They seem to be used more casually today, in conversation, on TV. Is this acceptable?

2. What about the emphasis on gender-neutral words, like *fireperson* instead of *fireman*?

3. "Private products," for both men and women, are advertised openly. Is this a good idea?

4. What do the responses you receive tell you about language change?

Language Change

Later in this chapter, in "When Some of Them Don't Speak English," Larry Andrews discusses how we can help students for whom English is a second language. In this application, however, I'd like to reverse the emphasis and ask what we might do in the classroom with those "first languages." For it is on these other languages that the richness of English is based. This is not to deny the beauty of the Anglo Saxon and Norman heritage of our language, but it is to say that the vast influence of contemporary English today can be explained in part by its remarkable ability to assimilate words and structures from other languages.

I'd like to suggest, therefore, that our students can benefit from understanding something about the history of words, and to make the point I'd like to refer to a small booklet, now unfortunately out of print, called *Answering Students' Questions about Words* (NCTE, 1986). Part of NCTE's "Theory and Research into Practice" series, this short work by Gail E. Tompkins and David B. Yaden, Jr., offers a brief and readable history of the English language, followed by a series of "extension" exercises in which students explore questions about words in English. The limitation of the exercises, as you will see, is that they seldom go beyond look-up work. Nonetheless, the selection of words and advice on research is impressive. I'll be referring to two sections here: etymologies and loan words.

An etymology is the story of how a word took on the meanings associated with it, and some of those stories are quite interesting. Tompkins and Yaden provide lists of such words, with some advice on exploring their etymologies by using unabridged dictionaries. In particular, they provide "extrapolations," which are essentially translations of the abbreviated language of the dictionary. Hence: "deer [ME *der*, OE *deor* beast]" is extrapolated as "Our word *deer* originated as the Old English word *deor*, indicating any beast or animal. In the Middle English period, the word was written *der*. Today the word *deer* has become more specialized, referring to a particular kind of animal" (p. 27). Tompkins and Yaden argue that in examples like these students can come to appreciate the very concept of language change.

In a multicultural context, the process of language change can be illustrated through the study of "loan" words—that is, words from other languages. According to Tompkins and Yaden, "Perhaps as many as three-quarters of our words have been borrowed from other languages and incorporated into English" (p. 30). They cite *taco* and *spaghetti* as examples, but the concept goes well beyond the obvious instances of foods. Words are "loaned" and "borrowed" as cultural groups come in contact with each other—through travel and commerce, and (as is apparent in the U.S. experience) through immigration. Thus, the language provides a window into the diversity of American cultures. Certainly the student who exhibits anti-Hispanic attitudes should know that he cannot speak of his beloved guitar or eat a taco without using Spanish words.

Though I am not so naive as to think that understanding language is going to rid the world of bigotry, I do believe that the more one knows about how languages work, especially one's own, the more likely one is to be tolerant of how others speak. And perhaps it is not naive to go a step further, suggesting that the study of language, like the study of literature, is essentially a broadening experience. And one of the first steps in that process is to understand that words are not static: They have histories, and their meanings change over time. Moreover, in a world characterized by rapid change, many words are likely to change in a student's own lifetime.

Some Things to Consider About the History of Words

1. Look at the first etymology extension from Tompkins and Yaden's book. Look up three of the terms in the dictionary you ordinarily use and in an unabridged dictionary in a library. Comment on what you learn, including the difference in using the two dictionaries.

2. Look at the second etymology extension, the one that has to do with meaning changes. Look up three of these words, using two dictionaries (as in question 1). Then write a comment, including your thoughts on how technical you would want students to be in their understanding of ideas like rising, falling, widening, or narrowing.

3. Look at the first extension on loan words. Choose five of the words and look them up in an unabridged dictionary. Write what you learned. You do not have to use a map, but you should have some sense of where, geographically, these words came from. What is the value of this kind of activity?

4. In the second extension activity on loan words, Tompkins and Yaden attempt to vary the "look up" nature of the activity by suggesting that students "construct a matching game or puzzle using these and other animal names and etymologies." How else might you vary the activities? For example, how might you get students to do some writing based on the study of words and their histories?

Etymology Extensions*

1. Have students locate the etymologies for these words:

angel	manufacture	quick
biscuit	mercury	robot
caterpillar	mermaid	salary
dinosaur	muscle	sherbet
gossip	music	silly
helicopter	nice	sinister
humor	noon	tennis
husband	nostril	villain
ink	penguin	window
lord	pepper	world
lunatic	poodle	zodiac

Next, ask students to extrapolate using the information contained in the etymologies. How is salt related to salary? What mistake was made in naming the penguin? How could a muscle look like a little mouse to the Romans? Why was the word *mercury* chosen to name both a planet and an element?

2. The meaning of a word can change in four ways: it can (1) rise, (2) fall, (3) widen, or (4) narrow. For example, *nice* once meant "foolish or ignorant," and long ago the word *meat* was used to refer to food in general. Have students check the etymologies of these words to see how the meanings have changed:

adventure	flesh	nice
angel	fowl	notorious
barbarian	governor	silly
barn	knave	sly
brave	knife	smug
cavalier	marshall	starve
deer	meat	stink
disease	mischief	trivial
fabulous	naughty	villain

Loan Word Extensions*

1. Have students determine the source of the following words, write the words on small cards, and attach the cards to a world map according to country of origin.

assassin	frolic	mumbo jumbo
atom	get	noodle

---

*From *Answering Students' Questions about Words* by Gail E. Tompkins and David B. Yaden, Jr. (Urbana, IL: ERIC/NCTE, 1986), pp. 29–30, 32–33.

bagel	goulash	opossum
balcony	gymnast	orange
bandanna	hallelujah	outlaw
banjo	hammock	pajamas
barbecue	hibachi	paprika
bazaar	hula	parka
beige	hydrant	pastrami
bungalow	igloo	pentagon
cake	jaguar	piano
casserole	jubilee	piranha
chic	kayak	polka
chocolate	khaki	potato
chop suey	kimono	prairie
chutzpah	kindergarten	pretzel
cobra	kiosk	raccoon
cocoa	knife	ranch
coleslaw	law	restaurant
coyote	lei	rhyme
cul-de-sac	llama	robot
curry	macaroni	rug
czar	mosquito	Santa Claus
epidemic	motto	scold
extravaganza	mukluk	shampoo
sherbet	thug	vanilla
sister	tomahawk	violin
skate	tundra	waffle
skin	typhoon	waltz
skoal	ugly	wampum
skunk	ukelele	yacht
solo	umbrella	zenith
tepee	vampire	zero

2. Many animals have unusual or interesting names. For example, when Captain James Cook was exploring Australia in the eighteenth century, he reportedly asked his native guide the name of the large, jumping animal he saw. The guide replied, "Kangaroo," which meant "I don't know" in his language. The name has remained, and the kangaroo is the "I-don't-know animal" (Sarnoff and Ruffins 1981). Have students discover the etymologies of these animal names:

> *aardvark*: earth–pig (Dutch)
> *alligator*: lizard (Spanish)
> *beetle*: biter (English)
> *caterpillar*: hairy cat (Latin)
> *cobra*: snake with hood (Portuguese)
> *crocodile*: worm that crawls in gravel (Greek)
> *duck*: diver (English)
> *elephant*: ivory (Greek)
> *hippopotamus*: river horse (Greek)

leopard: lion–panther (Latin)
lobster: spider of the sea (Latin)
moose: he strips off bark (Native American)
octopus: eight feet (Greek)
opossum: white beast (Native American)
porpoise: pig–fish (Latin)
rhinoceros: nose horn (Greek)
spider: spinner (English)
squirrel: shadow–tail (Greek)
penguin: white head (Welsh)
porcupine: spine–porker (French)
walrus: whale–horse (Danish)

Language at Work in the World

Here is a joke: Two men sat at the far ends of a bar in New York City—a Jew at one end, a Chinese man at the other. They drank their beers in silence until the Jew got up, walked down toward the Chinese man, and suddenly socked him in the mouth, knocking him off his stool. The Chinese man struggled to his feet and asked, "What was that for?" "That was for Pearl Harbor," answered the Jew. "Pearl Harbor?" said the Chinese man, "That was the Japanese! I'm Chinese!" "Chinese, Japanese," said the Jew, "all the same to me." They both returned to their beers, but after a while the Chinese man stood up, walked toward the Jew, and socked him in the mouth, knocking him onto the ground. The Jew struggled to his feet and asked, "What was that for?" "That was for the Titanic," said the Chinese man. "The Titanic?" retorted the Jew, "that was an iceberg!" "Iceberg, Goldberg," said the Chinese man, "all the same to me."

Language can do so much. It can make things seem alike ("icebergs" and "Goldbergs"), but it can also pull things apart ("Jews" and "Chinese men"). It can make us laugh, but it can hurt us as well—and sometimes it can do both at the same time. The point is that language is always doing something; or rather, we are always doing things through the use of language.

Sometimes what language does is political in the ordinary sense of the term: It urges us to "stay the course," "support the troops," or "buy American." It can, as George Orwell pointed out in "Politics and the English Language," obfuscate and mislead. Every year, for example, an NCTE committee gives a "Doublespeak Award" to someone or some group that is deemed to have used language in a particularly misleading manner. But language is political in a broader sense as well—for example, in the way it supports or challenges distinctions in race, creed, and gender.

So language sells *ideas*—but, even more obviously, it sells *things*, especially nowadays when young people buy clothing less for its style than for the language that, literally, appears on it. Students know this, of course: They are savvy about advertising even as they are being manipulated by it. But the language of the marketplace is still worth exploring, as is the language of music and sports and anything else that teenagers find fascinating. In drawing out the implications of the language of commerce and advertising, we teachers can help students gain a little more control over the way it works in their lives.

Jokes are especially interesting because the implications are often concealed beneath the surface of good humor and fun. Thus, the joke at the start of this section may or may not offend you. If it does not offend, it is because in "telling" the joke I left out some stereotyping markers, like the term *Chinaman* or the Yiddish and Chinese accents that might be used as embellishments. Moreover, the danger of telling this particular joke is defused by the fact that it undercuts its own genre: It is an ethnic joke that ridicules the idea of ethnic stereotypes. But for all that, the joke is still a minefield of potentially explosive ideas—about the way men behave in bars, our tendency to lump people together, the legacy of World War II, and the power of getting the last word. Nothing here is really neutral or free of value, and that is what makes the joke worth analyzing.

Would treatment of a joke like this be too political for the classroom? I think not, although we should not be naive. If we worked with this joke, we might very well hear someone say that this is just the way Jews or "Chinamen" really are, and we would have to deal with that. My point is that in the study of language, the same kind of values and issues are encountered that arise in the study of literature. The risks are real, but in the end I do not think we can duck the responsibility of helping students see how language makes things happen in the world.

Some Things to Consider About the Social Uses of Language

1. Choose a joke and be prepared to tell it to the class, explaining how its language works, what audience it is aimed at, and what view of the world it supports or challenges. Remember that some jokes are more politically charged (and hence more likely to offend) than others. What are the pros and cons of dealing with jokes in the classroom?

2. Think of a product or advertising campaign and explore its use of language. This might involve a brand name (why should *B.U.M.* sell clothing?), a phrase ("*Be all that you can be*"), or a recurring pattern of language (words like *performance, power*, and *handling* in car ads). Make a list of products that might be interesting for students to work with.

3. Find out more about doublespeak. You might read Orwell's "Politics and the English Language," consult *English Journal* for more on the NCTE Committee on Public Doublespeak or consult its *Quarterly Review of Doublespeak*, or read through recent news reports on the lookout for misleading language. Write a paragraph describing what you learned.

4. Consider the issue of sexist language, describing how you would handle the following: the use of *he* as a generic pronoun; the use of gender in salutations to business letters; and the replacement of terms like *mailman, freshman*, or *congressman* in ordinary discourse.

5. Think about language as it works in the classroom. For example, how will you address students and how will you expect them to address you? What does it mean to "speak out of turn" in class? What kind of language is appropriate or inappropriate for the classroom? What kind of language rules will you enforce in your classroom?

6. Create a lesson in which you ask students to explore the language of some area that might be of interest to them—sports, advertising, technology, mu-

sic, and so on. At the heart of the lesson there should be an activity that leads students deeper into the language itself. You might need to set up some ground rules about what kind of language is acceptable.

Parsing the Question: "Why Teach Grammar?"

Russell Tabbert

In "Parsing the Question," Russell Tabbert makes one main point, but it is a crucial one. He distinguishes among the various ways in which the term grammar *is used, labeling them* grammar-1, grammar-2, *and* grammar-3. *As you read, pay close attention to these three meanings of the word; we will refer to these definitions in the various applications in this chapter.*

This essay appeared in English Journal, *Vol. 73, No. 8 (December 1984); copyright 1984 by the National Council of Teachers of English. It is reprinted with permission.*

In one sense, the question is academic. We teach grammar because the public wants us to, indeed demands it. For if there is a literacy "crisis," then the obvious solution must be to get "back to the basics." And what could be more fundamental to language arts instruction than a rigorous component of "grammar"? (In addition to phonics, of course.)

But that's not good enough. The wide and uncritical public acceptance of the need for grammar instruction should not make the question "Why?" a moot one for us, the language instruction professionals. We must have *academic* answers to justify spending the time, a rationale which explains how studying grammar fosters skills or enriches content we want students to learn. Further, I believe that we have the professional obligation to try to clarify the discussion of this part of the curriculum for the benefit of both the

education establishment as well as the public. Such clarification is badly needed, for there is considerable confusion about what "grammar" is and about what benefits its study provides.

First, what do people mean by *grammar* when they insist that it be in the curriculum? Consider the following typical outcries:

1. These kids need to study grammar. They can't even put together a basic English sentence.
2. These kids need to study grammar. They can't even diagram sentences or identify the parts of speech.
3. These kids need to study grammar. Their speech and writing are full of mistakes.

Though the remedy in each case is said to be "grammar," the symptoms are diverse enough that we should look closely at the basis of the supposed maladies to see if the same kind of pill is being requested for each.

In order to take the first literally—that the children can't construct basic sentences—the word *grammar* has to mean "the set of organizing principles which native speakers intuitively follow." In this sense *grammar* is the unconscious knowledge which we learned as very young children during language acquisition. From the spoken language around us we were able to discover, in some amazing and little understood way, what the elements and rules are for forming utterances.

No one taught us, and the ability is not open to inspection. Yet obviously speakers of the language share a complex, highly structured system, the abstract structure of the language itself—the *grammar*. To distinguish this sense of the word from others to come, we will call it *grammar*-1.

Now admittedly some congenital defect of infant trauma may prevent normal acquisition of *grammar*-1. Children thus deprived may literally be incapable of putting together a basic English sentence. But such children are comparatively few, and they have almost always been identified early and accommodated in special programs. The English speaking children who are in our regular classrooms—because they are within the limits of normal educability—all have *grammar*-1; they can all put together basic English sentences. Of course, students who are from homes in which English is not the actively used language are in quite another situation. But it is simply wrong to assert that our ordinary English speaking Johnnies and Joanies can't form basic sentences. We may not like some features of those sentences. Or we may want them to be more effectively constructed. Or we may wish the content were different. But none of that is *grammar*-1.

However, when it is charged that students can't diagram sentences or identify the parts of speech or words in them, there is good reason to accept this assessment, for now *grammar* is being used in quite a different sense. Whereas *grammar*-1 was the abstract underlying structure, here *grammar* means the theory of that structure, the concepts, terminology, and analytic techniques for talking about the language. *Grammar*-1 is unconscious knowledge; it is *knowing how*. *Grammar*-2, as we can call this second sense, is conscious knowledge; it is *knowing about* the language according to a particular descriptive model. In our society, as in most literate societies, we have developed the strong expectation that an educated person should know a basic set of concepts and associated terminology for commenting on sentence features. Of course we don't come by this *grammar*-2 naturally, because it isn't any part of the language acquisition process. We have to go to school to learn it. However, many students have difficulty doing so, few retain the knowledge for long, and hardly anyone finds it very exciting—teachers nor students. Yet its place in the curriculum is probably secure, at least during the foreseeable short term, for the assumption is widely held that a heavy dose of *grammar*-2 is very important for improving language skills, especially writing. We will examine the possible connection between *grammar*-2 study and writing improvement in a moment.

First, however, we must notice still a third kind of lament over a deficiency in "grammar." It is frequently pointed out that students confuse *lie* and *lay*, do not choose *who* and *whom* correctly, say *infer* instead of *imply*, mismatch subjects and verbs, mix up pronoun reference, use double negatives, etc., and that these mistakes are evidence of their need to study grammar. In such a claim we have *grammar* being used to mean not "underlying structure" (*grammar*-1) or "theory of the structure" (*grammar*-2) but "linguistic etiquette," the rules of "proper" verbal manners which tell us what to do to be correct but most frequently what to avoid. This collection of "don'ts" is popularly called "grammar," and in fact must surely be what most people think of when the term is used. So here we have *grammar*-3, and here the other grammar responsibility assigned to the schools. However, the distinction is usually considerably blurred. We don't find separate *grammar*-2 and *grammar*-3 textbooks. And sometimes single lessons will mix description and pre/proscription, especially in using concepts and terminology from *grammar*-2 to explain the *grammar*-3 errors. But the two are fundamentally different in nature.

Most people, including educators, do not feel any need to justify teaching grammar. Thus the possible benefits remain unspecified and their validity unexamined. My purpose in what follows is to attempt to state precisely the range of possible justifications for including grammar study in the curriculum, keeping in mind that they are not mutually exclusive. First for *grammar*-2.

Either or both of two general benefits have been claimed for consciously knowing about the structure of sentences. The first is that it has humanistic value, that it is liberating knowledge for its own sake. This lofty view was expressed strongly in a statement from the NCTE Commission on Composition (1974, no. 12):

> The study of the structure and history of language, including English grammar, is a valuable asset to a liberal education and an important part of the English program. It should, however, be taught for its own sake, not as a substitute for composition, and not with the pretense that it is taught only to improve writing.

Or more eloquently, Bradford Arthur in *Teaching English to Speakers of English* (1973, p. 150):

> The study of language need not be justified by its effect on learning academic skills. If man needs or desires to understand himself and other human beings and if education helps satisfy this need, then the study of language does not have to be an aid to reading or writing, or to anything else. Our ability to think, act, feel, and interact as human beings is bound up

with our ability to speak to and understand each other. In learning about language, a student is learning about himself: no further justification is necessary.

But if the continued funding of grammar teaching depended just on its humanistic value, we would see its place in the curriculum shrivel to insignificance. We are a much more pragmatic people than that; almost all the support that exists for grammar instruction rests on the belief that knowing grammar contributes to improving language use, especially writing. However, much less clear, because seldom discussed, are the exact ways in which grammatical knowledge may aid writing improvement.

Two pragmatic ends are offered for knowing *grammar*-2, one productive and the other editorial. The stronger claim is that knowing *grammar*-2 enables the writer to consciously and actively choose from a wider range of structural resources, the result being more direct, sophisticated, varied, and well-structured sentences and discourse. For example, knowing how subordinate clauses are formed in English allows one to structure interrelated propositions effectively and precisely. Or being aware of the devices for attaching free sentence modifiers improves the use of detail in descriptive writing. Some approaches actually require students to practice using these structures in specific ways. However, mostly it is assumed that the knowledge itself is sufficient and that it will transfer when appropriate writing situations arise. In the words of one widely used text:

> Just as there are careful and effective drivers who do not know what makes a car run, so there are those who, through practice and skillful observation, have become satisfactory, even effective, writers with very little un-

derstanding of the mechanics of the language. But it follows that the more you know about the form and function of the parts that make up the larger unit, the sentence, the better equipped you are to recognize and to construct well-formed sentences.... (Emery, et al, 1978, p. 1)

The weaker, but more common claim, is that the ability to analyze sentences grammatically helps the writer to recognize problems and to understand how to remedy them. These may be stylistic problems, such as monotonous patterns or awkward passives or front-heavy subjects. However, by far the most frequent application of *grammar*-2 knowledge is in learning the "mechanics" of standard written English, primarily punctuation and correct linguistic etiquette (*grammar*-3). Because we don't acquire these editorial rules naturally, we have to learn them consciously, usually in school. But to be teachable, the content must be analyzed and be specified with a nomenclature. This is precisely what *grammar*-2 provides—the shared concepts and associated terminology by which the linguistic preferences of the elite can be objectified as rules learnable by anyone. As John Warriner (n.d., p. 8) puts it: "The chief usefulness of grammar is that it provides a convenient and, indeed, as English is taught today, an almost indispensable set of terms to use in talking about language."

To summarize, the justifications for teaching *grammar*-2—that is, conscious theoretical knowledge about the structure of the language—are that

1. The knowledge has humanistic, liberating value for its own sake; *and/or*
2. the knowledge improves language use, especially writing,
   a. by making the writer aware of the grammatical resources available for creating effective sentences, *and/or*

b. by providing the student and teacher with a common basis for recognizing and analyzing sentence problems and for learning to remedy them.

The obvious justification for teaching *grammar*-3—the collection of linguistic behaviors to be avoided—is that we want our students' writing to be free of the sorts of errors that would mark them as uneducated. However, when we examine attitudes towards the teaching of linguistic etiquette, we find two sharply differentiated assumptions. The prevailing belief is that the rules should be taught as absolutes, what Joseph Williams (1981, p. 166) has called the standard of "Transcendental Correctness." Thus, as much as possible, all rules are treated as having about equal validity and each as being applicable in virtually all writing situations. Opposed to this, however, is the view that the teaching of *grammar*-3 should have a relativistic justification, what can be called the standard of usage. If we are training our students for the real world of writing, then our instruction should be based on—and should reflect—what successful writers actually do. Therefore, how the rules are justified will depend on whether specific ones are generally heeded, generally ignored, heeded variably according to context, or heeded by some writers and ignored by others.

There might be still other justifications offered for teaching grammar, such as that it exercises some general analytic or reasoning faculty or that the knowledge is simply an essential mark of an educated, cultured person. However, I believe that the reasons specified above account for the preponderance of attitudes and assumptions about why American students should be taught grammar.

The question now remains: can any of these justifications, alone or together, support a prominent place for grammar instruction in the curriculum? I leave aside here the important question of whether, in fact, teaching grammar achieves the ends claimed. There is a long history of research attempting to measure the alleged practical benefits of studying English grammar. These research results are reviewed and assessed in a number of places, including Braddock, et al. (1963), Sherwin (1969), Elley, et al. (1979), and Kolln (1981). Overall the research gives little cause for optimism. But for my purposes this doesn't matter. Let's assume that the research designs were faulty or that the wrong kind of grammar was used or that the teaching method was bad. Let's assume that grammar instruction *is* effective. I want teachers, administrators, and the public to seriously consider whether the ends that are claimed justify the time and resources required to achieve the necessary level of knowledge and skill.

As a linguist I would enjoy being able to plump the importance of part of my stock in trade, grammar. However, in my short career I have seen the pendulum swing from one grammatical excess to the other in the American school curriculum. In the late 1960s and early 1970s the salvation was to be "linguistic" grammar. If traditional grammar hadn't worked, it was because it was the wrong grammar—prescientific, prescriptive, Latinate. What was need was the "new grammar," descriptions of English according to the structural or transformational models then current or evolving in linguistic research. They came, and though many of the textbook versions were superficial and poorly done, there were several thorough treatments which, within the limits of theory and knowledge then available, accounted for large amounts of English structure, and quite systematically and explicitly too. The epitome of the trend was the kindergarten to high

school *Roberts English Series*, which immersed the students in detailed information about the structure of English presented within the framework of early transformational grammar.

For many reasons, some of which should have been obvious early on, the "new grammar" failed. The fad quickly passed, hastened by the growing perception of a "crisis" in the reading and writing abilities of the students of the mid and late 1970s. Obviously if the "new grammar" hadn't succeeded—in fact, according to some, had contributed to the problems—then the direction to go was back to the old grammar, the "traditional grammar" with its relatively few, relatively familiar terms and concepts and especially with its no-nonsense emphasis on "correctness." The pendulum has swung, and now with overwhelming public and establishment support, grammar again rides high in the textbooks being published and in curricular changes being made or urged. Like phonics, grammar (this time "real" grammar) is one of the "basics" that we are getting back to.

What can we expect from this renewed stressing of the old grammar? Will literacy improve? Will verbal test scores rise? Will the impatient public be satisfied that language arts teachers are using the appropriate means to achieve the right ends?

Since standardized tests almost always check on the control of correct punctuation and linguistic etiquette, it is possible that a wide, sustained instructional emphasis on *grammar*-2 and *grammar*-3 could result in somewhat improved verbal scores. If we started the drilling and memorizing early and insisted more strongly on the importance of the skills, then we could reasonably expect that more students would retain more of it. That is the direction we seem to be going, and if this trend lasts long enough, then we will likely produce young writers who are better able to edit the surface features of their writing.

Will the public be satisfied? Probably yes, at least partly. The expressions of concern about writing are almost never occasioned by, or exemplified by, problems such as poor organization, inadequate development, inappropriate tone, etc. Rather, the handwringing attaches to bad spelling and punctuation and to the grosser errors in linguistic etiquette. If we can show that language arts instruction has improved on these problems, then public criticism will, I think, be considerably diminished.

But will literacy have been improved significantly? That, I think, is the serious question which we must raise both for our own professional consideration in rationalizing our instructional goals and methods and also for the larger public policy discussions. For I sense that once again unrealistic hopes are being raised for "grammar." I have tried to show through my close specification of answers to "Why teach grammar?" that the benefits which can possibly be claimed are few and modest, even when accepted collectively. But especially when we consider the benefit which overwhelmingly justifies grammar instruction—error avoidance—we see how narrow is the base on which such great expectations are founded.

I am not saying that we shouldn't teach grammar. We should, both *grammar*-2 and *grammar*-3. And we should do it more interestingly and effectively so that in fact our students *are*

more knowledgeable about the structure of English and *are* better editors. But we should not allow the current enthusiasm for grammar to distort the curriculum. True literacy is more than the negative virtue of not making mistakes, and it cannot be attained primarily through analyzing sentences and memorizing rules. Reading and writing must remain the center of the language arts curriculum, "basics" which we must be prepared to explain and defend to colleagues, administrators, school boards, and the public.

REFERENCES

Arthur, Bradford. *Teaching English to Speakers of English*. New York: Harcourt, 1973.

Braddock, Richard, R. Lloyd-Jones, and Lowell Schoer. *Research in Written Composition*. Urbana, Illinois: NCTE, 1963.

Elley, W. B., I. H. Barham, H. Lamb, and M. Wyllie. *The Role of Grammar in a Secondary School Curriculum*. Wellington: New Zealand Council for Educational Research, 1979.

Emery, D., J. Kierzek, and P. Lindblom. *English Fundamentals*, 6th ed. New York: Macmillan, 1978.

Kolln, M. "Closing the Books on Alchemy." *College Composition and Communication* 32 (May 1981): 139–151.

NCTE Commission on Composition. "Teaching Composition: A Statement." Urbana, Illinois: NCTE, 1974.

Sherwin, J. *Four Problems in Teaching English: A Critique of Research*. Scranton, Pennsylvania: International Textbook, 1969.

Warriner, J. E. "The Teaching of Composition." Pamphlet published by Harcourt School Department, n.d.

Williams, J. *Style: Ten Lessons in Clarity and Grace*. Glenview, Illinois: Scott Foresman, 1981.

For Further Thought

1. Think about Tabbert's distinctions among the various meanings of "grammar." Explain grammar-1, grammar-2, and grammar-3 in a paragraph each. Cite an example of each that is not mentioned in the article.

2. Tabbert says that grammar-2 and grammar-3 are "fundamentally different in nature" (p. 246). We can grant that point, and yet it seems that some concerns of grammar-3 can be explained in grammatical terms. For example, at

the start of that same paragraph he mentions the confusion of *who* and *whom*. Is this simply a usage rule to be taught separately, or might it be taught more systematically in a grammar unit on "pronoun case"?

3. Tabbert raises, but does not pursue, the possibility that grammar instruction might have benefits other than reducing errors in writing—for example, in the study of a foreign language. Discuss those possible benefits. You might want to look at Constance Weaver's comments in the opening section of the next essay, "Teaching Grammar in the Context of Writing" (pp. 255–257).

4. Think about what your teachers seemed to believe about grammar. Did they seem to work from the kinds of distinctions that Tabbert discusses, or did they take a monolithic view of grammar? Did they say that learning grammar would improve your writing?

5. At this stage in your thinking about grammar, what do you think are the implications of this article for teaching? Which, if any, of these grammars could (or should) be explicitly taught?

Application 5.2:
Grammar for Teachers?

Reviewing Traditional Grammar

> . . . *teachers need not to teach grammar so much as use their knowledge of grammar in helping students understand and use language more effectively. (Constance Weaver,* Grammar for Teachers, *pp. 5–6)*

Weaver's position could be restated this way: Regardless of what we require of students in respect to grammatical knowledge, teachers need to have a firm understanding of grammar. After all, we still need to talk to students about sentences—the parts of a sentence, the relationship of those parts to each other, the conventions of punctuation that show those relationships. These are all grammatical concerns. Although we might want to bypass the terminology and formal rules of traditional grammar as we talk with students, it would be difficult to help them with sentence-level concerns without some understanding of English grammar.

In this respect, any English grammar would be helpful. One could even argue that transformational grammar offers potentially deeper insights into the complexities of English sentences than does traditional grammar. But in practical terms, we need to recognize that traditional grammar, for better or for worse, is still current in the teaching of English. Even if you choose to avoid the formal grammar instruction, some students (though perhaps not many) will know something about traditional grammar and will expect you to know it. On an even more practical level, parents, administrators, and fellow teachers might well have the same expectation. This suggests that it would be wise for you to know something about traditional grammar.

These latter reasons might seem self-serving or even cynical. Still, it is good to know what is expected of you. If you doubt that, look ahead at the Petruzzella article and review the comments of the cooperating teachers about their student teachers (pp. 273–274). Do you really want to be characterized this way by your colleagues? And regardless of what people might think of you, the main reason for knowing grammar is that you need to know as much as possible about the way sentences work. Again, your knowledge of the subject does not determine a student's need to learn it. By analogy, if you are to teach *Romeo and Juliet,* it could help you to know a great deal more about Shakespeare than students ever need to know. The same might be true of grammar.

As you take the grammar test (below) you might experience one of two emotions. If your knowledge of traditional grammar is shaky, perhaps because you didn't ever "get it" in seventh and eighth grade, you might feel discouraged. You might say: "I can write sentences, but I don't know most of this stuff! How will I ever teach it?" Or you might experience the opposite reaction, feeling elated that you did well on the test. "Look at that," you might say, "I'm prepared to teach grammar!" Although it is obviously better to do well on the test than to bomb it, neither of these reactions is totally appropriate. The test is designed to review a few aspects of traditional grammar, not to test your understanding of language. I am certainly not urging you to teach these concepts to students. It is a question of your own understanding of traditional grammar: How much do you know and how comfortable are you with the state of your knowledge?

Some Things to Consider About Traditional Grammar

1. Take the review test that follows. Then comment on the test itself and the state of your own grammatical knowledge. How much of this, if anything, would you want students to know?

2. Recall your own experiences with grammar. How well did you learn it? Was it rewarding or disheartening? In what sense, and for whom, is grammar fun?

3. Rei Noguchi, in *Grammar and the Teaching of Writing* (NCTE, 1991), suggests the following components of a basic, working grammar for the schools: *sentence, nonsentence (fragment), modifier, subject,* and *verb* (p. 34). What do you think of this pared-down grammar? What would you add or remove?

4. Sentence diagraming has a bad reputation, whether it be traditional (Reed-Kellogg) diagraming or transformational (tree) diagraming. Yet some people feel that a way of representing a sentence visually would help some students. Take any three of the sentences in the test and represent their structure visually, using a standard format or some kind of map of your own. Then comment on the usefulness of this approach.

5. Think about the attraction that grammar holds for many teachers. What is it about the discipline of English that creates in many teachers a *need* to teach grammar?

A Test of Traditional Grammar

The following is a test of some aspects of traditional grammar. Take it with or without reference to a grammar book, depending on what your instructor says. Note that each section has two parts.

1. Parts of Speech
   (a) Identify the part of speech for each word in the following sentences: noun, pronoun, verb, adjective, article, adverb, preposition, conjunction, and interjection. Decide for your-

self how detailed to be (e.g., whether it's a "proper" or "common" noun).

The boy who was wearing the red sweater left quickly.

The: _____   the: _____
boy: _____   red: _____
who: _____   sweater: _____
was: _____   left: _____
wearing: _____   quickly: _____

Oh, Albert and I were in deep trouble.

Oh: _____   were: _____
Albert: _____   in: _____
and: _____   deep: _____
I: _____   trouble: _____

(b) Describe the function of each of the words above. Try to use your own words, not the definition from a grammar book.

2. Dependent and Independent Clauses

    (a) Underline the dependent clause (if there is one) in each of the following sentences.

    You'll recognize it when you get there.
    He who laughs last laughs best.
    Caesar came, saw, and conquered.
    If at first you don't succeed, try, try again.
    Time flies.

    (b) Using your own words, explain why each of the three dependent clauses above is "dependent." In each case, what is the relation of this clause to the independent clause? Then explain what makes the independent clauses "independent."

3. Phrases

    (a) Identify the italicized phrase in each sentence.

    Without my date book, I'm totally lost. _____
    Swimming alone can be dangerous. _____
    Jones, *the pitcher of record,* lost the game. _____
    They traveled westward, *driving Route 66.* _____

    (b) Using your own words, explain how each of the phrases above relates to the rest of the sentence.

4. Verbs

    (a) For each of the following sentences, (1) underline the verb; (2) if it is the verb "to be," describe its function in the sentence; (3) if it is an action verb, indicate whether it is transitive or intransitive—and if it is transitive, whether it is in active or passive voice.

    The Twins defeated the Yankees.
    They have only won twice this year.
    In fact, they have been beaten at least once by every team they have faced.
    The team was long overdue for a victory.

    (b) In your own words, explain how you knew a verb was transitive or intransitive, active or passive.

Traditional Grammar Exercises

Here is a situation: You have recently been hired to teach ninth-grade English. One of the first things you learn from the other English teachers is that you are expected to teach grammar (traditional grammar, of course) and to use the textbooks the other teachers use. Looking through the book, you find that the work consists largely of exercises (a sampling of which is included here). You are the "new kid" in the school and are eager to get along with the other teachers.

There are lots of problems with grammar exercises. There is something unreal about the way language is used in them: They are usually written, not to make sense, but to focus attention on some point of grammar. Moreover, exercises do not in themselves connect very well to what students are writing: This is somebody else's language on somebody else's topic, focusing on matters that are not necessarily relevant to what a student is reading or writing. And finally, as you have seen, there is reason to doubt whether teaching grammar in isolation can have much effect on students' ability to write.

You might therefore be tempted to avoid grammar instruction entirely, yet this is not always possible or desirable. As the preceding scenario suggests, you might very well be asked to teacher grammar, whether you want to or not. And, as Constance Weaver points out in the next reading, it may not be good to give up on grammar prematurely: There might well be points of connection between grammar and writing, insofar as each is concerned with the fashioning of sentences. If instruction takes place in the context of meaningful writing projects for students, then minilessons on points of grammar and usage might have a role in the curriculum.

The preceding situation poses the teaching problem in the baldest possible terms. As a teacher, you are clearly constrained—told what to teach and required to use certain materials. Yet even within this straitjacket situation, you have some freedom. You are not told when to teach the various points of grammar (though in some schools this might be the case). You are not told that you must use only the textbook. And, most importantly, you are not told how to use the textbook.

It is well to remember, too, that a situation like this is not just a problem (a negative view); it is also a problem to solve (like a puzzle). As is often the case with teaching, we are presented with a less than perfect situation—but part of the fun of teaching is using creativity to solve the problem, making a virtue of necessity by adapting materials to suit our own goals.

Some Things to Consider About Grammar Exercises

1. Think about the situation illustrated in the opening paragraph of this application. First, do you think it is reasonable or unreasonable for new teachers to feel this kind of pressure? Second, what are some of your alternatives within the situation? Third, which course of action would you adopt?

2. Look at the sample grammar exercises that follow. As the instructions indicate, each works in a slightly different way: identify the error, fill in the blanks, and choose the alternative. What are the advantages and disadvantages of each approach?

3. We know that good writing and correct writing are not necessarily the same thing, and these exercises sometimes make the point dramatically. Locate in the exercises where a standard of correctness is being promoted even when sentences are poorly written and ineffective. (The first sentence in the first group is a case in point.) What would you say to students about these sentences?

4. Adapt the exercises to improve them and make them fit with your goals in teaching. For example, which sentences would you drop entirely? Which would you change? Would you alter the instructions? Explain your choices.

5. Find a grammar book, preferably one that is used in the local schools. Describe the kinds of grammatical issues covered by the book and analyze at least one exercise as you did in question 3, adapting it as you did in question 4.

6. Create a minilesson on a point of grammar or usage. You could use one of the ideas from these exercises—pronoun case, sentence punctuation, or subject–verb agreement—or come up with an idea of your own.

Sample Grammar Exercises

I. This is an exercise in pronoun case. Decide whether the underlined pronouns are in the correct case. If so, write C for *correct* after the sentence; if there is an error, write the correct form of the pronoun after the sentence.

   1. *They* and *he* were the first to arrive.
   2. I was bewildered by *him* asking that question.
   3. Did you know that *me* and Bob were cousins?
   4. *Whom* do you think he came with?
   5. They left it up to Bill and *I*.
   6. The ball belongs to *us* boys.

II. This also is an exercise in pronoun case. Fill in the blank with a pronoun of the correct case. Vary your pronouns.

   1. Once we had picked up Erika, _____ girls drove to the party.
   2. Erika was late, _____ having waited for her friend, Janet.
   3. So we all walked in with Erika and _____.
   4. _____ do you think was there?
   5. The first person to see _____ was Janet's old boyfriend, Todd.
   6. _____ and Erika turned and walked out.

III. This is an exercise in subject–verb agreement. Choose the correct form from those listed within the parentheses.

   1. Where there is no evidence to the contrary, the presence of dark spots (suggest, suggests) a harmful condition.
   2. Specialists who see this condition frequently (recommend, recommends) immediate treatment.

3. These treatments, which (cost, costs) a great deal, are highly effective.

4. Two thousand dollars (is, are) the cost of one week's treatment.

5. Few (has, have) enough insurance to cover this expense.

6. Thus a rich man and a poor man (do, does) not have equal access to treatment.

Teaching Grammar in the Context of Writing

Constance Weaver

In Grammar for Teachers *(NCTE, 1979), Constance Weaver analyzed the available research on the relationship of grammar to writing, recasting the whole debate in terms of reading and writing theory. Her latest book,* Teaching Grammar in Context *(Boynton/Cook-Heinemann, 1996) extends the ideas of the earlier work. This* English Journal *article does not cover all the topics of the book, but it does lay out Weaver's basic positions. Like Tabbert, she sees in the research data no clear relationship between isolated grammar study and writing improvement. She does not conclude that grammar is useless for writers, but she has some definite ideas on how and when grammar should be taught. The title contains the main idea, but there is more to it than that: As you read, think about what she says about learning theories and be prepared to discuss the classroom practices that she cites.*

This essay appeared in English Journal, *Vol. 85, No. 7 (November 1996); copyright 1996 by the National Council of Teachers of English. It is reprinted with permission.*

While I was doing research for my book *Teaching Grammar in Context* (1996b),

I was surprised to discover that during the Middle Ages, grammar was considered the foundation of all knowledge, the necessary prerequisite for understanding theology and philosophy as well as literature. As Jeffrey F. Huntsman (1983) puts it, "grammar was thought to discipline the mind and the soul at the same time" (59). I was even more surprised to discover that a major publisher of textbooks used in home schooling and in fundamentalist schools describes a certain middle grade grammar and writing program (*God's Gift of Language Series*) by saying that "Grammar is taught with the purpose of making clear to the students the orderly structure of their language, a picture of God's orderly plan for the world and for their lives" (A Beka Book, 1996, *Home School Catalogue*, 36). Clearly some people think that grammar should be taught as a formal system because it represents order, authority, and something that—to them—seems absolute, without question (Chapman 1986; Holderer 1995; Gaddy, Hall, and Marzano 1996).

With such deep-seated beliefs, some parents and community members argue vociferously for teaching grammar as a system—formally, and not necessarily in conjunction with writing. They argue for grammar on what, for them, are moral and religious grounds. And when other stakeholders in education realize that grammar is not being taught as a formal system and that students are not necessarily mastering some of the conventions of edited written English, it is easy for them to simply assume a causal relationship and believe that English teachers are not doing their duty when they don't teach grammar as a complete subject.

As professionals teaching the English language arts, we too are sometimes convinced that *we* learned practical things about sentence structure, style, and editing from doing exercises in our grammar books; for instance, I can tell you very specifically some of what I learned that has helped me as a writer (though I'll admit I only needed one or two semesters of intensive grammar study to reap its potential benefits, not the six semesters to which I and my classmates were subjected). Because some of us are convinced we benefitted at least somewhat from the formal study of grammar, it can be difficult for community members and English teachers alike to believe what decades of grammar studies tell us: that in general, the teaching of grammar does not serve any practical purpose for most students (Hillocks and Smith 1991). It does not improve reading, speaking, writing, or even editing, for the majority of students—nor does the teaching of English grammar necessarily make it easier for students to learn the structure of a foreign language (indeed, many students who have studied English grammar consciously *learn* the structure of English for the first time when studying a foreign language).

THE RESEARCH

Typically the research studies have not been fine-tuned enough to reveal that the study of grammar does have at least limited benefits for a few of us as writers. But even this more optimistic conclusion is called into question somewhat by a landmark study done by Findlay McQuade (1980). He taught an elective, junior-senior level Editorial Skills class that enrolled students who, it appears, were typically college-bound. The students reviewed parts of speech and basic sentence structure, then dealt with application of such principles as "agreement, reference, parallel construction, tense, case, subordination" to the task of finding errors in sentences written expressly for that purpose. Students, parents, and the teacher were happy with the course, until some students who had succeeded in the Editorial Skills class were assessed in reading, writing, mechanics, and vocabulary, then assigned to a course in writing mechanics on the basis of that assessment. This unhappy result led McQuade to investigate the effects of his course.

What he found was startling. Overall, students showed as much gain on their Cooperative English Tests in years that they hadn't taken the Editorial Skills class as in the year that they had (McQuade 1980, 28); the ES class seemed to make no difference in students' preparation for the College Entrance Examination Board's Achievement Test in Composition (29); the class average on the pre-test was actually higher than the average on the post-test (28); most of the reduction in errors was a reduction in relatively simple errors (mainly capitalization) by just a few of the students (29–30); and though the students' pre-course essays were not spectacular, their post-course essays were "miserable" and apparently "self-consciously constructed to honor correctness above all other virtues, including sense" (29). No wonder that this and other studies have led research summarizers like George Hillocks (1986) to conclude that:

None of the studies reviewed for the present report provides any support for teaching grammar as a means of improving composition skills. If schools insist upon teaching the identification of parts of speech, the parsing or diagramming of sentences, or other concepts of traditional grammar (as many still do), they cannot defend it as a means of improving the quality of writing. (138)

Or to put it even more bluntly, "School boards, administrators and teachers who impose the systematic study of traditional school grammar on their students over lengthy periods of time in the name of teaching writing do them a gross disservice" (Hillocks and Smith 1991, 248). (For other choice quotations from research summaries, see my fact sheet on the teaching of grammar that NCTE published as a SLATE Starter Sheet in the spring of 1996.)

What, then, are teachers to do? Should we teach formal grammar to all our students, knowing full well that only a few are likely to make practical use of what we've taught? Or should we abandon the teaching of grammar entirely, unless we teach it as a subject for inquiry (Postman and Weingartner 1966) or as a subject simply of intellectual interest, if not religious/moral value?

Probably neither extreme is the best option. In an article critiquing the earlier research summaries, Martha Kolln (1981) pointed out that teaching grammar in the context of writing might be much more effective than teaching grammar as a separate subject (as evidence, she cites, for instance, a study by Roland J. Harris [1962], which is reported at length in Richard Braddock, Richard Lloyd-Jones, and Lowell Schoer 1963). Later studies by Warwick B. Elley *et al.* (1976) and by McQuade (1980) do not invalidate this point. On the other hand, it is by no means clear that "application" of selected aspects of grammar cannot be done just as effec-

tively, and a lot more efficiently, without detailed, explicit grammar study, as illustrated by Frank O'Hare's experiments in sentence combining (1973). This is the argument advanced by Rei Noguchi (1991), and it's the argument advanced in my new book as well (Weaver 1996b). Though the research investigating this issue has been meager, it is definitely promising. For example, Lucy Calkins (1980) found that third graders learned punctuation much better in the context of writing and "publishing" than by studying punctuation rules in isolation. Furthermore, an experimental study at grades four through six showed that students who were taught the conventions of language in the context of their writing generally made better use of writing mechanics than did students who had studied these skills in isolation (DiStefano and Killion 1984).

WHAT ASPECTS OF GRAMMAR SHOULD WE TEACH?

Of course some educators may still want to teach at least an elective course or unit in the structure of the English language, simply on the grounds that studying the language is interesting and/or intellectually challenging—or can be made so (Postman and Weingartner 1966). What all students need, however, is guidance in understanding and applying those aspects of grammar that are most relevant to writing.

Teaching Grammar in Context includes suggestions that we teach a minimum of grammar for maximum benefits (Weaver 1996b). This is what I call a "scope-not-sequence" chart, covering relevant concepts that might be taught sometime between kindergarten and graduate school. The chart includes five categories:

teaching concepts of subject, verb, sentence, clause, phrase, and related concepts for editing;

teaching style through sentence combining and sentence generating;

teaching sentence sense and style through the manipulation of syntactic elements;

teaching the power of dialects and dialects of power;

teaching punctuation and mechanics for convention, clarity, and style.

The partial chart presents details for the first of these categories.

While this full chart (Weaver 1996b, 142–144) includes most of the grammatical concepts needed for sentence revision, style, and editing, and while some concepts are listed in the developmental sequence found in research studies, neither the sets of objectives nor the detailed lists should be understood as presenting a sequence for instruction. What's appropriate at any given time will vary considerably from school to school, class to class, and especially from individual to individual. Therefore, I would suggest that teachers consider the chart, examine their own students' writing, and offer the kinds of guidance their students need—mostly at the point of need (though some basic grammatical concepts may need to be taught aside from the writing process itself).

At the very least, I would recommend that teachers in a school or school system decide what their own students should be taught at each level, with considerable overlap. Better yet, teachers could collectively decide what the teachers at each grade level should be responsible for teaching, but only to the students who demonstrate the need or readiness for these predetermined concepts and skills in their writing.

UNDERLYING LEARNING THEORY

There are no miracles here. That is, teaching grammar in the context of writing will not automatically mean that

---

> **TEACHING CONCEPTS OF SUBJECT, VERB, SENTENCE, CLAUSE, PHRASE, AND RELATED CONCEPTS FOR EDITING**
>
> Objectives
>
> - To help students develop sentence sense through wide reading.
> - To help students learn to punctuate sentences correctly (according to accepted conventions) and effectively (judiciously violating the rules on occasion, for rhetorical effect).
> - To help students learn to make verbs agree with their subjects.
> - To help students learn conventions for punctuating subordinate clauses.

---

once taught, the concepts will be learned and applied forever after. On the contrary, grammatical concepts must often be taught and retaught, to individuals as well as to groups or classes, and students may long afterwards continue to need guidance in actually applying what they have, in some sense or to some degree, already learned. There is no quick fix.

In part, this is because the learning of grammatical concepts is so complex. For example, Muriel Harris and Katherine E. Rowan (1989) point out that practice, practice, and more practice usually does not promote adequate understanding (see also Kagan 1980). In part, this is because the practice exercises in grammar books are carefully crafted to be relatively easy; they do not give students the opportunity to grasp the critical features of a concept like "sentence." In their study of college students' concept of sentence, Harris and Rowan found that many students were confused by the meaning-based definitions of sentence that they had been taught ("A sentence is a group of words that expresses a complete thought"). Many of the students could not reliably differentiate between grammatical sentences and fragments or a run-on or comma splice. In order to understand the concept of "sentence," they also needed to understand what was *not* a sentence, and vice versa—but they had a firm grasp of neither.

I am convinced that one reason our traditional teaching of grammar has little transfer to writing situations is the underlying behaviorist learning theory. We have simply taken for granted the behaviorist ideas that practice makes perfect and that skills practiced in isolation will be learned that way and then applied as relevant. We have assumed that this is the way teaching and learning should work, despite the overwhelming evidence that it doesn't. With respect to grammar, Harris and Rowan (1989) show quite convincingly that a conscious grasp of grammatical concepts requires a depth of understanding that is not often gained through practice exercises alone.

The list titled "Ends of Behavioral-Constructivist Continuum" reflects one of my attempts to contrast a behaviorist, transmission theory of learning and teaching with the constructivist, transactional theory that better reflects how people learn in general and how teachers may better promote the learning of concepts and complex processes. The learning of grammatical concepts is itself a complex process.

Ends of Behavioral-Constructivist Continuum

• BEHAVIORAL PSYCHOLOGY	• COGNITIVE PSYCHOLOGY
• Transmission	• Transactional
• Reductionist	• Constructivist
• Habit formation	• Hypothesis formation
• Avoiding mistakes prevents formation of bad habits	• Errors necessary for encouraging more sophisticated hypotheses
• Students passively practice skills, memorize facts	• Students actively pursue learning and construct knowledge
• Teacher dispenses prepackaged, predetermined curriculum	• Teacher develops and negotiates curriculum with students
• Direct teaching of curriculum	• Responsive teaching to meet students' needs and interests
• Taskmaster, with emphasis on cycle of teach, practice/apply/memorize, test	• Master craftsperson, mentor: emphasis on demonstrating, inviting, discussing, affirming, facilitating, collaborating, observing, supporting
• Lessons taught, practiced or applied, then tested	• Mini-lessons taught as demonstration, invitation; adding an idea to the class pot
• Performance on decontextualized tests is taken as a measure of learning of limited information	• Assessment from a variety of contextualized learning experiences captures diverse aspects of learning
• Learning is expected to be uniform, same for everyone; uniform means of assessment guarantee that many will fail, in significant ways	• Learning is expected to be individual, different for everyone; flexible and multiple means of assessment guarantee all will succeed, in differing ways
• Adds up to a failure-oriented model, ferreting out students' weaknesses and preparing them to take their place in a stratified society	• Adds up to a success-oriented model, emphasizing students' strengths and preparing them to be the best they can be in a stratified society

(Weaver 1994, 365; Weaver 1996b, 149)

Certain aspects of the constructivist theory of learning seem especially relevant for the teaching of grammar. One is that the learner must form hypotheses about concepts in the process of coming to understand them. This means that we teachers must give a wide range of examples to illustrate a concept (such as "grammatical sentence") and also that we must contrast these with common non-examples that are frequently mistaken for instances of the concept (such as a dependent clause, which has a subject and predicate—often part of the handbook definition of a sentence—but which is grammatically not complete as a sentence). Another significant implication is that errors are common and probably even necessary in the process of formulating more sophisticated hypotheses—or to put it more simply, errors are a necessary concomitant of growth (Shaughnessy 1977; Kroll and Schafer 1978).

Thus we should not be surprised if students make new kinds of errors after we have taught a "new" syntactic structure or editing concept, nor should we penalize students for taking the risks that have resulted in these errors. Instead, we should praise students for what they've attempted, then gently show them how to eliminate what we perceive as error (Weaver 1982). We also need to adopt a stance of humility before we undertake to "correct" students' writing, or to help them "correct" it themselves. As Robert J. Connors and Andrea A. Lunsford (1988) put it:

> Teachers' ideas about error definition and classification have always been absolute products of their times and cultures. . . . Teachers have always marked different phenomena as errors, called them different things, given them different weights. Error-pattern study is essentially the examination of an ever-shifting pattern of

skills judged by an ever-shifting pattern of prejudices. (399)

And this doesn't even begin to address the issue of dialect differences.

KINDS OF LESSONS: SOME EXAMPLES

The kinds of grammar lessons I suggest in *Teaching Grammar in Context* are incidental lessons, wherein (for example) grammatical terms are used casually, in the course of discussing literature and students' writing; inductive lessons, wherein students may be guided to notice grammatical patterns and derive generalizations themselves; teaching grammatical points in the process of conferring with students about their writing; mini-lessons, which present new and useful information (to a class, group, or individual) in a brief format (Atwell 1987; Calkins 1986); and extended mini-lessons, which typically involve students in trying out or applying the concept, briefly and collaboratively, in order to promote greater understanding. Here, I would like to offer three examples of extended mini-lessons, which are common and often productive. Individual conferencing is perhaps even more valuable, as illustrated with one example. These lessons were taught by teachers from fifth-grade to upper-level undergraduate, but all are appropriate for secondary students. Each example reflects one or more of the principles of constructivist learning theory. Each also illustrates the teaching of a grammatical concept, an editing concept, and/or a stylistically effective use of language.

Ann

Ann, a fifth-grade teacher, had noticed that when her students answered comprehension questions in reading, science, and social studies classes, they frequently responded with dependent clause fragments, especially those starting with *because*. She admits that when students wrote subordinate clauses for answers, she used to add independent clauses in red ink "to help them see the error of their ways. But to no avail: the subordinate clauses keep coming with all the tenacity of the Energizer Bunny."

Before taking a course in grammar and teaching grammar, Ann had been inclined to think that she should teach grammar as a formal system in order to help students eliminate such fragments from their writing. As a result of research read and ideas discussed in the class, Ann decided to teach just extended mini-lessons on areas of particular concern: in this case, writing grammatically complete sentences instead of dependent clause fragments. She taught two such lessons, one focusing exclusively on the subordinating conjunction *because*, since it is so often used in answers and in other writing. She had students work in pairs and added a peer editing component, asking pairs to trade and check one another's work.

Ann learned several lessons as a result of this experiment. First, the students understood the examples very well and asked a lot of questions about applying the "rules" to their writing. However, Ann also discovered that her transparencies involved, perhaps, too much information for her fifth graders. Furthermore, though the worksheets seemed simple and obvious to Ann, some kids had trouble, especially with the terms and concepts of *subordinate clause* and *independent clause*. And in spite of the mini-lesson examples and the examples at the top of the activity sheets, some students forgot capitals, commas, or periods, others misplaced commas, and still others capitalized the subordinating conjunctions in the middle of sentences. Furthermore, many of these errors were overlooked during peer editing. Ann also discovered that the practice took longer than she had anticipated—almost half an hour. In other words, neither Ann's lesson nor the students' responses achieved perfection.

"Lastly," Ann reports, "on subsequent student writing the Bunny was back. Students were still using subordinate clauses as sentences." However, Ann did not become discouraged, for she knew better than to expect one mini-lesson to produce mastery, even when extended with some practice. Ann writes:

> As Lois Matz Rosen puts it, "Learning to use the correct mechanical and grammatical forms of written language is a developmental process and as such is slow, unique to each child, and does not progress in an even uphill pattern." (1987, 63)

Sarah

Taking the same course in grammar and teaching grammar as Ann, Sarah had likewise been inclined to teach traditional grammar; in fact, she admits that "Last year, I have realized, I did too much traditional grammar, and sadly enough I am afraid I did not teach my students how to become better writers." So it became her goal to improve her teaching of writing and not concentrate on the traditional grammar lessons. She writes:

> Already this year, it has been exciting to watch the difference in my classroom as I implement new teaching ideas. This year I see much more enthusiasm for writing and grammar because the students are not fully aware they are being taught grammar. Disguising my grammar lessons behind the mini-lesson format in the writer's workshop has prevented me from having to endure a repetition of last year's groans regarding how boring grammar is.

Sarah had previously encouraged her seventh graders to use adjectives and adverbs in their writing but found that often her students' "descriptive" poems or paragraphs included little description and no details to make the pieces come alive. When it was suggested that she guide her students in writing a "five senses" poem about fall, Sarah decided to experiment with two different ways of encouraging students to use adjectives and adverbs. First, she asked the students to write about fall but gave them little direction, except for mentioning, "Be sure to use those adjectives and adverbs for detail!" The students turned in their writings at the end of class.

About two weeks later, Sarah guided the students in writing their second fall poems, the "sense" poems. She explains:

> The Monday before, I had each student bring in one or two leaves, so by Wednesday we had a large basket of them. Before writing on Wednesday we did prewriting exercises together as a class. My students loved it! We threw the basket of leaves in the air and watched them fall in different directions. Then the students took turns placing their leaves on the hot air register and watched as their leaf got blown up toward the ceiling. After this they went around the classroom sharing a favorite fall memory or Thanksgiving tradition. Finally, with that introduction, I explained the writing assignment as using the five senses and they began writing. Those that had trouble with the first fall writing assignment now had previous knowledge and ideas from the prewriting activities on the five senses to provide organization. The difference in their writings was amazing as shown below.

Tom's Poems

Before

It is fall you rake the leaves crustily over a pile "o" mud. It is nearly ear

shattering when you rake the flames on the ground. How chilling it be, no one knows. It (fall) is so unpredictable.

After

Smells like destruction when burned.

Clogging your lungs.

Tastes like the dirt of the earth, destroying your taste buds.

See the leaves on the trees fall effortlessly to the ground,

Where they will be raked, mulched, and burned.

Touch them—they feel like razor blades, when you jump on them.

Hear them? You can't!

But if you can't hear them, do they really fall?

Amy's Poems

Before

Fall is the leaves changing colors; they can be green, yellow or red.

Fall is the cold and the freezing at night.

Fall is when your backyard is covered with leaves.

After

I can smell the apple pie baking in the oven.

I can smell the burning leaves in the neighbor's yards.

I hear the leaves crackling under my feet as I trudge through the yard.

I hear children yelling as they jump in a pile of leaves.

I see blended colors on the leaves like someone painted them.

I touch the leaves and I feel the veins.

I touch the leaves and sometimes they break in my hands.

I taste the turkey as the grease runs down my throat.

I taste the pumpkin pie and now I know it is fall!

One important thing to notice is that many of the descriptive words in the "after" poems aren't necessary adjectives or adverbs; they are nouns ("razor blades") or verbs ("mulched"), as in the sense poem from Tom, a student in Sarah's lower language arts class, who disliked writing and reading. Another important point is that while the "before" poems used some adjectives and/or adverbs, the "after" poems used a much greater variety of constructions that function adjectivally, to modify nouns, or adverbially, to modify verbs or whole clauses. One example is the participial phrases in the "after" poem by Amy, a student in Sarah's advanced language arts class. (The non-italicized phrases in both "after" poems are present participle words and phrases functioning like adjectives, to modify the preceding nouns.)

What is to be learned from Sarah's experience? Several things, I think:

1. Various kinds of prewriting experiences can greatly enhance the quality of students' writing. This is something Sarah already knew and *typically* practiced.
2. A variety of adjectival and adverbial constructions will probably emerge when students are guided in focusing on the details of experience, rather than on grammar.
3. Asking students to focus on "adjectives" and "adverbs" might actually limit students' use of the more sophisticated structures they would use naturally.

Renee

Secondary teacher Renee uses a conference approach to teach writing, including sentence revision and editing. The excerpts show a first draft of a sophomore's paper and the beginning of a much longer sixth draft.

First, Renee suggested to the writer that he consider an opening that "grabs the reader's attention." She further suggested that conversation can do that. In working with a later draft, Renee guided the writer in seeing how to put the reader "there," in using participial phrases to convey narrative detail, and in using punctuation conventionally. In a subsequent conference, she and the writer might still consider whether one or both of the comma splices should be left as is or eliminated (Weaver 1996b, 84–85).

My University Classes

In teaching upper-level undergraduates who are preparing to be teachers, I have often found that even these students do not evidence much concern for the mechanics of writing before they have "turned in" their papers. (This is in so-called content area classes, wherein I do not routinely lead students through stages of the writing process unless they request or obviously need such help.) The motivation is somewhat higher when students have gotten their papers back with "corrections," accompanied usually by an explanation and occasionally by the general reminder that "You need to get a grasp on this, because it's something you'll be expected to teach even elementary-level students!"

At this point, I have found some success with in effect treating the returned paper as a not-quite-final draft (for many related ideas, see Rosen 1987). So far, I have developed information sheets on two of the most common "errors" in mechanics: use of just a comma between two independent clauses (the "comma splice") and absence of the apostrophe in possessive nouns.

First, I distribute the handout(s) to students and explain the concept(s), using the examples on the sheet(s), which have been taken from actual student papers. Then I organize the students into groups and invite them to

One day when I was riding in my
moms car coming home from Kalamazoo° we looked
behing us and we saw ~~~~~~ smoke coming out
of the back of the car. We didn't know
what it was from so we kept on driving
wondering what it was from. We saw people
on the other side of the road suerving away
from us and the guy in front of us was
trying to stop us. So we stopped on the
side of the road and smoke rolled over the hood
we jumped out of the car and saw our
car go up in flames. We called the fire department
and they put the fire out. My moms car was
~~~~~~ totaled ~~~ ~ but the insurence company
payed for another one.   [end of 1st draft]

Sophomore's first draft (Weaver 1996b).

play around with correcting the other sentences, which again have been taken from students' papers, as in the handout on comma splices (see p. 266). I also give each group a grammar handbook, asking them to check the phenomenon in question, and/or to look up other kinds of "errors" that have been marked. The students are also asked to discuss with each other what needs correction in their own papers (not necessarily just comma splices or possessives), to determine what they still don't understand, and to ask me for clarification and help as I circulate around the room.

I encourage students to help each other edit future papers, to use a grammar handbook to help with grammatical problems they *know* they have, to seek my help in an individual conference if needed, and to take risks with grammatical constructions.

This procedure has typically reduced the incidence of these kinds of errors in subsequent papers—not only the one or two kinds of errors on my handouts, but other kinds as well. In addition, though, I usually find "new" kinds of errors, such as students punctuating ordinary plurals and verb endings with apostrophes, not just using the apostrophe in possessive nouns. My favorite overgeneralization is from the earnest young man who wrote "mathematic's" after learning about the apostrophe in possessives (e.g., "the mathematician's knowledge"). I greet such new kinds of errors with a smile and a chuckle, reminding the pre-service teacher that new errors will occur, almost inevitably, as writers try to apply concepts that are new to them and only partially understood. I remind them that as teachers, they too should encourage risk-taking and growth in the

> ### The Flaming Engine
>
> We ran out of the car looking for someone to help, yelling at them to call 9-1-1. "We already did," they told us. Then they asked, "What happened, what happened?"
>
> We were coming home from the mall, driving on Shane Road, when the stoplight ahead of us turned red. We stopped, waiting for it to turn green. The light turned green, and then we slowly pulled away, going faster, we accelerated to fifty-five miles an hour. My mom looked in the rearview mirror and asked my brother to look behind us and see if the smoke was coming from us. "I think so," he said. Then we looked ahead and the guy in front of us was waving his hands and pointing to the side of the road. "I think we should get out," my mom said. My mom stopped the car and we all jumped out of the car. My brother and I ran to the back of the car, and my mom ran to the front. [end of 1st paragraph]
>
> Then we heard the firetrucks coming. They stopped, then two guys, already dressed in their fire equiptment, jumped off the truck, got the water hose and started to put out the fire. While they were doing that one of the

Beginning of sophmore's sixth draft (Weaver 1996b).

use of language by responding to children's new errors in a similar manner.

CONCLUSION

As I indicated before, there are no miracles here. No matter how students are taught grammatical concepts, syntactic constructions and stylistic devices, or language conventions and editing concepts, they will not automatically make use of these in their writing. However, the relevant research confirms what everyday experience reveals: that teaching "grammar" in the context of writing works better than teaching grammar as a formal system, if our aim is for students to *use* grammar more effectively and conventionally in their writing.

HANDOUT ON COMMA SPLICES

Comma splices

A "comma splice" occurs when two grammatically complete sentences (independent clauses) are joined with just a comma.

On rare occasion, comma splice sentences are found in published writing. This usually occurs only when the two grammatically complete sentences are short and, for the most part, grammatically parallel. Examples:

1. The students that need to touch the book can, the children that need to verbalize their thoughts are responded to.
2. And they learn on their own, they in a sense teach themselves.
3. These children are not stupid, they just learn and understand in different ways.

Usually, however, comma splices are considered a "no no." Below are examples of comma splice sentences that don't meet the conditions for acceptability: ones that should be "corrected." With a neighbor, please consider effective ways of eliminating these comma splices by using different punctuation, restructuring the sentence, or adding a connecting word.

1. I was very impressed, the teacher pointed to the words as the students said them.
2. Then the students were blindfolded and given a button, they had to name the characteristics they felt the button contained.
3. This little exercise really worked, as soon as she started singing the children started singing right with her.
4. My first expectation was the shared book experience, this seems to be one of the most fundamental aspects of whole language.
5. The first is a poetry notebook, it is the first item on the agenda that day.

NOTE

The author wishes to thank Renee Callies, Ann Miner, and Sarah Woltjer for permission to describe some of the ways they teach grammar in the context of writing.

WORKS CITED

A Beka Book. 1996. *Home School Catalog.* Pensacola, FL: A Beka Book.

Atwell, Nancie. 1987. *In the Middle: Writing, Reading, and Learning with Adolescents.* Portsmouth, NH: Heinemann.

Braddock, Richard, Richard Lloyd-Jones, and Lowell Schoer. 1963. *Research in Written Composition.* Urbana, IL: NCTE.

Calkins, Lucy M. 1986/1994. *The Art of Teaching Writing.* Portsmouth, NH: Heinemann.

———. 1980. "When Children Want to Punctuate: Basic Skills Belong in Context." *Language Arts* 57: 567–573.

Chapman, James A. 1986. *Why Not Teach Intensive Phonics?* Pensacola, FL: A Beka Book.

Connors, Robert J. and Andrea A. Lunsford. 1988. "Frequency of Formal Errors in Current College Writing, or Ma and Pa Kettle Do Research." *College Composition and Communication* 39: 395–409.

DiStefano, Philip and Joellen Killion. 1984. "Assessing Writing Skills through a Process Approach." *English Education* 11: 98–101.

Elley, Warwick B., I. H. Barham, H. Lamb, and M. Wyllie. 1976. "The Role of Grammar in a Secondary English Curriculum." *Research in the Teaching of English* 10: 5–21. (Reprinted from *New Zealand Journal of Educational Studies*, May 1975, 10, 26–42).

Gaddy, Barbara B., T. William Hall, and Robert J. Marzano. 1996. *School Wars: Resolving Our Conflicts Over Religion and Values.* San Francisco: Jossey-Bass.

Harris, Muriel and Katherine E. Rowan. 1989. "Explaining Grammatical Concepts." *Journal of Basic Writing* 8.2: 21–41.

Harris, Roland J. 1962. *An Experimental Inquiry into the Functions and Value of Formal Grammar in the Teaching of Written English to Children Aged Twelve to Fourteen.* Unpublished doctoral dissertation, University of London.

Hillocks, George, Jr. 1986. *Research on Written Composition: New Directions for Teaching.* Urbana, IL: ERIC Clearinghouse on Reading and Communication Skills and the National Conference on Research in English.

Hillocks, George, Jr. and Michael W. Smith. 1991. "Grammar and Usage." *Handbook of*

Research on Teaching the English Language Arts. James Flood, Julie M. Jensen, Diane Lapp, and James R. Squire, eds. New York: Macmillan. 591–603.

Holderer, Robert W. 1995. "The Religious Right: Who Are They and Why Are We the Enemy?" *English Journal* 84.5 (Sept.): 74–83.

Huntsman, Jeffrey F. 1983. "Grammar." David L. Wagner, ed. *The Seven Liberal Arts in the Middle Ages*. Bloomington: Indiana University Press. 58–95.

Kagan, Dona M. 1980. "Run-on and Fragment Sentences: An Error Analysis." *Research in the Teaching of English* 14: 127–138.

Kolln, Martha. 1981. "Closing the Books on Alchemy." *College Composition and Communication* 31: 139–151.

Kroll, Barry M. and John C. Schafer. 1978. "Error Analysis and the Teaching of Composition." *College Composition and Communication* 29: 242–248.

McQuade, Finlay. 1980. "Examining a Grammar Course: The Rationale and the Result." *English Journal* 69.7 (Oct.): 26–30.

Noguchi, Rei R. 1991. *Grammar and the Teaching of Writing: Limits and Possibilities*. Urbana, IL: NCTE.

O'Hare, Frank. 1973. *Sentence Combining: Improving Student Writing Without Formal Grammar Instruction*. Research Report No. 15. Urbana, IL: NCTE.

Postman, Neil and Charles Weingartner. 1966. *Linguistics: A Revolution in Teaching*. New York: Dell.

Rosen, Lois Matz. 1987. "Developing Correctness in Student Writing: Alternatives to the Error-Hunt." *English Journal* 76: 62–69.

Shaughnessy, Mina P. 1977. *Errors and Expectations: A Guide for the Teacher of Basic Writing*. New York: Oxford University Press.

Weaver, Constance. 1996a. *On the Teaching of Grammar. SLATE Starter Sheet—Fact Sheet Series*. Urbana, IL: (Spring): 7–8.

———. 1994. *Reading Process and Practice: From Socio-psycholinguistics to Whole Language*, Second edition. Portsmouth, NH: Heinemann.

———. 1996b. *Teaching Grammar in Context*. Portsmouth, NH: Heinemann.

———. 1982. "Welcoming Errors as Signs of Growth." *Language Arts* 59: 438–444.

Weaver, Constance, ed. Forthcoming. *Lessons to Share: Teaching Grammar in the Context of Writing*. Portsmouth, NH: Heinemann.

For Further Thought

1. Weaver cites a number of research studies, among them McQuade's 1980 experiment with the study of grammar. How would you explain McQuade's findings? Is it necessary to reach the same conclusion as Hillocks (p. 257)?

2. Weaver mentions five concepts that might be included in a "minimal grammar" for the classroom. Using Tabbert's vocabulary (*grammar-1, grammar-2,* and *grammar-3*), discuss these five concerns.

3. Weaver contrasts a constructivist theory of learning to a behaviorist theory, clearly favoring the former. What do you think? Is it clear that the constructivist approach is superior for the teaching of grammar? Why or why not?

4. Think about the three teachers whose work is cited in the article. How successful was each? In what ways is each of them dealing with grammar?

5. Weaver provides a tip sheet on common-splice sentences. How would you describe this handout: constructivist, behaviorist, or neither? How useful do you think it would be? How would you adapt it for use in your classroom?

Application 5.3:
Dealing With Error

Analyzing Student Errors

Alot has changed from hunting now, and hunting in my grandpa's day. Like places, weapons, and the game itself.

The places have changed alot. My grandpa built his own blinds and his own decoys. Now you can go to places where you can just go to already built blinds and you can buy decoys in the stores and you can go alot more place now then you would then.

The weapons I don't think thes have changed that much. Back then they were heavier and had a lot more kick. But now there lighter and easier to carry, but still have quite a kick. He gave me sum of his guns, the only real differences is the price. There worth more then my new guns. I like my newer models of guns better cause there easier to hunt with.

They're is a big difference in game. There was lots of ducks and geese, but now there isn't half as many duck's and geese. I think its cause there are alot of poachers and stuff like that. And also cause of the different shots. There is either lead or steal.

My grandpa used lead shot back then, cause it was all they had, but now it is outlawed because ducks that get wounded would die of lead poisoning. We have to use steel so they don't die of lead poison ing. Thats a nother reason for the change in game.

I think I would have rather hunted back then because the abundance of game. And you had to build you own supplys. Also you could take more birds and stuff and there weren't as many poachers. (A paper by a tenth-grade student, submitted in handwritten form and typed by me.)

You saw in the previous application that correct writing is not the same as good writing. A piece of work can be error-free and yet fail utterly to achieve its purpose, or it may have many errors and still succeed to a degree. Correctness for its own sake is not the main idea to foster in student writers. And yet no one would want to argue specifically against correctness. Violations of rules, whether in spelling, grammar, or usage, are often perceived by readers to be the hallmark of poor writing. We might argue that there are more important concerns, but we would not want to mislead students into thinking that errors do not matter. We must take the issue of correctness seriously—seriously enough to examine the errors students make and seriously enough to try to understand them. It is not very helpful merely to say that a student's writing is "full of errors" or that it reveals "bad grammar." More to the point, as teachers we need to ask what kind of errors we are talking about. Until we know that, we can hardly be of much help to the student.

And that brings us to the paper on hunting. This student, whom we will call Jeff, was given a comparison/contrast assignment in which he was asked to discuss changes that have taken place in a subject that interests him (see Appendix 5). An avid hunter, he produced the paper you have read. For Jeff, this is not a rough draft. Earlier he had written a very disorganized piece, which with the help of a peer-response group he then revised. Measured against Jeff's previous work, this second draft is a fairly well-organized essay on changes in the sport since his grandfather's day.

It is important to begin this way, to notice what Jeff is doing well, for it is tempting to focus attention immediately on all the things that are going wrong here. We need to tell Jeff that his paper makes sense but also to acknowledge that it needs to be rewritten—not so much to change the content and structure but to alter the language itself. Jeff is using the language in nonstandard ways, making errors that will have serious consequences for him in his life after school. But in order to help him rewrite, we need to make some distinctions about what he has done.

There are, for example, a great many misspelled words here. In this, Jeff's paper is typical: Misspellings are the most common errors of all. But even in regard to spelling errors, some distinctions are in order. Some of them are mechanical, in the sense that his handwriting is poor; these are analogous to "typos." Others seem to represent uncertainty about how to spell a word, whereas still others indicate that Jeff does not have a clue about how to spell the word. So once we get beyond the mere identification of errors and ask ourselves the diagnostic question—Why did Jeff do this?—we find that things are more complex than they first appeared to be.

This complexity is even more apparent once we get beyond spelling, which is, after all, not a grammatical concern. Problems with sentence punctuation—which *do* relate to grammar—are not simple. The sentence fragment in the first paragraph is probably an error, not a stylistic choice, and its solution is not difficult to describe. But what about the first sentence in the third paragraph? Does Jeff need some punctuation after the initial phrase or is there a problem with the internal grammar of the sentence? There are other, more subtle problems to be tackled here, some of which have less to do with formal grammar than with standard usage. To my ear, there are two such problems in the first sentence of the last paragraph. Finally, there are the correct but ineffective passages, which might well be the most important things for Jeff to work on. The last sentence in the second paragraph is a case in point.

Some of these problems Jeff can be expected to handle on his own, without much help from the teacher; others seem to call for some direct instruction. In either case, however, we need to begin with some understanding of the classes of errors to be dealt with. It simply will not do to lump them together as if they had the same cause and the same kind of solution. In short, we must begin with what we know about grammar and style to sort things out—not so we can give Jeff more terminology (heaven forbid!), but so we can figure out how to help him edit his own work.

Some Things to Consider About Errors

1. List the errors in Jeff's paper, categorizing them this way: misspellings, sentence punctuation errors (run-ons and fragments), other grammatical errors (agreement problems, for example), and nonidiomatic English (wrong word). Then consider at least one instance in each category, explaining the cause of the error—that is, what Jeff might have tried to do that led to this problem.

2. Which kind of error do you think is the most important for Jeff to work on? Which is the least important? How would you convey to Jeff what you believe to be the relative importance of each kind of error?

3. Reread the short stories written by the seventh graders (Appendix 2). As a group, what kinds of errors are these students making? How would you rank them in importance? Then consider the particular cases of two of these students: Claire (who has a serious learning disability) and Diane (who is a very reluctant writer). What attitude would you take toward the errors in these papers?

Helping Students Correct Errors

So far we have been concerned with understanding and diagnosis—that is, realizing that any sentence-level error takes place in a context and for a reason. Students do not make errors to irritate teachers (though that is frequently the result); rather, they are trying to say something and the language has gone awry. Still, as we have seen, errors are important. If you doubt that, read Jeff's paper again, or perform the experiment I did a while back—rewrite the paper, correcting the errors. I think you'll see what a difference these surface blemishes make. Or look at some of the less extreme cases among the papers in the appendixes. I have left these unedited to illustrate how little editing many students do. Our job, then, is to help them become better editors of their own work, and to achieve that goal, we have a number of tactics available.

We can begin by thinking about what we say and do about the errors we see in a student's work. Should we correct them, deliver a lecture but leave the correction to students, or mark them in some other way? A great deal depends on the nature of the assignment and the needs of the particular students, but as a rule I'd say that it is not our business to correct student work, except perhaps for the purpose of modeling. Nor do lectures and threats seem to have much effect. Unless we are dealing with a capable writer who is just being lazy, a little more guidance than "clean up your grammar" would be in order. Some kind of signaling, or *flagging* at least some of the errors, would seem to be a reasonable way to begin. Many teachers underline or circle errors in the opening paragraphs; others put check marks in the margins next to any line that contains an error, instructing students to find and correct each problem. Flagging errors narrows the field a bit, while still leaving the work of correction up to the student—and that is often sufficient. Certainly, before we take a more directed approach, we want to know if a student can find and correct errors on his or her own.

Whatever we write on students' papers, however, we need to bear in mind the advice given by Nancy Sommers (pp. 152–153): The state of the draft is a primary consideration. Thus it is appropriate to work on editing with Jeff because he has already revised for content. We might wish that he would do some research on hunting or probe his ideas more deeply; we might even suggest a third draft before editing. But the final decision is his, and in this case he has signaled that the content and organization are more or less stable. In addition, we need to be clear about priorities—in two senses. Students need to know the relative importance of the errors in their writing (they can be negligible or hugely significant), and then, in each case, we need to help students see which are most deserving of attention.

In a case like Jeff's, flagging some of the errors probably will not solve the problem. He might find some of the obvious handwriting mistakes and a few of the stranger misspellings, but in all likelihood Jeff would be over-whelmed by the sheer volume of check marks and would not know where to begin. This suggests that a *conference* is in order. We could begin by get-ting Jeff's opinion of the draft—asking what he likes and dislikes, and whether he realizes how many errors there are here. It might also help to have Jeff read a portion of the paper aloud, to get a sense of what he can find on his own. In my experience, many students will *see* typos and *hear* certain kinds of errors, like subject–verb agreement problems ("There was lots of ducks and geese"). We can then point out and explain the most important un-detected errors and perhaps do some modeling, showing Jeff how we would go about correcting them. The conference should end with an assignment: Jeff needs to go home and work on the paper, showing the teacher how much editing he can do on his own. Deadlines and follow-up are crucial.

A conference like this can be quite time consuming, although subsequent meetings can (and should) be brief. After all, you are likely to have more than one Jeff in each class, and with five or six classes to teach, meeting with each of them can be a daunting task. Hence one advantage of the workshop approach: While students are writing, you have time for a ten- or fif-teen-minute conference with Jeff. Outside of your own class time, the school day provides few opportunities for conferences, though something might be done during study halls, during hall duty, and before school hours. (For a tenth grader like Jeff, the afterschool times are usually impossible to schedule, even if you are not busy with an extracurricular activity.) Real-izing that editing skills are important to all writers, we are best advised to schedule some class time to help students individually.

Another way to approach error, this time with the whole class, is through *minilessons*. Here again, it is important to begin with some kind of diagno-sis. It makes little sense to schedule a minilesson on pronoun case before we have seen this problem in students' writing. When, however, we notice a consistent pattern of error in the work of many students, a minilesson might well be the best and most efficient way to tackle the problem. Of course, all students will not need the lesson, so we could split the class, leaving some students to write while the others do the activity, or enlist the more capable students to present the lesson. These are judgment calls. It is most important to remember that a minilesson, by definition, is *short* (try limiting yourself to fifteen minutes) and *applicable* (it needs to be followed by some application to the real writing students are doing at the time).

All these techniques follow the same basic pattern: diagnosis, explana-tion or modeling if necessary, and application to the work at hand. This, you might say, is common sense, and yet so much of what we teachers do in re-sponse to error defies common sense. Grammar drills conducted in a vac-uum, exercises on errors that do not appear in student writing, or indeed any grammar or usage activities that cannot be related to the work at hand are not likely to help anyone, and they take up precious time. It makes more sense to save time in the curriculum for thoughtful written responses on pa-pers and strategic conferences with students like Jeff. Perhaps then, if we can find strategies that actually help students improve their work, we can get over our irritation with errors in writing and treat them as an opportunity for further learning.

Some Things to Consider About Error Correction

1. One of the key issues for a teacher is helping students decide when to edit their work. Students sometimes want to jump to editing prematurely, although at times the teacher wants to push the process to a close before the student feels the content is ready. Choose two papers from any of those in the appendixes—one that you feel is ready for editing and one that needs another "content draft." Then write a note to each student explaining your idea about each paper.

2. Review Nancy Sommers's article, "Responding to Student Writing" (pp. 148–156), with special attention to what she says about the state of the draft. Then choose two papers from any of the sets that seem ready for editing. Using a flagging technique of your own, indicate to the students the kinds of errors that need correction. Then explain your technique to the students in a brief comment.

3. Devise a plan for helping Jeff edit his paper. You have already made some decisions about the relative importance of each kind of error in the paper; now think practically about how you will help Jeff.

4. By now you have read most, or all, of the papers in the appendixes. Focus on one set of papers (except the rough drafts in Appendix 1) and consider one of the recurring problems in that set. Then devise a minilesson of no more than fifteen minutes in which you address that problem.

5. In the end you will have to evaluate student papers in some manner, and that work will never be error-free. Take one set of papers in the appendixes and discuss how errors will figure in your evaluation criteria.

Grammar Instruction: What Teachers Say

Brenda Arnett Petruzzella

For years there has been a kind of "disconnect" between some teachers and university professors about the relationship between grammar instruction and writing improvement. Some professors cite the research findings that grammar study in isolation does not seem to help writing; this is heard by some teachers as "Don't teach grammar." Some high school teachers say that grammar and usage rules have a place in process-oriented instruction; this is heard by some professors as "They persist in teaching grammar whether it helps or not." In "Grammar Instruction: What Teachers Say," Brenda Petruzzella discusses this tangled argument. Petruzzella clearly sides with the teachers, casting blame in the other direction. As you read, think about the various levels of mis- *understanding. What is it about grammar that causes this kind of feeling?*

This essay appeared in English Journal, *Vol. 85, No. 7 (November 1996); copyright 1996 by the National Council of Teachers of English. It is reprinted with permission.*

There are sometimes significant differences between what colleges teach prospective teachers in education courses and what practicing teachers in schools actually do. Nowhere is this more evident than in the area of grammar instruction. As both an undergraduate and graduate student, I had college classes which explicitly discouraged the teaching of grammar. However, high school English teachers I know continue to feel the need for some grammar instruction in their classes.

ATTITUDES TOWARD TEACHING GRAMMAR

In times past, English teachers had no doubt that formal grammar instruction belonged in the curriculum along with reading and writing. I learned the eight parts of speech, the intricacies of case and mood, and how to diagram sentences. It was not until college that I encountered the idea that grammar instruction was a waste of time. In 1963, Richard Braddock, Richard Lloyd-Jones, and Lowell Schoer published, through NCTE, *Research in Written Composition*, an ambitious attempt to summarize research findings about the teaching of writing. Among other things, these authors found widespread agreement among research studies that teaching grammar had no positive effect on student writing. It seemed to follow that grammar instruction could therefore be abandoned. Numbers of professors, teachers, and prospective teachers, I believe, greeted this suggestion with glee, because they and many of their students found grammar both difficult and dull.

In my own classes, I found many students remarkably resistant to learning grammar. I would painstakingly prepare and teach a lesson on nouns and verbs, using the most creative and relevant examples I could think of, and many students would fail the quiz. I was quite willing to abandon the formal teaching of grammar in favor of writing instruction—my students had good ideas and interesting things to say—but I found it very difficult to assist them in polishing their work without a common vocabulary of grammatical terms. How could I talk to them about the most basic writing concepts or discuss sentence fragments or run on sentences without using words like *subject* or *verb*?

Like many other teachers, I tried first one thing and then another, depending on the individual class. Sometimes I used a grammar book; some-times I didn't. Some years I taught prepositions; some years I didn't. Mostly I tried to teach grammar in the context of writing, the course recommended by most of my graduate school classes, but I had received little practical instruction about how to do this, and I often felt inadequate to the task. What seemed to make the most impact with students was individual discussion about their papers, as suggested by the various "workshop" approaches which became popular in the 1980s. This, however, was difficult to arrange in a class of 30 students, half of whom would be looking for ways to goof-off or cause disruption while I was occupied on the other side of the room. And always, there was the problem of how to explain and discuss grammatical concepts with students without using grammatical terms that they didn't know. I was always grateful for those few students who had acquired a modicum of knowledge, either from reading, from some instruction in middle school, or simply from a home where people tended to speak in standard English.

Professional reading was not particularly helpful because even researchers are not in agreement about grammar instruction. The debate in scholarly journals has, at times, become quite acrimonious. (There are numerous examples; two good ones are Martha Kolln, 1981 "Closing the Books on Alchemy," *College Composition and Communication*, 32.2, May; and Patrick Hartwell, 1985, "Grammar, Grammars, and the Teaching of Grammar," *College English* 47.2, Feb.)

School systems are nothing if not diverse, and while some simply ignored research findings and continued teaching grammar as they always had, others virtually abandoned grammar instruction. As a doctoral student, I worked recently for several quarters as a student teacher supervisor. Several of my prospective English teachers had received little systematic grammar instruction but were now placed in settings where it was part of the curriculum, and they were in trouble. One of my student teachers wrote in his journal that the university "really pisses me off. All my ed. courses said grammar wasn't important, and now I find out that it is!" On the student's evaluation sheet from the cooperating teacher I found this comment: "Needs to work on grammar basics—fragments, run ons, comma splices, etc. His spelling is weak and he misses many misspellings on student essays. He also needs to rid himself of the sub-standard English he uses in speaking." Another cooperating teacher said about her student teacher, "He has no clue about grammar, usage, and punctuation. The university's 'grammar doesn't count' attitude is a great disservice to new teachers ... Sadly, my seniors have a better working knowledge of grammar, usage, and punctuation than my student teacher."

RESEARCHERS VERSUS CLASSROOM TEACHERS

The point is, despite research studies and college classes which disparage it, large numbers of classroom teachers have continued to teach grammar in some form. In an effort to assist my student teachers, I began asking cooperating teachers about their beliefs and practices concerning grammar instruction; how they defined "grammar"; whether they were aware of controversy about the usefulness of teaching grammar in school; and what they did in their own classrooms.

Every teacher I spoke with insisted on the need for some grammar instruction in the teaching of writing, and their reasoning was remarkably similar, whether they were veteran teachers or relatively new, male or female, in urban or suburban schools.

I concluded that researchers and classroom teachers often have different

definitions of grammar or grammar instruction. When a study concludes that "formal grammar instruction" has not shown measurable improvement in students' writing, it is often not clear exactly what "formal grammar instruction" means, but it usually seems to refer to isolated memorization of rules and terminology and pages of skill and drill practice. Many of the studies reviewed by Braddock *et al.* dealt with skill and drill exercises in isolation and with some of the more esoteric terminology such as predicate objectives or gerunds. Classroom teachers, on the other hand, tend to use the term *grammar* for what might be more properly labeled *mechanics*—usage skills such as subject–verb agreement, punctuation, and even spelling—which obviously do affect the readability of writing.

However, teaching these skills is conducted quite differently from the traditional grammar instruction many had in school. All of the teachers I talked with spoke of the necessity for teaching grammar in the context of writing and individualizing instruction as much as possible. Several spoke highly of the usefulness of sentence combining. From the 25 or so teachers I interviewed over the course of two quarters, I have selected six who seem to illustrate the prevailing opinions.

WHAT TEACHERS SAY

John, a veteran teacher in a suburban school, said:

> It seems to me that the grammar debate is almost a moot point—it is debated now for the sake of debate, between highly traditional people interested in structure for the sake of structure and those philosophically opposed to structure. I don't think the majority of English teachers see any purpose in the discussion.
>
> The guidelines for our district require no formal grammar study, but

do require mastery in terms of writing skills—subject–verb agreement, punctuation, etc. . . . I teach grammar with the understanding that it helps us express our thoughts precisely. Commas and question marks do have rational functions. We have to have some basic terminology—the parts of speech and their functions—to discuss writing.

Tom, a younger teacher in a similar school, said:

I agree that as a set of prescriptive rules to be followed for a writer, [grammar] is not useful. But if you teach grammar as a description of what a writer does, and as a vocabulary to talk about writing, it's very useful. In fact, you can't teach writing without it. If you have students diagram sentences before they write, you're wasting time. But after they begin writing, when they're ready, diagraming sentences can be very helpful. Beginning writers tend to use the same type of sentence patterns over and over. When they're ready to move on and learn something new, you can show them a diagram of what their sentences do. They can see that they're all the same. Then they can learn a new pattern. I love sentence combining for this; it's fun, and the kids love it, too.

That's one of the myths about grammar—that it's hard. It's not really hard, it's easy. But the writing comes first. Teaching the rules first is like giving a sixteen-year-old a manual of traffic laws and saying, "Now you know how to drive." The rules don't mean anything unless the students see how they can apply them in their own writing.

This instruction needs to be individualized in personal conferences. On every assignment, I have a conference with each student at least once. If you're really reading students' papers, not just grading them, you'll see what their patterns are. As I watch students write over the course of the year, I know when one is ready to

learn to use semicolons. If you try to teach semicolons to the whole class, you're going to lose half of them.

Ann, a teacher in a large, affluent school where almost all the students are college bound, observed:

I usually think of grammar in terms of mechanics and usage—writing skills. I am aware of the studies which show that teaching grammar does not improve writing, and I think they must have just used grammar drills in isolation. In college, I was taught that grammar drills don't help, and I agree, *if* the students are not shown how to *apply* the practice. Of course we should teach grammar, and of course it applies to writing. If a student doesn't know where to put apostrophes, how are you going to explain it except by teaching the rule? I teach subordinate clauses with sentence combining. I don't necessarily have them do a lot of labeling. I don't really care if they know it's an adverbial clause, as long as they know how to do subordination. *Everybody* needs to know the basics of usage, capitalization, punctuation, and be able to produce writing which is mechanically correct.

Janice, an experienced teacher in an urban school, noted:

Every English teacher I know thinks that you have to teach some grammatical skills in order to teach writing. I use worksheets in class—not the fill-in-the-blank kind, but the kind that require students to write a sentence of their own. When I identify a particular problem with a student, I try to discuss it individually. They often don't pay attention to the comments I write on their papers. I find that the students tend to pay more attention to grammatical concepts if we talk about them in the context of a paper they're working on, although there are some kids who just won't learn some things, like apostrophes and homonyms. No matter how I explain it, I have some students who just won't learn the rules. They don't expect to do any writing after high school, and they just don't care. They enjoy sentence combining, and that really helps a lot of students.

For Michelle, a young teacher in a large urban school, "the controversy about teaching grammar is just silly." She continued:

All "real" writers know grammatical conventions. You have to know the rules, even though you may sometimes choose to break them. Of course our students need to know some grammar. They need some terminology to talk about writing. They have to be able to use basic terms like *subject, verb, noun*. I think the controversy is really about how much to teach, and how to do it. You can't teach it now the way it was traditionally taught, at least to the type of students we have at this school.

I learned a lot by acquisition, by reading, and my students never read for pleasure. When I went to school, we learned the rules. My students now just won't do that. With more advanced kids, I can teach grammatical concepts, and it will transfer to their writing, but not with lower ability students. We can do a lesson on capitalization, and it just doesn't dawn on them to use the same rules in their own writing . . . so I individualize as much as possible. One-to-one conferencing about a paper is the best way. The big problem is not enough *time* to do that. I believe that achievement is directly related to class size. If I really try, I can get to half my class in one period.

Linda began teaching in an urban classroom four years ago. She, and several other teachers, pointed out that our colleagues in the foreign language department are often distressed that we don't have students conjugate verbs any more, but she said,

Grammar, to me, now means mechanics: capitalization, punctuation, subject–verb agreement, how to write

a complete sentence. If you're going to teach writing, you have to teach some grammar. I think students need more instruction, particularly in the lower grades . . . not complicated stuff, just the basics like when to use apostrophes, paragraphing, and the difference between *there* and *their*.

It's hard to teach this to non-readers. Many of my students don't read, so they don't know how things are supposed to look and they write what they hear, or think they hear, and since many of us are very sloppy about the way we speak, kids write things like *wanna* and *gonna*. They can't just go by what sounds right, because they have no good role models for speaking, and you have to be pretty careful if you're criticizing the way people speak in a student's home.

I don't find peer revision very helpful, but students enjoy sentence combining and usually do well on the exercises. I've also found that using the computers really helps students see their errors and be willing to correct. But it would be a lot better if we had more computers—or fewer students—so we could have one for each student in a class.

DISCUSSION

Obviously, these teachers seldom think of grammar in the linguistic sense as a description of the structure of the language, but rather as mechanics and usage: subject–verb agreement, plural formation, even spelling, capitalization, and punctuation. They speak of these conventions as "writing skills," "grammar skills," or "mechanical skills," and they see these skills, not as the most important thing, but as an essential part of good writing.

It is unfortunate that researchers have not always clearly distinguished between the formal study of descriptive grammar and the practical application of usage skills. The result has been much wasted ink in scholarly journals as well as teachers who feel that scholarly research has little relevance to their classrooms. Attacking grammar instruction in the article referred to earlier, Hartwell said:

> Those who defend the teaching of grammar tend to have a model of composition instruction that is rigidly skills-centered and rigidly sequential; the formal teaching of grammar, as the first step in that sequence, is the cornerstone or linchpin ... first grammar, then usage, then some absolute model for organization, all controlled by the teacher at the center of the learning process. (108)

This simply does not describe the opinions or practices of the teachers I spoke with, although they all said they teach grammar. Indeed, Tom articulated very clearly that writing must come *before* instruction in grammar. Teachers have internalized the point of the many research studies which illustrate the uselessness of grammar drills by themselves. No teacher I talked with defended teaching grammar for its own sake, which is probably a distinct change from the prevailing assumptions twenty or thirty years ago, and none of the curricula for the schools specifies teaching grammar per se. All the teachers I spoke with believe that grammar skills are best taught in the context of the students' own writing, though drills or worksheets may be used to reinforce specific concepts. The teachers maintained that clear, coherent content is the most important component of good writing, but that control of the mechanical conventions is also essential for clear communication.

Ann's anger about what she saw as the abandonment of grammatical instruction by the academic community may not be fair, but it was real:

> I think it's just a fad to say we don't need to teach grammar and when new teachers actually start to work they

find they need it, and they don't know it themselves. I'm very disappointed that I was allowed to graduate from college as an English teacher without a good background in grammar ... Even if *everybody* doesn't need to know what a participle is, *English teachers* certainly should know.

It should be noted, however, that several of the teachers I spoke with said that their college courses had *not* attempted to discourage them from teaching grammar, so perhaps what prospective teachers are taught about this issue depends somewhat on the courses they take and the particular professors they have. Our education colleges need to clarify that abandoning formal, traditional grammar instruction does not mean abandoning all attempts to teach the conventions of standard English. As one of my student teachers noted rather bitterly, "The professors tell you not to teach grammar, but if you make a mistake on one of your papers, they sure do mark it!"

The teachers I spoke with agreed that they teach more grammar terminology to higher-ability students than to lower-level ones. The rationale for this is that the college-bound students need it more, and the lower-level students are more resistant to learning it. As one teacher explained:

> Traditionally, the upper half of society has always learned more grammar—back when they had to learn Greek and Latin, for example. But 80% of our society now is not into academic rigor. Our school system is experimenting with heterogeneous grouping, and dissecting gerunds in mixed classes is just a swamp. I now deal primarily with usage issues.

The teachers from the urban schools have, by and large, given up teaching all but the most basic skills, and there is still a fair amount of frustration about students who refuse to learn even those skills. The urban teachers spoke often about the benefits of using computers in writing classes with less able or more reluctant students.

CONCLUSION

It is time for professionals to agree that isolated grammar drills may be useless in English classes but that accuracy in usage is desirable and can be taught effectively in the context of writing. Many teachers know this, have determined their own lists of the necessary rules and basic terminology, and employ effective techniques such as sentence combining and individual conferencing about papers to meet the needs of their students. I think many teachers wish that we could finally put the great grammar debate to rest, and consider more pressing problems, like how to get composition classes down to reasonable sizes where individual conferencing is practicable, how to get word processors in the hands of all our students, and how to get our students to read more.

For Further Thought

1. What do most of these teachers mean by *grammar*? (Tabbert's terms—*grammar-1*, *grammar-2*, and *grammar-3*—will prove useful here.) What general attitude do they take toward the teaching of grammar?
2. Both Tabbert and Weaver are linguists and college professors. Do they represent what teachers think university professors say about teaching grammar? Ask your instructor what he or she thinks about the subject.
3. Petruzzella quotes a student who is "pissed off" because his grammar and usage skills are weak—and his professors implied that this was not serious. Is he talking about *grammar-2* or *grammar-3*? How just is his criticism? Think about what an English teacher needs to know about grammar.
4. Specifically, what do these teachers say they do about teaching grammar? Are these activities in line with Weaver's recommendations, or not? For an explanation of sentence combining, look forward to the next application (below).
5. Petruzella says that with thirty students in a class, the workshop approach is not realistic. Some teachers, Nancie Atwell included, might challenge that statement. What do you think? Could an adaptation of the workshop be effective in these circumstances?

Application 5.4:
Sentence Fluency

Consider the following passages. I have adapted them from the work of a nine-year-old, a thirteen-year-old, and a seventeen-year-old, and they are listed in that order. (1) "There was a dog in the alley. He attacked me. I was playing there with my friends." (2) "I admire Michael Jordan because he's just what I would like to be. He's great at defense, but his shooting is the best. When he goes up for a dunk, he's awesome." (3) "If I had been Helen Keller I don't know if I'd ever be able to learn. Because being blind, deaf and mute I would never have realized there was language and would have thought there was complete darkness around everybody. That is, I'd think the whole world was like me. But by feeling people's lips moving, she realized they had a way of communicating with each other."

As students grow older and have more experience with reading and writing, the way they fashion sentences changes. In the preceding passages, the nine-year-old tells his story as it occurs to him, using the *primer style*, in which each sentence states one main idea. The thirteen-year-old is better able to show the relationships of one idea to another, and so he uses a more *embedded style*, in which there is a hierarchy of ideas related to each other in causal or temporal ways. The result is what we call, in traditional grammar, more "complex" sentences. The seventeen-year-old is dealing with an even more complex web of ideas; to get at them, she tries a number of grammatical strategies that do not seem to occur to the nine- or thirteen-year-olds—participial phrases ("being blind, deaf and mute") or gerunds ("by feeling"), conditional clauses ("If I had been"), and explanatory restatements (the "that is" part of the sentence). Of course she makes a number of errors along the way, but that does not alter the fact that her style is more syntactically mature than that of the other writers.

This kind of development, which I call sentence fluency, tends to occur without much formal instruction, provided students continue to read and write regularly. It is tied, no doubt, to cognitive development (notice how the ideas become more complex as the writers grow older), which suggests that grammatical fluency is connected in some manner to thinking. But the main point is that we should be looking for this progress in students, fostering it in whatever ways we can. And because many students do not do much reading and writing outside of school, we cannot expect that progress in the fashioning of sentences will happen "naturally." It is part of our job to help it along.

How to do that has been a subject of debate for three decades now. For some, direct grammar instruction has been the answer, although we have seen that this solution is questioned by many. Others have looked for a more holistic, less analytical approach to sentence study. One such approach that was popular in the 1970s, called generative rhetoric, attempted to combine a simplified grammar with pattern practice and a great deal of modeling. Those of us who tried this technique found that it did indeed affect students' writing style, at least in the sense that it illustrated to students who were "lagging behind" what kinds of sentences they might be creating. But the exercises were complicated, and generative rhetoric did not seem to connect well to all kinds of writing. So it went the way of other educational trends.

Then came sentence combining, a technique that has had more success. The idea of taking short sentence kernels and combining them into longer units had been around for some time, but it was promoted vigorously in the 70s and 80s by two scholars, Frank O'Hare and William Strong. O'Hare conducted an influential study of the technique and produced a book, *Sentencecraft*, in which he presented a number of cued (directed) exercises. Strong favored uncued (free) sentence combining and later extended the practice to include units of discourse longer than the sentence. If you look at the sample exercises at the end of this application, you will see immediately how sentence combining works. The idea is to give students practice in using the "internal grammar" they already possess, thus fostering sentence maturity without recourse to much formal instruction in grammar.

Sentence combining seems to have some staying power; that is, the technique still shows up in textbooks, and many teachers, including those interviewed by Brenda Petruzella, think that it helps students write more sophisticated sentences. But it is obviously no panacea for students' sentence-level problems. For one thing, it seems that sentence combining needs to be done with some regularity to have much effect on students' style. So although it might be helpful to do some minilessons in combining just to illustrate stylistic resources to students, a one-shot dose probably won't have much effect on basic writers who are really struggling with sentence problems. More importantly, sentence combining will not do much for students unless they keep working on pieces of their own. In this sense, sentence combining activities are no different from regular grammar exercises. We have accomplished very little if students become adept at doing exercises but don't transfer those skills to their own writing.

I suspect that, in the end, the value of any such technique depends on our expectations. If we ask too much of sentence combining, we are bound to be disappointed. If, on the other hand, we are modest in what we expect, sentence combining might be worth a try. Surely exercises like these have an illustrative value, and they can provide worthwhile practice for many students. Perhaps more importantly, they can foster a useful playfulness in students, getting them to stretch their stylistic wings a bit. Risk taking with sentences almost always leads to errors at first, as we saw with the seventeen-year-old at the start of this section. But this, I think, is a good kind of error. We would surely not want her to revert to a less mature style to express what she wants to say. Rather, we'll want to reward her for the risks she takes, and then help her play some more games with her own sentences, combining and recombining them in ways that are more effective and more correct.

Some Things to Consider About Sentence Maturity

1. Play with the three passages at the beginning of this section. Write at least two versions of the nine-year-old's and the thirteen-year-old's work, using a more mature style and explaining what you did. Then rewrite the seventeen-year-old's passage, punctuating it correctly.

2. Look at the seventh-grade papers in Appendix 2. Brad's paper is clearly different stylistically from some of the others. Identify some of the features of Brad's style and then compare it to the work of one of the other seventh graders.

3. Do the following sentence combining exercises. Which do you prefer—the cued or uncued exercises? Discuss sentence combining as a general technique. Would you use it? Why or why not?

4. Consider the attempt to extend the combining principle to longer units, for example, the "fact sheet" on whales. Do this exercise and then discuss it, indicating how effective you think it might be. For more exercises like this, consult Strong's *Creative Approaches to Sentence Combining* (NCTE, 1986).

Cued Sentence Combining*

Lesson 8   *That, the fact that*

   Example   Peter noticed something.
               There were nine golf balls in the river. (*that*)
               Peter noticed that there were nine golf balls in the river.

---

*Frank O'Hare, *Sentencecraft*. Needham Heights, MA: Silver, Burdett and Ginn, 1975.

Lesson 10   *Who, what, where, when, why, how*
Example   Something worried the climbers.
            The odd light meant something. (*what*)
            What the odd light meant worried the climbers.

Lesson 19   *Which/that, who, whom*
Example   Some of the engines were scheduled to be scrapped this year.
            The saboteurs have demolished the engines. (*which*)
            Some of the engines which the saboteurs have demolished
            were scheduled to be scrapped this year.

Lesson 22
Example   The girl suddenly began to scream in terror.
            The girl was *walking through the park*.
            The girl walking through the park suddenly began to scream
            in terror.

Open Sentence Combining*

Rock Concert

1. The singer was young.
2. The singer was swarthy.
3. He stepped into the spotlight.
4. The spotlight was red.

5. His shirt was unbuttoned.
6. The unbuttoning bared his chest.

7. Sounds ballooned around him.
8. The sounds were of guitars.
9. The sounds were of drums.
10. The sounds were of girls.
11. The girls were screaming.

12. He nodded.
13. He winked.
14. The wink was to his guitarist.
15. The drummer responded with the beat.

16. The singer became animated.
17. His legs were like rubber.
18. His body jerked.
19. His head was thrown back.

---

*William Strong, *Sentence Combining: A Composing Book*. New York: McGraw Hill, 1973.

Sentence Combining Fact Sheet*

Fact Sheet: Whales

are among the most intelligent animals
have no ears
use sound signals to communicate
use sound signals to navigate
are the largest living creatures
strain plankton from the seawater
are mammals
can sometimes be found in fresh water
have voices
may become extinct
have teeth
eat fish
have fishlike bodies
have paddle-shaped flippers
range in size from the porpoise to the blue whale
can hold their breath up to two hours
are insulated by a layer of blubber, or fat

are aquatic animals
have lungs, not gills
have horizontal tail fins, unlike fish
are different from fish
have thick, smooth skin
can dive to depths of 4,800 feet
do not see very well
range from 4 feet to 100 feet in length
are social animals
may weigh as much as 150 tons
cannot smell
have nose openings, or blow holes, atop their heads
are hunted for oils in their bodies
live in all of the world's oceans

At level   Students are to
   A   use five facts in no more than four sentences.
   B   use ten facts in no more than six sentences.
   C   use fifteen facts in no more than eight sentences.
   D   use twenty facts in no more than ten sentences.
   E   use twenty-five facts in no more than twelve sentences.

---

*From William Strong, *Creative Approaches to Sentence Combining*. Urbana, IL: NCTE–ERIC/RCS, 1986.

When Some of Them Don't Speak English

Larry Andrews

In the general introduction to this chapter I alluded to Larry Andrews's Language Exploration and Awareness: A Resource Book for Teachers, 2nd edition (Lawrence Erlbaum Associates, 1998). The following article is the final chapter of that book, which explains the unusual format. Andrews provides a prereading scenario, as well as materials at the end—review questions, advice from an elementary ESL teacher, and two language exploration activities. Hence I have included no applications of my own. In the essay itself, Andrews offers what he calls "a practical and introductory guide for the classroom teacher" of students whose first language is not English. His assumption is that we will have some ESL students in our classes, and that they will be best served if we treat them not as "remedial" students but as mature language learners.

Copyright 1998 by Lawrence Erlbaum Associates. This excerpt from Language Exploration and Awareness: A Resource Book for Teachers, *2nd edition, is used with permission.*

"Well, then, why ain't it natural and right for a Frenchman to talk different from us? You answer me that."
—Mark Twain, *Adventures of Huckleberry Finn*

Before you read the following chapter, consider the following telephone conversation:

"Dr. Andrews, this is Jane Doe, the high-school counselor at Midway High School. We have three new students from (name a country) who came to school just two days ago to begin school here and their English language proficiency is, well, very limited. Their teachers aren't sure how to help them in their classes. Can you give us some, like, really quick advice?"

I've had several conversations like this one. In this example, I've changed only the names of the counselor and the school.

What advice would you give to the counselor and to the teachers?

Because of the enormity of the United States, many of us spend our lifetimes immersed in a monolingual, English-speaking environment.[1] For example, I can get in my car and drive for six hours in *any* direction, get out of my car and the language I'll hear spoken on the local main street, radio or television, or read in the local newspaper will be the same language I routinely speak and read. I'm not unique. Many people in the United States, perhaps you, too, can make the same comment. With only one or two exceptions, however, few people in the rest of the world can make this generalization. In that regard, then, several of us in the United States *are* unique.

People in other parts of the world, on the other hand, can drive for six hours—or even much less—in any direction and encounter *several* language groups. What this illustrates is that many of us in the United States are linguistically landlocked. Except for those of you living near ethnic enclaves in major metropolitan centers or those of you living in a border state, we in the United States are largely, but not totally, of course, surrounded by linguistic sameness: the English language.

I do not mean to suggest that we are inherently stupid or lazy people because of our lack of experience with other languages and cultures. It is unfortunate, however, that this lack of experience with other language groups causes us, sometimes, to view other languages and other cultures as being of little or no value or importance, and causes us either to ignore or to avoid those who do not speak fluent English.[2]

In some cases, according to Betancourt, there are openly antagonistic attitudes toward persons of other languages. She suggests that especially in those states that have enacted English as the "official language," the discussions have encouraged hostile feelings toward non-English speaking citizens.[3]

THE GROWING NUMBERS OF SECOND-LANGUAGE LEARNERS

This is no small issue. According to the U.S. Census Bureau, in 1994, fully 8.7% of those living in this country were born in other countries. Approximately 31.8 million people in the United States speak a language *other than* English in the home. Some have estimated that as many as one third of all of the students attending urban schools use English as their *second* language.[4]

Even in the relatively sparsely populated state in which I live, both the larger and the smaller school districts are facing a common challenge: meeting the learning needs of a growing number of children whose first language is not English.

I know of two smaller school districts serving towns with populations in the 5,000 to 6,000 range. If anyone had suggested to school personnel in these districts a decade ago that among their greatest challenges in the late 1990s would be trying to meet the needs of English as a Second Language (ESL) learners, they would have laughed at the suggestion. They certainly couldn't laugh today, however, as the telephone conversation reported at the beginning of this chapter illustrates.

What all of the above tells me is, I believe, fairly clear. Unless or until there is a dramatic reduction in immigration quotas that might be established by the U.S. government, I can guarantee you that sooner or later—and it's likely to be sooner—you will have a student, perhaps several students, for whom English is their second (or third, or fourth) language, and, further, their English language proficiency will not be the same as that of your native-English speaking students! What do you do, then, when all of your students don't speak English?

I cannot deliver in this single chapter a complete K–12 teacher-education program that will certify you as an ESL teacher. If you are interested in such a program, your state colleges or universities may offer one. Because one chapter in one book can't tell you everything you need to know about second-language acquisition and pedagogy, I'm going to inject a subtitle for this chapter: *A Practical and Introductory Guide for the Classroom Teacher*.

Who Are These Students?

Who are these children and young adults who look to you to help them learn in school? They are the sons and daughters of immigrants from Bosnia, Russia, Ukraine, Croatia, Mexico, Vietnam, Haiti, and a host of other nations. They may have come to the United States with the assistance of family members who immigrated earlier, years ago. Or, they may have come with the assistance of a local social service agency or church. Or, they may have immigrated to the United States completely on their own.

Further, remember that each family has a *story*. Some of the stories are narratives of dogged determination and achievement. Some of their stories are nothing less than horrific! As John Skretta, a local high-school teacher and a graduate student who teaches me a lot, wrote in his ESL internship journal: "That human beings could endure, or should have to endure and overcome the physical, emotional and psychological threats some of my ESL students have faced, is testimony to the incredible resiliency of the human spirit."

Finally, but by no means conclusively, some of these learners—a number of whom have never before attended school—are in your community and school because they want to be there and are happy to be there. They have come to the United States and have, consequently, avoided the life-or-death threat of "ethnic cleansing," or, they have rejoined their family, or they have new-found opportunities for education and for employment.

On the other hand, some are here against their will; their parents made the decision to immigrate to the United States and the son or daughter had absolutely no vote in the matter. They were finessed. When they came to the United States, they left behind their best friends, their own culture and customs, and their own language. In the words of a well-known science fiction writer, Robert Heinlein, they are strangers in strange land . . . and they may not like this strange land!

SOME NOTIONS ABOUT ESL LEARNERS IN YOUR CLASSROOM

As we begin our *Practical and Introductory Guide for the Classroom Teacher*, there are a few notions worth remembering about the ESL learners in your classroom.

ESL Learners Are, First of All, Human Beings; They Are People.[5] This may seem obvious, but, sometimes, it is either forgotten or ignored. For example, I have seen a 15-year-old immigrant student placed in a 5th grade classroom. His English language proficiency wasn't the same as the native English speakers of the same age. He was, clearly, the oldest and the largest learner in the room, much too large for the flip-top desk he tried to cram his body into. Further, he had the interests of a 15-year-old person, not a 10-year-old. He had no friends in this room. He was clearly embarrassed and anxious. For him, school was not a "safe place."

I have seen a 12-year-old student from Bosnia placed in a classroom dedicated to the needs of "retarded" learners. Because of her limited English proficiency, she was classified by the school as a "retarded" learner. This young woman knew what was happening to her, and she resented the treatment she was receiving.

Both of these learners, however, are *people*, just like their American agemates. Their only "problem" was that they didn't speak fluent English. The schools forgot they these students were human beings with the same needs and interests of their native English-speaking peers.

In addition to these violations of human relationships, there is a significant linguistic fault: The two young people I've described needed to be placed with first-language students; the ESL students will learn a lot of English from them.

ESL Students Learn English in Order to Accomplish What They Need and Want to Accomplish With Those Who Speak English.[6] ESL learners need to learn English that will help them *now*, not someday in the future.

To illustrate: One of my students shared with the class one night the first sentence he learned in a foreign language course, which was, (translated into English) "I have a green pencil box." Twenty years later, he said, he's still *waiting* for an opportunity to use that sentence! As you might imagine, he may need to wait a few more years.

ESL learners need to do *immediate* things with English; how to ask for help or for directions, how to ask a question in class, how to go through the lunch line and ask for a preferred entrée, how to ask for a bus transfer slip, how to give an answer to a question in class, and the like.

The ESL Student's Growth in English Proficiency Develops Globally, Not Linearly.[7] ESL learners don't acquire English in a linear sequence by learning nouns first, verbs second, adverbs thirdly, then pronouns, etc. They learn "chunks" of language in meaningful contexts. Please, do not waste their time by assigning drills and worksheets that focus on isolated fragments of language; rather, keep them engaged in talking and writing activities with their English-speaking peers in which they must use English in order to satisfy age-appropriate, meaningful classroom learning assignments.

Won't these activities present a variety of challenges to the ESL learners and to their English-speaking peers? Of course; next question?

In time the ESL learners will learn both English and content, more rapidly than you might assume. Plus, peers are effective—and relatively more patient—mentors than you or I might be.

Language Develops in a Variety of Contexts.[8] When you were acquiring language, you did so by playing different types of games with your family; by listening to read-aloud poems and stories and by talking about them; by looking at pictures in a variety of books; by going to the mall and talking about what you saw; by going to the grocery store; by riding in the family car or in a bus, by talking about what you were seeing.

I have a friend who teaches ESL science. The curriculum called for a unit entitled "The Rain Forest"; her stu-

dents from Iraq and Jordan recognized the words "rain" and "forest," but had little understanding of the larger, compound concept, "rain forest." She took the students to a nearby zoo that has a reconstructed Rain Forest. The students enjoyed the trip, had a meaningful experience, and the unit meant something to them.

All of the field trips you can arrange— or piggyback with another teacher in your building—will be useful, but the field trips don't need to be "fancy." A walk around the block, a trip to a local grocery store, fire station, hospital, a drug store, or even to your own home will provide your ESL learners with language-rich experiences. Further, keep a supply of word games available; take your old magazines to school. Bring the local newspaper and telephone book to class; they employ many uses of language you cannot assume your ESL learners are familiar with.

Focus Your Attention on General Literacy, Not Isolated Skills. Once again, review your own experiences, or, if you are a parent, those of your children. When language learners acquire language, their family members don't devote Mondays for reading, Tuesdays for talking, Wednesdays for writing, and the like.

In an English-speaking home with a younger language learner, literacy events take place in an integrated manner: A parent reads a letter from a relative, talks about the letter and the relative with the learner, then the child "writes" a letter, real or imaginary, using some conventional spellings, some not, maybe some invented spellings, or perhaps only what adults might call "scribbling."

In English-speaking homes, adults read to children, make shopping lists, and talk about what's for lunch. The children talk with the adults about the letters, the lists, and the menu; they'll frequently create their own stories, lists, and menus, in both written and oral forms.

I am not suggesting that you duplicate these illustrations in your classroom. If you think they'll work, try them. I am, however, suggesting that reading-writing-listening-speaking events are normally and naturally *intertwined*. Read aloud to your students, talk about what you've read. Use wordless picture books and invite the class to create the narration and dialogue. Have the students draw or write their own stories or poems. Discuss the stories. The students will learn language and conversational conventions, story structures, the differences between expository and narrative prose, the importance of sequence, and the like.

Include Your ESL Learners in All Classroom Activities. The vast majority of classroom teachers I know are humane, caring people who are dedicated to helping others to learn. They know that classrooms should be "safe" environments in which predicting, speculating, and exploring are to be encouraged, without the students fearing failure.

Further, they know that no learner should suffer embarrassment; learning is, among other things, emotional. When people are threatened, they learn little; when they are safe, people learn more.

Consequently, some well-intentioned teachers will not call on ESL learners in class discussions. Fearful that the ESL learner might not know an answer (as if all of the English-speaking students will!) or might mispronounce the language, the well-intentioned teacher doesn't call on the ESL learner as often. Let's avoid embarrassment seems to be the ruling assumption. On the one hand, this is understandable.

In the long run, however, strategies such as these, no matter how altruistic they may be, do not help the ESL learner. They push him or her to the social and educational periphery of the class. These "humanistic" attempts, in fact, remove the ESL learner from meaningful content-related discussions and from the culture of the classroom. You must include your ESL learners in all of the activities in your classes; the alternative is to harm them with misguided kindness, however well-intentioned, which makes them marginalized citizens in the classroom.

SELECTED CLASSROOM STRATEGIES

First of all, let me clear the chalkboard: Some teachers believe that fully-certified ESL teachers possess a mysterious repertoire of *magical* strategies enabling them to help immigrant/refugee children learn English. This is, however, not the way it is.

Certified ESL teachers are not wizards of the arcane; they do not employ academic alchemy. They modify successful, proven practices in order to meet the needs of their students. All good teachers do the same thing.

As a transition, revisit with me an early Indiana Jones movie, *Raiders of the Lost Ark*. In the first scenes we see Indy and his guide attempting to take a bag of jewels from a protected dais. Indy takes the bag, he and the guide race out of the cave—chased by a large, rolling boulder—only to be met by a dastardly villain. Indy heroically flees and runs as fast as he can to his airplane, parked on a conveniently nearby lake, and he escapes! Whew!

In the next scene we see *Dr.* Indiana Jones, an Ivy League Professor of Archeology, all tweedy and frumpy, leather patches at the elbows, delivering a lecture to his students. As Indy's lecture approaches a dramatic denouement, a rude school bell rings, interrupting and signifying the end of class.

The students gather up their notebooks, stuff them into their book bags, and start filing out of the room. As the students exit, Indy shouts after them, "Remember, read Chapter Six for the next class!"

That's how Professor Jones gives assignments to his students. It's a *counterexample* of effective practice, described here as a model to *avoid*. With all students in general, and with ESL learners in particular, the assignment phase of a reading assignment in any classroom is crucial. A more effective assignment will include the following:

• **The assignment will build on the learners' prior knowledge of the topic.** The teacher will describe in very direct language how the next assignment is related to the topic covered yesterday, last week, or in the last unit of study. Or, the teacher may ask the class to brainstorm about the topic of the next assignment, listing their comments on the chalkboard, then organizing these comments into related clusters. If the class lacks sufficient prior knowledge, provide direct experience that will give them the knowledge. (The trip to the zoo's rain forest, described above, is an excellent example.)

• **The assignment will introduce important new vocabulary words.** Presented in the actual context in which they appear in the text, the new words are introduced. Perhaps the students can figure out the meaning of the word by seeing how it is used in the sentence. If not, the teacher can provide the meaning. Be selective in choosing words, however. You can't teach your students all the words they might not know. Consequently, introduce vocabulary that name *key concepts* in the assignment and that are likely to be *encountered again* in the study of the subject at hand.

• **The assignment will provide clear direction, purpose, and meaning.**

Through the use of graphic organizers, Venn diagrams, structured overviews, and the like, the teacher can help the readers to focus their attention. For example, some reading materials compare and contrast two characters, two countries, or two forms of government; some texts provide a description of causes and effects of events in history or in proper versus improper nutrition. Some texts are organized by providing a list or a sequence, as in the ordering of the planets in our universe or in naming the characteristics of the more successful first colonies. When readers know beforehand that they are reading an assignment in order to determine one of these relationships as they read, their reading will have greater purpose and meaning, the underpinnings of successful comprehension.

• **The assignment will provide opportunities for the learners to integrate language activities.** After reading the text, the class may be asked to write a more complete description of how, for example, Jim and Huck Finn are similar and dissimilar characters (compare–contrast), or why the Battle of Bull Run took place and why it was significant (cause–effect). Some of these writings can be read aloud for further class discussion.[9]

FOR YOUR INQUIRY AND PRACTICE:

Review both the section "Some Notions About ESL Learners in Your Classroom" and the characteristics of effective assignments. In how many ways are the notions and the characteristics interrelated?

WHAT ABOUT GRAMMAR AND CORRECTNESS?

Second-language learners (L2 learners) aren't likely to be as proficient in their oral and written uses of English as their native English-speaking peers; they may never achieve that standard. What should we do, then, when L2 students make usage errors?

As one teacher describes it, "I was pleasantly surprised to learn there has recently been a shift away from preoccupation with surface errors in the teaching of L2 writers."[10]

Surface errors in usage should not be viewed as an L2 learner's failure, but as natural part of the language learning process. In fact, errors that do not get in the way of the L2 student's reading or writing comprehension are often overlooked.[11]

Many L2 learners are eager to achieve grammatical accuracy; they want the teacher to correct all of their unconventional usages, spellings, pronunciations, and the like. This is, however, a daunting task. Consequently, Leki makes two useful suggestions: First, focus your corrections on those errors that have the greatest social stigma; and, second, watch for patterns of errors L2 students may be making in your class. If patterns become obvious to you, then you can help your L2 learner(s) through a 15 to 20 minute minilesson addressing the matter.[12]

AND NOW, IN CONCLUSION . . .

The chapter has tried to provide some basic suggestions to teachers who have the responsibility for helping immigrant children whose first language is not English to achieve in school. For additional help, you should talk with an ESL teacher in your building or district. He or she can provide both collegial support and suggestions for teaching L2 learners. Also, don't forget the foreign language teacher. She or he is familiar with approaches to teaching in a second-language acquisition context; they'll likely be happy to help you.

Although L2 learners may, at first, seem to present a challenge you'll never be able to meet, in time and with patience and practice, both you and they will learn. They will be learning a lot about a new culture, the English language, and the content of your course. The beauty of your relationship with these students is so will you.

REVIEWING THE CHAPTER

1. Approximately how many people in the United States speak a language other than English in the home?
2. Is teaching ESL learners an experience relatively few teachers will have?
3. Do you believe ESL learners ought to be placed in special classes?
4. Should ESL learners be allowed to use their native language in school?
5. Will a fish out of water learn to swim better?
6. What should an ESL student learn first; accurate pronunciation or accurate spelling?
7. What's more important for the ESL student, to learn English for social purposes or for classroom purposes?
8. If you could select one major goal for an ESL learner, would it be improved speaking or improved writing abilities?
9. Should an ESL learner consult the dictionary whenever an unfamiliar word is encountered?
10. Does practice always make perfect?

***** ***** *****

If you have a younger ESL learner in your classroom, say from grades K to 6 or 7, you might want to consider these suggestions, offered by one of my ESL teacher friends, Rita Smith. If you believe that some of these ideas are not age appropriate for your students, adapt them and make them more appropriate.

PREPARING YOUR CLASSROOM FOR ESL LEARNERS

by Rita Smith, ESL Teacher
Meadowlane School
Lincoln, NE

Before Your Students Arrive:

1. Prepare a list to hang by the door that includes the students' names and bus number. Keep this list updated throughout the year!
2. Provide picture cues that include the daily schedule and other daily activities such as choices for Learning Centers.
3. Translate for parents notes that contain important school information. One way to do this is to assemble a bag that includes school forms and a translated description on a cassette tape of how to fill out the forms. A tape recorder should also be included.
4. If you are unfamiliar with the customs, eating habits, greetings, etc., of your new ESL students, read an appropriate *Culturegram. Culturegrams* are or should be available in your school media center or from your ESL teachers.
5. Ask ESL teachers, former students, or translators in your district how to say "hello" in your new students' first language.
6. Celebrate diversity! Show diversity in your classroom in the literature you choose, the pictures you hang, and in the activities you plan.
7. Label and picture objects and areas in your classroom.

On Your Students' First Day:

1. When the busses arrive, attach a name tag for each student in the bus windows. The name tag should include the student's name and bus stop address.
2. Give each student a button name tag that includes the student's name and

the teacher's name or classroom number.
3. If your students eat lunch at school, prepare a lunch chart that provides pictures of the choices on the school menu.
4. Prepare a Good Manner Chart with your students that has the classroom rules written and pictured. Role play the rules with the students.
5. Role play other classroom and school-wide activities, such as Friday Folders, Popcorn Friday, lunchroom routines, lining up, taking turns, etc.
6. Assign a buddy to each new ESL student. Buddies can help new students learn the routines of the classroom.
7. Establish a consistent routine in the classroom. Students will learn from "Saying, Watching, and Doing."

Other Ideas:

1. Use pattern books! Students enjoy and learn from books they can read again and again. *Brown Bear, Brown Bear, What Do You See?* is a good example of a pattern book. It is also fun to let the children make book rewrites with these books.
2. Use photos of all your students in books and room displays. An *Alphabet Name Book* is fun to make and students will read it over and over again!
3. Provide many hands-on activities and modify activities to meet ESL students' needs. For example, in a Food Unit, students could (1) walk to the nearest grocery store, (2) bake and eat different foods, (3) set up a "Classroom Cafe" to practice ordering food off a menu, and (4) sort food in different ways, by color, size, food groups, etc.
4. Read books such as *We Are All Alike, We Are All Different*. Have the children make paperdoll people that show the different colored skin tones and different dress of students in the room. Provide multicultural paint, paper, and/or crayons for students to use.

5. Provide modeling in all activities. Use "Read and Do" charts with your activities that show the directions in written and picture form.

6. Make picture/word charts for each unit and/or new vocabulary words in books you're using.

7. When printing material that students will see, make sure your printing is very clear and that each letter is separate, not connected as in cursive writing.

8. Use sign language when introducing new vocabulary words or new concepts. Students will enjoy learning the signs and the visual cues are helpful reminders.

9. Incorporate music whenever possible into your units of study. Students enjoy singing. The actions and repetition of words will be helpful to second-language learners.

STUDENT EXPLORATIONS FOR WHEN ALL OF THEM DON'T SPEAK ENGLISH

EXPLORATION: Tune in Next Week
DIRECTIONS: The teacher needs to bring to class a videotaped episode of a currently popular soap opera. Show some of the episode first with no volume and ask the class if it can interpret what the characters' moods and attitudes are based on their nonverbal behaviors, facial expressions, and the like. After this discussion, replay the videotape with the audio on.

1. How do the characters' body language support the spoken language used?

2. What are some relationships among body language, intonation, and communication?

***** ***** *****

EXPLORATION: Pause, and Take Five
DIRECTIONS: Select a paragraph from a book being used in class. Read the paragraph aloud with the students, clearing up any unfamiliar words or pronunciations. When the students are comfortable with the paragraph, copy it onto a transparency, breaking the sentences according to the natural pauses, not necessarily the punctuation marks, used in the oral reading.

> If your oral reading is typical
> you'll probably find
> that the sentences will assume
> a vertical form
> something like this.

1. Which words in the text's paragraph are emphasized when it is read silently? Why?

2. Are the same words emphasized when the paragraph is read aloud? How do we decide when to pause when reading aloud?

3. What are some of the differences between reading aloud and reading silently? Do these differences affect our understanding of what we read?

***** ***** *****

NOTES

1. Donna M. Brown, "One Person's Opinion," *English Journal* (December, 1996), 13.

2. Ibid., 14.

3. Ingrid Betancourt, *Wilson Library Bulletin* (February, 1992), 38.

4. "One Nation, One Language," *U.S. News & World Report* (September 25, 1995), 38–40.

5. Pat Rigg and Virginia G. Allen, "Introduction," *When They Don't All Speak English* (Urbana-Champaign, IL: National Council of Teachers of English, 1989), viii.

6. Ibid., ix.

7. Ibid., xi.

8. Ibid., xii.

9. For a more complete discussion of effective assignments and follow-up activities, see Suzanne F. Peregoy and Owen F. Boyle, *Reading, Writing and Learning in ESL: A Resource Book for K–12 Teachers* (2nd ed.,

White Plains, NY: Longman, 1997), 281–284.

10. Pamela Sissy Carroll et al., "When Acceptance Isn't Enough: Helping ESL Students

Become Successful Writers," *English Journal* (December, 1996), 28.

11. Ibid.

12. Ibid.

For Further Thought

1. Andrews believes that secondary ESL students should be treated as mature language learners—that is, that they benefit from the same activities that help native speakers. Still, some special help is needed. What examples of that special help does Andrews give?

2. Andrews suggests that peers—other students—can be the best helpers for ESL students. What do you think of that idea? What are some of the advantages and limitations of using peers as mentors or tutors?

3. Rita Smith, who provides the advice at the end of the chapter, is an elementary ESL teacher. Clearly some of her ideas are not applicable on the secondary level. Name two such ideas and explain why you would not use them. Then choose two that you could adapt to the secondary level and explain your adaptation.

4. In regard to correctness, Andrews advises us to concentrate on "those errors that have the greatest social stigma" (p. 289). In your opinion, which errors would fit that category? Give an example of each and explain why you think there is a social stigma attached.

5. Andrews clearly favors a mainstreaming approach to second language instruction. What do you think? Should ESL students be placed in special classes? If you have had contact with nonnative speakers of English, use your experience to support your ideas.

Writing Assignment: A Plan to Address a Problem

I think there is a natural tendency on the part of English teachers to avoid the issue of correctness—either that, or the countertendency to make a fetish of it. So there are those who like to focus on "the big things," hoping that in the long run "the little things" will take care of themselves. The problem here is that those little things can matter a great deal, and some of them stubbornly persist—yes, even in the writing of English majors! On the other hand, some teachers seem to focus only on the surface of writing, or at least that is how they are perceived by students. The problem here is that some very big things—knowledge, passion, logic, clarity—can take a back seat to fussiness about grammar and usage.

So obviously, we need to strike some kind of reasonable balance, recognizing the legitimate value of surface correctness without letting it get out of hand. In this regard, the teachers interviewed by Brenda Petruzzella can provide some overall guidance: What they say about usage seems quite reasonable to me. And we can take heart from the advice of Constance Weaver, realizing that a pared down, more focused "grammar" has more instructional value than a linear march through every issue raised by the latest edition of

Warriner's. And finally, we can hold onto some basic principles of instruction. For example, every effort to help students solve a problem with correctness should proceed in this manner: diagnosis of the problem, analysis of its causes and effects, and some plan of action followed by an application of the lesson to a real piece of student writing. The following writing assignment asks you to do just that.

* * *

Write a paper in which you tell how you will go about helping students with a sentence-level problem. This could be a grammar problem, a usage issue, or something to do with sentence maturity.

Your job is to find some pieces of student writing (you can work with the papers in the book) and identify something about the sentences that you would like kids to work on. Then you need to consider some different ways to help students, which might involve looking at some instructional materials (secondary textbooks, college composition books, handbooks, articles, materials you borrow from a teacher) if they are available. Eventually you will devise a plan for helping students, using and adapting your chosen materials in some way. The plan could involve one student as a tutorial or a larger group in a minilesson. Finally, you'll need to reflect on your own decisions.

The paper itself could take the shape of a narrative. You might begin with your reading of the student work and an identification of the problem, with specific examples from the student texts. This is your description of the diagnostic stage. Attach student samples as your first appendix. Then you could tell what kinds of instructional practices you considered and how you arrived at the materials you are using/adapting. If you are using textbook materials, attach an example as your second appendix. This phase describes your decision making. The third phase would be more expository: You will describe your approach to the problem. Describe your plan of action, attaching a lesson plan if your instructor so directs. Then conclude your narrative by explaining your current thinking on the approach you took, making sure that you critically evaluate its chances of success.

For Further Reading

Adger, Caroline, Donna Christian, and Walt Wolfram. *Dialects in Schools and Communities*. Mahwah, NJ: Lawrence Erlbaum Associates, 1999. A comprehensive discussion of dialects, with particular attention to reading and writing. "Language Variation in the United States" (pp. 220–233) is an excerpt from the first chapter of this book.

Andrews, Larry. *Language Exploration and Awareness: A Resource Book for Teachers*, 2nd ed. Mahwah, NJ: Lawrence Erlbaum Associates, 1998. Andrews believes in the active study of language. His book covers a wide range of language issues, with plenty of sample activities. "When Some of Them Don't Speak English" (pp. 283–292) is the final chapter of this book.

Baron, Dennis. *Declining Grammar and Other Essays in the English Language*. Urbana, IL: NCTE, 1989. A series of readable essays on language-related issues: lore (myths), usage, trends, and politics.

Cleary, Linda Miller, and Michael D. Linn, eds. *Linguistics for Teachers*. New York: McGraw-Hill, 1993. A good collection of scholarly essays on language issues as they relate to teaching.

English Journal. Periodically, *English Journal* devotes part of an issue to a particular aspect of teaching English. Note especially: "Language in Our Lives: Talkin' and Testifyin' " (January 1995) and "The Great Debate (Again): Teaching Grammar and Usage" (November 1996).

Hartwell, Patrick. "Grammar, Grammars, and the Teaching of Writing." *College English* (February 1985): 105–127. Hartwell discusses research findings on grammar and the teaching of writing, concluding that research alone will never resolve the controversy. Along the way, he covers the ground that Tabbert and Weaver cover, adding some other useful categories.

Noguchi, Rei R. *Grammar and the Teaching of Writing: Limits and Possibilities*. Urbana, IL: NCTE, 1991. Noguchi is trying to establish a middle position in the grammar wars: He believes it is possible to teach limited "writer's grammar" using test cases that capitalize on the grammar that native speakers already possess.

Strong, William. *Creative Approaches to Sentence Combining*. Urbana, IL: ERIC/NCTE, 1986. Strong discusses the research history of sentence combining and offers ways to use the technique with sentences and larger units of discourse.

Tompkins, Gail E., and David B. Yaden, Jr. *Answering Students' Questions about Words*. This book is discussed in Application 5.2 (pp. 238–242).

Weaver, Constance. *Teaching Grammar in Context*. Portsmouth, NH: Boynton/Cook, Heinmann, 1996. The first section of this book is an extended discussion of the issues raised in "Teaching Grammar in the Context of Writing" (pp. 255–267). The book also contains a detailed and rewarding discussion of "error."

Weaver, Constance, ed. *Lessons to Share on Teaching Grammar in Context*. Portsmouth, NH: Boynton/Cook, Heinemann, 1998. The more practical follow-up to *Teaching Grammar in Context*, this book is actually an anthology of essays on a number of aspects of the teaching of writing.

6

Joining the Profession

Introduction

> "Good luck!" God, that depresses me. Nothing is more depressing than people saying "Good luck" when they say goodbye. (Holden Caulfield in *The Catcher in the Rye*)

"No more advice!" I can almost hear you say it—and you are right. By now you have probably received a great deal of advice, from your instructor, from this book, from parents and friends, even from people you scarcely know. Get used to it. Like new parents, new teachers and student teachers are subjected to a lot of free (and sometimes conflicting) advice.

So there will be no direct advice in this closing chapter—no applications, just two articles, some voices to listen to. The first reading brings you back to a voice you have heard before: my own. In "Paradoxes of Planning," I pick up on a theme that is latent in John Rouse's description of Mrs. Martinez (see chapter 2), that is, her apparent lack of planning. If you have been in schools at all lately and if you have talked to any experienced teachers, you know what I mean. As a new teacher, you know that you need to plan carefully, yet the old hands seem to teach "naturally." How do you get there? "Paradoxes" is my way of wrestling with this dilemma, not to solve it but to shed some light on the problem. My method is to take you on a journey through my own experiences as a planner, beginning with my student teaching and ending with my practice as a college teacher.

Second, we come back to those three students you read about in "Where's That Fairy Dust When You Need It?" (chapter 1). Six months after the first interview, I met with Gabby, Debbie, and Nicole once more, to see how things were going. Two had finished student teaching, and the third had done some work in a field experience. They weren't exactly worry-free, but things had changed quite a bit.

The chapter ends with a brief writing assignment, but really that is about it. And it's enough, I think. If you are reading this chapter, then you are near the end of the course, and that probably means that you are nearing the end of your college career. You are ready to student teach or enter some kind of internship. Like Gabby, Debbie, and Nicole, you are about to become a teacher. Holden Caulfield would not let me say, "good luck," so I'll just say "bon voyage."

Paradoxes of Planning

Dan Sheridan

Writing this essay gave me the opportunity to think about the nature of planning and to reflect on the various ways I have prepared for classes over the years. Unlike some of the other readings in this book, it has a somewhat unfinished quality: I have not reached any definite conclusions about planning, and I certainly feel that, as a planner/teacher, I am still in the process of learning my craft. Yet so little has been written about actual planning practice that I include the piece here.

A friend and fellow English educator once told me that the focus of his entire methods course was planning. "If I couldn't do anything else, I'd focus on planning. It's what they most need; they need to know how to plan." That's the gist of what he said, and I remember feeling a bit uncomfortable as I listened. It isn't that I object to planning. I hope it will be clear as you read this essay that I do not. Nor do I object to asking "methods students," prospective teachers like you, to write lesson plans. Some of the applications in this book ask you to do just that. And I should hasten to add that I felt equally uncomfortable when a radical educator once said to me that we could solve a lot of problems in the teaching of English if we'd just "abolish the methods course and all that lesson planning." Whatever the solutions to the "problems with education" might be, I thought to myself, *that* surely isn't the answer.

So I guess I'm conflicted, as they say. Surely all teachers, beginners and old hands, should know how to plan. In fact, as I'll explain in a moment, they should also know more than that: They should know what it means to be prepared. But no one should be misled into thinking that lesson planning is just a matter of figuring out "what to do" or that having a lesson plan solves one's teaching problems. There are, as I hope to show, different ways to plan, but a good plan, of any sort, is much more than just a formula for getting things done. Moreover, (I hope this is so obvious that it needs no more explaining) the most thorough lesson plan in the world cannot ensure success—assuming success means thoughtful learning for students. That kind of success depends on so many things . . . and that, too, is a subject for later discussion.

The beginning teacher is therefore faced with a complex, even paradoxical, situation. On the one hand, you need to know something about planning; indeed, you need to be able to write lesson plans. But on the other hand, the effectiveness of a plan is contingent on a number of things that you can neither control nor (at this stage in your career) predict; indeed, the plans you write seem like fictions, formulas that might have no bearing on a real teaching situation. When you student teach, your cooperating teacher will probably want to see lesson plans, so it's good to practice a little beforehand. But until you are faced with a real teaching situation, it's hard to determine what it means, really, to plan a lesson. And so you might feel ambivalent about planning—as I do.

Let me confess right away that I can-not solve the problem that planning poses for the beginning teacher. The best I can do here is explore the mean-ing of planning and then tell you a story or two about my own planning prac-tices, offering (along the way) an insight or two about how you might go about preparing to teach. But there, I have done it! I have conflated two ideas: hav-ing a plan and being prepared. They are different things, so it would be wise to draw back and explain a bit.

Preparedness and Planning

Every teacher, I suspect, has con-ducted a successful class that seemed not to have been planned at all. More times than I usually care to admit, my planning has been hasty, done in my head while walking to class, and yet sometimes the class sessions have been marvelously (magically!) success-ful. At these moments I confront one of the paradoxes of planning, the appar-ently illogical relationship between what I have done to prepare and what actually happens. For what, I ask my-self, have I done all that planning? If it's this easy, if I can wing it, why bother planning at all? Normally on these oc-casions, I attribute success to the stu-dents, concluding that they bailed me out. And I tend to offer the same kind of explanation when the opposite oc-curs. I can recall many classes for which I had a thorough lesson plan but which did not go so well. In these in-stances, too, I want to hold the stu-dents responsible: They were unpre-pared; they didn't help me out. In my mind, you see, I have been consistent as a teacher (largely because I plan con-sistently), so I look to the students for praise or blame. I am predictable; they are the wild cards in the classroom.

These moments stand out against the background of everyday practice because of the elements of success and

failure, but in reality they may simply be the most striking instances of the general "disconnect" between the teacher's explicit plans and the actual way students learn in the classroom. Moreover, I suspect that the underlying causes of an unplanned success or a planned failure are less arbitrary than we imagine. Of course the students make or break our plans, and, equally of course, they are not very predictable. That's part of what I want to discuss. But there is another way to think about these instances, one that has less to do with blaming either ourselves or the students, and that is to consider the difference between "having a plan" and "being prepared."

Preparedness depends on our un-derstanding of the situation in all of its dimensions: the complexity of the sub-ject at hand, the state of our learning about that subject, the state of student knowledge, and the sometimes con-flicting roles we teachers play in stu-dent learning. If we have thought about these things—the subject, the students, and ourselves—we are generally pre-pared, whether we have a plan or not. Or rather, this kind of thinking serves as the basis for effective planning. The unplanned success, then, could have its roots in a kind of preparedness that goes deeper than a lesson plan, just as the planned failure could be rooted in a deeper state of unpreparedness.

That is a comforting thought to some, but, as I know from my work in education courses, it can drive teach-ers-in-training crazy. Specifically, you might have two complaints, both of which have to do with preparedness. "You want us to write lesson plans and teaching units," students in a methods course might say, "but we know we're unprepared." I could argue that pre-paredness is a relative term, not a pla-teau that one reaches with experience, but that seems dishonest. In my heart of hearts, I know that the beginning teacher is simply admitting the truth: To the extent that you have less experience with the subject, to the extent that you are unfamiliar with students, and to the extent that you are still coming to terms with your role as a teacher, *you are in fact unprepared*. The other complaint is related. "You want us to learn these ways to teach," they say, "but when we ask for specific direction, you can only say, 'It all depends.'" There is no answer to that charge; all I can do is remain silent. But that's the point, isn't it? Being prepared means knowing that "it all depends."

In its best and fullest sense, planning is a way of coming to terms with those things on which learning depends—the subject, the students, and the teacher. But because those components are complex in themselves and complicated in their relation to each other, planning means different things to different people. Indeed, planning seems to serve quite a different function, depending on the stage of one's teaching career. The best way for me to explain that is to tell you a story.

The Beginner as Planner

A while back, while in the process of moving from one office to another, I came across some twenty-five-year-old lesson plans. They had been written while I was student teaching at Von Steuben High School in Chicago. I have no idea why I kept them (the same reason perhaps that I have kept my college notebooks), but I'm glad that I did. One in particular, consisting of three pages of close hand-written notes on George Orwell's *Animal Farm*, serves as the exemplar of the beginning teacher's approach to lesson planning. It is a compendium of everything I knew about the novel, Orwell, and the Russian Revolution. The students, juniors in that north-side Chicago high school, hardly figure in the plan at all.

Subsequent experience, especially in supervising student teachers, has shown that this kind of content-oriented plan is typical of beginning teachers. The focus is squarely, almost exclusively, on the subject matter, as if the major issue were "what does the teacher know." The teacher summons up and records whatever he or she knows about the subject, an activity that looks, on the surface, like the transmission mode of teaching, what the Brazilian educator Paulo Freire calls the "banking" model of education. It looks as if I were saying to myself: If I know this about the literature, then students should know it too. In fact, however, that is not what I thought I was doing at the time. Although I do not remember this particular lesson, I know what my intentions were, and I would have been offended by the suggestion that all I wanted from students was to know the stuff I knew about *Animal Farm*. I wasn't lecturing. In my own mind, I was "running discussions," "putting students in small groups," "facilitating learning."

Perhaps I did run a good discussion; I could well have put students in small groups; I might even have facilitated their learning. No doubt there was some kind of action plan, since lost, that guided me through the actual class period. My point here is not that I was a bad student teacher (I think I did a pretty good job) or even that my practice fell short of my lofty student-centered theory (I take that for granted). No, my point is that these early plans reveal a profound disruption between two ways of thinking: There is the person with the student-centered philosophy and then there is the planner who is concerned primarily with himself—a person who is trying very hard to "authorize" himself as a teacher.

New teachers do this all the time. Uncertain of their own authority, they work to establish themselves as experts. Yes, they are concerned, unduly so, about discipline and control, but authority to speak on the subject matter is even more important—this, in turn, justifies the other forms of authority one exercises over students. Beginning teachers can be so concerned with their own teacherly role that the students are largely invisible to them. Hence the absence of students in my planning. In writing my *Animal Farm* plan, I was doing much more than boning up on Orwell; I was, almost literally, convincing myself that I was really an English teacher.

These habits of the beginning teacher seem perfectly normal to me. Across the span of twenty-five years, I can see, and even honor, this kind of planning for what it was: something that did a lot for me but precious little for those high school juniors. Or perhaps that is unfair. Because I could not have entered that classroom without having gone through this exercise, it was writing that *had* to be done. Indeed, there is a sense in which all planning is "for the teacher," a way of telling ourselves that we are teachers—and, later on, what kind of teachers we are. (For me, there was then, and is now, something talismanic about a lesson plan: Unless I commit some words to paper, I cannot walk into the classroom. Without the charm, I am not a teacher.) So what the content-centered plan reveals, more than anything else, is the difference between planning and preparedness: I could plan, but I wasn't really prepared. As a beginning teacher, I could not get myself off center-stage; I was rehearsing my lines, while the other actors, the students, waited in the wings.

Practice Into Theory

The next step, for me, was to focus more on activities. By the time I had been teaching two or three years,

mostly on the college level, planning had become something of a routine with ritualistic overtones. I would begin by writing the name of the course and the date at the top of a lined sheet of paper, underlining the course title. Then I would list the topic for the day, also underlined. (For reasons that remain mysterious to me, this underlining was—and still is—important to me. I suspect it is another talismanic activity.) The plan itself consisted of notes describing the activities for the day, numbered and listed in chronological order. For a few years I jotted down objectives beside each activity but ultimately abandoned this practice: the objectives were repetitive ("deepening insights" kept reappearing) or the reasoning circular ("students will work in groups to have the experience of working in groups"). Notes about the material were kept elsewhere, either on separate sheets of paper or in the textbook itself.

This form of planning, which I believe to be very common among high school and college English teachers, was clearly an advance over the *Animal Farm* note-taking with which I began. As the need to authorize myself became less pressing and the students became more visible, I became less fixated on my image and could focus more on what the students would do. In fact, one function of the lesson plan was to insist on the distinction between teacherly behavior and student learning; because I did not want to be the kind of teacher who lectured all the time, I began to deemphasize my own role and to think of each lesson in terms of students' behavior. (I note, too, an interesting shift in my sense of what was disposable. As a student teacher, I kept my *Animal Farm* notes and threw away the list of things to do; at this new stage I was tossing the notes on the material and filing away those activities.) As a result, my teaching practice was becoming more predictable. Oh yes, there were still plenty of mediocre lessons, but if I planned something (discussion or writing or group work or role playing or even a lecture), it was likely to happen.

But was I becoming more like the student-centered teacher that I envisioned myself to be? Was the gap between my theory and my practice lessening? The question is complicated. In one sense, the answer is yes: Students were becoming more visible to me, and the plans did concentrate on student activities as opposed to teacher knowledge. So I think I was becoming a better teacher—at least in terms of the rather fuzzy theory I espoused. But in my desire to build the largest repertoire of things that "worked," I became very eclectic in my approach. So long as something felt student-centered and seemed to work fairly well, I added it to my bag of tricks. In the beginning at least, I was not particularly concerned about building a coherent theory of teaching.

In this age of "theory," such a confession should make me ashamed, and yet I can scarcely manage a blush. For the fact is, whatever my highly theoretical colleagues might think of the way I went about planning and teaching, I was learning to teach. With the general idea of "student-centeredness" to keep me relatively honest, I was working out my ideas on the subject matter, the students, and my own role—that is, I was becoming better at preparing, and thus my actual planning improved. And when it came to the development of a more sophisticated theory of teaching, I found myself gravitating toward ideas that were consonant with aspects of my work that seemed effective and satisfying. Thus, the early work of composition theorists (proponents of the "process approach," like Donald Murray or Peter Elbow) and literary theorists (proponents of the "transactional" the-

ory, like Louise Rosenblatt) had a profound effect. Both schools of thought encouraged me to think of writing and reading as processes that students performed and learned from, rather than as subjects that I taught—attitudes that were already implicit in much of my practice.

As practice and theory interacted, the gap between them lessened, but even as that was happening, I was becoming aware of other kinds of gaps in my teaching. For one thing, I was developing a deeper appreciation of the sometime paradoxical relationship of teaching and learning. Why was it, I had to ask, that the most profound kinds of learning took place without the aid of teachers? Or sometimes in spite of someone else's teaching? This connected to the drift of my reading: Theorists and practitioners alike seemed to be urging me to let go, to orchestrate my work less around what I wanted to teach and more around what students had to do to learn. In the abstract, and in general, this was fine, but when it came down to actual planning, I kept encountering the same problem. How do you back off from teaching and still plan to teach? How do you "let go" and still think of yourself as a teacher?

Exploring the Land of "It All Depends"

There are several ways of addressing this paradox. Some would have us cut the Gordian knot decisively, by getting out of students' way, whereas others would reassert the more traditional need for scaffolding or teacher intervention. And what, I sometimes wonder, would Elbow say, for although his work on "contraries" has to do specifically with the evaluation of writing, that subject touches on my more general paradox. "Embrace the contraries! Understand that you play many roles! Use that understanding to advance student learning!" This seems like good advice, but I have yet to find a way to orchestrate my alternating stances in the classroom. And what does it mean for planning? Can I really plan "to teach" sometimes and "not to teach" at other times? I think I can, though not exactly in Elbow's manner. For I've come to see that the best kind of plan for me is the one that acknowledges the very problem that my education students complain of: the fact that "it all depends."

This realization has led to a slight adjustment in the way I plan for class. Yes, I still begin with the course and date underlined on the top of a page of lined paper. And, yes, I end up with something like a list of "activities," though I've now come to think of it as "work that students need to do that day." What differs is what I do after the underlining at the top. In the simplest terms, I engage in some freewriting (another influence from Elbow). Specifically, I begin by writing about the students and then, once I have fixed my attention on them and their learning, I write about myself. With my small handwriting, I can usually manage two decent paragraphs on a single page, with room for the notes on the work of the day at the bottom. Simple. Yet in many ways this is the most complicated thing I have ever done in my teaching career.

In terms of the class-in-preparation, this ritual has produced a series of small but significant results, all of which have to do with my stance, my attitude, my sense of my work. First, writing about students is part of that career-long process of making students more visible to me as a teacher. Sometimes I will focus on particular students—Jeremy, who seems disinterested; Emily, who is so very silent; Brad, who appears confused; or Jessica, who seems to ooze hostility. These students present "issues" (which might be mine, not theirs), and writing

about them can help. But more often I will write about each class as a group—trying, first, to imagine them, to conjure them up, to make them real to me; and, second, to assess the state of their learning, to figure out what they need. Thus a typical entry might begin with the informal question, "So where are we now?" I might refer to the last class session—the effectiveness of the discussion, the group work, the conferences (it depends)—or I might think more about the course in general. But the purpose is always to figure out what students need at this point.

Then, and only then, will I turn to myself, writing about my role in the course. If I need to do something—to provide some information, to be more or less directive in discussion, to arrange conferences (it depends)—then I can explore that through writing. Or if I need to back off, I can tell myself that, perhaps by writing "Shut up, shut up, shut up, shut up" repeatedly down the page. Or perhaps what I need to consider is not a course of action (or nonaction) but the very contradiction of teaching/learning itself. For there are times when the proper course is not "teach" or "let go" but to change the options so that I can learn something with the students.

As a result, one class session seems to follow more logically from the next because the writing forces me to make connections. I find myself better able to see the course of study as a whole and to communicate the state of affairs to students, to help students pull the various strands of learning together. And I seem to be more flexible nowadays. Although I will never be the kind of teacher who can enter the classroom without a plan of action, I know that having explored different courses of action in the freewriting allows me to let go of an activity without feeling that things are falling apart. In other words, I can follow the indicators of student learning, because that is where I began in my planning. And I'm more confident in changes of plan because I feel better prepared.

There is no magic in this. It is embarrassingly commonsensical. I can't even argue that it takes a lot of time and effort, for in fact my planning is more efficient now because I am less frequently baffled by all the decision making that goes into teaching. And I am certainly not arguing that a simple change in my planning habits has transformed me into one of those great teachers that we all admire. Would that it were so. On the other hand, I have learned quite a bit about myself as a teacher through this habit of writing-before-teaching. The binaries, the conflicting roles, are more apparent to me now, and when I write about them I feel less paralyzed. It helps to make a space for myself in my reflections on teaching; being student-centered, I've come to see, does not mean effacing yourself as a teacher. In the end, of course, writing this way is something I do for myself. This is the way I can bring planning more in line with a more thorough sense of preparedness.

Thus, despite all the differences, this mode of planning has returned me, in an odd way, to my earlier days as a student teacher. The students are much more real to me now, and I have gotten over some (not all) of that need to authorize myself. And I have acknowledged that "it" (what students will do, what I will do, who will learn what) does indeed "depend." But I am still exploring my sense of myself as a teacher, still creating and re-creating myself as a teacher. Those early plans, like the one on *Animal Farm*, were necessary to me; I couldn't have taught without them. Now I plan by writing; I couldn't teach without it.

REFERENCES

Elbow, Peter. *Embracing Contraries: Explorations in Learning and Teaching*. New York: Oxford, 1986.

For Further Thought

1. Think about the distinction between preparation and planning. Does this make sense to you? Can you think of teachers who have planned but seemed unprepared? How could you tell? Conversely, can you think of teachers who are prepared but seem not to have planned? Mrs. Martinez (pp. 72–78) seems to be a teacher of this sort.

2. Consider the *Animal Farm* plan that is described in the essay. Does it remind you of plans that you have written? What is the real function of a plan like this? Do you think that all new teachers have to focus first on the content of the lesson?

3. Do you think there are really stages in the development of a teacher? (I know I seem to imply this by saying that I went through various stages as a planner.) If you do believe in stages, which stage are you in?

4. The essay suggests that there is something paradoxical in planning to teach. We plan, I say, but in the end we know that "it all depends." On what do teaching and learning depend? What, after all, is the point of planning?

"I'm Going to Get Paid Today!" (Another Conversation About Teaching)

Gabrielle Albertsen, Debbie Luth, Nicole Poolman, and Dan Sheridan

You met Gabby, Debbie, and Nicole in chapter 1 when they discussed their hopes and fears about student teaching. That conversation took place at the end of a school year. Gabby and Nicole were scheduled to student teach the following fall semester, whereas Debbie would continue her studies and student teach a year later.

Six months later, the four of us sat down to talk about teaching once more. Gabby and Nicole had finished their student teaching, Gabby with seventh graders, Nicole with tenth and eleventh graders. I was their university supervisor, and, as predicted, they each did a really good job. Debbie had taken a thirty-hour field experience during the same semester. At the time of the interview, Gabby was "on vacation" and getting ready to work as a substitute teacher, Nicole was working as a long-term sub in the school where she had student taught, and Debbie, still in classes, was getting restless and eager to teach.

Dan: *When we first talked six months ago, you were concerned about a whole range of things that could be grouped under three headings: how much do I know, what am I able to do, and do I have the presence or personal authority to teach? You ended by talking about what your college coursework had done to prepare you, which seemed to be precious little. Now six months have passed. Can you talk about what, if anything, has changed?*
Nicole: Well, at first I was nervous that I didn't have enough coursework or background, but I found that much

of what you're teaching in high school would not have been covered in college, so you're starting from scratch regardless.
Dan: *Could you give an example of something that you wouldn't have learned in college anyhow?*
Nicole: Nonfiction. I had to do a whole unit on biography and autobiography and things like that. That wasn't covered in my courses; I had never seen them being taught, so that's what I had the toughest time with. Of course, it did amaze me the number of times I have gone with things professors or my high school teachers did with the material. I took that base and said, "OK, I *didn't* like what they did with the material, so I'll change it; or I *did* like what they did, so I'm going to model my lesson on that. But with a lot of it, like nonfiction or the Planters and Puritans in American Lit, I had no background in that at all, so I had a tough time and had to start from scratch.
Dan: *I'm not sure if you're saying you* did *or did not* know enough.
Nicole: I'm saying I didn't know enough, and it's not something to worry about. (Laughter) The other teachers don't know that much more than . . .
Dan: *Go ahead and say it.*
Nicole: . . . much more than you do anyway. (Breathes a sigh.) I'm hesitant to say it, but a lot of teachers, I realize now, aren't any different than I am in terms of their background knowledge.
Gabby: I have to agree with Nicole. It's not that I knew enough or did not know enough. I was teaching stuff that I would not have encountered anywhere in college, except in a methods class. We did seventh-grade short stories—

you don't get a lot of those in college. I used stuff that, based on my knowledge of the kids, I thought they would understand, and I had to do a lot of improvising. The example that I used with one class would not be one that I'd use with another class because each classroom had a different personality.

Dan: *How could you do that? You were the one who was saying six months ago, "I wish I had a big bag of tricks."*

Gabby: I guess when you look into their faces and they're looking *through* you and not *at* you, and you realize that they're not in the room with you anymore, that they're off, you know that what you're doing is really not working. You have to come up with something else that will bring them back to you.

Dan: *But Debbie (who hasn't student taught yet) is sitting here listening to you, and she's probably saying, "You're talking about magic again."*

Debbie: Yup.

Gabby: Well, as a matter of fact . . . yup.

Nicole: It's amazing how much you start to read the kids, start to read the chemistry in each class and know what's going to work for those kids.

Gabby: You have to get a feel for the kids and their personalities right off the bat.

Nicole: And it's not really as hard as I thought it would be.

* * *

Dan: *Debbie, these two have student taught now, and Nicole is a long-term sub in the same school where she taught, so she is a real teacher now. What's changed with you?*

Debbie: I've taught only one lesson in a field experience, but I have changed in a couple of ways. I'm starting to see more and more how kids remember so little of what the teacher said in high school, and I realize that I don't really have to worry so much about whether I know enough of what I'm teaching; it's going to be stuff like how to ask questions or think critically or express themselves clearly. So I think I'm changing my focus more toward teaching them how to be better learners—things they can carry on, instead of worrying so much about what I know.

Gabby: That's a good point. I did a short story and we watched a movie which was very different, and it's true—it's not so important that they remember the story as it is that they know how to do the comparing and contrasting, and to use that in the future.

Debbie: Also, when people ask me what I'm planning to do and when I say I want to teach in high school, they say, "You're kidding!"

Gabby: "They're so horrible!"

Debbie: "Why not some little *nice* children?" Before this field experience, it had been a year and a half since I'd been in a high school classroom and I was beginning to believe them. I thought I was going to go in there and, like piranha, they were going to eat me up. But it was so great to be in the classroom. I was amazed at the amount of respect they gave me. They asked me questions right off the bat. There wasn't some test I had to go through first. That was good for me too.

Dan: *That addresses the question of authority. When did you feel that you were a teacher and not someone playing a role?*

Nicole: The day you came up to me during student teaching and said that I had become a real teacher, I didn't agree with you. I thought it was later. It's when you stop worrying so much about knowing everything and you worry more about whether the kids are understanding it. You're looking at their faces instead of worrying about how professional you look.

Dan: *You thought I jumped the gun because, inside, you didn't feel that?*

Nicole: Inside, I didn't feel I was reading them—not as much as I am able to read them now. Like Gabby said, I have different tactics . . . hmm, not the greatest word . . .

Dan: *A little military.*

Nicole: It's the first term that comes to mind when I think of my fifth period. The chemistry in there is so different from the other classes. They need a completely different lesson plan. And I never would have done that in the beginning. I just would have gone to class, presented the material the same each time, answered any questions, and said, "Get to work." Now I'm much more ready to change the pace in the middle. I'm reading the kids more.

Dan: *What about you, Gabby, when did you know (that you were a real teacher)?*

Gabby: I don't really know. Probably when I quit writing lesson plans. I probably shouldn't say that.

Dan: *I'll have to erase that from the tape.*

Gabby: I only wrote lesson plans on the days you were coming.

Dan: *I'm so disappointed in you.*

Gabby: At first I would write down all the questions I wanted to ask and page numbers and every little detail that I thought I would need while I was standing there. And after a while, it would work in one class and not in another, and I would find myself skipping and throwing this or that out and I found that paper to be distracting—because if I'm looking at that, I'm not looking at my kids. And so then I thought, "Screw it. I have a general idea of what I'm doing and I'll write a couple of things down (just a basic 'Here's what you're supposed to be teaching today'), and we'll go from there." And the kids were fabulous about that; all of the classes, except one

group that was always a problem, would pretty much go along with me.

Dan: *But you would talk to Diane (your cooperating teacher) about what you were doing, right?*

Gabby: Yes, I'd come in the morning and she's ask, "Do you have a plan?" and I'd say, Yes."

Dan (to the others): *I keep waiting for her to say what I want her to say, but she never does. What I'm hearing you say is that you were prepared to teach even if you didn't have a lesson plan. So I want to know how you prepared yourself to teach in these different ways.*

Gabby: I'd go home at night, and while I was cooking supper, I'd think about what we had done that day, and what worked that day and what didn't. And if I had to, I'd go and make some notes. But most of all, I'd think about the day and what was coming next, whether it was short stories or grammar, and then I'd think about each class individually and what would work best for each class, and then I'd jot down little notes on stickies and I'd put those on the class seating chart. And that was about it.

*   *   *

Gabby: At times I had some grammar concept that for me was amazingly simple. There should have been absolutely no problem whatsoever. It was like trying to explain *nouns*. It was just that basic. And these kids were just sitting there and they had their mouths open and they were looking at me like, "You have horns on your head, Mrs. Albertsen." At one point it just frustrated me so much that I just stopped and I said, "OK guys, I'm just going to have to back up and punt. Somebody needs to tell me *why* this is so hard." I had tried three different things in each class, and they were all not getting it, so finally by sixth period, I said the heck with it, we're going to scrap this whole entire day, and start all over tomorrow. And that's what I did.

Dan: *So what did you do the next day that was different? Did you find the magic approach?*

Gabby: No, I don't think they ever got it.

Nicole: That's the hardest part of teaching a subject that you have always enjoyed and had an easy time with. For me grammar is so difficult to teach because in high school I wouldn't even (have to) pay attention. I would just go to the exercises and make the sentences look right. I never have had a problem with grammar and that is why it becomes very difficult to teach kids who have trouble with it, because you don't understand what it is that they don't understand. I think that's far more frustrating for me than it is even for the students. I get so frustrated when I can't help them.

Dan: *It's interesting that Gabby's example was from grammar. It does suggest that the people who say that grammar is an abstraction of language rules from actual use—that they might be right.*

Gabby: The problem with grammar is that you can teach these kids "This is grammar: It's a big bunch of rules, all the rules that will always work." But that's crap because it doesn't work that way. You say this is the rule for this, *but* the exceptions are this and this. You're teaching them parts of speech and you have words that can be adjectives and adverbs, and this word and that word, and the kids are thinking, "How the heck do *I* know what word that's supposed to be?"

Debbie: And it doesn't catch on. Yesterday in an education class, an English major taught a ten-minute mini-lesson on the parts of speech. There were two other English majors and we didn't want to answer everything, and eight other college students didn't know anything besides a noun and a verb. My mouth dropped open. I was helping this guy with an adverb. I said "Modifies a . . . ?" And he says, "Verb?"

Gabby: When you're trying to explain to seventh graders that an adverb modifies a verb, they're thinking, "What the heck does *modify* mean? We don't get that."

Nicole: Today, we were reading a Walt Whitman poem, and after lots of discussion about the poem when I thought we had come to a consensus about what Whitman was getting at, a student raises his hand and says, "Are there words on the page here that I'm not seeing?" And I said, "What is it that you you don't get?" And I thought, "It would be nice to get into his mind to figure out what I need to say to explain."

Debbie: Getting into their minds? Does that happen?

Nicole: Is that the real magic?

Dan: *That's advanced magic. But you do get better at it.*

* * *

Debbie: When I ran discussions in my field experience, I found I could work with students who don't want to say anything, but there are one or two students who answer everything, and it's hard because you can't say, "I don't want to hear from you. . . ."

Gabby: Yeah, you can.

Nicole: Sure.

Gabby: I mean, you don't say, "Would you shut up for once." You don't say it like that. You say, "Gosh you were so helpful. Thank you so much for all that you contribute. Maybe somebody else would like to start contributing."

Nicole: You don't even have to be that nice. You can say, "Thank you. Can I hear from somebody else?"

Dan (to Debbie): *Are you surprised that these two answered that way?*

Debbie (slowly): Yeah ... it would seem that after you try so hard to get students to respond to you, it seems odd to tell them not to. . . .

Gabby: But, you know, the ones that you say that to are the ones that from the first day of class are sitting there (ready to talk) or they walk in with their hands up. They're confident enough in their ability that they're not going to get hurt by that—because it's probably happened before.

Debbie: And then I was taught in methods class to wait students out. If you have a discussion question, just take your time and wait them out, but Mr. Jaeger (the teacher I observed) does not agree with that approach. If they don't talk, he'll answer. He doesn't want to waste time sitting there. I talked to him after class and I said, "I was taught that you're supposed to wait them out," and he said, "Hogwash. If they don't want to answer, they're not going to, so go on to a different question." (Laughs.) And I didn't know quite what to make of that. I don't know what's true.

Dan: *You're still looking for the truth, aren't you? Nicole, you're the teacher. What do you do?*

Nicole: If they don't answer one question, then I give a hint in the next question or I rephrase or I call on somebody. It depends.

Dan: *I hope you noticed that she said, "It depends."*

Gabby: Dan, you've actually been in the class when I've done this. I've asked a question and I did wait them out, but I wound up saying, "OK guys, here's the deal. You're being really quiet today, and I might not feel like talking. I'm going to sit here. The question I just asked was this, and I repeated the question. I said, "I'm sitting here until somebody answers it." (Laughter) And the kids just looked at me. I said, "Well, I don't have anywhere else to be today. So I can wait."

Debbie: Really?

Gabby: So they all sit there for a second and think, "Nah, she can't do it." And then eventually they start answering.

Dan: *Well, of course, that's partly Gabby, but it's also partly seventh graders. They'll sit and squirm and then they just have to talk. They have to be involved. But juniors might wait you out for a long time.*

Nicole: My eighth period class might wait the whole hour. Well, no they wouldn't really, but they would wait too long for *me*.

Gabby: See, I would still sit there and wait.

Dan: *Yes, you're more comfortable with that style.*

Nicole: She's tougher than me.

Dan: *We said she was tough six months ago, and she did turn out to be pretty tough.*

Gabby: But I was nice too.

Dan: *Yes, you were really nice to those students, but then I don't think tough and nice are contradictory terms.*

Gabby: Yes, I fell in love with them. They just had so much energy, and I thought that would drive me insane, but I loved their energy and enthusiasm. And they just like to *laugh*, and they like to give it to you and they liked to get it *back*. They're just a lot of *fun*.

Dan: *Nicole and Gabby seem to be saying that, if a kid is too talkative or not talkative enough, you don't have to make a big methodological mystery about it. You can be direct. You can talk to them as if they're human beings.*

Gabby: And actually, that's what works best. The best way to relate to people is honestly. And if you do things with humor and a smile on your face, they're not going to stand up and throw a desk at you ... very often.

* * *

Dan: *So was it important to be treated as a teacher?*

Nicole: The students just take that for granted. It is amazing to me what kids take for granted. You're up in the front of the room . . .

Debbie (referring to the first interview): "I know nothing," remember?

Dan: *They took for granted that you're a teacher?*

Nicole: I think so. They were pretty nice to me. I didn't have problems with the exception of fifth period—and now even my fifth period is fine. I think to a certain extent, if you are in front of the room and you start talking, they stop and they listen and do what you tell them.

Gabby: Well, that must come after the seventh grade. My kids wanted to know what my title was: if my title was as good as Mrs. Stoley's. I'm a student teacher, so does that mean I'm a student and not worthy of the teacher part? And they really had to know the entire dynamic of student teaching and how much authority does she really have.

Dan: *So how much did you have?*

Gabby: Thank God for Diane. She said, "She has just as much authority as I do. Whatever Mrs. Albertsen says is what you do. You treat her exactly as you would treat me."

Dan: *Did it work?*

Gabby: Absolutely. But they had to know all about the student teacher thing. And, "Aren't you old for a student?" A lot of them said that.

Debbie: They thought *you* were old!

Gabby: They thought I was ancient.

Dan: *Debbie, you were worried about how little and young you look.*

Debbie: Yes, I *am* little. The talkative boy in my field experience discussion asked me my name. "Debbie," I said. "I can't call you that," he said. And so I said, "Oh, Miss Luth." That's the first time in my life I've ever been called Miss Luth, and it sounded so odd every time they said it. I can't take it seriously. I don't feel like a Miss Luth.

Dan: *You'll get used to it, though it will always remain a sort of signature of the special role you play as a teacher.*

Debbie: It feels a little fake. You put on your teacher clothes, and they call you "Miss Luth," and you get to go into "the secret room"—the teachers' lounge—it's like a game.

Nicole: It is a completely different atmosphere and it took a period of adjustment, but it doesn't take long because you are surrounded by this atmosphere.

* * *

Dan: *So, Debbie, what do you see that's different in these two?*

Debbie: Confidence. Weeooh! They say, "I don't know much, I'm not sure what I'm doing, but it all works out"—which I find very inspiring, because I'm going to hold it as the law. I'll twinkle my toes and have it happen one day. But you guys *do* have a lot more confidence. I could tell that you would be really good teachers anyway and that you'll continue to progress.

Dan: *But they didn't seem to know that.*

Nicole: No, you just try to act competent, and then once you get to the point where you can look at the kids, then you feel comfortable enough. I think the kids were partly responsible for that because they give you confidence when they give you respect and listen to what you say. You read their essay tests and you say, "They were listening to me!" There are even minor victories, like when you have a kid who has a really tough time and he didn't remember the concept but he remembered the example that you gave to illustrate the concept—and so you know that they're listening. You say, "I'm not horrible." And you realize that you don't have to know everything, and they don't expect you to know everything. They are very forgiving—at least high school kids are. If you just say, "I don't know, let's go look it up." Once you realize that . . .

Gabby: . . . it gives you the ability to relax a little bit.

Dan: Nicole, you said a wonderful thing just then. You were asked how you learned to be confident, and you said that the kids made you confident. I think that's exactly right. Before you taught (take a look at that first interview sometime), the three of you were asking, "What can I do, what can the university do, what can the teacher education program do—what can anybody do to make me a teacher?" And, as happens so often in teaching when you ask a direct question and the answer seems to come from some place you didn't expect, you discover that the kids . . .

Debbie: . . . the kids teach you how to teach.

* * *

Dan: So do you want to teach?

Gabby: Do I want to teach? Absolutely. In the middle of student teaching, I thought, "There just really isn't anything in the world that would be as wonderful as teaching—for me anyway."

Nicole: Just the other day I was sitting in class and I thought, "I'm going to get paid today!" And I couldn't believe that I was getting paid to be there. It's a job that you would go to if you weren't getting paid. Maybe it's just that I'm accustomed to being in school . . .

Debbie: We don't ever have to leave school.

Nicole: Yes, I just think it's the greatest.

For Further Thought

1. Interpret Nicole's remark, "I didn't know enough, and it's not something to worry about." She doesn't seem to be excusing ignorance or lack of preparation. What do you make of this?

2. Look back at Gabby's description of how she prepared for a day's lessons. Does this seem like a valid way to prepare? Explain your answer a bit. And what about lesson plans? Gabby and her cooperating teacher thought that formal plans were not necessary. What do you think? (You might think about the previous essay, "Paradoxes of Planning.")

3. In the first interview, Nicole and Debbie expressed some serious anxiety about discipline. Yet each found the students were willing to accept them as teachers. This does not always happen, but in most schools it seems to be the norm. Why do you think students are so accepting? Under what conditions might they be less accepting?

4. The conversation is full of moments where "issues" arise—for example, the teacher who calls the university professor's advice "hogwash," or Gabby's admission that she only wrote lesson plans on the days I came to observe her. Yet no one, including myself, seems particularly worried about these issues. It is as if a general understanding has been reached that puts these differences into perspective. What are some of the common understandings about teaching that these three teachers have reached?

5. Think about these three people. Gabby is brash and loves to tease; Nicole is soft-spoken and self-reflective; Debbie is lively and full of irony. With whom do you identify? And what do you think is the relationship between a teacher's personality and his or her choice of methods? (Think, for example, of Gabby's "silent treatment" technique with her seventh graders, but remember that Nicole agrees with Gabby about being open and direct with students in the classroom.)

Writing Assignment:
A Philosophy of Teaching English

Each year, a new group of students at my university complete student teaching and enter the job market. And each year, they are required to include in their teaching portfolio, along with a resume and some sample lessons, a statement of their philosophy of teaching. They fuss and they fume, complaining that they have already written this kind of thing "dozens of times before"—when they applied for admission to the secondary ed program, when they applied for scholarships, when they applied for student teaching. "We're always *applying*," they seem to be saying. "When will it ever end?" Their instructors respond by reminding them that are now applying for a *job* (which carries with it a new sense of urgency), and when they get a job, well . . . maybe that's when it will end. And, anyway, shouldn't their philosophy of teaching change as they grow professionally? So the new professionals shrug and churn out yet another statement of their philosophy.

But recently I was taken aback when a student asked, "What exactly should be in a philosophy of teaching?" My first reaction was to laugh, for it sounded so much like a student trying to psyche out a teacher who had made a writing assignment. "What do you *want*? What should be *in* this paper?" As if a paper, or philosophy statement, were a container into which you put stuff that pleased the teacher. And yet the student had a point. A writing task like this is seldom one that we actually teach. We tell people to do it, maybe glance at the result, and correct a few spelling errors (typically "grammer"). It enters the portfolio or accompanies the resume and is never mentioned again. And since it had been over twenty years since I'd written a statement of philosophy, I figured I'd better try it myself.

I began by reviewing the kind of advice that I had given students over the years. It should be short, not over a page—preferably less. "Administrators or other people hiring you don't want to read a long philosophical treatise." It should refer to students. "Less about you, more about students and their learning." And it should have something to do with English. "You're not applying for a math or social studies position. You want to be an English teacher. Tell them what you hope to accomplish in the *English* classroom."

All this seemed like good advice, but when I tried to apply it to myself, I couldn't seem to begin. There I was staring at a computer screen with "Philosophy" neatly centered at the top, and the rest blank. What could I possibly say? All the words that came to mind seemed like cliches, the kind of bland educationese that I have grown so weary of. "Who made this stupid assignment?" I muttered, and stared some more. I thought of Donald Murray—the scene at the start of "Write before Writing" in which he looks at kids in school fiddling and fidgeting, delaying their writing. Clearly, I thought, I was receiving no signal that said "write." So I did what Murray recommends and delayed. In this case, it meant working on the turkey soup for dinner—and gradually the words started to come. First a lead ("I am a believer in language") and a follow-up ("I believe that language can help people make a difference in the world—indeed, it can make a difference for the person who uses it"). And by the time the soup was simmering on the stove, I was ready to go back to that blank screen.

I'll make the rest of the story short. The first draft came pouring out, an avalanche of ideas about what writing and reading could do for kids. Then I looked at my advice (keep it short, focus on kids, apply it to English), and realized that I had missed on two of the three. That guided my revision—the growing sense of audience. Someone might actually read this. Something might actually depend on this. This language might "make a difference in the world." A second and third version was cranked out, this time more slowly, and finally I was ready to show it to someone. Ah, I thought, the writing process in action. Donald Murray, Nancy Sommers, Peter Elbow, Nancie Atwell—they would all be proud of me. Now, as Ken Donelson says at the end of his essay (p. 92), go and do likewise.

Write a statement of no more than one page in which you explain your philosophy of teaching English. Be sure that you refer to students' learning. Make it applicable to the teaching of English. Write several drafts, and then bring it to another English teacher to critique. Remember that it might be read by someone interested in hiring you.

Appendixes

The six appendixes that follow consist of assignments given by secondary teachers and samples of the work students did in response to them. The assignments have been rewritten for the sake of regularity and clarity, but I have tried to remain true to the spirit and main idea of the originals. For the sake of anonymity, I have changed the names of the student authors, other students, and their schools. Otherwise, the student papers are just the way they were submitted—with the exception of the rough drafts, which have been adapted from the originals. Again with the exception of the rough draft adaptations, the papers are reprinted here with the permission of the students who wrote them.

In general, I tried to select a sampling of high, middle, and low papers from each set, but that does not mean that they follow a particular "curve." For one thing, the classes of students who wrote them, though nominally homogeneous, were actually quite varied in ability. Nor did I have grades in mind when I chose them. Rather, I worked holistically, looking for a variety of topics, issues for the teacher, and writing abilities.

Some of these papers appeared in the first edition of *Teaching Secondary English*, and a few readers (not just students) have suggested that they do not represent the complete range of writing abilities among American secondary students. In particular, a colleague who teaches an English methods course in a large city made such a comment. It is interesting to note that she did not say *which* ability levels were missing. I haven't asked, and I still don't know. My own students at the University of North Dakota often complain that this student work is almost universally "bad," though some change their minds when they confront the realities of student writing in real classrooms. My colleague from the big city might well have thought that the writing was too "good."

I really have no way of answering either of these charges. These papers seem to me to be fairly typical of the various grade levels—typical, that is, of students in the upper Midwest. I can see all kinds of things that are wrong with many of them, but I enjoy reading them. I hope you will too.

Rough Drafts
(Tenth Grade)

On the first day of school in the fall, a tenth-grade teacher asked his students to write a paper on "one thing you would like to see changed in school." He gave them time in class to jot down some notes and to begin writing. The papers, all of them handwritten, were handed in the next day.

From the teacher's point of view, this was just a quick start-of-the-year piece of writing. His students were new to the high school, all having attended junior high schools in other buildings, and he wanted to get an idea of what they thought about school in general. From our point of view, however, the papers can be treated as rough drafts. They have all the signs of early drafts (see Application 4.2) and seem to cry out for revision.

The rough drafts that follow are adaptations of the originals. They were written some time ago, in the early 1980s, but the issues they raise about schools are still relevant today.

Frank

Finding a topic to write on seems to be a problem because of all the problems at school. But it is the same in all the school systems in the United States.

Whether it is a big school or a little school they all have the one problem. Prejudice. Either the complaint is farmers and city folk or towners and out-of-towners. In the big cities it is gangs that go after each other.

Now to go on. In our school it is the same. Students from the military base are mistreated by people from town. Town people sometimes gang up and jump a guy from the base just to be nasty. I think students should get together. There are not enough clubs or social activities to bring these two groups together.

Teachers also go this way. Some teachers look down on students who come from out that way. Some even go so far as to give them a lower grade. Some teachers look at basers as troublemakers. If there is ever a fight against a baser or a towner some people might look down on a baser.

Basers present the same difficulty. Many will look at towners and spit on their shoes. Others will just walk away and not listen or something else like that. Basers have habits of forming their own cliques also. Here it is not as bad as in New York with its street gangs. But if we don't do something to control it, it might get out of hand.

To conclude I suggest that things be done to prevent it. Maybe students could get together and sort things out. But again we arise to that problem. A towner won't lower himself to talk with a baser and vise versa. This report is a little exaggerated, but maybe it should be to get the point across.

Gary

I think that the change they need in education is a relaxing class. They should have chairs that are cushioned so that the enviroment is comfortable. Then since you were pleased you probably listen and learn more. Do fun things like field trips, and going outside you can learn alot more outside and not under a roof most of your life. You can learn alot more if you are out by your self trying to survive then you can coming into the same old pail rooms and the same uncomfortable chairs. They should be able to go to a lounge where kids could smoke, although that is not legal in public buildings. But a lounge would be good because kids need a place to go. They need more classes like auto mechanics and carpentry etc. Those are the classes you would be able to use when you go out in the world. You will be able to live out in our society. Absences wouldn't be as bad because it would be a more enjoyable place to walk into for the years you have to spend here. I think that some teachers should try harder to make their class rooms a more liked place.

Heidi

I think one of the major changes in our education today, should be the fact that we need more classes that deal with the career we want. I mean what do some of us need with Biology, Physical Education, Poetry, Speech, American Lit., and any of these history classes. Cause I know I don't need any of them. Sure I do believe in taking them if we need them or if we could use them as electives. Cause I myself would need courses for drama and music. That is the main thing I am interested in. I guess speech you would need for drama. If kids would speak up and say what they think would be best for their learning and have teachers, parents, and anyone that has anything to do with the school. Maybe they would understand why some kids are not learning, or going to class, or even the fact that some kids dropout.

My mother sometimes wonders why I can't learn in my classes as well as I can the words to music.

Music is more fun, more interesting. I guess it sort of draws me into my own world outside of reality. The words in music aren't just words. It gives a message or a story. The way someone feels can be put to music.

With school it's different you must memorize things you may never need. Such as all the presidents, state flowers, birds, etc. It's nice to know those things but still, why teach the kids if they aren't going to learn.

If they teach us what we are interested in, we would be much easier to teach. The drop out rate would go down and so would the skipping problem.

I think that they should at least one day try it and see that it would work. I guess what it all amounts to is why not ask students how they feel about it then listen to what they have to say. Then maybe do something to improve their learning.

Irene

If I could change one thing in the school system it would be the way the teachers ask questions in class. Alot of teachers ask a question to a certain person even if they know they don't know the answer. Then when the person doesn't answer the question the teacher kind of gives the kid a look so the kid feels like crawling under his chair. Or else the teacher gets mad at him, and the kid begins to hate the teacher and starts to skip his class. Then the person doesn't learn anything at all. Or if the person still goes to class he feels like he is the dumbest person in the world, so he doesn't even try anymore.

I think if a teacher knows the person does not know the answer he shouldn't call on that person just to embarrass him.

I think the teacher should try to talk to the person after class or something. Then if the teacher finds out the person is not trying or doing his assignments or something then I think it would be O.K. to ask him a question once in a while but not all the time, and not just to embarrass him.

Jack

If I could change something in this education system of today it would be the teachers. Some teachers know too much about their teaching and others know too littel. Some spend too much time on one person; theres too little on the individual.

Some teachers, I won't use any names, know too much about what they teach. They ramble on about different signs and symbols without telling the students what they are—assuming the students have used these signs and symbols countless numbers of times when they (the symbols) are new. Some of these teachers know so much about what they're teaching that they start to ramble on without telling the student what he should know.

Some of the teachers know so little about their subjects that they either talk about something else (not within the subject)—thus not informing the student—and/or give huge needless assignments that don't help tell about what the teacher was supposed to teach that day, and inconvenience the students—especially those with jobs. These teachers seem to assume that reading chapters in a textbook will help. But what if the textbook is very unclear on the subject, and the teacher makes even less sense in the discussion the next day? There are such teachers.

I've met teachers that've been so wrapped up in only a couple students that they seem to forget the others. While pumping information into the few students (who might not be able to handle all of it) these teachers deprive the other students of their rights to help and more knowledge.

Some teachers seem to automatically put a standard on all of their students. To them all the students are one person with one grade,—with one mind. He neglects the fact that they are individual and only gives aid to the whole class on class time. If they need help he doesn't offer them the time before school or after school or during noon hour. At times the teacher is too wrapped up in where to take his wife, or his girlfriend (just the opposite depending on the teacher) that he doesn't hear, or even see, the individual student. Perhaps he's afraid to help.

These are just four categories of teachers. There are others: the temper-tantrums, the extremely passives, the whatever-you-says, the always debatings, and many, many more. If I had my way I'd get the teacher with a sound (maybe not too sound) teaching degree and background, and the type of psychology and philosophy that could make him more than just the student's teacher, but his honest-to-goodness friend.

Kelly

If I could have one thing changed in the educational system, I would put more emphasis on the basics, reading, writing, and arithmetic, and less emphasis on other subjects. Reading, writing, and arithmetic are essential for everyday use. If you couldn't read or write, it would be very hard to get a good job. Arithmetic is used in virtually every job and if you can't do at least a little arithmetic, you will be unable to get a good job. Other subjects aren't as important. Unless you're going into the field of science, science just isn't that important. Social studies and history classes teach you some important things, but it doesn't compare with reading, writing, and arithmetic.

Some people graduate from high school with out learning how to read or write. It is hard to believe they could make it all the way through high school. These people have a hard time getting a job and making it through life without reading and writing. People who can't do simple arithmetic also have a hard time in life. If they go shopping or do anything that involves money, they won't be able to know if they're getting a fair shake when it comes to getting change or collecting a bet.

We have to start teaching the basics more in school and teach the people to read, write, and do arithmetic. Maybe start a required class that would deal with these basic fundamentals. Also for the adults, you could start a night class dealing with the basics.

The effect that it would have could be rewarding depending on participation in the class. I think it would greatly help the people who couldn't read, write, and do arithmetic. It would also help high school kids and adults get jobs.

Laura

In some classrooms from Elementary to High School, students are constantly being yelled at and embarrassed by impatient teachers, when the student doesn't know something he should know. In one incident I know of, a teacher in a junior high told a student she was a liar when she didn't know an answer to a question. The teacher who embarrassed and yelled at the students, scared the whole class and no one would ask for help, and they all showed a drop in grades. The teacher also said "I get paid for teaching not popularity." When a student told him no one liked him because he was mean.

I can see the teachers point but if he doesn't have any patients when someone doesn't know the answer to a question and yells he should not be teaching.

I think that before a teacher can take on the job, he should have proof that he has patience, likes the job, not only the money and can get along with students. If a student feels comfortable in a class which is a class kept under control and to the point where teacher or student aren't tense he will learn more than in a class he's not comfortable in.

I think that some kind of interview with different people who have known the person who wants to become a teacher should be done. Finding out if the person qualifies.

This would cut down on impatient not understanding teachers. The teacher probably doesn't realize but that teacher could be ruining that students school years and cause him to have problems with other teachers.

So this should be changed so that the school system is more relaxed.

Matt

The one major change I would make in the school system, would be that all text books would be changed into visual materials because if text books would be put on tapes they would be easier to store, easier to use without opening pages, or covers.

The main reasons for this change would be that most kids really hate to read so most of the kids don't learn because they hate to read. So instead of reading a book they could just push in a tape and watch and listen to the book tell its story.

How I would do this would be by putting in all the data of a book and have a computer absorb it in then transfer it to another computer and have it make all figures of the book and combine them with the happenings of the story at the precise moments; and then after all that work was done the student could watch it on an almost cartoonish film so it would keep the kids interest going about the book.

In my own personal experiences I've found that watching a novel on TV was more excilerating than just reading the book, such Lord of the Flies and so on.

If it was possible I think more schools should go into this kind of learning. The people I know like to have slides and movies about their subject then just constantly reading out of a text book.

Although maybe the text would be more helpful as a combination with the film tapes because the text may be boring in some ways, but it has a lot to offer the kids that are still in school.

Teachers would have an easier job by using these films, it would be easier to make tests for the kids, easier note taking for studying for tests, if they want a review just rewind it, so its an all around idea, it could be good, but could be bad.

Nate

I think one major change that should occur in Education is that you can take a semester on a certain trade you are interested in. The school should have areas of different trades such as welding, brick laying, deisel mechanic, interior decorating and others. The school has a few trades they teach but they should have more.

The school should have one whole semester on just one trade not any other classes at all so that the students will find out what trade they like and what trade they can consider going in to.

The students should have some idea of what the trade is like before making the jump. The students should be taught the basics and the fundimentals of a certain trade. The class should consist of the machines and the proper tools or what ever you need. The class should have the proper atmosphere.

The class should run at least a semester. From 8–3:30 with breaks in that time. It has to run at least that long because in order to get the basic fundamentals down in just a semester it has to run at that time.

I think that the course can help the student choose what trade he would like to go into. The students should be able to go out and talk to people who have considered that same trade as the student.

At the end of the semester that student would go out and work in the place where he has chosen his trade, it might be a sales store or any place. The student should be graded on his ability his interest in the course and his improval in his studies. If the students were offered these facilities the student could get an idea of what it consists of before jumping into something he might not like.

Short Stories (Seventh Grade)

To accompany a literature unit focusing on the short story, a seventh-grade teacher decided to ask his students to write stories of their own. His major aim was to reinforce what students had learned about the short story form, but he wanted students to take the writing seriously as well.

To help solve the problem of what to write about, he used pictures from Chris Van Allsburg's *The Mysteries of Harris Burdick* (Boston: Houghton Mifflin, 1984). Years before, he had heard Jeff Golub, then a high school English teacher and now a university professor, make a presentation on this "children's" book with its evocative illustrations and slightly creepy titles and captions. The conceit of the book is that a writer named Harris Burdick approached a publisher with fourteen strange illustrations to go with fourteen different stories. Burdick was to come back with the accompanying stories, but he mysteriously disappeared. All we have for each story is the title, an illustration, and a caption to the picture.

Each student chose one of Van Allsburg's fourteen illustrations and was given a copy of it. The teacher then led students through a series of activities, from invention (naming characters or free writing about plot) to techniques (using dialogue, for example). These were side activities, completed between the reading of short stories from the textbook. After two weeks of this intermittent work, students handed in a draft, which the teacher read and commented on. Final versions were submitted a few days later; they had to be neatly handwritten.

Brad

Mr. Linden's Library

It was middle summer. The frost from spring, had melted away. It wasn't to return till fall.

Donna Ozier had just woken up to the sound of a robin chirping on her windowsill. She sat up and admired the bird. She was curious as to how the bird had gotten into her room. So, Donna looked closer. she remembered how she had left the window open the night before when she and her friends snuck out to Mr. Linden's house.

They would go to Mr. Lindens house every Friday & one Saturday each month. Every time they came he would fix them tea and they would tell scary stories. On that one Saturday he would take them to his magical library. He would let each of them choose a book and they would read for hours and hours. The children would read with excitement as the stories became reality before their eyes.

Now, Mr. Linden was a lonely person. After his wife died, he had no one to talk to. But, now that the kids are coming he feels happy once more. He is a mysterious secretive old man. He never would tell the kids how he lost his eye. Mr. Linden stands 6 feet tall. His long gray frizzy beard hangs down and rests on his chest.

This Saturday was special because, Mr. Linden was letting the children take home a book.

Donna had just gotten out of school and was preparing for the night.

Ten o'clock, finally the time was here. Donna was more ready than ever before.

Donna made her way to Mr. Lindens house. She carried with her a flashlight, a pencil, and a notebook. She walked slowly so she wouldn't attract attention.

10:15, she was at the door. Donna rang the bell, and Mr. Linden let her in.

They both went down to the library. Her friends met her there.

Everyone had chosen a book except Donna. She looked on every shelf till finally, Donna's eyes came upon a book called "Ivy Vines Grow There". She picked it up and was on her way home when Donna heard a faint but recognizable voice calling her name. It was Mr. Linden yelling, "Donna wait! You must not read that book!", but Donna ignored him. She just kept running.

When Donna got home she immediately started reading the book. Donna was very tired so, she fell asleep, book wide open.

Huge vines began to grow from the book entwining her body, squeezing it tightly like a vise, pumping the life out of her body.

Mr. Linden had warned and now her curiosity had killed her.

People in that small town of Martin, Tennessee still say Donna Oziers spirit lives in those ivy vines growing on her now condemned house.

Mr. Linden disappeared from town after that. No one know what happened to him, But I do!

Betsy

Under the Rug

"As you were saying?" said Charles. It was a beautiful day in the late spring and Charles and his wife were having some friends over, just because it was everybody's day off.

At about 4:00 pm every body was still here. In the meantime, Sam was telling us how he had lost his cat, Batman. I started to get sick of him going on and on, yack,-yack,-yack-all ten minutes long.

That night when everybody was gone I was thinking about where Sam's cat would have been.

The next day I was watching t.v. and I glanced to see what time it was and there was a big lump in the rug. I had looked under the rug and nothing was there, and the rug was flat. I didn't go to do any research on it because I wondered if it was a only once situation.

Two weeks later it happened again. I looked under the rug and there was nothing there. That's when I started to get suspicious.

The next day I immediatly went to the police station. I didn't know if it was appropriate but I thought it might do some good. We could find out what it was that was hiding under the rug.

That night the policeman came over.

One thing we found out was that there was a secret door under the rug right were the bump had been and I was so blind I hadn't even seen it.

Sam and the other policeman did some more investigating. The door under the rug was too small for us to fit and so they asked me if I had a basement and I said, "Yes." We decided we could look and try finding where the secret door led to and who or what was hiding there. We looked and looked for almost an hour then we were about to give up but I had been in the laundry room and I heard some sort of noise behind our canned foods cabinet and sure enough there hd been Batman meowing.

I had figured out that somehow Batman had crawled under the rug when I wasn't looking and then when he heard me coming toward him he would go down through the secret door.

It turned out that in the next couple of days it had seemed that the whole world know about Sam's cat. I heard him one time telling the story to our next door neighbor. He was telling how easy it was and how he had done the whole thing by himself.

Claire

The boy the dog and the harp

On an April Spring morning ben was just waking by in Ottumwa Iowa. He heard something out side his window so and his dog Buck went to see what it was. There was a forest back thier that said enter so they did. Ben and Buck whent inte the forest not knowing that theer was danger in the forest.

they whent on thier marry way. All of a sudden Ben looked back and could not see the house no more. ben got scared but him and Buck kept on going. Soon they came up to a buitufl stream with a waler fall and ben and buck started to drink it. the water tasted good. ben rembered what his grandfather tooled him before he died that not to dink the water in the pound ather wise the monster in the pound will put a curse on you and you will tun into a magic harp. when ben remebered this he stop drinking it and so did buck. they waited to see if the monster came up but nothing happened. So they started to drink it agin. All of a suden ben see this thing come up. it was big and agle. Ben started to sake the monst said some magic words. ben turned into a harp. buck did not now what to do. So buck just sat thier. ben was scared so he screamed and screamed and all that came out for buck to hear was music. back at bens house his mom and look all over for them and could not find them. Ben was thinking about what his grandfather tolled him. the only way the curse will go away is if you are kissed by a girl. ben said to himself how am I going to get a girl in to this forst. the day soon was over so ben whent to sleep. eraly the next morring ben hard a girl sing. he started to scream se the harp would play music. the girl picked up the harp and said I'm going to take this home. ben thought to him self where is home. He started screaming agin. the girl said don't cry I will care for you and she kissed the harp. All of a suden Been turned back into his old self. When the girl saw this she ran away and ben never say her agin. Now for ben he larned to lissen to his elders.

And so how the old tail goes don't dirnk the water in the pound in a strange forst or ether wise you will pay the councaquences.

the end

Diane

The Harp

One day Eric was reading a book and he heard about a place in England. There was a beauitiful maden playing a harp in a magical world behind a never ending brick wall with no door. Scientists have searched for years trying to find a way to get in but they couldn't. So Eric thought to himself one day "I want to go to Emgland and find that door to get in and I'll become rich." He went downstairs and asked his mom if they could go on a trip to Edinburg Emgland. His mom said "yes." They were on the way when Eric kept thinking about where to start looking. When I got off of the plame I took a taxi over to where the wall was. I saw a old abandoned house that nobody lived in. I went in the house and opened a closet door that was upstairs. When he opened it there was a beauitiful garden like place and a clear blue pond. And by the pond there was a harp a golden harp with a madin sitting by it.

So it's true he thought it's really true.

Edward

Ralee and the Writing Worms

As she did every day since the beginning of the school year, she walked the same old route. Walk two blocks from the east exit of school. After that she cut across a playground which she sometimes stopped at, and then went two blocks to her blue house.

Here she was two blocks away from home at the playground sitting on a swing. She thought of her old friend Miawho had moved away. Since then Ralee had been bored to death.

Her parents had been divorced for two <u>months</u>, and her mom worked double-shifts on Mondays and Wednesdays. It was a Monday. Her mom wouldn't be home until 8:45 the next morning.

An idea started to form in her mind. What would her mother know of she went on a trip into the big forest. What would she know, how could she know, why would she know?

Ralee got off the swing and started running. She ran out of her middle-class area, through a slum, into a rich area, and to the spread out super-rich area with the houses that made her feel unworthy, and finally she came to the countryside.

She stopped and drank some water out of a ditch. She looked ahead. The forest was about half a mile up. The road turned, and she'd have to cut through a field. The field was raspberries.

She'd have to be careful if she didn't want to get hurt, and she didn't want to. She took it easy eating berries along the way. She began daydreaming, and tripped over what she thought was a tree stump. She got up, and looked back. "For strange," she thought, "that a dollhouse would be sitting in the middle of a raspberry field."

She looked inside it, and saw a group of blue worms. She though," for gross," but then she thought, "for strange that there would be <u>blue</u> worms in a dollhouse."

The worms came out of little holes in the dollhouse, and Ralee backed away, but she fill again. When she started to get up she saw something that kind of half-scared, half-excited her.

The worms had shaped into a peace sign. She asked, "Who are you?"

They spelled out (three letters at a time), "We're the Writing Worms."

Ralee was unbelieving, so she asked a few more questions. "1. How did you learn to write? 2. How did you get the house? and 3. Will you come with me to the big forest?"

The answered, "1. We underwent tests at a science place. 2. We found the house here, and 3. We will come with you to the forest."

Ralee had wished that she would get more friends. Her wish had come true. "Can I pick you up? she asked.

"You can pick <u>us</u> up, but we're not only only one. You can call us the Oscars, because that's who taught us to write."

"Okay then, get on my hand Oscars, and let's go!!!" she said, now not only half-excited, but wholly excited.

By now it was 6-0-clock. The forest was withen 15 feet. She walked, and in a few seconds she was out of the sunlight, and into the shade of the forest. She was hungry, but not too hungry.

The forest started out flat, and the trees were spread apart. After a while they got thicker. And thicker. By 8:30 they came to a cave where they stopped. The worms asked her, "When are you going to light the fire."

"What fire?" she asked. "I can't light the fire. I don't have matches, I don't have a lighter, and I'm not strong enough to start one with wood. I want to stay. Can I?"

The spelled out, "No!"

She looked at their faces, and knew it was time to say goodbye. Sadly she looked at how the worms had spelled out goodbye in her hand.

She let them down and a tear came to her eye. Her friends were going to stay in the cave. The day became darker. She started running. The whole forest unthickened. The forest was behind her. The raspberry field was behind her.

When she stopped to get water near the road in the ditch it was pitch dark, and she now was hungry, but she kept on going. She ran towards the light of the super-rich houses that made her sick. She passed that section.

It was past eleven. She kept running. She passed the rich area, the slum, and into her middle-class area. She stopped at the swings, and swung. She thought of how all of her friends seemed to move further and further away. She though of how she had helped the worms moved.

Then she remembered that it was Tuesday and her mom got off at midnight. It must've been 12:05 when she ran that last block, but it was lucky she ran, because it was right when her mom came home that she got into her bedroom.

Childhood Toy Papers (Eighth Grade)

An eighth-grade teacher wanted her students to practice descriptive writing. She knew that thirteen-year-olds are beginning to think of themselves as young adults, thinking of their childhood as "another age," so she asked them to remember and describe a toy that they had when they were children. Feeling that they need a structure to work within, she asked for three paragraphs: "The first paragraph will give a history of the toy (who gave it to you, when did you first receive it, and memories associated with the toy). The second will describe the toy in its original condition. The third will tell us what happened to the toy." She had students do a variety of prewriting exercises in class and told them to turn in a rough draft in two days. The final version was due two days later, to be typed in the computer lab at the end of the week. This teacher also wrote a paper of her own, which (after some hesitation) she showed to students:

On my fifth birthday, I received a stuffed dog from my next-door neighbor and best friend, Jimmy Donaven. I remember his gift was the largest package sitting on the kitchen table that day. This dog that I named Samuel became my favorite toy. I slept with him; I dragged him with on all vacations and trips; I took him to "show and tell" each year in school, and he sat on my bed in my college dorm for four years. I remember holding Sam when I was scared at night, and I also painfully recollect how my older brother Curt ripped off Sam's ear one time when we were fighting. I was heartbroken, but my mom sewed the ear back on, and Sam was good as new once again.

Sam was a beautiful, cuddly dog when I first received him some thirty years ago. He was made of light pink fur, and he had pink satin on the underside of his big, floppy ears. On the bottom, he was covered with a soft, plaid flannel. His nose was a black, fuzzy ball, which was always falling off, and his tail was a mound of pink fur. His eyes and mouth were lines just stitched in black on his face. Around his neck was a bow of pink satin, which of course soon untied and was lost forever. His four paws stuck out from his body, and I often carried him by his front left paw.

Sam is no longer with me. When I was in my senior year of college, I threw him out. By then, Sam and I had traveled many miles and many years together. His pink fur was faded, dirty, and matted. The satin on his ears was worn thin, and his front left paw was ripping, so that stuffing fell out of him every time I moved him. His little black nose had disappeared years ago, and in its place was a glob of dried-up Elmer's glue. His back left leg was stained a dark brown from spilled Coke. I realized at the age of 21 that Sam had lived a full life, and that I could go on without him. However, whenever I go back home and listen to the wind outside howling, I wish that Sam were still around.

Penny

My Smurf

It was a Friday afternoon when I was five, and my mom and I were out at the mall. My mom had said that if I was good, I could get a toy. So I got a smurf. I was so proud! First thing I did when I got home was show my family. My mom said that if I was good, I could get one every pay day. I was thrilled! So I went to my room to pick out a place where my collection would go. I finally cleared my top shelf and decided they'd go there. After a half hour of positioning my smurf just right, I took it down to sleep with it. I took that smurf everywhere: to school, to the sitters, and when my mom would let me I'd bring it to the grocery store. In fact, I remember the first pay day I didn't get to get my smurf. I recall putting up a fit and getting sent to my room. But I got one the next pay day!

My first smurf was about two and a half inches tall. They were actually two inches tall, but Smurfette was on roller skates. She had two big yellow pony tails with red bows in them, and she was wearing a white dress. My second one was clumsy brushing his teeth. He had a tube of toothpaste in one hand and a big red tooth brush in another, and white all over his mouth. I have about thirty of them now and they're all different. Some are playing sports like football, baseball, and soccer. Others are doing things like playing cards, swimming, picking berries, and all sorts of things.

I still have my surfs. They are hanging on a shelf in my room. They don't sell miniature smurfs anymore. So when my mom sees one out at a garage sale or something she'll pick it up for me. Right now my smurfs are a little scuffed up from always falling off my shelf. Their little white hats and pants are now gray and on some of them paint is coming off. I am planning to keep my smurfs for a long time. They will be the first thing to be put in my hope chest.

Ray

My Wagon

When I was three years old I got my first wagon. When I got it, I thought that I was the luckiest kid in the world. In the department store, where I got it, my brother was pulling me in the wagon up and down the aisles all around the store.

My brother used to pull me around the ice on the road. When my neighbors got a wagon, too, we used to have races down the dyke, and the winner, which use to be me, got a big slice of watermelon. I also remember when my older brother use to pull me around in my wagon by the bumper of my dads car.

Now my wagon is in the shed, its color is bleached to pink the body is all rusted out, the sides are almost gone, the wheels are broken, and the handle is off. It was fun when I had it.

Samantha

My Blanket

My favorite toy when I was a kid wasn't really a toy. It was my blanket. I received my blanket when I was a baby, from my Great-Grandmother. I remember that that blanket never left my side until I was in kindergarten. Then of course I couldn't have it with me all of the time.

My blanket had The Three Little Pigs design on one side and it was yellow on the other side. It also had little yellow yarn strings on it and the little pigs were brown with yellow cloths on them. It was about the size of a baby's blanket, but a bite bigger.

I remember when I was about four years old I droped it in some orange paint so it had a big spot on it. I think if I ever saw my blanket again I would know it was mine.

When I was about seven years old I stayed at my cousins and forgot my blanket there and my aunt accidently gave my blanket to one of the kids she babysits and that was the last I have seen of my Three Little Pigs blanket.

Tom

My G.I. Joe Men

The toy I remember most is my G.I. Joe guys. I started collecting them in third grade. Some of the people who gave them to me were my mom, dad, sister, and cousin. One time I remember putting one of the guys in a parachute and throwing it up in the air, and it got caught in the wires. One other time, Nate was over at my house. We put the guys in our bike spokes and spun them really fast until they flew into the air and broke.

The G.I. Joe guys I usually got were camouflage and had little guns and backpacs and wore helmets. I had about fifteen guys. Some came with vehicles and each guy had a special name and back ground. Each guy had his own nationality. Some were from the United States and others were from different countrys.

A couple of my guys I lost or sold. The rest my mom put away in a box in our storage room about one year ago. Right now the guys are in pretty good condition. Some were missing arms or legs. Right now the guys are buried under about ten boxes and a whole lot of junk.

Wendy

Baby Chrissy

When I first received Baby Chrissy was on a calm Christmas Eve. My brothers and sisters were all excited to see what was in the humongous box, that also weighed a ton. When the time came for me to open it up, everyone came to help me out! Finally, we had all of the paper off, and I looked up and saw this doll that was the same size as me, look me eye to eye. After that day Chrissy was with me everywhere. The bathroom, my room, the basement and every other room in the house. I never took her outside of the house though, because I didn't want to get her dirty! I always had to keep my dolls cleaner than my sister Kayleen's, or else I would never hear the end of it!

Chrissy had long, brown-red hair, that also looked like it had copper wires in it. You could shorten her hair by pulling a string in her back, and you could lengthen it by just pulling her hair out. She also had eyebrows painted on, but her eyes were plastic balls, and her eyelashes were like soft straw. You could feel the outline of her nose, lips, and ears. I had pierced her ears, so she also wore earrings. She had a fat stomach, and chunky arms and legs. Her fingers were a little bit curved and so were her toes. Soon after that I was bored, so I painted her fingernails and toenails a kind pf purple-pink color.

When I was about 10 years old, I figured it was about time I got rid of her. But there was something inside of me that still wanted to keep her. So, I finally found out a way I could keep her, without being embarrassed about Chrissy when my friends came over. So, the next night I took Chrissy downstairs and put her in the closet. The only thing wrong with Chrissy is that her hair hasn't been combed in about 4 years and she probably has a whole bunch of dirt marks on her body. Sometimes I still wish I could have her with me. But I'm a big girl now! I don't need those silly toys anymore, or do I?

Aaron

G.I.Joe

G.I.Joe were little army men that I got for my birthday in second grade. I really liked it! So with my birthday money that year, I went out and bought some more of it. Then before I knew it I had a collection. I kept collecting it until fifth grade. I usually got them for gifts. One of the memories I have is setting a base up in the laundry room. Another one is playing with them outside and loosing stuff. The last memory is always forgeting to pick them up, then someone might step on them.

They were about three inches tall, the color was variable, they had movable arms, waists, legs, knees, and elbows. They were plastic and they came with little guns, helmets, and backpacks. You could buy tanks, planes, vehicles, choppers, and etc.

I gave all of my collection of G.I.Joe to my brother Brent, he doesn't use them very much any more, they mostly sit in the basement under the stairs.

Beth

My Cabbage Patch Kid

When I was about a third grader, I received a Cabbage Patch kid. I know I got it for my birthday, and it must have been when I turned about 8 or 9. I got it from my parents. My sister and I used to play ship with them. We have beds directly across from each other and we said the floor between us was the "water". We said the walls next to us had shelves full of food and candy. Anyway, we had lots of fun with that. Another thing we did was play house. The dolls were the babies and we were the mommies. The last thing we did was to take them for bike rides. We put them in our bike baskets and then went for bike rides. We had a lot of fun with that when we were little.

My Cabbage Patch Kid was really neat. Her name was Marilyn Vera. It came in a yellow jogging suit. The pants were baggy at the top but they got tight at the bottom. The shirt was yellow with white on the cuffs of the sleeves. Her shoes were little white tennis shoes. She also had little white socks. Her hair was light brown and curly on the top and her ponytails were just straight. On her ponytails there were white ribbons. She was soft and squishy and really cute.

Right now she is in fairly good condition. She and her sweatsuit and socks got kind of pilly, but otherwise she looks basically the same. I still have everything she came in. Right now she is on top of my curtains, above my window. So I still know where she is.

Cara

My Blanket

My blanket was my most loved toy. I don't really remember how I got it. I think my mom made it for me. I use to lug it around everywhere with me. Whenever I forgot it somewhere I would cry until one of my parents went to get it for me. It went through alot, being dragged around everywhere through rain, snow, and mud. It was washed so many times.

It was a very cute blanket. It was white with purple, yellow, blue, and pink clouds on it. It had a silky border around it, it smelled like baby powder.

It was a very sad night, when my mom said I had to say goodbye to my blanket. It was Christmas Eve I was 3 or 4 my mom put my blanket under the three, so Santa could take it to a kid less fortunate than me. Then a halfa year later I found it in my moms chest. I got really mad!! So I went and really got mad at her, but when I got done spazing I decided that I lived with out it this long and I really don't need it anymore. Well thats the story behind my blanket.

Danielle

My Favorite Blankey

I got my blanket from my mom's godmother at my mom's baby shower. One of the memories of my blanket is I always slept with it. Also I always would drag it where ever I would go. Another one of those speicail memories is that I always had my thumb in my mouth and in my other hand. I had my blanket. My final and favorite memory is that I always called my blankent, "Blankey."

When I got my blanket, it was small and white with little duckies. The female duckies had blue and pink dresses and is holding a little basket with flowers in them. The male duckies had black and white suits on. My blanket also had pale white satin around the edges and also was very soft.

My blanket is now in the bottom of our storage closset. The blanket is now torn in one corner and is faded into a grayish colorand you can still see the duckies. The blankent is now out of shape some of the cotton bading is coming out.

Ethan

My Pop Gun

A childhood toy that was extremely important and special to me was a Daisy brand pop gun.

This pop gun was shiny black steel with a smooth wooden stock. The gun was about two and a half to three feet long. The lever used to cock the gun was nice, and had a very strong pull. The trigger was sort of loose, so every time you would shoot, you would pinch your finger. When you pulled the trigger, it would make a loud "BANG!" sound. It had aiming sights just like a real gun!

I remember the day that I got it. I was about four. I remember my parents were outside and I was in the porch. Then the UPS truck drove up. I opened the quickly door and ran outside. The driver opened the back and got a box. He had my parents sign something. They gave it to me. I opened the box and inside was my gun! I spent long hours playing "Cowboys and Indians", "Hunting" and my favorite game "the Dukes of Hazzard" with my brother because he also had a gun. We had a lot of fun together.

The last time I saw it, was about five years ago. A lot of the shiny black paint was chipped away revealing patches of rusty metal. The lever used to cock the gun was even harder to pull, and the rusty trigger still pinched your finger. The barrel was bent and even rustier than the trigger. The wooden stock was no longer smooth, but it was scratched and scarred from many hours of play in the field.

My gun still popped! Right now I bet my gun is laying in the junkyard in back of the church, across from my house.

Hundred Year Birthday Papers (Tenth Grade)

A tenth-grade teacher began the school year with this assignment. It was, she said, "a chance for me to get to know you better and to find out how you write; a chance for you to have some fun."

Students first read a newspaper story about Maria Rude, a farm woman who had just celebrated her one hundredth birthday. The story began with Maria's plan to fly over the farm on her birthday, and then recapped her life, telling of her education, marriage and family, trials, tribulations, and triumphs. Students were asked to write a newspaper article in which they described their own one hundredth birthday celebration and then told the stories of their own lives.

The teacher then took students through a variety of brainstorming exercises in which they listed things they might have done in their long, eventful lives, and thought about how the world might have changed during their lifetimes. She mentioned the following kinds of details they might consider, including "jobs you've had, travel, your married life and family, places you have lived, unusual or interesting things you have done or seen, close calls with danger, chance events that turned out to be important, obstacles or problems you have overcome, things you still would like to do, education you've received, membership in groups or organizations, public recognition, how you celebrated your one hundredth birthday."

She also listed for students the following criteria for evaluation: (1) "Does it tell the story of your life in some detail?" (2) "Is that story easy to follow, with no big gaps or inconsistencies?" (3) "Are the sentences clear and relatively free of error?" and (4) "Does the paper give the reader a sense of the *kind* of life you've led?"

Jenny

Doctor Who Discovered Cancer Cure Turned 100

Jamaica—Doctor Jennifer "Jenny" H. Cousteau turned 100 years old yesterday. Her birthday celebration was held in her summer home in Jamaica. Over 1000 guests attended the one-day party.

Jenny Cousteau was born on January 15, 1976 in a small town in North Dakota. She lived primarily in the midwest, living in Montana, South Dakota, and Minnesota. At the age of three she almost drowned, near Pipestone, Minnesota. "I saw a girl jumping off a houseboat. It looked like so much fun. I thought I could do it too. The next thing I remembered was my dad's arms reaching down for me," said the centurian.

At age 13, Jenny moved to Valley, Minnesota; where she graduated from high school in 1994. She then went on to Harvard Medical School where she earned her degree in medicine. At age 23 she married 47-year-old Pierre Cousteau. They had two twin girls, LaToya and Keila.

Jenny and her family moved to Switzerland in 2029 after Pierre became President of the Swiss Bank. While in Switzerland Jenny received a $2 billion grant to work on the cure for cancer. In 2034, Jenny discovered that cancer could be cured with the help of a rare plant in the African Jungle. It was called Healus All-Of-Us. Also in Africa Jenny found Noah's Ark. "It was in the middle of this mountain cave. African headhunters had been using it as a temple. When they saw us, arrows began to fly. I don't know how we ever made it out of there alive."

Tragedy did strike this intriguing women. One month before receiving the Nobel Peace Prize for her work in medicine. Jenny's husband Pierre died from a Piranha attack while fishing in the Amazon River. "I felt so bad. One moment I saw him (Pierre) sticking his hand in the river to wash it. The next second I saw him floating. It was so horrifying." Said an emotional Jenny.

Dr. Cousteau recovered but not fully. She kept live Piranhas in her bedroom and never left the mansion until 10 years later.

Then in 2050, Jenny married Mr. Rodgers' grandson. She was divorced two weeks later after she found out that he would sing and throw his shoes up in the air every night before bed. "I got so sick and tired of this singing and playing catch with his shoes and *NOT ME*." said a blushing Jenny.

After her divorce she moved back to Valley, where she has been spending her later years. "I love the big city life and Valley has that to offer."

When asked what she's like to do with the rest of her life, she replied, "I want to bungee jump, and learn the Beer Barrel Polka on the accordion."

USA TODAY

Doctor Jenny Cousteau died at the age of 100 years old. She was bungee jumping in New Zealand where she apparently had a major heart attach. Funeral arrangements are made by Fly-So-Free Funeral Home in Valley, Minnesota. She was proceeded in death by her husband Pierre Cousteau.

Holly

"She Makes It to 100"

Holly McMahon celebrated her 100th birthday today by going to Chicago and seeing the Chipendales. She said, "I've never seen such out of shape, fat, and descrasible men!"

Holly was born April 21, 1976 in Fargo, N.D. She was the daughter of Peter and Judy McMahon. She moved to Valley, M.N. when she was 8. She went to school there from 4th grade until she graduated.

After graduation she went to the University of Minnesota with her 2 good friends, Jody Berger and Julie Weingartner for four years.

Holly went on to become a great English teacher and horse trainer.

When she was 22 she went to Tulsa for the world championship on her horse she did very well, after that she went on to win the Coppenhagen horse. She won $500,00 dollars, a new pickup, and a new horse trailer.

When she was 23 she met a man named Vance Vesey who was 24. They got married 6 months later. They moved to Oklahoma and bought a horse ranch.

She had 2 children a boy Christopher Jon and a girl named Katelynn Jo. Her son went on to become the world's best hockey player and her daughter went on to become one of the world's best horse rider.

Holly and Vance spent 65 years together. Vance died in a car accident at 85.

Holly has been living with her sister Marie who is 15 years younger. They've been very close and they've been living together for 15 years.

Have a great birthday and may you live another 100 years.

Cy

"Change Is Never Ending So If You Stop to Think About It, It Could Pass You By"

These are the words of the ever-so-changing Cy Gregory Winter. Born in the year 1975, Cy today is turning the ripe old age of one hundred and fifty. Although all his close friends have died quite the few years ago, he is throwing a birthday bash at his estate located on the island of Cyrus (historically known as Cyprus).

Cy Winter was born at the United Hospital in Minneapolis, Minnesota. When he was three he moved to the now happening town of Valley.

As a child Cy was always moving, always had a football, basketball or some form of ball in his little hands. At the age of six he started his basketball career. As he went through high school he was good but never outstanding. Then on June 3, 1995, he got a phone call from the head coach of the University of Minnesota, Clem Haskens, asking him to come play basketball for his team. He leaped for the opportunity. But then his Junior year rolled around and Cy got in a tragic accident while skiing down Mt. McKinley. Although he recovered remarkably with the rehabilitation, he went on to discover new things he enjoyed. He came to a conclusion that he wanted to pursue a different career. So he continued on through the four year college with a double major in business and architecture. He went on through college for twelve years before he ventured out into the business world.

He started out managing a big oil coporation down in Texas. And after three years of saving his money, he and a friend he met in Texas bought thier own land and started a childhood dream. They started their own restaurant called "The Eawania." It was a restaurant and a movie theater in one. It is a very upper-class restaurant, with many television rooms.

Cy has been married since 2012. His wife was tall, red hair and very beautiful. They met while attending the same college. Cy had two kids by the name of Helen and Zeus.

Cy has many plans for the future, although his main goal is to golf a round of golf with the great Michael Jordan.

Tanya

Life and Death of a Centenarian

We are all gathered here today to celebrate the 100th birthday of a woman who says that she thinks she is one of the luckiest people in the world.

Tanya Lansing was married for fifty three years, before her husband died. She has two children, Alex who is now seventy six years old and a daughter who is seventy three years of age. I got to meet them and their children.

Before Mrs. Lansing died she told us of her life and what it was like to be a child in the 1990's. This is how it started. In 1976 her parents Bonnie and Jerry Barton conceived her in Dallas Texas.

After they stayed there for a few months they decided they didn't like the environment for raising Tanya so they moved to a small town in Scotland. They lived there for three years and had a second girl named Julie. When Tanya was ten they moved back over to the United States to a town called Valley, Minnesota. Back then it was just a small quaint little town, but now it has one of the largest school supply production companies in the world. Tanya lived in Valley for eight years. After she graduated from high school she decided she wanted to go back to Scotland for college. Tanya went to the University of Scotland for four years to become a world famous Archeologist, and devoted her life to finding the lost city of BogaMonga. She found it only three years after graduating from college. Tanya found the city in a valley south of Mexico City. The president of Mexico was very grateful for what she had done for the country of Mexico. She got a two million dollar award for finding the city. She couldn't take the money so she gave it to the homeless people of Mexico.

By the age of twenty four she decided to move to Australia and get married to a wonderful man named Nick Lansing. They had their first child Alex, who is now a world famous artist. In the next couple of years Tanya discovered a lot more cities and articles that could change the world's thinking to a more positive way of living. When Tanya was thirty she had a second child named Catherine. By the age of forty Tanya decided it was time to retire from archeology. Tanya decided to end world hunger. She did, and won a Noble Peace Prize. At the award ceremony she said that it was hard at first, but after a while I was able to conquire it." You will be able to read all about her journeys through Ethiopia and Africa in her first book called "Helping all the Little Children."

Tanya at the age of sixty decided that she wanted to stay at home and spend time with her children and her grandchildren. She had great times with them telling them all about all her wonderful journeys and exciting expeditions she had been on as a young adult.

When her husband was fifty eight he and her father died in a plane crash over the Himalayas. Tanya went into a deep depression for two years, her children couldn't even help her. They decided it was time for her to see a psychiatrist. Tanya saw him for three years and finally she was cured.

For her one hundredth birthday her son took her to Egypt. (where they are now.) They climbed the tallest pyramid there. When they reached the top she told her son, "Alex I just want to tell you that I know that I am going to die and that I want you to know that I have lived the life some people dream of living and that I couldn't ask for a finer son and daughter. I am going to a better place now and I will always be watching over both of you." That was the last words of Tanya Lansing, I hope that we will all remember her in the finest ways possible.

Her funeral will be held in Scotland. She wanted her ashes spread over the Atlantic ocean.

Todd

A Golf Legon That Had a Few Set Backs

Minneapolis. Todd Meyer celebrated his 100 birthday yesterday by playing 18 holes at the local golf course where he grew up in Valley, Minnesota. He shot a 4 under 68. He was quoted saying, "I'm a little rusty."

He was born April 26, 1975 at University Hospital in Fargo, N.D.

Todd moved to Valley at age 9 and went to school at Holy Family until the first part of the 8th grade then went to Valley Middle School and on to the senior high. He then joined the golf team in 9th grade. He was not very good; he only played in 3 tournayments. In 10th grade he also was not so good but he did not give up. He made varsity in 11th grade and went to state and took 3rd place. When he became a senior in High school he went to state and took first place.

The University of North Dakota then made a golf team just because Todd was planning to go there. They also gave Todd a golf scalorship. He took first in 10 tournayments in college. He also was the best in the nation in his junior and senior year.

Todd joined the PGA at age 24. He was the top money winner five years in a row. Then on his 32th birthday, he got hit in the eye with a golf ball. The doctors were so dumb they put a glass eye in the wrong eye.

So he was blind in both eyes. Todd then sued the hospital and man who hit him in the eye for a million dollars each. But he only got money from the hospital. He lost most of it gamboling. So he took the rest of the money and learned brale. He then became an accountant.

Two years later he married Sue. They had four children, Maynard, Jason, Clerance, and Danny.

His father died when Todd was 50 and left millions of dollors behind for research on a plastic eye that helps you see. It took them 10 years but they found a way and Todd had the surgery.

Todd then took 5 years to get his golf game back in shape. He then joined the Senior PGA at 65. But he was never as good as before his injury. He now designs Golf Courses around the world.

Tammy

"Centurian Parties It Up at Estate in Sydney"

Sydney, Australia. Tammy Holmgren was born in St. Anne's in Alexandria, Minnesota on May 14th, 1976. She spent her childhood growing up in the wild, exciting town of Valley, Minnesota. Tammy had many pets, but she liked fish the best. She took up fish collecting as a hobby and now has a whole room in her estate full of aquariums.

Holmgren maintained an A average in school. In her sophomore year, he friend Julie Benoit, boyfriend Peter Holmgren, and herself tried to rip off luggage from K-Mart, but got caught. They would've been sent to jail, but they convinced a judge not to send them. After that, Tammy started the second hippie movement. Bunches of people turned into hippies and teenagers rebelled against their parents. The second hippie movement taught people to let go, follow their own opinions, and have their own personality.

Tammy and a bunch of other hippies wanted to get revenge on the "Guess" clothing company because they thought buying "Guess" apparel was a waste of consumers money. So on July 17th, 1992, the rebellious group had hippies from all over the world burned all the buildings where they manufacture "Guess" clothing to the ground.

In response to this, Tammy formed a company of her own called "What!". The company (still in business)—sells great clothes at low prices. The "What!" company has a great selection of "hippie" clothing. Her boyfriend's sister Lori took over as president of the company so Tammy could finish school.

Tammy graduated from the Valley Sr. High in 1994 with top honors. She then moved on to college in Denver Colorado (DU) where she majored in Biology.

Holmgren, who's maiden name was Gravseth, married her longtime boyfriend Peter Michael Holmgren in the year 2000. Peter had won the U.S. Open for tennis in 1994, 1995, and 1996. After that, he became a guitarist for E.I.D. (a heavy metal band.)

For their honeymoon, they sailed into the Bermuda Triangle on a houseboat. They reported seeing a serpent that "looked like a dragon and had shimmering green scales." Peter took numerous pictures of the serpent, also.

With the money Pete made from playing tennis and playing guitar and the money Tammy made from the "What!" company, the couple was able to do many things. They moved to California and took up many hobbies such as water skiing, mountain climbing, hang gliding, sky diving, and downhill skiing.

Tammy once went on an expedition into space. She few into a black hole and became the first person to make it out of a black hole alive.

In 2003, Tammy and Peter gave birth to a spanking baby boy who they named Corey Michael Holmgren. Two years later, Tammy had a baby girl that they named Courtney Kristin Holmgren.

In their 50's, the couple travelled the world for a few years and then retired on an estate in Sydney Australia, where Peter had lived his childhood.

To commemorate her 100th birthday, she and her husband went back to the K-Mart store in Valley (the one where they had tried to rip off luggage) for old times sake. Afterwards, they went back to their estate in Australia and threw a wild party. In two more years they are going to throw another party, because Peter will be 100.

When asked for a closing comment, Tammy (with bony hands forming a peace symbol) simply replied, "Make love, not war!"

John

President Kravits Turns 100 Today

WHITE HOUSE—It was 100 years ago today in 1975 when a boy named John Christopher Drayton was born in a hospital in Iowa City, Iowa. After hearing about his rough lives, it is hard to imagine that he would become the President of the United States of America and creator of universal peace among the galaxies.

John Drayton (the former life of Lenny Kravits) lived outside of the small town of Ely, Iowa as a child, until the age of 13. At the age of 13 he moved to the small town of Valley, Minnesota. We asked President Kravits about the childhood of his former life, and this is what he stated.

"I find it difficult to recall details of adolescence in my past life. I remember that I had only one goal in life, and that was to rule over everybody. I also remember that I was restless, so restless that I would often resort to violence in public places, especially restaurants and public restrooms. At the age of 16 my parental unit kept me constantly secluded from public, claiming that I died in a tragic accident while brushing my teeth."

There are no official records of John Drayton, other than his death certificate, past the age of 16. The story is that John ran away to Chicago after his parents faked his death in 1991. In Chicago, John got a job running errands for the Mafia. At first, it was only little things like collecting money from the local businesses, but it quickly advanced to things like doing hits, and dropping off bombs. He soon became a respected member of the Mafia. John made millions dealing drugs, and doing hits, but it wasn't until the age of 30 he made his first billion. His life seemed perfect, but nothing can stay that good for that long. A drug deal went bad, and John was shot and killed at the age of 47.

"Death was a major setback in my goal of total monarchy," stated President Kravits, "thank heavens for reincarnation. I still had my goal, but this time I was going to do it by the book."

Leonard Kilroy Kravits was born Jan. 6, 2022, in Fisher, Minnesota. As a boy, Lenny was the perfect example of an angel. He had perfect morals, self-discipline, a high I.Q., and a kind heart. This kid had high potential right from the start. Lenny whizzed through high school and college, and went on to law school at Harvard, where he graduated at the top of his class. Lenny then married Suzanne Applegate, the daughter of retired actress and model Christina Applegate. Once out of law school, Lenny became a politician and ran for senator of Washington. Lenny won easily and then served 2 flawless consecutive terms. After his 2 terms as senator, he ran for president. He was once again easily elected. His 2 terms as president flew quickly by, and it finally looked as if he would be out of the White House. Citizens were outraged! They demanded a third term. Congress listened and passed an amendment stating that Lenny Kravits would remain in the White House until his death.

Lenny could finally relax. He had fulfilled his ultimate dream of supremacy. It took him 100 years, and 2 lives to do it, but he did it.

President Kravits will be celebrating his birthday in the White House this afternoon with friends from both lives.

Jeremy

Ryan the Card Player

On Jeremy Ryan's 100th birthday he decided to throw a party with his old friends. When everyone came over they were all carrying little baggies filled with money and bottles of chew spit. It was poker at the Ryan's again. It was the first time in 85 years, everyone was a typical cheater when they had the chance.

It all started when Jeremy and his friends began to play hockey. Mr. Ryan would bring change along with all of his big bills. Everyone would play cards on the bus, to hockey and back from the trip.

Between cards and sports Jeremy Ryan was the best. Mr. Ryan did not need a job. Jeremy made all of his money playing cards.

When Mr. Ryan went to UCLA for football he lost a little but gained a little. Jeremy was receiving money from the Vikings so that he would play for there team.

The Vikings wanted Mr. Ryan on there team because he was the best. So through college they paid his way, also giving him girls.

At the end of college Jeremy was drafted #2 to the Vikings. There he played 10 years of fabulous football. Nine Super Bowls, eight MVP seasons, and leading rusher, passer, and sack leader. Then all the fame came to an end when Jeremy was caught for receiving money from the Vikings. So he was kicked out. Jeremy lost everything, his wife Kim, his money, and his lucky Quarters.

At the age of 45 Jeremy was living in the street collecting cans. Then Jeremy became famous all over again by buying lotto tickets with the money he saved and won. Jeremy opened up his own casino, making lots of money.

So there you have it Jeremy Ryan, son of Karen and John, has proven to the world to be the luckiest guy around.

Now Jeremy on the weekdays relaxes at his lake cabin playing cards with his old friends.

Susan

Being 100 Years Old

Susan Hernandez was found in Paris celebrating her 100th birthday, with her family. Susan had always wanted to go to Paris, so on her 100th birthday she got her chance to go. When asked how it felt to finally be in Paris, she said, "It's a dream that I thought would never come true."

Susan was born in Carrizo Springs, Texas on January 26, 1976. Her family moved to Valley when she was 11 years old. When Susan was 16 she went to visit a relative in Los Angeles for her summer vacation. One day while Susan was going to the store, she was caught in a crossfire. Lucky for her that she ran inside a building before she got shot. She claimed to have been very scared and was careful in the streets after that.

Susan graduated from Valley Senior High School in 1994. After that she went to California to attend the University of UCLA. There she studied art design. After college, at the age of 25, she moved to Miami, Florida to start her own business. There she met Ray Hernandez. He was 27 years old, born in Miami, Florida.

She went out with him for 2 years. Then in 1998 they decided to get married. They got married in Texas where Susan was born, so that her family could be there. After 2 years of marriage, Susan and Ray gave birth to a baby girl. They named her Jasmine.

At the age of 31, Susan still remembered the heat wave that hit Florida. Her baby almost got a high temperature. But Susan took her to the hospital just in time. Nothing bad happened to Jasmine.

At the age of 96, Susan suffered a heart attack. She was immediately rushed to the hospital. She got better after a month in the hospital. After that she recovered completely and quickly. Her doctor comments, "I've never seen a person that old recover so quickly from a heart attack. She sure is lucky."

Now Susan is 100 years old and happily living with her husband who is 102.

Her daughter Jasmine is happily married and living in Fresno, California.

Jodie

Mrs. Cartier Turns 100!!!

Jodie Lee Cartier will be celebrating her 100th birthday on Tuesday, June 3rd in 2076. On this particular day she plans on attending the championship beach volleyball tournament in Sunny California where she used to coach.

Her daughter, Jordan, took over her position. After this she plans on going skydiving. They are going to be flying over the Sahara Desert and dropping down from there. For her final excitement of the day she plans on joining her chiropractor for lunch at the Flamingo. When we asked the centenarian about how it felt to be 100, she simply answered "I feel no older than 18!!

When Jodie Lee was born a whole century ago, she lived in Greenland. Her mother and father died when she was 15 so she took care of her 5 younger brothers and sisters. When they were old enough to be on their own she decided to move to Valley, Minnesota. She moved in with her aunt and uncle. She attended school at the Valley Senior High. While there she participated in volleyball and basketball. When she graduated in 1994, she went to college at the University of Mexico. She went there and got a degree in Computer Programming. She met her husband Chuck while there. They were married on January 3rd, 1999, in the Sacred Heart Church.

They had their little homestead outside of town on a farm. There they had cows, pigs, chickens, and horses. They had their first child a year later. Then they had twins a boy and a girl named Jordan and Jamie.

When she was 53, she and her son went for a horseride. They were riding along when gunshots fired from the woods. She stated "It sounded like a war going on in our back woods." Well when they heard this the horse bucked her off and she cracked her head open. She came out with only minor cuts.

When she was 88, her husband died of a heart attack. She then was put in a Mental Institute because she didn't want to go on living without Chuck. After recovering from the Mental Institute, she was put in a nursing home in Erskine. She was named Elder of the Month. She has lived in the home for 12 years and will be for life. When asked how she liked it there she said, "I enjoy it, but I wish we could go dancing."

Then/Now–There/Here Comparison-Contrast Papers (Tenth Grade)

This assignment was given to a class of tenth-grade students. In many respects it is a standard comparison-contrast paper, but unlike most such assignments, it moves in the direction of autobiography. Students were asked to compare and contrast two experiences. One option was to write about an activity from the present day ("now") and a similar activity during their childhood or their parents' era ("then"). Another option was to work with a place they knew previously ("there") and a place they know now ("here").

Students had considerable freedom in choosing topics and were given about a week to complete the assignment, from brainstorming through peer response to revision of drafts. These papers are second drafts. The attitudes expressed in them are, needless to say, students' own.

Eddie

I'm from a city in Texas. I moved here with my Dad. I've been here since the beginning of August and I've been enjoying every minute of stay here in Valley. I plan to stay here for a long time.

I went to Washington High School but now I'm going to Valley Senior High. So far so good; I'm enjoying it here but its a big difference from the size of Washington.

Washington has about a square mile of school facilities and recreational grounds that make the school even bigger. On the other hand, Senior High is not as big but that's better than a big school because you don't get lost as easy. The first day I went to Washington I got lost. When I came to this school I found my classes without any problem.

The rules are also completely different because of all the drugs and violence and misbehavior. Washington has a tremendous amount of drug related problems. People were smoking weed in the hallways and in the classrooms. This problem isn't as bad here. There might be drugs here but not as bad as Washington.

The mental environment of Washington and the Senior High are basically the same. The majority of races in Washington are Mexicans, Blacks and, very few whites. They all get along except the Mexicans. It's kind of the same way here: Mexicans think they're superior to all people but there not. There are all types of people and they are all the same. There are alot of Mexicans here that think their race is superior.

The students here and there are kind of the same; it's just that there are more students in Washington than in Valley Senior High. Also it's a big city and Valley is such a small place. I think that Valley is such a nice place and I'll enjoy it until I have to move.

Gina

Living with one parent is extremely different from living with two. I especially see this when I compare my family to some of my friends' families or when I compare our family now to when my parents weren't divorced. I have been living with my mother, sister, and brother since I was eight, when my parents got divorced.

When living with only one parent your rules tend to be a little different from other families. In my case, I find mine to be a little more lenient, if anything. I usually don't have any trouble convincing my mom on a somewhat suitable curfew like some of my friends, and I never have to worry about convincing two parents on anything. As far as chores around the house go, we all pitch in pretty much. Sure, we need a little urging sometimes, but my mom usually doesn't have to assign us duties.

It seems when living with two parents you find an over-protective parent. Dad doesn't want you to go and mom is willing to let you. And sometimes mom doesn't think you're helping around the house enough and dad doesn't care. As a result, you have stricter rules concerning curfews, household duties, and independence.

Likewise, independence is an important quality in a single family. The independence my mother has gained has definitely influenced me and the way our family works. I have learned to stand on my own two feet. My mother has no problem when I tell her I won't be around the house much for the week, or when I make plans for myself. She knows I'm very capable. Therefore, independence is an important factor when it comes to rule-making at our house.

However, in two parent families sometimes the parents don't allow their kids to become independent since they tend to be dependant on each other. They don't show the characteristic too much since they can rely on the other parent. This can sometimes lead to a strict family with lots of rules.

On the whole, I think many single families are closer than some two parent families. There really is no two sides in a single parent family, therefore you either all work together or you don't have a family. Like when our family is having a big argument, my mom says it's either all of us or none of us. I think you pull closer to stay together. On the other hand, it gets tough and hard to keep together.

Lots of times in a two parent family you have a constant battle between two sides. Mom and daughter side against dad and son and so on. This results in a family without very many ties.

All in all, living in a single parent family isn't so bad. I'm not saying it's great, but living in a two parent family isn't always what it seems to be either. I guess I feel bad for my brother sometimes because I feel it's harder for him to miss out on a dad than for me or my sister. We're very lucky to have other family like my grandpa and uncles to make up for that. I guess you just accept the consequences and live with them To live with the consequences of a single family you pull closer together, forming a different kind of family.

Hillary

Listening to my parents recollect about their high school years. I undoubtedly notice that high schools and teenagers have changed in the last 20 years. Although basically the same, high schools in the 60's definately have their differences with high schools, today in the 80's.

Back in the 60's the school dress code was very strict. Girls were not allowed to wear pants except on storm or game days and their skirts had to be below the knee. However today girls can even wear shorts and jeans with holes in them. Back then boys weren't even allowed to wear jeans. Personally, I think fashion in the 60's had less of a variety compared to today in the 80's. Today girls perm and curl their hair with curling irons. The 60's girls did some real wierd things, they styled their hair in beehives, curled it with orange juice cans and literally ironed it with a clothes iron.

Entertainment 20 years ago was going to a drive-in movie. On the other hand, today you can just stop at your local video store and choose any movie you want to see and watch it at home on your own TV. Also, the music today is much different than the music our parents listened too. Todays heavy metal music greatly contrasts with the 60's songs written about love and peace.

There was alot of sex discrimination back in the 60's. For one thing there was no sports for girls and in alot of schools the female teachers were not allowed to get married or they could be fired. Girls weren't allowed to take shop classes as the boys couldn't take Home Ec. This was just a unwritten rule that not many questioned. A accepted stereotype in society. Luckily, today people have come to their senses.

In the 60's, teenagers were more motivated to go to college, because if you didn't you were most likely drafted for the Vietnam War. But, I think alot of kids in the 90's are going to college too to make better lives for themselves and their future families. We are the future and the future looks bright.

The pressures of sex, drugs and alcohol are stronger now than they were back in the 60's. Today teenagers are exposed to sex, drugs and alcohol nearly every day whether it be through commercials, TV programs, movies or the music they listen to. Not that the teens of the 60's weren't exposed to these pressures, but they probably weren't as strong.

On the whole, I think generally the pressures and emotions of todays teens are the same ones that teens 10, 20 and even 30 years ago went through. If parents, teachers, and other adults would only try to remember what it was like being a kid, there might be less of a generation gap.

Jeff

Alot has changed from hunting now, and hunting in my grandpa's day. Like places, weapons, and the game itself.

The places have changed alot. My grandpa built his own blinds and his own decoys. Now you can go to places where you can just go to already built blinds and you can buy decoys in the stores and you can go alot more place now then you would then.

The weapons I don't think thes have changed that much. Back then they were heavier and had a lot more kick. But now there lighter and easier to carry, but still have quite a kick. He gave me sum of his guns, the only real differences is the price. There worth more then my new guns. I like my newer models of guns better cause there easyer to hunt with.

They're is a big difference in game. There was lots of ducks and geese, but now there isn't half as many duck's and geese. I think its cause there are alot of poachers and stuff like that. And also cause of the different shots. There is either lead or steal.

My grandpa used lead shot back then, cause it was all they had, but now it is outlawed because ducks that get wounded would die of lead poisoning. We have to use steel so they don't die of lead poison ing. Thats a nother reason for the change in game.

I think I would have rather hunted back then because the abundance of game. And you had to build you own supplys. Also you could take more birds and stuff and there weren't as many poachers.

Karla

As I walked into my dance studio I suddenly had visions about how my old studio was like seven years ago. The difference in the size and the attitude of the dancers. And how many things stayed the same.

When I was three to seven years old I went to dance at a studio in my teacher's basement. The studio was small and had dull colors that seemed to make it a boring place to be. There were pictures on the walls showing off how great my teacher's daughters were. Along the entire front wall there were mirrors. I used the mirrors to follow the steps my teacher was doing. However, we didn't really seem to care about what we were doing. Maybe it was because it didn't seem like we were taking lessons because we were in the basement of a house. Or maybe it was just the fact that we were to young to understand.

Since then things have drastically changed. Now my studio is in a big business building. And I feel I have a lot more room to move since the studio is much bigger than the old one. The bright pastel colors of the studio make me feel warm and happy inside. The same pictures of my teacher's daughters still hang on the wall. Now I don't need to look at the mirrors to follow steps. By now I know the steps and use the huge wall of mirrors to see what I'm doing wrong. Suddenly all the dancers care about how they dance. We all want to be the best or get the biggest part.

It is very clear to see that we have improved. In fact I believe the improvement came with the improvement of the studio. Knowing that it is bigger and better I feel more confident in what I do.

Leanne

The loud music and the shouting of voices suddenly got to me and I had to get out. I left the small confines of the bathroom and made my way to the basement. I strained my neck above the many heads and through the smoke. Finally, I found my ride home. He got up from the chair he was sitting on unsteadily walked over to me. I smelled the strong alcohol on his breath when he slurred, "Do you want me to take you home now?"

I felt sick to my stomach. I wanted to hit him. How could he do this to me? I had to be home in twenty minutes and I knew deep down that he was too drunk to drive. Yet, I was tempted to let him. The last thing I needed was a lecture from my mom on being late. I didn't know what to do. With tears in my eyes I ran back into the bathroom, shut the door, and slid down to the floor. My head was pounding.

I hated him. I hated myself for coming to the stupid party. I wanted to die. I thought about all of the problems I had been having lately. My mom and I were always arguing. Whatever I tried to do it's never good enough for her. She questions everything I do and everywhere I go. We can't even talk anymore without being hostile or sarcastic. I though about school and some of the classes I was having problems with, and my grades. It seems like there's tests every other day and I can't keep up. On the days that I work, the last thing I want to do is come home and study. When I do, I get to bed really late and I'm exhausted the next day. I can't quit my job because my mom and dad have money problems and it's really important to have that extra money. I then thought about my boyfriend and friends and all the pressures. I get pressured about everything. To lie, to drink, to try marijuana, and to have sex. I now have so many important decisions to make. Decisions that could affect me for the rest of my life.

I folded my knees to my chest, resting my chin on them. I remember grade school when I was about nine years old. Everything was so much easier. Grades weren't so crucial and they won't hardly effect your future. My friends didn't put all of these pressures on me to do things I don't want to do. I never worried about drugs or drinking because the oppurtunity was never there. My mom and I got along really good. We talked about everything like friends. I remember we used to have what she'd call "girl talks". Now, I could never imagine doing that, it would only end in an argument. Fashion wasn't so important then. I mean, I just wore jeans and a t-shirt and no one cared. Boys were definitely the farthest thing from my mind when I was nine. I almost wish it could still be that way.

Sometimes I don't think that parents or adults realize how stressed a teenager is. They always say, "These are the best years of your life." I'll agree in some ways that they are but if you really stop and think about it, they're not. The pressures and decisions that are put on teenagers are so heavy. It happens all of a sudden, too. One day you're not worrying about much and the next day everyone wants to know what you want to do with your life, if you'll drink and smoke pot, if you'll have sex, and if you're getting good enough grades to get into a decent college. Some people can't handle it and maybe that's why the statistics for teenage suicide is so high.

A loud rapping on the door startled me and I jumped to open it.

"Well are you coming or what?"

I observed his drunken state and answered, "No. I'll find my own way home." I then went into an upstairs bedroom and called a good friend of mine to come and pick me up.

Marissa

It was Saturday night, and my mom and I were sitting at the kitchen table, looking at her old yearbooks. My mom graduated in 1969, and just had her 20 year reunion this past summer. It was obvious to me that there was a lot of differences in the 20 year span.

20 years ago there was no such thing as girls sports. All they had were cheerleading and pom pom girls. But they did have a club called the GAA (Girls Athletic Association) which met about once a week after school. The club only consisted of high school girls. They were led by the school gym instructor and they played volleyball, basketball, badminton and tumbling with the gymnastic equipment. Their club sponsored a school dance. My mom was a cheerleader and lettered but she doesn't remember going to a banquet.

Times have changed, and there are now many girls sports, such as basketball, volleyball, golf, tennis, crosscountry, track and figure skating. I've lettered in figure skating in the last 2 years. I know times are really different when a girl goes out for the wrestling team! And when one of my girlfriends played on the ninth grade football team.

Next, my mom did a lot of social activities within her church youth groups. They had a couple of hangouts, like "A & W". She sometimes went to dance at the Armory. Fights sometimes occured between the boys.

Right now, and throughout the whole school season, I'm really busy between sports and school. But when I'm not at practices or doing homework, my friends and I sometimes go to movies, shopping or go out to eat. I think we talk on the phone the most!

Finally, classes were indeed a problem in mom's years at the high school. Boys weren't allowed to take Home Ec classes and girls weren't allowed to take shop classes. Chorus was a regular class, but band had to be done before school started.

Now boys are allowed to take the Home Ec classes and girls can take shop classes. In seventh, eight and ninth grade those two classes are required. There is also computer classes that are optional.

I think that I would rather stay in the 80's, because of more privilages for girls, and more technology in the school.

Ned

I got to thinking over the long summer of going back and forth between Clear Lake and Valley to visit my moms husband to be who owns a construction company, which I liked better Clear Lake or Valley and figured out there was more to do in Clear Lake during the summer. In the summer in Clear Lake swimming is the best. We would go to all kinds of rivers to swim, but the best was the Big Bend River where we would jump off a 40 foot cliff into a big pool of water that was once a waterfall. In Valley it's pretty fun swimming in the river but nothing like Clear Lake.

I do a lot of biking in the summer so I compared them. In Clear Lake we did a lot of mountain biking up huge hills where we would sometimes get going up to speeds of 50 miles an hour and barely staying on the bike. Biking in Valley isn't quite as exciting because there aren't that big of hills here and we mainly use the bikes around here to get somewhere.

I love fishing so this subject really made a differance in my decision. Fishing in Clear Lake has to be one of the primest places to fish in Minnesota. I caught a 9½ pound lake trout downrigging fishing on the lake and it was one of the biggest fish I ever caught. Valley fishing isn't that fun all you can catch here is catfish and carp in the river.

With these subjects I found there is more to do in Clear Lake in the summer but in the winter there is a lot of stuff to do in Valley. So, if you want to have a fun summer go to Clear Lake if you like to do some of the stuff I mentioned.

Pete

When I was in Junior High a lot of things were different then they are now in Senior High.

When I was in Junior High the building was badly lighted and smelled very bad. There were two gyms in it which was very nice, but it had three floors. Because of all the floors your classes were sometimes a marthon to get to before the bell rang.

Undoubtedly the teachers were very nice. They seemed to feel sorry for the small 7th graders that are there. Even so they would laugh at them behind there back a lot too. Unquestionably the teachers made the class a lot more fun as the years went by. Obviously some of my favorite teachers were Mr. H., Mr. B., and Mr. E. In fact the classes with these teachers were the finest.

There wasn't a lot of learning in Junior High. The teachers merely gave homework because they would let you do your assignment in class and everyone would get done. Thus the only time I got homework is if I missed a day or didn't feel like doing the work in class.

In Senior High the building seems a lot more smaller with only two floors and one big gym. The building smells a lot better and the lighting is very good in it.

The teachers at the Senior High want to teach a lot more. Some teachers are a lot meaner and don't talk to the students enough. The other teachers talk to much and wast a lot of time and as a result give you big homework assignments.

I get homework every night from almost all of my classes. But somedays they are nice and I don't get any but that is very rare.

The students are a lot nicer at the Senior High. I am friends with a lot of the Seniors but, all the Juniors hate me.

Senior High is a lot better than Junior High for the way the kids act. But I would rather be in the Junior High for the work. They both are fun schools to go to in your school years.

Randy

My dad started to hunt when he was about 11, in 1950. He said, "I can remember sitting out there and shooting 10 ducks a day." Now you can only shoot 3. Before, when you shot your ducks it didn't matter what kind they were. However, now if you shoot 3 ducks only two of them can be mallards.

Today every stuble field up north by Canada is posted. Back then nothing was posted, you didn't even have to look around the corner to check. My dad says that the big reasons for all the posted land, is ever since the air base came, they started posting it cause the basers would drive over the crops, throw all there litter, shell boxes, and leave lots of ducks in the slews if they didn't have waders.

But it hardly matters if you shoot a duck in the slews, cause theres hardly any water, on the other hand, when my dad hunted, every mile road would have a least 3 slews. Now the farmers are burning up all the ditches and haying the bottoms of the slews which I don't think any of the hunters like. The farmers have this thing called the swamp busters program, its where all the farmers in there township get together and say we'll burn up all the ditches and slew bottoms and wont let hunters hunt on any of their land.

Now you have to use steel shot, when ever you hunt waterfowl. That rule just went into effect, cause when the ducks go down to the bottom of the slews and it eats the bb's thinking there rocks to grind up the food and they get lead poisoning. If you get caught hunting geese in a field with lead shot you can get a serious fine, cause if you shoot at a goose and one bb hits him and sticks in his body and he lands in water and the bb falls in, one of the birds could be poisoned.

I say that hunting has got worse, in the last thirty years, with low population of waterfowl, the only positive thing about it is the steel shot law and even some people don't obey it. The DNR tries to put refugees up for the birds, give them land to feed on but some people ruin it and hunt on it anyways or take to many ducks or liter I think if the hunters co-operated, that in 20 years it would be just like it used to be.

Literary Analysis Papers (Eleventh Grade)

This assignment was given to a class of high school juniors toward the end of the year. As part of her instructions, the teacher said, "Your job will be to choose one or more pieces of literature we have read this year, analyze something about the literature, and present your analysis in a well organized and thoughtful paper. You must use quotations to support your interpretation." Students were also given the option of comparing a work they had read to another work of literature or some other work of art with a similar theme.

Students were given a series of steps in the prewriting process: (1) choose one or more works that they had read in American Literature; (2) decide what interested them and find quotes to illustrate the point; (3) copy the quotes and jot down notes beside each one; (4) reread the quotes and decide on a thesis; and (5) outline the paper. They were given examples of thesis statements and a sample outline. One of the examples had to do with foreshadowing.

Sam

Hangin' Out in Salem

Arthur Miller's "The Crucible" is an ample show of how little disruptions can expand into huge problems in a society that strives for perfection. In this paper you'll see how some little girls dancing turns into people being killed for being a witch or wizard.

Dancing was the spark that set ablaze the town of Salem. "You permit dancing?" (Miller 38) was said by Mr. Hale, a man who came into Salem to save it from the devil. "You'll only be whipped for dancing' . . ." (Miller 19) was said by one of the girls who was dancing. In Salem children were to be seen and not heard, to walk with their hands at their sides and head and eyes down. Also in Salem books were not allowed and "The creed forbade anything resembling theater or "vain enjoyment"." (Miller 4) These examples show how strict the town was.

The dancing incident soon turned to scares of witchcraft. The scares were not taken lightly either, the town promptly called Reverend Hale (a witchcraft specialist) to find the devil in Salem and quickly exterminate him. The town will not put up with the devil in a "perfect puritan" society. In Salem "Witchery is a hangin' error . . ." (Miller 19).

Mr. and Mrs. Proctor, Giles Corey, and George Jacobs were a few of the people who went to their deaths because the group of girls couldn't tell the truth and take their whipping. Mary Warren (one of the accused) said, "I never saw no spirits" and "that were pretense, sir." (Miller 89) when she was asked about her accusations of the people who were to be hung. Mary was soon overthrown by the rest of the accusing girls and the people hung anyway.

In conclusion. many loved ones were lost and disgraced by being called witches and wizards. There was no reason for these deaths. If the town had not been so hung up upon being perfect, the dancing incident would have blown over quickly, but it was twisted and turned and many people were forced to 'hang out in Salem'.

Travis

The Crucible

Arthur Miller's "The Crucible" tells, among other things, how a little lie can turn into something extremely serious.

This story begins with girls dancing in the woods. Dancing was considered a sin in Salem, which was the same as breaking a law. Reverend Paris finds the girls dancing in the woods and that's how the whole ordeal starts. The girls claim that they were being persuaded by the devil who was working through a long list of "witches" in Salem.

The girls kept telling lies to cover themselves and it became more and more serious. No one in the court even began to think that the girls were lying until they started accusing practically everyone in town of being a witch.

One of the first people to say that they were lying in court was Francis Nurse who said to the Head Judge, "Excellency we have no proof for your eyes, God forbid you shut them to it. The girls, sir, the girls are frauds" (Miller 87). Both John Procter and Mr. Nurse were in the court room with Mary Warren, one of the girls who was dancing and now lying. John and Francis convinced her to tell the truth about what the girls were doing. Mary Warren told the Judge that the girls had lied about seeing people with the devil.

This was the first time Danforth, the head judge, considered that the girls could be lying. He said, "Then you tell me that you sat in my court, callously lying, when you knew that people would hang by your words" (Miller 101).

When the girls entered the court room, shortly after Mary had told the truth, they accused Francis, John, and Giles Corey, who was also in the court room at the time, of being witches.

Later when John and Elizabeth, his wife, were talking in John's cell, John asked about Giles. She said that they pressed him, when John asked what pressing was, she said, "Great stones they lay upon his chest until he pleaded aye or nay (to being a witch). They say he gave them but two words. More weight and died"(Miller 135).

At the end of the book many people are hung because of lies, including John Procter.

It amazes me that people can be so stupid and so stubborn. All Giles Corey had to do was repent and he wouldn't of been crushed, but he chose to die instead of save his life by lying. Also I ponder on how a judge can be so incredibly stupid to believe teenage girls over grown men and women. But in conclusion I guess that we cannot judge the people of the past by our present day standards and morals.

William

Comparison Between Faulkner and Borland

Wm Faulkner's "The Bear" and Hal Borland's When the Legends Die were both written about the wilderness and how it compares to the bears harbored within. Native American Culture also plays an important role in these stories.

Borland writes about the White culture as being afraid of the wilderness. Both authors compare grizzly bears to the wilderness to add to this fear. ". . . Then the boy [Tom] saw the She-Bear. She was dead . . . The man walked around her *afraid* even though she was dead." (Borland 33) Faulkner talks about how the wilderness is being destroyed, ". . . The doomed wilderness whose edges were being constantly and punily gnawed at by men with axes and plows who feared it because it was the wilderness." (Faulkner 1)

In "The Bear", Sam Fathers is a teacher to the boy. Sam is the "son of a slave woman and a Chickasaw chief."(Faulkner 1) He is an expert woodsman and knows many of the legends of the wilderness. The Boy hunts with Sam and learns everything he needs to know to kill Old Ben, the bear.

Tom Blackbull is the hunter in When the Legends Die. He was also and Indian. He learned the legends and skills from his parents before they died. He adopted a bear when he lived alone in the wilderness. After he came back from his rodeo career, he hunted an older larger grizzly. Whether or not it was *his* bear is arguable.

He closed his eyes, fighting with himself. *I came to kill the bear!* His throbbing pulse asked, *Why?* He answered, *I must!* And again his pulse beat, *Why?* He answered, *To be myself!* And the pulse asked, *Who . . . are . . . you?* He had no answer. The pulse kept beating the question at him. Angrily he said, *This bear has made trouble!* The question beat back, *To . . . whom?* And his own biter answer, *To me!*

> Then the question, as before, *Who . . . are . . . you?* And he, having no answer he could face said, whispering the words aloud, "This bear did not make trouble. The trouble is in me." And he lowered the rifle. (Borland 206–207)

The bears meant something to each of the characters. To Sam Fathers and The Boy it was part of the wilderness. Tom Black thought of the bear as part of himself, his troubled part. Neither of them shot their bear. They had too much respect for them. They gained their respect from their Native American culture.

Works Cited

Borland, Hal. <u>When the legends die</u>. New York: Bantam Books, 1985.
Faulkner, Wm. "The Bear." Glenview, Illinois: Scott, Foresmon and Company, 1989.

Amy

Judy Loses on Life and Love . . .

Scott Fitzgerald's "Winter Dreams" is focused on lessons of life and love. Remember this: selfishness gets you know where.

> Judy Jones was a beautiful tease right from the beginning of her time: There was a general ungodliness in the way her lips twisted down at the corners when she smiled; and in the—Heaven help us!—in the almost passionate quality of her eyes. Vitality is born early in such a women. It was utterly in evidence now, shining through her thin frame in a sort of glow (Fitzgerald 588).

You could tell that even when Judy was young, she was higher than anybody else was. People put her on a pedestal. She has a look to her that tease men and she always gets what she wants. Judy is a Goddess. She is uncaring of the way her actions hurt people. As she grew her beauty grew even more:

> She was arrestingly beautiful. The color in her cheeks was centered like the color in a picture—it was not a "high" color, but a sort of fluctuating and feverish warmth, so shaded that it seemed at any moment it would recede and disappear. This color and the mobility of her mouth gave a continual impression of flux, of intense life, of passionate vitality—balanced only partially by the sad luxury of her eyes (Fitzgerald 591).

She was a beautiful princess. People compared to a perfect painted picture. The way she was shaped and curved was unbelievable. Men fall all over her beauty and body. She attracts many men. Although it seems like none of them are good enough. She cared for a man once, when he told her that he was as poor as a church mouse, he wasn't good enough anymore:

"There was a man I once cared about, this afternoon he told me out of the clear sky that he was poor as a church-mouse. He'd never even hinted it before" (Fitzgerald 593).

She went on to say, she would have of cared for him if he told her in the beginning. It seems she doesn't know what she wants. While she finds this out, she leads men on left and right.

Judy realizes her beauty and uses it against men and uses them:

"I'm more beautiful than anybody else, why can't I be happy? "I'd like to marry you if you'll have me, Dexter. I suppose you think I'm not worth having, but I'll be so beautiful for you, Dexter" (Fitzgerald 600).

She manipulates men, she leads them to believe that she likes them. She does that all the time, especially when they don't have 100% of their attention on her:

. . . Varying dozen who circulated about her. Each of them had at one time been favored above all others . . . Whenever one showed signs of dropping out through long neglect, she granted him a brief honeyed hour, which encouraged him to tag along for a year or so longer (Fitzgerald 594).

The way Judy turns out to be, is the opposite of what the story leads you to believe:

"Awfully nice girl," brooded Devlin meaninglessly, "I'm sort of sorry for her."
     "Why?" Something in Dexter was alert, receptive, at once.
     "Oh, Lud Simms had gone to pieces in a way. I don't mean he ill-uses her, but he drinks and runs around—"
     "Doesn't she run around?"
     "No. Stays at home with her kids."
     "Oh" (Fitzgerald 601).

I feel Judy got a little taste of her own medicine. The story goes on to say she has lost her beauty:

"Lots of women fade just like that," Devlin snapped his fingers.
     "You must have seen it happen. Perhaps I've forgotten how pretty she was at her wedding. I've seen her so much since then, you see. She has nice eyes" (Fitzgerald 601).

This story sent out a great message, beauty is a gift and it can be washed away with over use and selfishness. Judy was a great beauty. She took that to her advantage and lost. Now her life is unhappy. She lost her beauty, a chance of a good life, and love.

Bethany

Night

Elie Wiesel's "Night" is a book that shows how people struggled through the hard times, and how they need their families' support to keep them moving on and not to give up when the hard times came.

In the story, Elie shows the reader how much concentration camp inmates struggled. And you can see this by everyone telling each other "We must keep going, we must keep going" (Wiesel 18). People would comfort each other saying that everything will be all right. When Elie was crying, a boy named Yechiel said "Don't cry, don't waste your tears . . ."

"Not cry? were on the threshold of death . . . Soon we shall have crossed over . . . Don't you understand? How could I not cry" (Wiesel 33). people were starting to give up. Thinking that there is no chance for them. In the beginning people had high hopes and there was no way that they were going to give up. For many people such as Stein of Antwerp he says "The only thing that keeps me alive is that Reizel and my children are still alive" (Wiesel 42).

"I can't go on any longer. My stomach's bursting . . ."

"Make an effort, Zalman try . . ."

"I can't . . ." he groaned (Wiesel 82). And at that point he gave up and lost his life. These people were tortured very badly to the point where they couldn't stand it much longer. They were treated bad. They hardly got any food, so they were almost starved to death. They worked from the time they woke up to almost the time they went to bed. They were always on the go. They couldn't stay in one place for very long. And when they had to travel it wasn't easy. Probably the worst time was during the Ten day March. They couldn't take a break whenever they wanted or they would be shot. They couldn't even slow down, it was almost always at a running pace. But when they did stop sometimes people would stop right where they were at. They just wanted to sleep. They also didn't get very much sleep during all of this. So, when they happen to get to stop Elie's father fell onto the snow filled ground. Elie said "Come on, father, its better over there. We can lie down, a bit, one after the other. I'll watch over you, and then you can watch over me. We won't let each other" (Wiesel 85). During all of this they have to look after each other or they wouldn't make it though alive. There was almost no hope towards the end. Many people just didn't care about their lives anymore and they just gave up. As one man said "It's the end. God is no longer with us" (Wiesel 73).

The last few days were the worst; none of them had eaten for six days, except a bit of grass or some potato peelings near the kitchens. But on the sixth day they were free. For at least those who survived.

In conclusion you see they way that these people in the concentration camps had to struggle in order to save their lives and their familys. Also how they had to help each other pull through and not to give up their life. And just keep going and not to stop.

Cody

Night: Finding the Strength in People

In the book Night, Elie and his family were put through a lot of things that were terrible. Elie was the only one that made it through the whole ordeal. Elie showed his strength when he had no reason to keep on going. Even when his family was split up and his dad was killed, Elie kept on fighting to stay alive.

Elie had to do a lot of things to stay alive in the concentration camps. His people were treated really bad and used for bad things. They would have to watch people get punished and watch them die. They even had to run naked and be humiliated in front of the Nazis. At the beginning the Jewish people were very hopeful. Even when they were brought to the camp and when people would say things like "Poor devils, you're going to the crematory" (Wiesel 30), they still kept hope that they would make it through it. Elie was put through many tests. When he was in those camps Elie lost faith in his religion and his hope at the end, because of all he went through. The only reason why Elie stayed alive was because of his father.

When the Wiesels were still in Signet life was okay. They thought that the Nazis couldn't make it to Signet. They thought that it was going to be over in a matter of weeks. Until the Nazis came and put all the Jewish people together in a little community and cut them off from the rest of the town. The place was called a ghetto. At first the people thought that it was okay and that it was kind of nice. The Germans took away all of the Jewish people's valuables and crowded them together. To think that people were saying things like, "The Germans won't get this far. They'll stay in Budapest. There are strategic and political reasons . . . ," Wiesel 7). The German soldiers put on an act for the Jewish people, so not to get them scared away. They actually fell for the Germans fake charm. The Jewish optimists were rejoicing and saying things like, "Well there you are, you see! What did we tell you ? There they are your Germans! What do you think of them? Where is their famous cruelty?"(Wiesel 7).

At the end Elie described himself as a living corpse. That's what the Germans did to him. Elie was strong and even though he just barely made it out of that whole ordeal alive, I think he learned that if you lose hope or love it's not worth it. The main reason why Elie kept fighting was because of his dad and at the end his dad was killed. I don't think that he would've kept on fighting for his life after his dad died. He really didn't have anything or anybody then.

The Germans were cruel and pure evil to the Jewish people. Its amazing how Elie just barely made it out of this experience alive. All the tests that his strength was put up against and how he was beaten physically and emotionally and made it. I was surprised at how much Elie could hold on and keep fighting. To me, I thought he had a lot of strength.

Dustin

Of Mice and Men, Foreshadowing

The book, Of Mice and Men, has many good examples of foreshadowing. Foreshadowing is when something happens at the beginning or earlier in the book and hints at what is going to happen later in the story.

One example of foreshadowing is when Lennie is in Weed and he sees the woman with the red dress. It looked soft to Lennie, so he grabbed it and the woman screamed. Lennie got all worked up and scared, so he wouldn't let go of the dress. This foreshadowed what would happen later when Lennie killed Curleys wife.

—You get into trouble. you do bad things and I got to get you out.—(pg. 12.)—George

—Jus wanted to feel that girls dress- jus wanted to pet it like it was a mouse.—(pg. 12)—Lennie

Another example was when Carson took Candy s dog and shot him in the back of the head. He did this because the dog was old and suffering. This foreshadowed George shooting Lennie in the back of the head because Lennie killed Curleys wife and Curley wanted to shoot Lennie in the guts. George didn t want Lennie to suffer so he shot him. And by shooting him in the back of the head he wouldn t feel a thing.

—Look, Candy. This ol dog jus suffers hisself all the time.—(pg. 49.)—Carson

—Tell you what. I ll shoot him for you.—(pg. 49)—Carson

One last example of foreshadowing in this book was when Curley picked a fight with Lennie and Lennie broke Curleys hand. Lennie got all worked up again and would not let go of Curleys hand. This happened when he killed Curleys wife also.

So in conclusion, this book did a very well job of foreshadowing. There were many other examples of foreshadowing besides the examples that used. Foreshadowing is a good tool to use when writing a book. It make the reader want to read on and on.

Eve

The Foreshadowing of Steinbeck

John Steinbeck's OF MICE AND MEN is an unusual story that foreshadows the death of a big guy that is to strong for his own good (Lennie). Some of the foreshadowing events include George, Lennie's companion, warning Lennie of were to go if they got in trouble, Lennie uncontrollably crushing Curley's hand (the boss's son), and Curley's wife always wanting attention from other men.

in the beginning of the story George and Lennie stop at a river for some water. While at this river they discuss their future plans and about how,

"Guys like us got no fambly. they make a little stake an' then blow it in. They ain't got no body in the worl' that gives a hoot in hell about 'em . . . But not us . . . We got each other." (Steinbeck 114) Most importantly they discuss the trouble in Weed and what to do if he got in trouble again, "Lennie—if you just happen to get in trouble like you always done before, I want you to come right here and hide in the brush." (Steinbeck 17)

After being on the ranch only a couple days Lennie is already getting into trouble. Curley comes into the bunk house and for no reason jumps all over Lennie. To save George and Lennies job slim warns, "I think you got your hand cough in the machine." (Steinbeck 71) after Lennie grabs and crushes Curleys hand in self defense.

The death of Lennie was partially to blame on Curleys wife. "Married two weeks and got the eye." (Steinbeck 31) She presses Lennie to feel her soft, pretty hair. Her death is the result of Lennies uncontrollable reaction to her getting upset.

While going through the story Steinbeck foreshadows Lennies death by the potential danger in the events throughout the book.

Josh

Of Mice and Men paper

Of mice and Men was written by John Steinbeck.

It starts off in Weed, California. That is where George Milton and Lenny Small work at. George is a small and quick man. He is dark in the face, with restless eyes and sharp, strong features. Every part of him was defined.

Lenny is a large and unintelligent man. He is a very strong worker in the fields lifting heavy bags of grain. For being so slow in the head, Lenny is still a very nice guy. He will help out on lifting bags for others and he does what ever is needed to be done. He has many different personalities as he will flip out if he gets scared. He likes to feel soft things such as rabbis, dogs, and mice. The only thing bad about that is that he mainly pets them to hard and ends up killing them. He was feeling Curly's wife hair in the barn one time and he got nerves and squeezed her to hard and killed her.

Kyle

Interpretive Essay on The Night Thoreau Spent in Jail

In Jerome Lawrence's and Robert E. Lee's The Night Thoreau Spent in Jail, there are many political, social, and philosophical ideas that should ring true even in today's modern times. Some of these ideas or similar thoughts to these ideas have appeared in other literary works, plays, movies, and music. The idea of rebelling against the system and the ageless debate of who is right and who is wrong, also the conflict of modern vs. traditional practices are being tested in places around the world even as you read this. Practices and approaches should be challenged everyday until the best sequence is found, which should never happen. Things should always be changed and need to be changed for a society to grow. The system needs to always be challenged to find its flaws and to repair them. All of these ideas are thoughts that Thoreau believed in and preached about to who ever should be listening. Here a couple of stories and situations that tend to follow Thoreau's pattern of thinking. the first story has to do with the education of America. How Thoreau wanted his students to be able to think for themselves. In his book he says, "My students have the ache of curiosity, which I'm afraid your proscriptions will not sure (Thoreau 21)." The second involves two very politically outspoken music groups in America today. These bands, like Thoreau, feel very strongly about the politics of this country, as well as other countries in the world. In The Night Thoreau Spent in Jail, Henry says, "What law ever made a man free? Men have got to make the law free. And if a law is wrong, by heaven it's the duty of men to stand up and say so. Even if your oddfellow society wants to clap him in jail (Thoreau 66)."

In the movie "Dead Poet's Society," Mr. Keating was a radical new teacher in a very traditional ivy league school. When he arrived at this school, he challenged his students to think for themselves, which some felt uncomfortable with. As he was there longer, he began to have a real impact on his students and encouraged them to go for their goals, or as he put it, "Carpe Diem." Some of his most loyal students formed a club that Mr., Keating was in when attended that very school, dubbed the Dead Poet's Society. This club was frowned upon by the elders of the school and caused much controversy between the students and the students. One of the members wanted to join a play in which he succeeded in getting the lead role. This was a direct violation of this boy's father's wishes, and he was told he'd have to quit a week before opening night. With such a short notice he performed in the play against his father's orders and did a very good job, but was caught by his father. He was immediately taken home and scolded, but his parents couldn't understand his newly found love in the theater. The boy felt that he couldn't go on with his life under his father's oppression and chose to end his life. Immediately Mr. Keating, as well as the Dead Poet's Society was the center of the controversy. In the end Mr. Keating was wrongly fired and indirectly blamed for the death of one of his most loyal students. All Mr. Keating was trying to do was to get his students to see life in a different view, think for themselves, and seize the day. The elders and the boy's father felt otherwise, however. They felt that the students should be in the classroom with books and pencils, just as Deacon Ball felt. Of course when that young student took his life, people couldn't believe it was the father's fault, so they had to find a scapegoat, and that scapegoat was Mr. Keating. This is like Thoreau saying that change must come in the practices and you must take the classroom outside sometimes to get his students to experience life, nature, and to form their own opinions.

Politics has and always will be a very controversial subject in today's societies, everyone has an opinion. These differing ideas on how the country should be run in newspapers and magazines, pondered in discussion groups and television talk shows, and even written about in music. Two bands come to mind when I think of politically opinionated groups: "Rage Against the Machine." and "The Beastie Boys." "Rage" is very critical about the

American and Mexican governments and their practices. If you ever see one of their videos on MTV, you'll find that they will have a statement on the situation of some area of the world. "Freedom," the band's first video, told the story of how American armies forced the native Americans off their lands and killed many in the process. In the song, the leader singer sings; "Freedom, yeah Right." this is an obvious statement contradicting the government's promise to grant the Native Americans their freedom in this country. This feelings that this band holds about the government are so strong that on an appearance of "Saturday Night Live," they hung American flags upside down on their amps. This was noticed seconds before going on and resulted in the m their first song without their flags and being kicked off the show before they could perform their second song. This was done as a statement against NBC's parent-company, General Electric, for their ties to the defense industry. When the band teamed up with the controversial group, "Wu Tang Clan," lead singer of "Rage," was sold bold as to say, "the tour is going to incorporate everything which the rich, wealthy classes in America fear and despise (Rolling Stone sept. 4, 1997, pg 38).

"The Beastie Boys" are also politically out spoken about the current situations of the world, particularly the pole in Tibet, which is held by communist China. Each summer since 1996, this group has held the Tibetan Freedom Concert, featuring many popular bands which raise money for the liberation of Tibet. These shows are full of music and chants by monks as well as some footage taken of monks being tortured by the Chinese military in the Tibetan temples. This festival will be held again this summer in New York and looks to become an annual event.

What I'm trying to get across with these examples is that similar practices to Thoreau's are still being used today. His ideas should be recognized as almost timeless, as they still can be applied to today's modern problems and conflicts which won't go away. Even if the problems in society go away, brand new ones will always surface. Whether it's found in movies, books, magazines, or music the ideas, that have evolved from such philosophers as Thoreau will always be around. In conclusion,k I think Thoreau was a man ahead of his time, and his ideas and practices should be looked upon and practiced for years to come.

Lana

The Night Thoreau Spent in Jail

The Night Thoreau spent in Jail represents Henry David Thoreau's total individualism. He took a stand against the government. By not paying his taxes, Thoreau showed everyone what kind of an individual he really was. He also believed that not just himself, but that everyone else should be an individual too. Everyone should stand up for what they believe in. He showed his individualism in many ways.

If everyone in this world agreed with one another it would be a boring place to live. Thoreau was quoted by saying "And if you never disagree, it's only like breathing in and never breathing out! A man could suffocate on courtesy." (Lawrence and Lee 14) This shows to me that individualism was at the top of his list. It's almost like saying if you are not your own person, you're not complete. When he was a teacher for awhile, he really stressed being yourself.He said things like if I were one of his students, they would have really stuck in my head. Thoreau said things like "If you want to take notes, go ahead. But no because I'm doing it or because I told you so." (Lawrence and Lee 30) Thoreau was a very smart man. He made a lot of people think whenever he would open his mouth.

One of his quotes that showed his anti-government was when he was talking to his mentor, Waldo Emerson. He said, "Waldo! What are you doing out of jail?" (Lawrence and Lee 73) Waldo was asking Thoreau what in the heck was he doing in jail. But Thoreau comes back with an awesome quote. He was telling Waldo that he should stand up for what he believed in. Emerson was against the war, but he didn't stand up for it publicly like Thoreau did. Thoreau went to jail because he wouldn't pay his taxes. He didn't pay his taxes because it went towards the Mexican/American War. The war was over getting Texas as a state. If we would get Texas from Mexico, then it would become a slave state. Thoreau was against slavery. He showed that by going to jail. He made a statement to show his support for anti-slavery and to show people how much he was an individual.

Thoreau was a very unordinary man. He had a lot of cool ideas. His quotes really made you think. I love his thoughts on individualism. It's so rue on what he said about it Everyone really should be their own person. I really admire Thoreau for what he believed in and what he stood up for. Thoreau is a role model for all of us. If I could go back in the history of the world and there would be only one person I could meet; it would probably be Henry David Thoreau.

Author Index

Subject Index